A TEACHER'S GRAMMAR OF ENGLISH

linking grammar with communication

K R Narayanaswamy
(formerly, Bayero University, Kano, Nigeria)

Orient BlackSwan

The answer key with supplementary notes is available separately.
Please email enquiries to chennai@orientblackswan.com

ORIENT BLACKSWAN PRIVATE LIMITED

Registered Office
3-6-752, Himayatnagar, Hyderabad 500 029 (A.P.), India
e-mail: centraloffice@orientblackswan.com

Other Offices
Bangalore / Bhopal / Bhubaneshwar / Chennai,
Ernakulam / Guwahati / Hyderabad / Jaipur / Kolkata,
Lucknow / Mumbai / New Delhi / Noida / Patna

First published by Orient Longman Private Limited 2004
First Orient Blackswan impression 2013

ISBN: 978 81 250 2664 8

Typeset at
Devi Information Systems
Chennai 600 106

Printed in India at
Graphica Printers and Binders
Hyderabad 500 013

Published by
Orient Blackswan Private Limited
3-6-752, Himayatnagar, Hyderabad 500 029 (A.P.), India
e-mail: hyderabad@orientblackswan.com

Foreword

A Teacher's Grammar of English is for teachers of English teaching at primary, secondary or tertiary levels. The book is also for teachers teaching subjects other than English in English-medium schools and colleges. Setting standards in English and helping to maintain them is the job of the English teacher as well as teachers of other subjects.

The book is based on the idea that grammar is a means to fluent and accurate communication. An effort has been made to strike a balance between traditional concepts and latter-day insights, and between descriptive grammar and grammar in use.

Ideally, grammar should teach the learner (a) the form; (b) the meaning and (c) what a given formally correct sentence achieves in terms of communication. This is what has been attempted in the present book. To educated users of the language, form and structure are certainly important. Each chapter of the book thus begins by setting out the forms of the grammatical class or category it deals with. It then goes on to explore their meanings with a variety of illustrative examples, and finally it touches on the communicative uses that the given forms have and their appropriateness to certain situations.

An example would be the passive. Most pedagogic grammars treat passivisation, among other things, as simple exercises in conversion. They do not tell the learners the subtle differences in meaning and emphasis between the active and the passive; they do not tell them when the active is to be preferred to the passive and vice versa. The result is that the learners are left with the impression that the two forms mean the same and are therefore freely interchangeable.

Another special feature of the book is that it deals with both spoken and written communication. The sections devoted to contracted forms, tag-questions and modal auxiliaries deal largely with spoken English. There is a pronounced tilt, however, towards the written mode, and the tilt is deliberate. The reasons have been explained in the introductory chapter.

All adult communication is really a question of exploring possibilities of sentence construction. The English sentence is extremely plastic and opens up many possibilities to learners of English. What a learner is called to do is to internalise the basic sentence patterns of the language and to learn to expand them through a process of modification and transformation. This assumption is basic to the author's approach to the learning and teaching of grammar and accounts for the emphasis throughout the book on transformations. These range from the simpler transformations (that is, those in which the subject–predicate structures are unchanged, or least changed, as for example in noun, adverb and adjective clauses), through not-so-simple transformations (as for example, in active–passive and direct–indirect patterns) to more complex ones (such as the participle and infinitive phrases in which the subject or the finite verb is reduced or omitted).

The importance of transformations cannot be exaggerated. Transformations are the grammatical equivalent of an extensive vocabulary. Basically, what language does is to make available to learners two choices: choice of words and choice of sentence-structures. An extensive vocabulary ensures a wide variety of words for learners to choose from; the ability to transform would ensure for them a similar freedom of choice with sentence-structures.

The concept of a teacher's grammar of English is a comparatively novel one. There is the teacher's perspective on grammar as surely as there is the learner's, and both find a voice in this book. The book seeks to teach grammar and to teach it well by providing a variety of material for both the purposes. One of the important aims has been to simplify the teaching and learning of grammar as a whole as well as complex areas such as prepositions and prepositional phrases.

By way of value addition to the book are three appendices: a glossary of grammatical terms for ready reference, a note on concord or agreement of subject and predicate and a set of tables giving the basic forms of irregular verbs, grouped according to the type of irregularity they show.

It is the author's hope that at least some teachers will say, after reading this book, "I never imagined grammar could be so interesting!"

K R Narayanaswamy

to

A.E.S

Contents

1 Introducing Grammar

Language is a 'rule-governed activity' and grammar is a code of rules which help us to tell a sentence from a non-sentence, and a well-formed sentence from a not-so-well-formed sentence, in a given language. Our concern in this book is with English and we may therefore define English grammar as a set of rules which establish meaningful relationships between the parts that make up the sentence, which in the final analysis are real-life relationships between persons, things, and events. Take, for instance, a simple string of words like:

John loves Mary.

We call the above an English sentence: the words are all English and they are arranged in a manner in which words can be, and often are, arranged in English. We say that 'John' and 'Mary' are nouns; that noun 'John' is the subject, and noun 'Mary' is the object, of the verb 'loves'; that 'John' being the subject is the 'lover', the one who does the loving, and 'Mary' being the object is the 'loved one'. We also say that 'loves' is a transitive verb, and the action indicated by it transits or moves across from the subject ('John') to someone beyond the subject, namely, the object ('Mary'). The grammatical terms 'subject', 'object' and 'transitive verb' help us in this instance to establish a meaningful relationship between the parts that make up the word-group: John loves Mary.

Grammar does not, however, stop with merely setting up a meaningful relationship between subject-noun 'John' and object-noun 'Mary'; it points to a real-life relationship between two persons known to the speaker. By saying 'John loves Mary', the speaker is not mechanically practising a pattern of English sentence (N–V–N) but communicating important information about two real-life people known to him/her. Grammar, thus, is a means to communication and that is the most significant part of grammar.

We learn grammar so that we may communicate fluently and accurately; we teach grammar so that our learners may learn to communicate fluently and accurately.

As a matter of fact, there is grammatical meaning as distinct from real-life meaning, from meaning as we ordinarily understand by the term.
Look at these two lines from the famous Jabberwocky poem of *Lewis Carroll:

'Twas brillig, and the slithy toves
Did gyre and gimble in the wabe.

Would you call the first half of the first line ('Twas brillig,) or for that matter, the rest of the lines (the slithy toves did gyre and gimble in the wabe), an English sentence? Probably not. There are no such words in the English language as 'brillig', 'slithy', 'toves', 'gyre', 'gimble' and 'wabe'—no dictionary lists them. The lines therefore do not make any sense. They do not relate to real life, and we expect a sentence to relate to real life, to have real-life meaning, in other words.

*Lewis Carroll: pen-name of C.L. Dodgson (1832-98), author of *Alice's Adventures in Wonderland*

And yet the lines, nonsense though they are, disturb us in a curious way. Along with the nonsense words listed above are words that are recognisably English—structure words like 'it', 'and', 'the', 'in', the linking verb 'be' (as in 'Twas brillig') and the 'do' auxiliary (as in 'did gyre and gimble'). Interspersed with these real English words are the nonsense words, and the two groups of words are so interspersed that they occur in ways that we recognise as typical English sentence patterns. Thus, ''Twas brillig' is modelled on the sentence pattern:

impersonal 'it' + verb 'be' + adjective ('It was hot'; 'It was cold').

In the same way, 'the slithy toves did gyre and gimble in the wabe' is modelled on a sentence pattern like this:

article + adjective + noun + verb (made up of auxiliary 'did' plus main verb 'gimble') + prepositional phrase ('in' plus article plus noun).

Suppose we substitute for these nonsense words real English words, thus:

It was bright and the young people
Did sing and dance in the valley.

We then get a meaningful English sentence. The point to note is this: 'brillig' and 'slithy' look and sound like English adjectives; 'wabe' could be an English noun even as 'gyre' and 'gimble' could be English verbs. The fact that they are not real English nouns, adjectives and verbs makes the lines nonsense but the lines themselves, grammatically speaking, are an authentic English sentence made up of two main clauses joined by the co-ordinate conjunction 'and':

main clause 1	conj.	main clause 2
'Twas brillig	and	the slithy toves did gyre and gimble in the wabe

The lines, in other words, make grammatical sense; they have grammatical meaning.

Let us take a similar word-string:

The bink ropped the garst and swiggled it in one fug.

This, again, sounds like an English sentence. 'Bink' sounds like an English noun, so does 'garst', and they both fill the same slots in the sentence as nouns ('bink' is subject, and 'garst' is object, of the verb 'ropped'); 'ropped' and 'swiggled' could easily be English verbs, judging from their '-ed' ending and the position they occupy in the word-group; 'it' is personal pronoun standing for the object-noun 'garst' and 'in one fug' looks like a prepositional phrase with an adverbial function. The whole word-group conforms to a familiar English sentence pattern:

N (subject) + V (transitive) + N (object) + adverbial

and the sentence could be interpreted thus:

Someone or something called 'bink' did something called 'ropping' to someone or something called 'garst'; the same 'bink' did something more to the 'garst' called 'swiggling' and the 'bink' did it 'in one fug'.

Compare the above word-string with a proper English sentence like:

The snake seized the frog and swallowed it in one gulp,

and you realise how close the nonsense string is to a meaningful English sentence. This closeness arises from the fact that the nonsense string conforms to the same sentence pattern as 'The snake seized the frog and swallowed it in one gulp', the nonsense words being formally identifiable as nouns and verbs filling the same slots in the sentence as real English nouns and real English verbs.

We now move on to yet another example of a grammatically meaningful sentence, this one from Noam Chomsky*:

Colourless green ideas sleep furiously.

The Chomskyan sentence is an improvement on:

The bink ropped the garst and swiggled it in one fug

as well as the sentence from the Jabberwocky poem in that it is wholly made up of real English words. It is nonsense nevertheless. Ideas are neither green nor colourless; if they are green, they cannot be colourless and if they are colourless, they cannot be green; ideas, green or colourless, do not sleep, let alone furiously. The sentence conveys no meaning to us, and yet it is a grammatically meaningful sentence made up of real English words conforming to a familiar sentence pattern in English:

adjective + adjective + noun (subject)+ verb (intransitive) + adverb

We thus see that there is grammatical meaning, as distinct from semantic or real-life meaning, and an acceptable English sentence is one which is both grammatically and semantically meaningful like this one:

Guileless little children sleep peacefully

and our business as English teachers is to teach our learners to make up sentences that are both grammatically and semantically meaningful; our business, in other words, is to teach them to communicate, and communication happens only when meaning enters into what we say or hear.

No sensible teacher or learner of English looked upon grammar as an end in itself. Grammar was, and has ever been, a means to an end: indispensable as a means but a means nevertheless, the end being communication.

Once grammar is understood as a means to fluent and accurate communication, the relevance of grammar both to the learner and the teacher of English becomes apparent. How does grammar help the learner of English? What is grammar supposed to teach the learner of English so that he/she is better able to communicate fluently and accurately?

Ideally, grammar should teach the learner a. the form; b. the meaning; and c. what a given formally correct sentence achieves in terms of communication.

By 'form' we mean the formal characteristics of the various parts of speech, of phrases, of clauses, and of sentences. The learner should, for example, learn to identify on the basis

---

*Noam Chomsky (1928 -), US linguist, known for his *Syntactic Structures* (1957), in which he put forward his theory of transformational-generative grammar

of form, nouns, verbs, adjectives etc; tell an infinitive phrase from a participle, prepositional or gerundial phrase; tell a noun clause from an adjective or adverb clause; tell a simple sentence from a complex or compound sentence. The learner should know besides that verb phrases like 'has been doing', 'will have done', 'is being done' are formally correct but not 'has do', 'will have doing', 'is being doing'. He should also learn to tell a formally correct sentence like:

He and I weeded the garden

from an incorrect one like:

Him and me weeded the garden.

Secondly, learners should be taught the meaning of a given form. For example, they should learn the meaning of tense, of voice, of mood. What does the present simple tense mean in English and how is it different from the present continuous tense? What does the simple past tense signify and how is it different from the present perfect tense? How is the interrogative different from the imperative? Do the active and the passive mean the same?

Finally, the learner should be taught to discriminate between two or more formally correct utterances in terms of their overall communicative effect. Teaching this would go well beyond teaching the meaning as such of the utterance. Look at the following pairs of sentences:

1. a. I have written a dozen letters since morning.

   b. I have been writing letters since morning.

2. a. The Prime Minister was greeted at the airport by a large crowd.

   b. A large crowd greeted the Prime Minister at the airport.

Sentences 1 (a) and 1 (b) share in common a core meaning, so do sentences 2 (a) and 2 (b). But 1(b) does not mean the same as 1(a) any more than 2 (b) means the same as 2 (a). The speaker of 1 (a) communicates a sense of achievement ('I have written a dozen letters since morning and I'm rather pleased with what I have done'), while the speaker of 1 (b) stresses the activity that he/she has been engaged in since morning ('You ask me what I have been doing since morning? Well, I have been writing letters'). Similarly, in 2 (a), the focus is on the Prime Minister, rather on the event of the Prime Minister being greeted by a large crowd, while in 2 (b) the focus is on there being a large crowd to greet the Prime Minister. Sentence 2(a) clearly suggests that the Prime Minister is a draw, a crowd-puller; 2(b), on the other hand, is more in the nature of a factual report.

One can go on multiplying examples. Supposing you are writing a testimonial about a student of yours who is both intelligent and lazy, would you say:

Kumar is intelligent but lazy? (or)
Although Kumar is intelligent, he is lazy? (or)
Although Kumar is lazy, he is intelligent?

All the three sentences are formally correct and they mean roughly the same but only roughly. If you opted for the first sentence, you would be giving equal importance to Kumar's intelligence and his laziness; you would, in other words, be factual, non-committal, non-judgmental. If you opted for the second, you would in effect be damning

Kumar, playing down his intelligence and playing up his laziness. By opting for the third, you would be helping Kumar by subtly suggesting to whoever reads the testimonial that Kumar's laziness is nothing to worry about, that the important thing about Kumar is his intelligence. This difference in the final meaning or message communicated arises from the fact that in the first sentence each of Kumar's qualities is expressed in a main clause and thus receives equal main-clause emphasis, while in the other two sentences one or the other quality of Kumar is expressed in a subordinate clause and thereby understated.

There nearly always is a reason why a given construction takes the form it does or means what it means. The reason may be logical, psychological, or sociological. Sometimes, the reason is purely historical: it has to do with the way the language has evolved over the centuries. The point to remember, however, is that there nearly always is a reason, and the teacher who can explain to the class the why and wherefore of a construction or usage will carry conviction to the class, besides helping it to learn and memorise the construction with relative case. The Indian teacher of English cannot, when confronted by a learner asking 'Why so?', claim the native speaker's privilege of saying, 'It's so in my dialect; that's how we say it'.

How is the teaching of grammar relevant to the teacher of English? There are doubtless people who speak good English without ever having consciously studied grammar as a subject at school. But I doubt whether there are, or ever can be, teachers of English who have made a success of teaching English at the school level without a thorough knowledge of grammar.

Broadly speaking, there are two schools of thought among experts and teachers regarding the role of grammar in English language teaching. There are those who are totally opposed to the formal teaching of grammar (the anti-grammar brigade) and there are those who say that the teaching of grammar is a regrettable necessity (the apologists who are wary, defensive about having to teach grammar). The anti-grammar brigade may comprise the native speakers of the language, usually British or American, who say: 'We didn't learn English grammar at school, we know no grammar and yet we use the language competently. If we can do that, why can't you?'

Implicit in this kind of reasoning is a fallacy and a misplaced analogy. The native speakers of the language may not have learnt grammar at school but they do know grammar. How else do they communicate? They are speaking and using grammar all the time without knowing it. All that they really mean when they say they know no grammar is that they cannot articulate their knowledge of grammar, they cannot make it explicit. They may not, for instance, be able to tell gerund from participle, or object from object complement but they can generate dozens of sentences with object and object complement on the lines of a basic sentence pattern like:

The party elected Mrs Tanya leader.

This is because by virtue of being born of English-speaking parents and/or having grown up in an English-speaking country, they have internalised the grammar of English, even as Indian children internalise the grammar of their first language, for example, Tamil, Telugu, Bangla, Hindi, without ever being formally taught it. This is what Chomsky calls the language user's 'competence', the implicit knowledge that native speakers have of the rule system underlying their language. While competence in Tamil or Bangla comes naturally and effortlessly to a Tamil or Bengali as a result of his/her growing up in a Tamil-speaking or Bangla-speaking environment, there is insufficient exposure to English, and competence in English may have to be acquired mainly through a systematic study of grammar.

For the teachers of English, competence in the language alone is not enough. They need to make their competence (that is, the implicit knowledge of the underlying rule system) explicit. They must know how the language works; they must know its forms, its regularities and contrasts, and the way it is used. In short, they must acquire language awareness.

One way of acquiring language awareness is through analysis – you analyse particular samples of language and then discover the general rule or principle behind the particular samples – the inductive way. A more direct – and probably more effective and certainly less time-consuming – way of acquiring language awareness is through a systematic study of modern English grammar which formulates its rules on the basis of a close and extended examination of the language as it is used today.

English teachers need to acquire language awareness for themselves, and they have to promote it among their learners. This book advocates teaching grammar systematically as a school subject, the way it was taught many decades ago. It is based on the premise that the grammar we teach through readers and workbooks is bound to be highly selective and therefore incomplete. The items selected for study are partly determined by the text under study. The text in turn finds a place in the reader on the basis of considerations such as how readable it is, how easy or difficult it is in terms of the vocabulary and structures used and whether the learner can easily relate to the subject-matter. This kind of learning is insufficient for imparting language awareness. We need to teach grammar systematically, not as an examinable subject or as an end in itself, but as a means to fluent and accurate communication. The readers and the workbooks may then supplement what is formally taught, thus extending and deepening the learner's language awareness.

The ultimate test of the learner's knowledge of grammar is his or her ability to tell a sentence from a non-sentence or a well-formed sentence from a not-so-well-formed sentence. This is at the receptive level, at the level of the learner as listener/reader. At the productive level, learners as speakers/writers will be able to generate or produce the kind of sentence they want in a given situation in response to a particular communicational need. Knowing English grammar is knowing the English sentence, the basic unit of communication; knowing grammar is being able to make sense of any and every English sentence and being able at the same time to produce any and every kind of sentence that makes sense to the listener or reader.

When native speakers of English speak of their ability to use their language competently without having learnt grammar at school, they usually mean the ability to speak, not the ability to read or write. This is true of all of us; we speak our first language with no overt or formal training in grammar but how many of us can read or write our first language without acquiring these skills through conscious effort and practice?

When Harold Palmer speaks of our 'natural, universal, spontaneous capacity' for language learning, he means our capacity for learning to speak the ordinary everyday form of the language. There is nothing natural, universal or spontaneous about learning to read and write. The native speaker of English has no natural advantage over the non-native speaker, an Indian or African, in the matter of reading and writing.

Reading and writing are precisely the skills that the non-native learner of English needs most today. One can speak English for ordinary everyday purposes of communication with a little grammar and a limited vocabulary but it is difficult to see how one can build one's reading and writing skills on this fragile foundation. Writing in particular calls for accuracy apart from fluency and one simply cannot write unless one has a thorough knowledge of grammar.

What kind of grammar should we teach: the grammar of spoken English or the grammar of written English? It should be both but with greater emphasis on the grammar of written English for two reasons. The dominant goals of ESL (learning English as a second language) today are reading and writing, and a grammar of written English therefore is more appropriate and in tune with current learning objectives. Secondly and more importantly, written English exploits and exhibits the possibilities of sentence construction that the language makes available to us: in writing, the sentences tend to be longer and more intricately constructed.

The English sentence is extremely plastic. It can be stretched as much as is needed. It can be made as long and as complex as necessary depending on one's communicational needs and purposes.

The interesting point, however, is that all such sentences, however long or complex, are derived from basic sentence patterns through a process of expansion and transformation which can be repeated. The basic sentence patterns are just a few; they occur in formations according to fixed rules. The process of expansion and transformation, again, is carried out according to a small number of fixed, learnable rules. A grammar of written English exhibits these rules more fully in action and is better able to give the learner an insight into the underlying rule system, which is the proper purpose of all grammar teaching. When we teach a language, we cannot teach the whole manifestation of the language. We would not be able to. What we try to do instead is to impart to learners an insight into the rule system underlying the language, in the light of which they can make sense of any and every manifestation of the language.

One final question remains to be answered: Should the grammar we teach be prescriptive or descriptive?

Grammar through the centuries and until the end of the nineteenth century was prescriptive. Grammarians like Robert Lowth, author of *A Short Introduction to English Grammar*, 1762 and Lindlay Murray, author of *English Grammar adapted to different classes of learners*, 1795 prescribed or laid down the law in regard to what is correct English and what is not. They defined grammar as the art of writing and speaking English with propriety. They were so influential that the educated users of the language, including professional writers of the calibre of Addison, Swift and Dryden, obeyed them. Murray's grammar in fact set the norm for the later textbooks like Nesfield's in the nineteenth century and these books attained almost Biblical authority.

The prescriptive grammarians did not prescribe in vain. They managed to banish from the language the double negative: 'She didn't know nothing', 'Nobody never told me'. Similarly, they banished the double comparative ('more nobler', 'more abler') and the double superlative ('the most noblest', 'the most ablest'). All these usages were common in earlier English—a double or multiple negative was thought of by earlier writers as more of a negative, just as a double comparative or superlative ('the most unkindest cut of all'—Shakespeare) was thought of as intensifying the comparison. But the grammarians' objections stayed and the aforesaid forms disappeared from the language. They, the prescriptive grammarians, nearly banished from the language one of the most idiomatic constructions in English—the practice of ending a clause or sentence with a preposition:

> Houses are built to live <u>in</u>, not to look <u>on</u>.
> The painting that you are looking <u>at</u> is a fake Turner.

This was prescriptivism with a vengeance, and naturally there was a reaction against it towards the end of the nineteenth century. Henry Sweet (*New English Grammar*, 1892) was the first to depart from the prescriptivist tradition. He confined himself to a statement and explanation of the facts; he did not attempt to pronounce on the relative correctness of different usages. Sweet pioneered the descriptivist tradition, which continued into the twentieth century. But as it often happens, the reaction in favour of descriptivism and against prescriptivism was carried to extremes. The latter-day descriptivist grammarians went to the extent of saying that whatever <u>is</u> (i.e. exists)among native speakers is right. Thus was born the myth of 'native speaker infallibility'.

What do we do as teachers of English? We need to strike a balance between the two extreme viewpoints.

Grammar has to be authoritative and must pronounce on what is unquestionably correct and what is unquestionably faulty. Thus, 'He is used to working long hours' is correct, while 'He is used to work long hours' is not, and there can be no argument about it. Similarly, the failure to maintain concord between subject and verb in the following sentence is a serious error:

> I personally do not feel that <u>either</u> of these critics <u>make</u> my flesh creep. (John Wain, in an article in 'Encounter')

Teachers should be able to state their views about usage. They should be able to support their views with reasons for their preference but without being dogmatic. They must allow for the possibility that a construction currently regarded as incorrect may one day become standard.

The teacher must also allow for dual standards, one for formal writing, and one for informal speech, at any rate in the higher classes. Thus, the class must be told that while 'Who do you want?' and 'Who did you give the book to?' are standard in conversational English, these should give way to the grammatically correct 'Whom do you want?' and 'Whom did you give the book to?' in formal written English. In the same way, the use of 'like' as a conjunction (as in 'Speak <u>like</u> I do if you want to improve your pronunciation') may pass muster in conversation but not in writing.

As a matter of fact, there has been in recent years a new movement towards prescriptivism which steers clear of the dogmatism of the grammarians of the eighteenth and nineteenth centuries as well as the permissiveness of the latter-day descriptive grammarians of the twentieth century. The new prescriptivists do no hesitate to say what is right and what is wrong but they are willing to supplement and if necessary, to modify their description of language in the light of a close study of the language in action. This new prescriptivism, in other words, is based on an objective study of the facts of language as they are today. For example, unlike the earlier grammarians who spoke of direct and indirect speech as though they were two modes of speech presentation in writing, mutually exclusive and collectively exhaustive, the new grammarians allow for variations in the traditional modes such as these:

<u>free direct speech</u>

Ever live by play? Not more than other gentlemen do.
Ever borrow money of the prisoner? Yes. Ever pay him? No.
–Charles Dickens, *A Tale of Two Cities*

<u>free indirect speech</u>

Was it possible, he wondered, that he had been too strict with his children? No, he hadn't. Why then did they hate him so?

<u>mixed modes</u>

'Is there anything I can fetch you?' the doctor asked, and, the old man replied, he had everything he needed.
–Graham Greene, *A Burnt-out Case*

We have been looking at two schools of thought among language teaching experts and teachers on the role of grammar in English language teaching. There is a third school which believes that no serious teaching or learning of English is possible without the teaching of grammar as a school subject. In most schools English is a serious subject of study, a necessary tool of survival in the highly competitive environment of today and an indispensable aid to career advancement in a globalised world. Fortunately for them and for the country, the teachers of English in the Indian subcontinent by and large belong to the third school. A large majority of these teachers believe strongly in the teaching of grammar. There is probably no teacher who believes that grammar is dispensable. However, many teachers feel that they do not know enough grammar to be able to teach it. The present book is designed primarily to help them. It is hoped that even those teachers who are not intimidated by the prospect of having to teach grammar will find the book useful, illuminating and enjoyable.

2 The Sentence

An English sentence is a group of words with a *subject* and a *predicate*. The subject is a person or thing we speak about, and the predicate is something we say about the person or thing. The subject usually comes at the beginning of the sentence, followed by the predicate.

subject (S)	predicate (P)
Dogs	bark.
The little girl	hates onions.
The captain	called the sergeant courageous.
Abdul	is a doctor.
The other child	looked unhealthy.

An English sentence, in other words, consists of a predication. Something is *predicated*, or said, about a subject. Thus, in 'Dogs bark', we are saying something about 'dogs' (subject) and what we are saying about 'dogs' is that they 'bark' (predicate).

To find the subject of the sentence, ask who or what we are speaking about. To find the predicate, ask what is predicated or said about the subject.

Exercise 1

Write a suitable subject for each of the following predicates and complete the sentences.

a. ______________ were pleased with the progress report of their son.
b. ______________ finally lighted upon a clue to the crime.
c. ______________ were declared unsafe by the Corporation and demolished.
d. ______________ came up in the course of the discussion.
e. ______________ have agreed to most of your suggestions.
f. ______________ waved to the soldiers marching by.

Exercise 2

Write a suitable predicate for each of the following subjects and complete the sentences.

a. The angry young man ______________________________________.
b. A dog on a chain ______________________________________.
c. A man in Delhi ______________________________________.
d. The three old women ______________________________________.
e. The girl ______________________________________.
f. The large dog ______________________________________.

A sentence normally is an independent unit of thought or feeling expressed through a logically related subject and predicate. The sentence therefore is the basic unit of communication in English.

2.1 Basic Sentence Patterns

Every day, all over the English-speaking world, countless sentences are spoken and written. Yet at the base of nearly all these sentences are two statements:

Statement 1: Somebody or something *does* something.

Statement 2: Somebody or something *is* something.
or Somebody or something *seems* (to be) something.

Every sentence, spoken or written, is only a variation on one or the other of these two statements.

Statement 1 may take the following variations:

1. Dogs bark.	(noun as subject) plus (verb intransitive)	(N-V)
2. a. The child chased the dog. b. The dog chased the child.	(noun as subject) plus (verb transitive) plus (noun as object)	(N-V-N)
3. John gave Mary a letter.	(subject-noun) plus (verb transitive) plus (object-noun 1) plus (object-noun 2)	(N-V-N-N)
4. a. The Menons named their baby Sudha.	(subject-noun) plus (verb transitive) plus (object-noun) plus (noun as object complement)	(N-V-N-N)
b. Parents consider their children special.	(subject-noun) plus (verb transitive) plus (object-noun) plus (adjective as object complement)	(N-V-N-Adj)

Statement 2 may take the following forms:

5. The king was a tyrant.	(subject-noun) plus (linking verb) plus (noun as subject complement)	(N-LV-N)
6. The crowd seems (to be) restless.	(subject-noun) plus (linking verb) plus (adjective as subject complement)	(N-LV-Adj)
7. The man is here at home.	(subject-noun) plus (linking verb) plus (adverbial: adverb and/or adverb phrase)	(N-LV-Adverbial)

Sentences 1–7 are a set of basic sentence patterns in English. Observe them closely, and you will notice that the core of the English sentence consists of the subject and the predicate. (By the 'core of the sentence' we mean the part that is essential to the sentence, the part that we cannot do without.) The subject at its barest minimum is a noun (or a pronoun) and the predicate at its barest minimum is the finite verb, as in basic sentence pattern 1: 'Dogs bark'. In patterns 2–4, the finite verb is followed by one or more words completing the predication. Thus, in pattern 2 the extra word is a noun (called an object). In pattern 3, we have two words following the finite verb, both nouns functioning as objects, while in pattern 4 the finite verb is followed by an object-noun plus a noun or adjective functioning as object complement. *Notice that the finite verbs in 1–4 are all verbs of doing.*

As for basic sentence patterns 5–7, they have a different kind of finite verb: a verb of being, not a verb of doing. This verb of being is called a linking verb. Preceding the linking verb is a subject-noun, and following it is a noun, adjective or adverbial functioning as complement, this time as subject complement.

The basic sentence patterns by themselves do not make for good communication. In normal conversation we are unlikely to use such brief sentences as 'dogs bark' or 'birds fly' to communicate, but are more likely to say:

> The dogs in this street bark right through the night, making it impossible for the residents to sleep in peace.
>
> Frigate birds fly at a speed of 100–160 kmph.

Sentences like the above sound more like normal communication *and yet they are both basic pattern* 1 *expanded.* That is what we do all the time: we expand the basic sentence patterns. We expand them so that we may accommodate or do justice to our ideas, which are necessarily more complex. The more complex our ideas, the longer and the more intricately constructed our sentences. The complexity of our ideas has to be matched by a corresponding complexity of sentence structure. The point to remember is this: all grammatical or well-formed sentences, however long or complex, are nothing but changes repeatedly rung on the basic sentence patterns through expansion and transformation. (You will learn a lot more about these later on in the book.) It is therefore important that we familiarise ourselves with the basic sentence patterns. Here are some preliminary explanatory notes to help you understand the bps (basic sentence patterns) with a view to eventually internalising them.

2.1.1 Finite and Non-Finite Verbs

The predicate at its simplest is a finite verb, as in bp 1. More usually, it is a finite verb followed by:

1. an object-noun (bp 2)
2. two object-nouns (bp 3)
3. an object-cum-object complement (bp 4) (or)
4. a subject complement (bp 5–7).

What, then, is a finite verb? How is it different from a non-finite verb? Non-finite verbs are of four kinds in all:

1. the infinitive ('to go')
2. the present participle ('going')
3. the past participle ('gone')
4. the perfect participle ('having gone').

These are called non-finite because none of these verbs by itself can make a statement about a subject. For instance, we cannot say:

a. He to go home
b. He going home
c. He gone home
d. He having gone home

but we can very well say:

e. He has to go home.
f. He is going home.
g. He has gone home.
h. He went home.

The word-groups a–d do not make statements because they are non-sentences; e–h are proper sentences and they make statements. The difference between the two sets of word-groups is this: the word-groups e–h have a finite verb each. The word-groups a–d have only a non-finite verb: *to go, going, gone, having gone.*

Another difference between finite and non-finite verbs is that a finite verb expresses person and number and it has more than one form:

a. He is going home. (3rd person, singular)
b. I am going home. (1st person, singular)
c. They are going home. (3rd person, plural)

A non-finite verb, on the other hand, has only one form. Look at the non-finite verb 'to see' in the following sentences:

d. He is going home to see his parents.
e. I am going home to see my parents.
f. They are going home to see their parents.

Finally, finite verbs *alone* can be put in various tenses—like present and past (simple, continuous, perfect, perfect continuous).

2.1.2 Verbs of Being and Verbs of Doing

In bp 1–4, the subject is said to *do* something:

1. Dogs bark.
2. The child chased the dog.
3. John gave Mary a letter.
4. The Menons named their baby Sudha.

We therefore call the verbs in these basic patterns **verbs of doing.**
The subject in bp 5–7, on the other hand, does not do anything, the subject simply *is* or *seems* to be something:

5. The king was a tyrant.
6. The crowd seems restless.

The verbs in these patterns express a *state* or *condition*, not an *action*. They are therefore called **verbs of being**.

Verbs of being belong to a larger group called **linking verbs**. They are so called because they link or join what goes before them (the subject) to what comes after them (the complement):

The king was a tyrant. The crowd seems restless.

The commonest linking verb is the verb 'be' (*am, is, are, was, were, will be, shall be, would be, should be*). Many other verbs are used as linking verbs: verbs like *seem, become, feel, look, remain, appear, continue, grow, sound, smell, taste*. For example:

The man seems/appears (to be) a stranger to the place.

The days became warm as the summer advanced.

I feel hungry.

She looks sad.

The parents remained tense and anxious.

The weather on the mountain continued to be calm and sunny.

The night grew cold. (meaning 'became')

The idea sounds good.

The perfume smells nice. (meaning 'the perfume is nice, judging by the smell of it')

The medicine tastes bitter. (meaning 'the medicine is bitter, judging by the taste of it')

Note

A verb of doing need not always express a physical activity like *bark, chase, give*. Verbs like *hope, love, like, hate, know, understand* are also verbs of doing, except that they express a different kind of activity, mental or emotional.

Verbs like *smell* and *taste* are verbs of doing, as in these examples:

I smell something burning. Something, I suspect, is on fire.

He is smelling a perfume.

A tea-taster tastes teas to test their quality.

All royal households had on their payroll a food-taster whose job was to taste the food meant for the king to check for food-poisoning.

So is the verb *grow*, as in this example:

The farmers *grow* potatoes in this part of the country. (meaning 'cultivate')

All the three verbs in the above examples (*smell, taste, grow*) take an object after them and consequently the sentences conform to bp 2 (N-V-N).

Note the finite verbs in each of the following pairs of sentences:

The perfume smells nice. N-LV-adj (complement) bp 6	He is smelling a perfume. N-V (transitive) – N bp 2
The medicine tastes bitter. N-LV-adj (complement) bp 6	A tea-taster tastes teas ... N-V (transitive) – N bp 2
The night grew cold. N-LV-adj (complement) bp 6	The farmers grow potatoes ... N-V (transitive) – N bp 2

2.1.3 Transitive and Intransitive Verbs

Verbs of doing are of two kinds, transitive and intransitive. Look at the verbs in bp 2–4 and compare these with the verb in bp 1.

A	B
The child <u>chased</u> the dog.	Dogs bark. (bp 1)
The dog <u>chased</u> the child. (bp2)	
John <u>gave</u> Mary a letter. (bp 3)	
The Menons <u>named</u> their baby Sudha. (bp 4)	

The verbs in column A (*chased, gave, named*) are called transitive verbs. They take an object after them. 'Transitive' means 'going across'. When a verb is used transitively, the action expressed by the verb goes across from the subject to the object:

<u>The child</u> chased <u>the dog.</u>		<u>The dog</u> chased <u>the child.</u>	
(doer of the action)	(receiver of the action)	(doer of the action)	(receiver of the action)

To find the object, ask the question 'Whom?' or 'What?' after the verb:

The child chased. What? (What did the child chase?)
Answer: the dog

The dog chased. Whom? (Whom did the dog chase?)
Answer: the child

The verb in bp 3 ('John gave Mary a letter') has two possible answers:

To <u>whom</u> did John give a letter?
Answer: Mary
What did John give Mary?
Answer: a letter

The verb *gave* takes two objects after it: 'Mary', and 'a letter'.

Unlike verbs like *chase, give, name*, the verb *bark* in bp 1 does not take an object after it. You cannot possibly ask the question 'Whom?' or 'What?' after the verb 'bark'. The action of barking does not go across from the subject ('dogs') to anything beyond the verb 'bark'. 'Bark', in other words, is an intransitive verb here. Some other verbs of this category are:

go jump roar wake come fly creep sit stand

2.1.4 Direct and Indirect Objects

Of the two objects the verb *gave* in bp 3 takes, the first one ('Mary') is called an *indirect object* (IO) and the second ('a letter') a *direct object* (DO).

The object that comes first after the verb and which answers the question 'to whom' or 'for whom' is the indirect object. The object which comes next and answers the question 'what?' is the direct object. A better way of explaining the difference between the two kinds of objects is that the indirect object is not essential to the sentence with a transitive verb while the direct object is.

Exercise 3

The verb 'give' is one of approximately eighty verbs in English which take two objects. Here are some of these verbs. The objects coming after the verbs are underlined for you. Indicate which one is a direct object (DO) and which one is an indirect object (IO). Try to read the sentence, first with one object, and then with the other, and see which of the two readings makes sense.

a. Could you please pass me the mashed potatoes ?
b. Mother baked her cousin a pie.
c. Ravi bought his sister Radha a present.
d. The witness told the court the truth.
e. We owe you an apology for coming late.
f. Can you book me two second-class tickets?
g. The accused handed his lawyer a note.
h. They showed the visitors some rare paintings.

2.1.5 Subject and Object Complements

The verbs of being in bp 5–7 belong to a large group called linking verbs. They link or join what goes before them (the subject) to what comes after them (the complement):

subject	linking verb	complement
The king	was	a tyrant.
The crowd	seems	restless.
The baby	feels	hungry.
The days	grew	warm.

We call the words in the last column complements because without them the sentences would be incomplete. We cannot possibly say 'The king was', 'The crowd seems', 'The baby feels', 'The days grew' and stop there. We need a word or words ('a tyrant', 'restless', 'hungry', 'warm') to complete the sentence. The word or words that help to complete the sentence are called complements. 'That which completes' is a complement. The complements in the above examples refer to the subject and are therefore called subject complements (SC). A subject complement either describes or represents a subject.

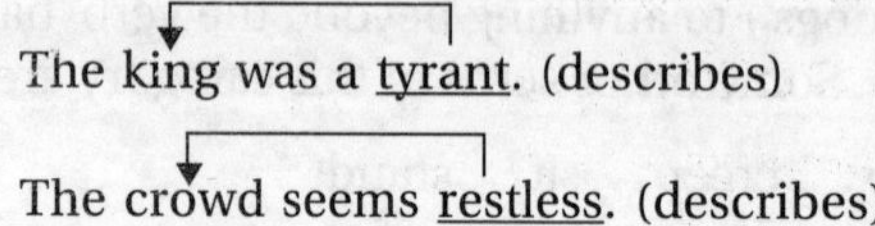

I am he. (represents)

There is another type of complement, the object complement. The object complement refers to the object of a transitive verb, as in bp 4:

The Menons named their baby Sudha.

Parents consider their children special.

The words 'Sudha' and 'special' are obviously complements, since without them the sentences would be incomplete and largely meaningless. However, these are complements with a difference. Unlike the complements in bp 5–7, these refer to objects – 'baby', object of the transitive verb 'named'; 'children', object of the transitive verb 'consider' – and are called object complements (OC). We have a small number of verbs in English which take an object and object complement after them:

The people elected him their leader.
The company appointed Mr Sharma manager.
The Sahgals found their house burgled.
The manager thinks Rose trustworthy.
The world called Tenzing Norgay a hero.
The club made Mr Pai an honorary member.

All the above sentences conform to the pattern in bp 4, as you can see from the following analysis:

subject	predicate		
	verb	object	complement
The people	elected	him	their leader.
The company	appointed	Mr Sharma	manager.
The Sahgals	found	their house	burgled.
The manager	thinks	Rose	trustworthy.
The world	called	Tenzing Norgay	a hero.
The club	made	Mr Pai	an honorary member.

Note

A complement is not a part of speech like a noun, verb or adjective. It is a term we use to indicate a word or word-group that comes after the verb (in the case of a verb of being) or a verb plus object (in the case of a verb of doing) to complete the sentence. It may be:

1. a noun — The man over there is the newly inducted minister. (SC)
   The trainers named the elephant Hima. (OC)
2. a pronoun — The actor much in demand today is she. (SC)
3. an adjective — She is clever. (SC)
   Her teachers think her clever. (OC)
4. a phrase — He is in a great hurry. (SC)

His sole aim is to make money. (SC)
We found the story hard to believe. (OC)

5. a clause — The fact is that we cannot count on a normal rainfall this year. (SC)

Exercise 4

Underline the complements in the following passage and say whether they are subject or object complements.

Tenzing Norgay, co-conqueror of Mount Everest, was a Sherpa. The Sherpas are a people, a tribe. Their present homeland is Solo Khumbu, in north-eastern Nepal. Solo Khumbu is actually two places, Solo and Khumbu, and Tenzing himself came from Khumbu.

Tenzing's very first expedition to Mount Everest was in 1932. He was eighteen then. During the next twenty years, he made five other unsuccessful attempts on the mountain. His sixth attempt was in the autumn of 1952, this time with the Swiss expedition. The Swiss had made him a full member of the expedition. The following year, in his seventh attempt on the mountain, he succeeded in getting to the top, which he did with Edmund Hillary. The world called Tenzing a hero and hailed his great achievement. Starting as a humble mountain porter, a bearer of loads, he had become the co-conqueror of the world's highest mountain. Tenzing, however, remained a simple man. He did not consider his ascent of Everest a conquest. To him the ascent was but an old childhood dream come true.

We now return to a consideration of the seven basic sentence patterns. Tabulated below are the seven patterns with brief descriptions of each and their symbolic representation:

Note

basic pattern	symbolic representation	description	illustrative example
1	N-V (intrans.)	noun+intransitive verb	Dogs bark.
2	N-V (trans.)-N (object)	noun+transitive verb+ noun as direct object	She photographed the tiger.
3	N-V (trans.)-N (IO)-N (DO)	noun+transitive verb+ noun as indirect object +noun as direct object	The children gave the elephant peanuts.
4	N-V (trans.)-N (DO)-N/Adj. (object complement)	noun+transitive verb+ direct object+noun or adjective as object complement	• We consider him a hero. • The teacher thought the book interesting.
5	N-LV-N (subject complement)	noun+linking verb+ noun as subject complement	• The man was a detective. • The woman seemed a stranger.
6	N-LV-Adj. (subject complement)	noun+linking verb+ adjective as subject complement	• The crowd was restless. •The sky appears blue.
7	N-LV-Adv. (adverb or adverb phrase)	noun+linking verb+ adverbial (adverb or adverb phrase)	• The man is here. • The woman is in a foreign country.

1. The symbol N in the basic sentence patterns stands for:
   a. a noun: Sekhar, Ruma, sky, crowd, truth
   b. a pronoun:

• *personal*:	he, she, it, I, we, you, they, him, her, it, me, us, you, them: He called her a genius .(bp 4) She called him hard-working .(bp 4) They were rotten mangoes. (bp 5) They were cheap. (bp 6) We bought them. (bp 2)
• *demonstrative*:	this, that, these, those: I like that. (bp 2) These are the reasons. (bp 5)
• *indefinite:*	somebody, someone, anybody, anyone, everybody, everyone, something, anything, everything, one, each, either, neither, many, most, much, several, some etc: They tried everything. (bp 2) Nothing worked. (bp 1) We had invited everyone. (bp 2) Some came. (bp 1) Most were absent. (bp 6) Several sent their apologies. (bp 2)
• *possessive*:	mine, ours, yours, his, hers, theirs, its: This pen is mine. (bp 5) That pen is yours. (bp 5) Yours is the better pen. (bp 5) I like yours. (bp 2)

2. The symbol N may be preceded by a determiner. By determiners we mean a whole class of words which always come before nouns, for example:

• *articles*:	a, an, the: A man showed up. (bp 1) The man was from Timbuctoo. (bp 7)
• *possessive adjectives*:	my, our, your, his, her, their: The Board thought your plan feasible. (bp 4) I gave Priya her due. (bp 3)
• *demonstrative adjectives*:	this, that, these, those: The usher found us this seat. (bp 3) These oranges are good. (bp 6)
• *indefinite adjectives*:	some, several, any, no, every, each, much, either, neither, few, a few etc: She gave each boy his share. (bp 3) Some people are clever. (bp 6) Some people are hard-working. (bp 6) Only a few people are clever and hard-working. (bp 6)

Exercise 5

Write the following sentences. Identify the basic pattern of each sentence by writing the appropriate labels. The first two are examples.

a. The story sounds interesting.

Answer: The story / sounds / interesting. (bp 6)
N / LV / Adj. (subj. compl.)

b. Mother bought me this dress.

Answer: Mother / bought / me / this dress. (bp 3)
N / V (trans.) / N (IO) / N (DO)

c. The lights went out.
d. Mr Pai was the club's first honorary secretary.
e. The waiter handed him a plate.
f. The teacher named Ravi the monitor of the class.
g. His explanation rings true.
h. The teacher thought the movie boring.

Exercise 6

Rewrite these sentences in the correct order. At the end of each rewritten sentence, write within brackets the basic pattern number. The first one is an example.

a. looks/Dennis/hungry

Answer: Dennis looks hungry. (bp 6)

b. pop music/Father/too noisy/considers
c. found/ a job/his wife/he
d. a party/his friends/Hari/gave (*two possibilities*)
e. the children/the teacher/a story/read
f. Arun/promised/a bicycle/Mother

Exercise 7

In the light of what you know about the English sentence, fill in the blanks in the following quiz. The answers are given at the end of the quiz but in jumbled order.

a. The ____________ is the basic unit of communication in English grammar.
b. English sentences naturally divide into the ____________ and the ____________.
c. The three basic sentence elements are the ____________, the ____________ and the ____________.
d. The normal word order of the three basic sentence elements is____________.
e. In the sentence 'The child chased the dog', 'child' functions as the ____________.
f. In the sentence 'The dog chased the child', 'child' functions as the ____________.
g. Word order therefore determines the ____________ of a sentence.
h. In the sentence 'The Pope crowned Henry King of England', 'Henry' is the ____________ and 'King of England' the ____________.

Answers: 1. subject-verb-object/complement 2. subject;

predicate 3. subject 4. object 5. meaning 6. sentence 7. subject; verb; object/complement 8. object; object complement

Exercise 8

Write sentences according to the following directions.

a. Use 'child' as an indirect object in the pattern N-V-N-N (bp 3).

b. Use the adjective 'faultless' as an object complement in the N-V-N-Adj. pattern (bp 4 b).

c. Use the verb 'spared' in the N-V-N-N pattern (bp 3).

d. Write sentences in which the verbs 'selected', 'elected', 'appointed' and 'found' are used with object complements in the pattern N-V-N-N (bp 4 a). Suggest three other verbs that may be used with object complements in the same pattern.

To sum up, the core of the English sentence consists of the subject and the predicate. The subject at its barest minimum is a noun (or pronoun) and the predicate at its barest minimum is a finite verb. Thus, the noun and the verb are the two parts of speech that form the core of the sentence. There are other words which cluster around the noun and the verb:

a. the words that modify the noun and the verb: the parts of speech called **adjectives** and **adverbs**;

b. the words that act as connectives between these four parts of speech, called **prepositions** and **conjunctions**.

We now look at these parts of speech.

3 Nouns

A noun may be defined on the basis of its meaning, its form, or its function. These are the three bases of our definitions: notional, formal and functional.

By notional definition we mean a definition based on the meaning of the word, rather our understanding of what the word stands for in the real world. By formal definition we mean a definition based on form, sounds in the spoken language and spelling in the written. By functional definition we mean a definition based on what the word does in the sentence and its relation to other words in the sentence.

Notionally, a noun is the name of a person (Ram), place (Delhi), animal (dog) or thing (table). Formally, a noun is a word that forms its plural by adding –s and its possessive by adding 's. Functionally, a noun is a word that serves as subject of verb, object of verb, object of preposition, subject complement, object complement, and so on.

a. The girls[1] in uniform[2] are nurses[3].
   (1. subject of verb 2. object of preposition 3. subject complement)

b. The party elected Mrs Kumar[4] leader[5].
   (4. object of verb 5. object complement)

None of these definitions – notional, formal, functional – may define a noun (or other parts of speech like verb, adjective, adverb) adequately, so in practice we use sometimes one definition and sometimes another, and sometimes a combination, depending on the circumstances.

3.1 Types of Nouns

Based on meaning, nouns may be classified in a number of ways, as shown below:

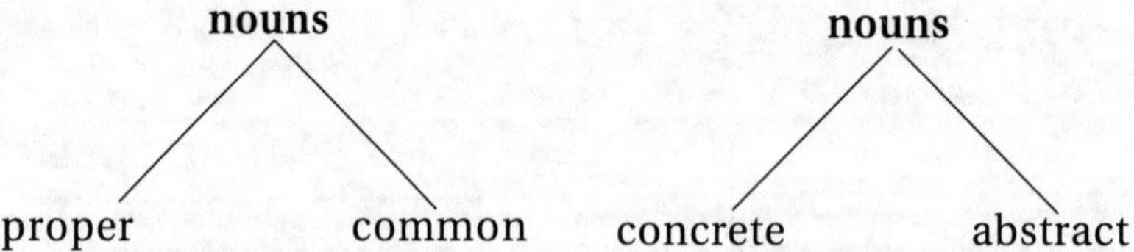

We have a fifth type called collective nouns. Some nouns may belong to more than one of the types mentioned above.

3.1.1 Proper and Common Nouns

A proper noun is the **particular name** of a person or thing and in writing, it begins with a capital letter. It may include:

names of persons (Vivek, Kamala, Yasmin)

names of tribes, nationalities, religions (Toda, Burmese, Islam)

names of places, cities, countries, rivers, seas, mountains, mountain ranges, islands, island groups (Chowringhee Lane, Chandigarh, India, Japan, the Ganga, the Arabian Sea, Everest, the Alps, Sri Lanka, the Andamans)

names of the days of the week (Thursday), months of the year (November)

names of special days (Christmas, Holi, Republic Day)

As opposed to proper nouns, all other nouns are common nouns. Words like *man, woman, street, city, country, river* are all common nouns. The word 'man' is the name of any man, so is the word 'river' the name of any river, unlike 'Vivek', which is the particular name of a boy or man, and 'the Ganga', which is the particular name of the river flowing through the plains of North India.

3.1.2 Concrete and Abstract Nouns

A concrete noun is a word that stands for an object that exists in the real world, something that we can see, touch, smell: *house, flower, basket* and so on. An abstract noun, on the other hand, is a word for a concept or idea which exists in our minds only: *truth, beauty, justice* and so on.

3.1.3 Collective Nouns

A collective noun is a word for a group of people, animals, or objects of the same class taken together and thought of as a single unit. Here are some examples of collective nouns:

audience	crowd	group	nation	team
assembly	family	herd	pack	class
flock	jury	committee	government	mob
public				

A collective noun, when used as a subject, may take a singular or plural verb. In American English the verb is usually singular:

The government **has decided** to enforce more strictly the immigration laws.

British usage prefers a plural verb:

The government **are considering** tougher measures to deal with traffic problems.

Here is a rule-of-thumb to follow. If the group is thought of as a single unit acting collectively, use a singular verb:

The committee **has** unanimously **decided** to reduce the club membership fee.

If, on the other hand, the focus is on the individual members of the group, use a plural verb:

The committee **were** bitterly **divided** on the question of admitting new members to the club.

Collective nouns may be used in the plural:

All the select **committees have submitted** their reports to Parliament.

All the **teams are gearing** up for the World Cup.

Exercise 1

Fill in this form about yourself. You will observe that there are plenty of proper nouns closely connected with you.

Your first name: ____________________

Your surname: ____________________

Place of birth: ____________________

Date of birth:

Birth sign (sign of the zodiac you were born under): ____________________

Lucky day of the week: ____________________

Favourite newspaper, magazine, book: ____________________

Favourite film star: ____________________

Favourite TV programme: ____________________

Exercise 2

For each of the common nouns in column 1, write an appropriate proper noun in column 2. The first one is an example.

common nouns	proper nouns	common nouns	proper nouns
city	New York	car	
ocean		film	
leader		dog	
writer		street	
king		shop	
island		mountain	

Exercise 3

Use the correct collective nouns from the box to complete the following phrases.

bunch	block	book	bundle	flight
fleet	heap	herd	litter	pack
pride	pile	sheaf	stack	string

a. a ____________ of pearls
b. a ____________ of cards
c. a ____________ of flats
d. a ____________ of lions
e. a ____________ of coins
f. a ____________ of rubbish
g. a ____________ of coupons
h. a ____________ of puppies
i. a ____________ of letters
j. a ____________ of clothes
k. a ____________ of birds
l. a ____________ of newspapers
m. a ____________ of keys
n. a ____________ of ships
o. a ____________ of cattle

Note

In present-day English 'data' and 'media' are often used as collective nouns, with either a singular or plural verb:

The media, the visual media in particular, *is/are* thought to be responsible for the spurt in crime.

The latest census data *shows/show* that more rural people own telephones than ever before.

Careful writers, however, use the plural verb with 'data' and 'media', these being the plural forms of 'medium' and 'datum'.

Exercise 4

The headlines below appeared in various newspapers highlighting a civic problem faced by residents of a locality. Expand each of the headlines into a complete sentence. The first one is an example.

a. Steep Rise in Number of Street Dogs. Janakapura Residents Alarmed

Ans: The residents of Janakapura are alarmed at the steep rise in the number of street dogs.

b. Street Dogs Chase Pedestrians, Cyclists, say Janakapura Residents

c. Janakapura Streets Unsafe after Dark for Pedestrians and Cyclists, Complain Local Residents

d. Janakapura Residents Concerned about Pedestrians' Safety Demand Action by the Corporation

e. Corporation Aware of the Problem and Concerned but Helpless: Reason Dogs not Wild Animals

Exercise 5

Choose the most likely alternatives to complete the following sentences.

a. As soon as the police arrived on the scene, the crowd was/were running in different directions.

b. The university faculty is/are united on the issue of a raise in salary.

c. The city corporation has/have adequate funds to repair the roads.

d. The press is/are here waiting to see you.

e. The audience was/were distinctly restless. The concert apparently was not a success.

3.1.4 Countable and Uncountable Nouns

There is yet another way of dividing nouns. Nouns may be divided into **countable** and **uncountable** nouns. This division of nouns is particularly useful to the learner from the point of view of usage.

Countable nouns refer to persons or things that can be counted: *boy, apple, tree.* A countable noun usually forms its plural by adding 's':

boy – boys   apple – apples   tree – trees

A singular countable noun is usually preceded by an article: *a, an* or *the.*

For example:

a. A dog, unlike a cat, is a friendly animal.
b. They went sailing down the river.
c. He lives in a house with a garden in front.

Plural countable nouns, however, do not usually have the definite article before them:

d. She likes cars but does not care for two-wheelers.
e. Living in apartments is convenient but it could get lonely for single occupants.

If, however, the plural noun is made specific, the definite article is a must:

f. The cars that you see on the city roads are mostly imported ones.
g. The apartments on the sea-front cost a fortune.

Uncountable nouns refer to things that cannot be counted: *sugar, butter, water, wood, cloth.* Such nouns are always singular and never used in the plural.

One type of uncountable nouns is known as **mass nouns**. Mass nouns are words for concrete objects which are referred to as a mass, as quantity. These usually do not carry an article before them.

He lives mostly on coffee and biscuits.
He likes tea but not coffee.
Cheese is good food but high cholesterol.
They do not grow cotton in this country, so cloth is rather expensive.

Mass nouns are sometimes used to refer to quantities of a particular kind of food or drink. When so used, the words can appear in the plural, or attract an article before them, if used in the singular:

a. 'How about a coffee before we go?'
'Yes, why not?'
'Waiter, two coffees please.'
b. The supermarket stocks a variety of cheeses.
c. A tea-taster makes a living by tasting teas to judge their quality.

An uncountable noun can, however, be made countable by adding certain words to it. 'Luggage' (meaning a number of travel things such as suitcases and bags) is uncountable in English but we can make it countable by saying 'a piece of luggage'. 'A piece of luggage' is one item of luggage, more than one item of luggage is 'pieces of luggage'. Look at these examples:

uncountable noun	**countable noun (singular)**	**countable noun (plural)**
clothing	an article of clothing	articles of clothing
shopping	a bag of shopping	bags of shopping
rubbish	a pile of rubbish	piles of rubbish
news	an item of news	items of news/news items

Here are some more ways of making uncountable nouns countable:

uncountable noun	countable noun (sing.)	countable noun (pl.)
bread	a loaf of bread/ a slice of bread	loaves/slices of bread
chocolate	a bar of chocolate	bars of chocolate
paper	a sheet of paper	sheets of paper
string	a ball of string	balls of string
cloth	a roll of cloth	rolls of cloth
milk	a bottle/glass of milk	bottles/glasses of milk
water	a glass/bucket of water	glasses/buckets of water
rice	a bag of rice	bags of rice
fruit	a basket of fruit	baskets of fruit
sugar	a kilo of sugar	kilos of sugar
petrol	a litre of petrol	litres of petrol

Some nouns may be used as both countable and uncountable nouns, for example, nouns like *stone, glass, cloth.* These nouns are uncountable when they refer to a substance or a material, and countable when they refer to separate items made of the same substance or material:

uncountable nouns	countable nouns
All these houses are built of **stone**.	There is **a stone** in my shoe and it is hurting.
The windows are made of **glass**.	Quick, get me **a glass** of water.
Cloth is sold through a network of fair price shops.	Clean the table with **a cloth**, not a sponge.

'Chicken' meaning 'bird' is countable but 'chicken' meaning 'bird meat' is uncountable:

The children loved to chase the **chickens** round the farm.
For dinner, we had fried **chicken** and roast potatoes.

Exercise 6

Use each of the words in box A below twice over, once as a countable noun and once as an uncountable noun, and complete the sentences. Remember to use suitable words from box B before some of these nouns to make them countable. The first one is an example.

A

ice	news	iron
furniture	wood	paper
	brick	

B

cube	chips	item
rods	sheet	bits
	piece	

a. 1. It's so cold. The water is frozen into ice.

2. Can I have a cube of ice, please? The water is not cold enough.

b. 1. No __________, they say, is good news.
2. Did you see __________ in today's 'Express' about a man being chased by a monkey at the local zoo?

c. 1. The house does not go with __________. You will have to buy it or hire it yourself.
2. There was not __________ that the burglars had not removed from the house.

d. 1. What is the melting point of __________?
2. The __________ that were left out in the rain had become rusty and were falling to pieces.

e. 1. Houses here are generally made of __________.
2. The carpenter had made a mess of the room and there were __________ lying all over the place.

f. 1. During the rains we used to launch toy boats made of __________.
2. Please give me a __________ to write my list.

g. 1. The walls are very strong. They are made of __________.
2. __________ and cement had fallen from the broken wall, there was debris everywhere.

All countable nouns have a singular and a plural form. However, all countable nouns do not form their plurals the same way.

As a rule, nouns in English form their plurals with the addition of -s to the singular:

boy – boys   girl – girls   tree – trees

However, there are several exceptions to the rule.

a. If the singular noun ends in -s, -ch, -sh or -x, we add -es:

class – classes   church – churches   lash – lashes   box – boxes

If the final -ch is pronounced k, we add only -s:

monarch – monarchs   stomach – stomachs   epoch – epochs

b. After a final –o, we sometimes add -es:

mango – mangoes   hero – heroes   potato – potatoes
tomato – tomatoes   echo – echoes   veto – vetoes

But if the final -o is preceded by a vowel, or if the word is a term used in music, we add only -s:

zoo – zoos   radio – radios   studio – studios   piano – pianos   solo – solos

Some other words ending in -o take either -s or -es to form the plural:

cargo – cargos/cargoes   volcano – volcanos/volcanoes
motto – mottos/mottoes   mosquito – mosquitos/mosquitoes
manifesto – manifestos/manifestoes

c. In some one -syllable nouns, the final -f or -fe becomes -ves in the plural:

life – lives   wife – wives   calf – calves   leaf – leaves   half – halves thief – thieves   loaf – loaves   shelf – shelves   wolf – wolves

Other one-syllable nouns ending in -f take only the regular -s ending:

chief – chiefs   cliff – cliffs   roof – roofs   proof – proofs

A few words take either form for the plural:

dwarf – dwarfs/dwarves   scarf – scarfs/scarves
wharf – wharfs/wharves   hoof – hoofs/hooves

d. If the singular noun ends in -y preceded by a consonant, we change y to i and add -es:

army – armies   fly – flies   hobby – hobbies   country – countries

If final -y is preceded by a vowel, we must add -s:

valley – valleys   boy – boys   donkey – donkeys   attorney – attorneys

e. With some nouns the plural has the same form as the singular:

sheep – sheep   deer – deer

f. With some nouns the singular has the same form as the plural:

series – series   means – means

Note

The regular plural ending -s or -es is pronounced in three different ways, depending on what sound comes immediately before it: sound /s/, sound /z/, or sound /iz/.

Thus, we have the /s/ sound in *cats, mats, roofs, proofs, cliffs, stomachs*;

the /z/ sound in *dogs, boys, tomatoes, zoos, leaves, scarves, valleys, series, means*;

and the /iz/ sound in *buses, classes, churches, lashes, boxes.*

All words ending in -s, -ch, -sh, or -x form the plural with the addition of -es.

g. **Irregular plurals**

Some nouns do not form their plurals the regular way. We call them irregular plurals. Irregular plurals may take the form of:

i. an internal change, that is, a change within the word:
   man – men   tooth – teeth   goose – geese   louse – lice   mouse – mice   foot – feet (or)

ii. an -en ending:
   ox – oxen   child – children.

h. **Foreign plurals**

Many foreign words, that is, words borrowed mainly from Latin and Greek, retain their plurals in English:

- stimulus – stimuli   radius – radii   nucleus – nuclei   focus – foci
- memorandum – memoranda   datum – data   medium – media
  aquarium – aquaria   referendum – referenda

- larva – larvae vertebra – vertebrae
- crisis – crises parenthesis – parentheses basis – bases
  hypothesis – hypotheses axis – axes
- criterion – criteria phenomenon – phenomena

i. words standing for items with two parts are always plural:
   scissors, pliers, tweezers, trousers, spectacles

j. Words like *news, mumps, measles, economics, politics,* although they end in -s, are singular uncountable nouns, so are *aerobics, billiards,* and *draughts.*

Exercise 7

Complete the following passages with the plural forms of the words in brackets.

a. __________ (kangaroo) are found in Australia and the nearby islands.
   They have large powerful hind__________ (leg) and move by leaping. Outside Australia they are mostly found in __________ (zoo).

b. 'Please get me a dozen __________ (box) of matches and a packet of (candle,') Ravi said to Mohan.
   'Anything else?' asked Mohan, who knew his brother was in the habit of remembering things only after he left.
   'Yes, now that you ask me, I need two __________ (loaf) of bread, a dozen __________ (handkerchief), a kilo each of __________ (tomato) and __________ (potato) and... well, that's all for today.'
   'Are you sure, Ravi?'
   'Yes, I am... but wait, Mohan. I've just remembered. Get me a couple of __________ (scarf) from Bhojson's.'

c. What are __________ (hobby)? One person's hobby is another person's work.

d. What, then, are the __________ (criterion) for judging, from among the many and diverse __________ (activity) that people pursue, which of them are __________ (hobby) in the real sense of the term? Is catching __________ (fish), __________ (mouse), or __________ (butterfly) a hobby? That would depend on the catcher and what he does the catching for. A Wodehouse* character is so crazy about __________ (newt)* that he collects them by the hundreds.

---

*Wodehouse: P.G. Wodehouse (1881-1975), an English novelist who wrote hilariously funny novels; the creator of the immortal Jeeves, butler to Bertie Wooster

* newt: a small creature, short-legged, long-tailed, living partly on land and partly in water

Exercise 8

In column 1 are a number of sentence openings. In column 2 are the sentence endings. Match each of the openings with an appropriate ending and complete the sentences.

1	2
a. News	1. is a fashionable game.
b. The media	2. about the hole in the ozone layer are rather disturbing.
c. Geriatrics	3. is a nasty disease that usually affects children.
d. Billiards	4. has just been received of the chairman's arrival in the city.
e. My trousers	5. are faded.
f. Mumps	6. are usually blamed for any spurt in crime.
g. The latest data	7. is all about the care of old people.

3.2 Nouns: Gender

English nouns are not classified as masculine, feminine and neuter the way nouns in some other languages such as Sanskrit, are. Every noun in Sanskrit has gender (masculine, feminine, or neuter) and the classification is not based on actual sex. Thus, in Sanskrit 'taru' (meaning 'tree') is masculine, 'nadee' (meaning 'river') is feminine, and 'mitra' (meaning 'friend') is neuter. This is known as grammatical gender. English has no grammatical gender.

Gender in English nouns is generally based on sex. It tells us the sex of the person or thing referred to by the noun. In life we think of people and things as:

a. male b. female c. either male or female d. neither male nor female

Corresponding to these divisions in real life, we have masculine gender (*boy, man, bull*), feminine gender (*girl, woman, cow*), common gender (*doctor, parent, teacher*), neuter gender (*chair, basket, cloud*). A noun in English belongs to one of these four genders. Nouns belonging to the neuter gender generally refer to inanimate or non-living things. Gender in English corresponds to sex as a general rule but there are exceptions to the rule. Here are two of them:

a. Babies and the lower order of animals are generally neuter gender.
b. Ships, cars, trains are regarded as feminine in some contexts, especially in the speech of their crew.

3.2.1 Ways of Indicating Gender in English

There are three different ways of indicating gender in English:

a. by adding the suffix -ess to the masculine:

host – hostess lion – lioness shepherd – shepherdess
heir – heiress steward – stewardess

Remember to drop the vowel of the masculine ending ('e' or 'o') before adding the suffix to these nouns:

waiter – waitress   actor – actress

Note

In present-day English there is a tendency to make less and less use of the suffix '-ess ' to indicate the female sex. Thus, we generally use the words *author, actor, manager* for both sexes . In cases where the gender label is necessary, we generally say 'woman manager' for example, or depend on the pronoun and other indicators. For example: The author is interested in wildlife. She is a keen photographer.

b. by adding a word before or after:
billy-goat – nanny-goat   peacock – peahen
bull elephant – cow elephant

c. by using two different words, one for the male and one for the female:
father – mother   son – daughter   husband – wife
brother – sister   nephew – niece   boy – girl   fox – vixen
gander – goose   drake – duck

Note

Another method of indicating gender is to use the word '-woman', as in 'policewoman' and 'needlewoman'. The masculine ending'-man' is no longer considered appropriate in contemporary English, so we now say 'chairperson' and 'spokesperson' rather than 'chairman', 'spokesman'.

3.3 Nouns: Possessive Forms

Formally, a noun may be defined as a word that forms its plural by adding –s or its possessive by adding 's. Why is the possessive form used?

We use the possessive form for saying that something belongs to someone or something is associated with someone:

The **policeman's function** primarily is to maintain law and order.
That is **Susan's handbag**, not mine.
By beating **Ravi's record** in pole-vault, ten-year-old Mohan became the **school's youngest champion pole-vaulter.**

We indicate possession or association by adding an apostrophe (or apostrophe plus 's') to the noun in question. Here are a few simple rules to remember when adding the apostrophe (or the apostrophe plus 's') to nouns:

a. Add 's to the singular noun (boy – boy's): the boy's mother.
b. Add ' alone to the plural noun ending in 's' (boys – boys'): the boys' mother.
c. Add 's to the irregular plural not ending in 's' (children–children's): the children's room
d. Add ' or 's to proper nouns ending in 's' (Dickens – Dickens'/ Dickens's): Dickens' novels/Dickens's novels
e. With the group of words functioning as one unit, add 's to the last word of the

group (the President of India – the President of India's): the President of India's official residence, the Rani of Jhansi's place in history

Using the apostrophe is one way of indicating possession or association in English; the other way is using the phrasal possessive or the 'of possessive'.

Compare the following pairs:

his father's ancestral house/the ancestral house of his father

Mumbai's Sahara Airport/ the Sahara Airport of Mumbai

3.3.1 Uses of the Possessive Forms

a. We normally use 's when the noun refers to a person or animal:

Arun's mother   the nurse's uniform   the tiger's roar
the elephant's memory

b. With things we normally use the phrasal possessive:

the leg of the table (not the table's leg), the foot of the mountain (not the mountain's foot), the top of the hill, the pages of the book

c. We can use either 's or the 'of possessive' with nouns denoting countries, cities, groups of people working together:

India's foreign policy (or) the foreign policy of India

the committee's proposals (or) the proposals of the committee

the ship's crew (or) the crew of the ship

the paper's sports editor (or) the sports editor of the paper

the bank's expatriate clients (or) the expatriate clients of the bank

d. We also use 's with words or expressions signifying time:

a month's holiday   an hour's drive
a day's journey   today's TV show

e. We use only 's in these expressions:

a stone's throw away (The club is only a stone's throw away from my house.)

to keep out of harm's way (He managed throughout his school years to keep out of harm's way.)

to keep someone at arm's length (Avoid that man, keep him at arm's length.)

to one's heart's content (They ate to their heart's content.)

f. We use 's alone to indicate a place of business:

at the chemist's (meaning 'at the chemist's shop') near the grocer's

next door to the dentist's (meaning 'next door to the dentist's clinic')

g. With words referring to natural phenomena, we use 's:

the sun's rays   the earth's atmosphere   the moon's orbit

h. We may use 's with 'of' in a double possessive:

a friend of John's (meaning 'one of John's friends')

Exercise 9

Put the following in the possessive form using ' or 's. The first one is an example.

a. the games of children (children's games)
b. the uncle of Charles
c. the plays of Kalidasa
d. the order of the commander-in-chief
e. the clothes of men
f. the waiting-room for women

Exercise 10

Insert apostrophes in the appropriate places.

a. The womens hostel, unlike the mens, was very large.
b. I saw her at the doctors. An hour later, I saw her at the chemists with the doctors prescription.
c. The policemens quarters are just ten minutes walk from here.
d. Did you watch yesterdays programme on TV?
e. It is just a days journey from Bangalore to Mumbai.

Exercise 11

Combine the words in brackets at the end of each of the following sentences into the 'apostrophe possessive' or the 'of possessive'. The first two are examples.

a. The umbrella the man is carrying is strange. It looks like a ____________. (child, umbrella)
   Ans: It looks like a child's umbrella.
b. Where shall we sit ? In front or at the ____________? (auditorium, back)
   Ans: back of the auditorium
c. Don't forget to buy me ____________ on your way back home. (cake, soap)
d. Do you know anything about the ____________? (new admission policy, school)
e. Can you wait while I repair your shoe ? It is just ____________. (work, ten minutes)
f. I wish I could buy a radio but it is not possible on a ____________. (teenager, pocket money)
g. He has gone on a ____________. (long leave, year)
h. He is not expected back before ____________. (May, the middle)

3.4 Function and Position of Nouns

A noun can fill one of these six positions in a sentence, **depending on its function.**

Look at the noun 'boy' in the following sentences and note its **position and function** in the sentence:

a. The **boy** belongs to a well-to-do family from East Africa. (comes before the verb, function: subject of verb)
b. The parents adored the **boy**. (comes after the transitive verb 'adored'; function: object of verb)
c. The parents were very fond of the **boy**. (comes after the preposition 'of'; function: object of preposition)
d. The parents found the **boy** a good school. (comes immediately after the transitive verb 'found' and before the second object 'school'; function: indirect object of verb)
e. Rahim is a tall **boy**. (comes after the linking verb 'is'; function: subject complement)
f. The teacher considered Rahim a quiet **boy**. (comes after the transitive verb plus object, 'considered Rahim'; function: object complement)

The above a-f, are the chief functions of a noun. Notice that the position of the noun 'boy' in each of the above examples is determined by its function.

Additionally, and less importantly, a noun may function as an appositive, as an adjunct to another noun, or as a vocative.

g. **as an appositive**:
Delhi, India's federal **capital,** is a fine city.

Both 'Delhi' and 'India's federal capital' refer to the same geographical area in the north of India. The second noun 'capital' is in apposition to the first noun 'Delhi' and it is called an appositive.

Notice the position of the appositive noun. It comes immediately after the first noun to which it is in apposition.

h. **as a noun adjunct**:

Suresh is now a **college** student. (noun adjunct to the other noun 'student')

She wore a **cotton** sari.

He behaves very much like a **music** teacher.

By 'noun adjunct' here we simply mean a noun used as an adjective before another noun, the two together forming a noun compound. Notice the position of the noun adjunct, it comes immediately before the noun to which it is adjunct.

i. **as a vocative:**
Susan, come here.
Come here, **Susan**.

A noun is said to function as a vocative when it is used in direct address, like 'Susan' in the example. The vocative noun always comes at the beginning, or the very end, of a sentence.

3.5 Markers of Nouns

By 'marker' we mean a structure-word that marks or signals the part of speech of a word following it. And by 'structure-words' we mean words like articles, prepositions, possessives, demonstratives etc which do not contribute much meaning to the sentence as a whole, but which are nevertheless an essential part of sentence-structure. Thus, in the sentence:

The old woman lived **in a** house **at the** edge **of a** forest

we have seven structure-words (**in bold type**) and six non-structure words.

Nouns are marked or signalled by **determiners** and **prepositions.** You know what prepositions are but what are determiners?

Determiners are a small group of structure-words which help to identify, **in a general or specific way**, the persons or things that the nouns refer to. A noun in English refers to someone or something. We may refer to this someone or something **in a specific way** knowing that our listener knows which person or thing we are talking about.

Here was **this** man striding up to me in the middle of the street and putting out his hand, asking for money.
The woman chased **the** thief down **the** street, **the** people cheering her along.
These ties are no longer in fashion.
I know all too well **his** views on **the** subject.

Who is this man the speaker refers to in the last example, whose views are well known to him? Whoever he is and whatever his views on whatever the subject, they are just as well known to the listener as to the speaker; theirs is shared knowledge. In the same way, the speaker and the listener know about the woman chasing the thief down the street, the thief that is being chased, and the street down which he is being chased. The structure-words 'this', 'the', 'these' and 'his' help to identify the persons and things that are being talked about, in a specific way.

Alternatively, you can refer to someone or something **in a general way**:

The crowd consisted mostly of women; there were **a few** men, though.
At the end of the day there was **an** unclaimed parcel/**one** unclaimed parcel.
Living is not growing like **a** tree.

We use determiners **before** nouns in order to refer to someone or something in a general or specific way.

3.5.1 Determiners

Given below is a list of determiners:

1. Articles: a, an, the (**a** girl, **an** elephant, **the** game)
2. Demonstrative adjectives: this, these, that, those (**this** book, **those** houses)
3. Possessive adjectives:

   a. pronouns: my, our, your, his, its, their (**my** car, **our** house, **your** handbag, **their** children)

   b. nouns: mother's, Vivek's, the country's (**mother's** hope, the **country's** import bill)

4. Indefinite adjectives: some, several, few, more, many, any etc (**some** men, **several** groups, **many** options)

5. Numerical adjectives:

   a. cardinal: five, twenty-one, thirty-seven (**five** rows)

   b. ordinal: fifth, twenty-first, thirty-seventh (the **fifth** row)

6. Interrogative adjectives: what, which (**What** men are you talking about? **Which** house are you thinking of buying?)

7. Relative adjectives: whose (This is my uncle **whose** son you met and had dinner with in New York.
   An equilateral triangle is a triangle **whose** sides are equal.)

Apart from determiners and prepositions, descriptive adjectives too help to mark the nouns that follow them.

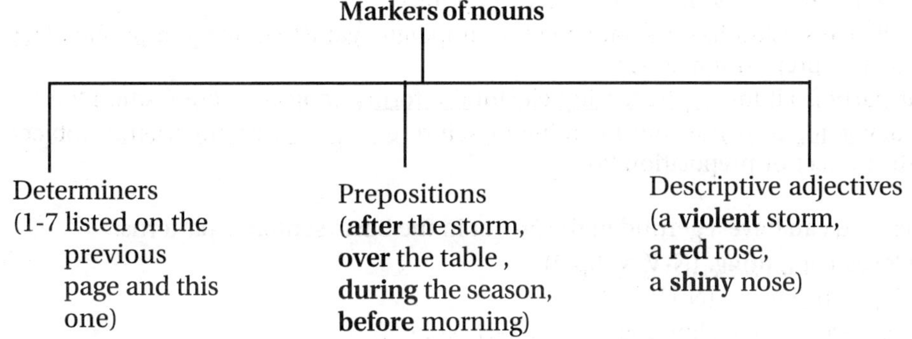

You will learn more about determiners in the unit on noun phrases.

3.6 Gerunds or –ing Nouns

Among the non-finite verbs, we saw earlier, are three participles: present, past and perfect. Two of these, present and perfect, can function as nouns.

They are called **verbal nouns**, or **gerunds**, or **–ing nouns**. Of these the term 'gerund' is the most commonly used.

Look at the underlined words in the following sentences. The noun-function that each of them does in the sentence is indicated in parentheses.

1. Swimming is a good exercise. (subject of verb)
2. I like swimming. (object of verb)
3. I am fond of swimming. (object of preposition)
4. The exercise I like best is swimming. (subject complement)
5. He stands in knee-deep water and splashes about, and he calls it swimming. (object complement)
6. He likes only one exercise, swimming. (noun in apposition)

We call 'swimming' in the above examples a gerund because it is a present participle performing one or the other of the half-dozen functions associated with the noun.

Apart from the present participle of the verb, the perfect participle too (but not the past participle) can function as a gerund:

> He regrets having wasted his time in college. (object of verb 'regrets')
>
> For the rest of her life she kept congratulating herself on having said no to cakes. (object of preposition 'on')

The more common form, however, of the gerund is the present participle.

You can have a gerund phrase instead of a gerund. A gerund phrase is a phrase or word-group headed by a gerund.

> Reading is a good habit. (gerund)
> Reading a few hours every day is an excellent habit. (gerund phrase)
> The old man enjoys walking. (gerund)
> The old man enjoys walking in the morning. (gerund phrase)

Here are some more examples of the gerund phrase:

> The Beavers' Club has just launched a campaign against smoking in public places. (object of preposition 'against')
> Our party is all for implementing electoral reforms. (object of preposition 'for')
> I enjoy going to parties but I confine myself to going out with my friends. (object of verb) (object of preposition 'to')

Note that you can have a gerund in the N-slot in the basic sentence patterns:

> He loves computing. (N-V-N; bp 2)
> Seeing is believing. (N-LV-N; bp 5)
> She considers rock-climbing fun. (N-V-N-N; bp 4)

Exercise 12

Underline the gerunds/gerund phrases in the following sentences and identify the noun-function that each of them does in the sentence. Note that all participles/participle phrases are not gerunds/gerund phrases. The first two are examples.

a. Riding a bicycle is an exciting adventure to a five-year-old. (gerund phrase, subject of 'is'. Note that 'exciting' is NOT a gerund, it functions as an adjective modifying the noun 'adventure' and therefore not a gerund.)

b. Do you honestly look forward to spending a whole week in the countryside? (gerund phrase, object of the preposition ' to ')

c. In June 1969, the Central American football teams of Honduras and El Salvador played a series of matches qualifying for the World Cup.

d. The games were closely fought and El Salvador finally won after being awarded a disputed penalty.

e. The awarding of the disputed penalty led to large-scale disturbances.

f. Rioting broke out on the ground and the fighting spilled into the streets.

g. In July, war was declared between the two countries, and 200 people were hurt in the fighting.

Exercise 13

Tina and Roshan are part of a team interviewing college students on behalf of a TV channel. Here they are, interviewing Kamal and Hassan on campus. Complete the dialogue with suitable gerunds/gerund phrases. Check with the verbs in the box if you need help.

Tina: I am Tina and this is Roshan.

Kamal: And I am Kamal and this is my friend Hassan.

Tina: Do you enjoy ___________ in college, Kamal ?

Kamal: I didn't at the ___________. There were those long lectures and the equally long sessions in the lab.

Roshan: You obviously were not interested in ___________ practicals. Am I right ?

Kamal: Yes, what I particularly disliked was ___________ to stand on the lab floor for two hours at a stretch proving Archimedes right.

Tina: And now ? Do you like college now, I mean, the lectures and the lab sessions?

Kamal: I'm not exactly happy about ___________ to my professors or about ___________ lab work but I've got used to them both.

Tina: How about you, Hassan ?

Hassan: I love ___________ practicals , and I don't mind ___________ to some of my professors. As a matter of fact, I enjoy ___________ my English classes. Most of our professors are quite interesting. We have no choice anyway and over time one does reconcile oneself to ___________ the rough with the smooth.

Tina: Do you watch...?

attend	be	begin	do
have	listen	take	

4 Pronouns

4.1 Introduction

Pronouns are a very small class of words but they are used quite frequently. When we want to refer to people or things, we use nouns in the first instance; the second or third time we want to refer to the same people or things, we use **pronouns**.

Sometimes we need to refer to a person or thing several times and we cannot repeat the same noun every time the reference is made. We use pronouns instead. Pronouns help us to make our discourse less repetitive and boring. (By 'discourse' we mean a piece of language, spoken or written.) For an example, look at this paragraph:

> The expedition led by Richard Burton made an important discovery: it discovered Lake Tanganyika. Speke on his own discovered another stretch of water to the north-east of Lake Tanganyika. He called it Lake Victoria. It was much larger than the Tanganyika and Speke, somewhat rashly, claimed that it was the source of the Nile.

If we were to dispense with the pronouns and use nouns instead, this is how the paragraph would read:

> The expedition led by Richard Burton made an important discovery: the expedition led by Richard Burton discovered Lake Tanganyika. Speke on Speke's own discovered another stretch of water to the north-east of Lake Tanganyika. Speke called the stretch of water to the north-east of Lake Tanganyika Lake Victoria. The stretch of water to the north-east of Lake Tanganyika was much larger than the Tanganyika and Speke, somewhat rashly, claimed that the stretch of water to the north-east of Lake Tanganyika was the source of the Nile.

The pronouns coming in the place of nouns not only help to make the discourse economical, less repetitive and more readable but they better demonstrate the *connection between ideas*: the connection between one word and another within the sentence, between one sentence and another within the paragraph, and sometimes between one paragraph and the next. *Remember pronouns are important reference words* and by referring back and forth to nouns already stated, or yet to be stated, they help to establish the interconnectedness of our ideas, and the *continuity of theme*.

4.2 Definition

The pronoun is traditionally defined as a word that takes the place of a noun. This is no doubt true of some types of pronouns, the types of pronouns, for instance, used in the first of the paragraphs you have just read, but not of others. A better way of defining a pronoun is with reference to its position and function. Defined that way, pronouns are a subclass of nouns; they occupy the same positions, and perform the same functions, as nouns in the sentence. Study the noun and the pronoun underlined in each of the following sets of sentences with respect to their position and function:

a. 1. Mr Sharma is a dentist. (noun, subject)

2. He is a dentist. (pronoun, subject)

b.1. People respect Mr Sharma for his professional skill. (noun, object of verb)
  2. People respect him for his professional skill. (pronoun, object of verb)
c.1. Mr Sharma is very friendly with his patients. (noun, object of preposition)
  2. Mr Sharma is very friendly with them. (pronoun, object of preposition)
d.1. It is Susan. (noun, subject complement)
  2. It is she. (pronoun, subject complement)
e.1. Shankar , the man I was just speaking to you about, is here. (noun, in apposition to 'Shankar ')
  2. Shankar, he of whom I was just speaking to you, is here. (pronoun, in apposition to 'Shankar ')

Even this definition of pronouns as a subclass of nouns is not wholly satisfactory. There are important differences *in form* between nouns and pronouns: many pronouns inflect far more than nouns for *person, number, gender* and *case*. A word is said to inflect, or be inflected, when its form or ending changes with a change in its grammatical function. For example, the first person pronoun is 'I' in the singular and 'we' in the plural. It is 'I' when it comes as subject of verb (nominative case) but 'me' as object of verb (objective case). The third person pronoun is 'he' for masculine, 'she' for feminine, and 'it' for neuter. The possessive forms of pronoun, again, inflect; 'my' and 'mine', 'our' and 'ours', 'your' and 'yours', and so on.

Note

Most English nouns form their plural with the addition of –s, and their possessive with the addition of 's. Most English verbs form their past tense with the addition of –ed. Personal pronouns have 'I', 'we', 'he', 'she', 'they' in the nominative case (i.e., when they function as subject) and 'me', 'us', 'him', 'her', 'them' in the objective case (i.e., when they function as object of verb or preposition).

A language is said to inflect, or be inflected, if it has words in it that change their forms or endings with a change in their grammatical function. Despite the presence of a few inflectional endings, Modern English is not an inflected language like, for example, German or Sanskrit. Of the few inflectional endings still present in Modern English, pronouns have more of them than nouns.

Even among the pronouns there are important differences: some (like the personal pronouns) are inflected while some (like the indefinite pronouns) are not; some (like personal and relative pronouns) substitute for nouns while some don't. However, there are two features shared by most pronouns. One is they are weak in meaning; whatever meaning they have is derived from the context in which they occur. Secondly, they may stand alone like nouns and function like nouns.

4.3 Types of Pronouns

4.3.1 Personal Pronouns

Modern English uses the following forms as **personal pronouns**.

	1st person singular	2nd person singular	3rd person singular
Nominative case	I	you	he, she, it
Possessive case	my, mine	your, yours	his, her, hers, its
Objective case	me	you	him, her, it
	plural	**plural**	**plural**
Nominative case	we	you	they
Possessive case	our, ours	your, yours	their, theirs
Objective case	us	you	them

Personal pronouns refer to:

a. the speaker, called the first person (I, we)

b. the person spoken to, called the second person (you)

c. the person or thing being spoken of, called the third person (he, she, it, they)

4.3.2 Possessive Pronouns

Personal pronouns have, apart from subject and object forms, possessive forms (see table below). These forms are called **possessive pronouns.** We use possessive pronouns when we talk of possession or physical ownership of something. When someone says ' This book is hers', he means that the book belongs to her.

Tabulated below are possessive pronouns:

possessive pronouns			
	singular	**plural**	**examples**
1st person	mine	ours	These coins are **mine/ours.**
2nd person	yours	yours	I think that hat is **yours.**
3rd person	his, hers, its	theirs	The car is **hers**, not **his.** The house is **theirs.**

Exercise 1

Vinod is on a train to Bombay. He finds a woman sitting in his seat. The woman refuses to get up, saying that the seat is hers. Read the conversation between the two and underline all the possessive pronouns.

Vinod: Excuse me. I think this seat is mine. You're sitting in my seat.

Woman: No, this can't be yours. This seat is mine.

Vinod: Are you sure? I saw the chart outside, and among the names listed was mine. What's your seat number?

Woman: It's F67.

Vinod:	Mine is also F67. How come?
Woman:	You can't depend on computers. But I'm sure my memory is correct. You see, I remember my seat number because my age is also 67.
Vinod:	I see... Here's my ticket. Can I look at yours? ... Just as I thought. F67 is not your seat number. F is for 'Female' and 67 is your age. Your coach number is S4.
Woman:	Oh, I'm so sorry. Now I must find S4.

Exercise 2

Rewrite the replies to the following questions using appropriate possessive pronouns. The first one is an example.

a. Is this your book?
No, it does not belong to me./It isn't mine.

b. Is this Susan's pen?
Yes, I think it belongs to her./ ______________

c. Whose two-wheeler is this?
It belongs to him./ ______________

d. Is this your house?
Yes, it belongs to us./ ______________

e. Is this your car key?
No, it belongs to you./ ______________

f. Whose umbrella is this?
It belongs to me./ ______________

g. Is Ravi the sole owner of the property?
No, I think Ravi and Priya jointly own the property. / ______________________

Exercise 3

Fill in the blanks with suitable possessive pronouns.

a. The purse belongs to my father. It is ______________. But the money in it is not ______________, it's my mother's.

b. The red saree she wore for the meeting was not ______________, it was her sister's.

c. The house that Keshav and Kusum live in is not ______________, it's ______________ in fact.

d. 'He dazzles everyone with his brilliant smile.'

'Does he? But remember that the teeth that he is flashing are not ______________. He uses false teeth.'

4.3.3 Demonstrative Pronouns

The words 'this' and 'that' and their plural forms 'these' and 'those' are used to point out someone or something. The words also stand for the people or things pointed out:

This is Mohan, captain of the school cricket team.

These are the people from Delhi I told you about.

That is a lovely view.

Those are protected trees.

The words in bold type are called **demonstrative pronouns.**

'This' and 'these' refer to what is near at hand, 'that' and 'those' refer to what is farther away in space or time.

Demonstrative pronouns, like personal pronouns, are reference words and may at times point to a part of a clause or an entire clause:

You say that you are going to live within your income. Tell me how you propose to do <u>this</u>. (to live within your income)

<u>This</u> may shock you. Your best friend in town has been held on a charge of speeding. ('This' refers to the entire clause that follows: 'Your best friend...charge of speeding')

Apart from 'this' and 'that', 'such', and 'so' may also function like demonstrative pronouns:

I was very angry with him for what he had done and I told him <u>so</u>. (meaning 'this' or 'that'; notice that 'so' refers to the opening clause 'I was very angry...he had done')

<u>Such</u> was to be the pattern of Stanley's marches through Africa: the quick advance, the shooting down of any African tribes that opposed him, the heavy loss of life among his own men, and the final reaching of the objective. (Notice that 'such' refers forward to the entire clause: 'the quick advance,... reaching of the objective'.)

Exercise 4

Read the following story about circus animals and circle all the pronouns (personal, possessive and demonstrative).

Every evening Hema Malini performs the fire dance. She also leaps over wooden blocks, performs balancing tricks, does the high jump, and crashes through a ring of fire amidst deafening applause. The ten-year-old lioness has been performing at the circus ever since she was bought from the Gwalior zoo as a cub. In her younger days, she roamed round the circus compound with her companions and went through a course of training at the hands of experts. At the age of four Hema gave birth to Raj.

Circus animals are named after film stars. They are treated with great care by circus owners and in course of time the animals develop a very close relationship with those in charge of them. The ringmaster even talks to the animals in a language they understand. 'While Hema knows Hindi, most elephants understand a Bihari dialect,' he says. 'It has all to do with the region their ancestors came from, not their place of birth. For instance, you cannot talk to a rhinoceros in Hindi, because for generations it has been living in Assam.'

4.3.4 Reflexive Pronouns

Look at the *underlined* words in the following sentences:

a. Trying to swat a fly off his arm, Sridhar struck <u>himself</u> hard.

The word 'himself' stands for 'Sridhar' so that the sentence means:

b. Trying to swat a fly off his arm, Sridhar struck Sridhar hard.

Compare:

Sridhar struck the ball hard. Sridhar struck himself.

The word 'himself' refers back to Sridhar. Sridhar is both the 'striker' and the 'struck'. The action begun by Sridhar reflects back to Sridhar; 'himself' is therefore called a **reflexive pronoun**. It is the object of the transitive verb 'struck'. Most transitive verbs can take a reflexive pronoun.

The reflexive pronoun generally refers to a living thing, usually a person. It consists of the personal pronoun plus the suffix '-self' or '-selves'.

	singular	plural
1st person	myself	ourselves
2nd person	yourself	yourselves
3rd person	himself, herself, itself	themselves

Here are some more examples of the use of the reflexive pronoun:

He stretched himself comfortably on the divan. (object of 'stretched')

Trying to cut a pumpkin, Saroj cut herself. (object of 'cut')

They gave themselves more time. (indirect object of 'gave')

John mixed himself a coffee. (indirect object of 'mixed')

John mixed a coffee for himself. (object of the preposition 'for')

You must learn to do your homework by yourself. (object of the preposition 'by')

Exercise 5

Use the correct reflexive pronouns to complete the sentences.

a. According to Karl Marx, history repeats ___________, the first time as tragedy, the second time as farce.

b. Laila bought ___________ a dress from the supermarket.

c. I cut ___________ while I was shaving.

d. Whenever anything goes wrong, don't be in a hurry to blame others for it; instead ask ___________ why and how it went wrong.

e. The child fell off the swing and hurt ___________.

Exercise 6

Complete the following sentences with the appropriate personal or reflexive pronouns.

a. Born poor, ___________ had no formal education. He had to educate ___________.

b. After retirement she built ___________ a small house in the country, where ___________ lived for the rest of her life.

c. With the money he had won in the contest, ____________ went on a round-the-world trip with his family. It was something he had promised ____________.

d. By the time he was seventeen, ____________ had established ____________ as a world-class player.

e. The first time he hit a century, ____________ felt proud of ____________. In subsequent years century-making became almost a habit with ____________.

4.3.5 Interrogative Pronouns

The words 'who' ('whom', 'whose'), 'what' and 'which' may be used to ask direct questions. They are then called **interrogative pronouns.**

Who made that noise?

Whom did you meet on your way back home?

Look at that newly painted house. Whose is it?

It's the old question, again. Which came first, the chicken or the egg?

Tell me, what do you really want?

The forms 'who', 'whom' and 'whose' refer to persons only. When they are used to ask questions, we expect the answer to identify the person or persons:

Father: Who is at the door?

Son: I think it's the postman.

The interrogative 'whom' is mostly a feature of written English; it is seldom used in spoken English. The usual form in spoken English is 'who' for the more grammatically correct 'whom':

Who did you see on your way back home?

Who were you talking to at the meeting last night ?

The interrogative 'which' refers to both persons and things:

Which of these girls is the cleverest ?

Which of these shirts would you have? The light green one.

The form 'what' refers to things only:

What does he want? Mr Gupta's telephone number.

What does your pet rabbit eat? Carrots and turnips.

Exercise 7

Turn the following into questions, asking about the underlined words. The first is an example.

a. Sheila has taken the tape-recorder.
   Ans: Who has taken the tape-recorder?

b. I met your long-lost friend Ajay in the market.

c. Nancy is engaged to be married to Alex.

d. A plane figure with three straight sides is a triangle.

e. She said that she was planning to go abroad for higher studies.

f. The bag contained a large sum of money.

g. Several people called while you were away.

Exercise 8

Here are the answers given by a candidate, who was being interviewed for the post of a Senior English Teacher. Complete the dialogue with appropriate questions.

Interviewer: ________________________?
Candidate: Sudha Manohar.
I: ________________________?
C: My father is a civil engineer.
I: ________________________?
C: My mother teaches in a primary school.
I: ________________________?
C: I spend hours listening to classical music. My other hobbies are dramatics, reading and writing, in that order.
I: ________________________?
C: I read mostly light fiction.
I: ________________________?
C: Agatha Christie and P.G. Wodehouse are among my favourite authors.
I: ________________________?
C: I write poetry and an occasional humour piece.
I: You speak excellent English. ________________________?
C: Mr Ravi Paramjyoti taught me English at school.
I: ________________________?
C: In my view, the single most important thing in teaching is winning the trust and affection of one's students.

4.3.6 Indefinite Pronouns

Read this dialogue between a postman and a teacher:

Postman:	Is there anyone called R. Kumar in this class, sir?
Teacher:	Is he in the 'A' division of Class 6?
Postman:	I don't know for sure. Someone over there said he is in the 'A' division.
Teacher:	I'm new to the class. Let me find out. (goes inside) Anyone here called R. Kumar?
Class:	No one, sir.
Teacher:	(going back to the postman) Sorry, he isn't here. Try the 'B' division. The trouble is these days nearly everyone is a 'Kumar'. We have over a dozen of them in Class 6 alone.
Postman:	You're right, sir. I am a Kumar myself and I should know.

The underlined words in the above dialogue are all **indefinite pronouns**. They are pronouns in the first place because they stand for nouns and function like nouns. They are 'indefinite' in the sense that they do not refer to any definite person.

Indefinite pronouns may refer to indefinite things as well—pronouns like 'something', 'anything', 'nothing', 'everything'.

The indefinite pronouns are:

somebody	nobody	anybody	everybody
someone	no one	anyone	everyone
something	nothing	anything	everything

Note that 'no one' is two separate words. You may, if you like, use a hyphen, 'no-one'.

We use indefinite pronouns when we want to refer to people or things without saying exactly who or what they are:

'*Someone* called and asked for you.'
'Who was he?'
'He didn't tell me. It could be almost *anyone*.'
'Didn't he say what he wanted to talk about?'
'No, he said *nothing*.'

When an indefinite pronoun functions as subject, it always takes a singular verb:

Everyone in the locality *knows* that the man is trustworthy.
Is anyone in?
How *is everything*? *Everything is* just fine.

However, when you refer back to an indefinite pronoun, you use a plural pronoun or a plural possessive:

If you follow the example of *someone*, you behave in the same way as *they* did, or in a similar way.
Has *everyone* paid *their* dues as *they* were asked to?

This may be illogical, a plural pronoun or possessive standing for a singular indefinite pronoun but it is neat and convenient. Consider what a cumbersome alternative you have before you if you stick to logic and the singular, as some people still do:

If you follow the example of someone, you behave in the same way as *he* or *she* did, or in a similar way.
Has everyone paid *his* or *her* dues as *he* or *she* was asked to?

Exercise 9

Fill in the blanks with suitable indefinite pronouns.

a. A man was taking a walk along the street when ________ hit him. He soon realised it was a big ball. ________ had thrown the ball out of the window, from the fourth floor of a tall building.

b. 'Can I do ________ for you?' The receptionist asked the visitor.
'Yes, you can do ________ for me,' said the visitor affably.

c. 'I agree with ___________ he has said.'
'Surely you don't mean that?'
'Yes, I do.'
'Is there ___________ at all in the report that you might object to?'
'Just ___________.'
'You remember he said ___________ about the way the management handled the strike. Do you go along with that? Remember you are part of the management.'

d. 'I smell burning, ___________ is alight somewhere.'

e. It was too late by the time they sent for the doctor. The doctor tried ___________ he knew but he couldn't do ___________ much to help.

Exercise 10

Use the verb in brackets in the correct form and complete these sentences.

a. Nobody ever ___________ (listen) to me any more.

b. Time was when everybody in the family and in the neighbourhood ___________ (be) all eager to consult me in all matters.

c. Now no one, just no one ___________ (seek) me out.

d. Nothing ___________ (be) so hurting as being left out in the cold by one's own people.

e. This is what Shakespeare probably meant by the phrase 'old age in corners thrown'. Well, nothing that he said ___________ (ring) truer.

Exercise 11

Complete the following with appropriate personal pronouns and possessives. The first one is an example.

a. If anyone telephones you and leaves a message asking you to call back, be sure that the business is more important to them than to you.

b. Inform everyone that ___________ must come with ___________ testimonials in original.

c. I won't be back home for hours. If anyone comes home while I am away, tell ___________ that ___________ shouldn't waste ___________ time waiting for me.

d. Nobody rushed to the meeting hall. ___________ couldn't care less; to ___________ it was just another routine thing ___________ saw or read about in the papers every day.

Indefinite pronouns, besides referring to indefinite persons and things, may refer to indefinite quantities or numbers. Here are some examples.

any	some	much	many	more
most	little	a little	few	a few
several	a lot (of)	lots (of)	plenty (of)	enough
all	each	none		

The last three pronouns in the box – 'all', 'each', 'none' – are by no means indefinite pronouns but traditionally they have been treated as such.

Some of the indefinite pronouns in the box stand for countable nouns (CN), some for uncountable nouns(UCN), some for both. Here are some illustrative examples:

a. *any, some*

1. 'Is there any food left over, mother? I'm very hungry.'
   'No, there isn't any.' (UCN, singular)
   'Let me see...... yes, there is some. You're lucky.'(UCN, singular)
2. At one time I knew some of the people in the village; now I hardly know any. (CN, plural)

b. *much, many*

1. There is enough rice in the godowns but much of it has gone bad. (UCN, singular only)
2. Over a thousand students wrote the entrance exam. Many of them didn't get through. (CN, plural only)

c. *more*

1. We have twenty men at work but we need more if we are to complete the building on time. (CN, plural)
2. Apart from more of men, we need more of cement, too. (UCN, singular)

d. *most*

1. We have over five hundred students in the Arts section but most of them are not present today. (CN, plural)
2. People these days hardly ever read, they spend most of their leisure time watching television. (UCN, singular)

e. *little, a little*

'Is there any milk in the jug?'
'Yes, there is a little.' (some but not much) (UCN, singular)
'There is little.' (hardly any) (UCN, singular)

f. *few, a few*

1. Some five hundred people had gathered in the hall to listen to the speaker. By the time he finished, there were few left. (hardly any) (CN, plural)
2. We bought six packets of milk in the morning and we still need a few more. (a small number) (CN, plural)

g. *several*

Several of the athletes who took part in the competition were from North India. (CN, plural only)

h. *a lot (of), lots (of), plenty (of)*

1. A lot of people are coming today to meet the minister. (CN, plural)
   Lots of people have come from the villages to take part in the rally. (CN, plural)
   There are plenty of applicants even for small jobs these days. (CN, plural)
2. You need a lot of sugar/plenty of sugar to make a cake. (UCN, singular)

i. *enough*

'Have you got enough of men for the job?' (CN, plural)
'Yes, but not enough of money.' (UCN, singular)

Exercise 12

Mohan owns a guest-house in Goa which he rents out to visitors. His friend Venkat wants to know some details about the guest-house. Complete the dialogue between Mohan and Venkat with suitable indefinite pronouns.

Venkat:	How many rooms are there in your guest-house, Mohan?
Mohan:	Five double rooms. Five families can stay there comfortably.
Venkat:	How about furniture? How ____________ of furniture is there?
Mohan:	There is quite ____________ of furniture. There is a double bed, a table, chairs, a cupboard, and a TV set in__________ of the rooms.
Venkat:	Are there many people visiting Goa?
Mohan:	There are ____________ of them. A number of new hotels have come up in Goa and the place is becoming a popular tourist resort.
Venkat:	Are ____________ of them equally good?
Mohan:	I wouldn't say that. ____________ of the new hotels are very good and come up to international standards.____________ of them are not quite upto the mark but____________ of them, believe me, are fully occupied during the tourist season. Such is the rush. I think there will be ____________ and ____________ of visitors, particularly foreigners, coming in the future and we will need ____________ of hotels and guest-houses, in fact ____________ of everything.
Venkat:	How do you find the experience of running a guest-house in Goa? Is it just fun or ____________ of work and worry?
Mohan:	It meant a great deal of work and worry when I started it but now it is ____________of fun and ____________ of work.

4.3.7 Emphatic Pronouns

Emphatic pronouns have the same forms as reflexive pronouns but the two are different, although some grammar books treat emphatic pronouns as one kind of reflexive pronouns.

We use an emphatic pronoun to emphasise or intensify a noun or pronoun in the sentence:

Did **you** write this essay **yourself**?

The question roughly means the same as 'Did you write this essay?' The questioner, however, is not sure, so he/she adds 'yourself' just to make sure, to emphasise the subject 'you'. Emphatic pronouns are different from reflexive pronouns. Compare the following:

	reflexive pronouns	emphatic pronouns
a.	He hurt himself.	He did it himself.
b.	We must depend on ourselves.	We must build the road ourselves.
c.	She bought herself a dress.	She bought the dress herself.

The differences between the two kinds of pronouns may be summarised thus:

1. Reflexive pronouns are an *essential part of the sentence*, emphatic pronouns are not. We can remove the emphatic pronouns and the sentences will remain the same, only the emphasis will be missing. (He did it./ We must build the road./ She bought the dress.) But we cannot leave out the reflexive pronouns. We must supply an object to the verb or the preposition. (He hurt himself./ We must depend on ourselves.) We can no doubt say 'She bought a dress' but it will not mean the same as 'She bought herself a dress'. The first sentence conforms to basic pattern 2, the second to basic pattern 3.
2. A reflexive pronoun is always the object – direct or indirect – of a verb, as in (a) and (c), or of a preposition, as in (b). The emphatic pronoun, on the other hand, is merely the emphatic equivalent of the personal pronoun.
3. An emphatic pronoun can change its position in the sentence but a reflexive pronoun cannot. You may say 'He did it himself' or 'He himself did it' or even, though less usually, 'Himself he did it'.

Here are some more examples of emphatic pronouns:

a. 'It's a lovely dress. Who made it for her?'
'She made it <u>herself</u>.'

b. 'You say that Ramesh is in town. I don't believe it.'
'Well, I saw him <u>myself</u>.'

Exercise 13

Say whether the pronouns (in italics) are reflexive or emphatic.

a. You are *yourself* to blame for what happened.
b. You are to blame *yourself* for what happened.
c. A house divided against *itself* cannot stand.
d. He built *himself* a house.
e. He built the house *himself* brick by brick.
f. The principal *herself* announced the holiday.
g. He drives his workers hard but you must admit he also drives *himself* hard.

Exercise 14

Choose an emphatic pronoun to complete these sentences.

a. The President of the Selection Board announced the results ________.
b. I don't look forward to telling her the news but I must do it ________.
c. The villagers built the road ________.
d. Rumu is under orders of transfer. She told me so ________.
e. Did you draw the picture ________? It looks so professional.
f. Don't tell me these boys made all these delicacies ________.

4.3.8 Relative Pronouns

Relative pronouns are different from other kinds of pronouns (like personal, possessive, demonstrative etc) in that they function like a subordinate conjunction introducing a subordinate clause:

a. The woman **who** lives next door is very friendly.

b. The book **that** you see on the table is mine.

c. The house **which** stands across the road is his.

d. The girl with **whom** you waited at the bus-stop is my sister.

The boxed words in the above examples do two things:

1. They relate the subordinate clause to a noun in the main clause:

	main clause	subordinate clause
a.	The woman is very friendly	who lives next door
b.	The book is mine	that you see on the table
c.	The house is his	which stands across the road
d.	The girl is my sister	with whom you waited at the bus-stop

2. They serve as subject or object in the subordinate clause, thereby functioning like a noun:

boxed words	noun function performed
a. who	subject of the clause
b. that	object of the verb 'see'
c. which	subject of the clause
d. whom	object of the preposition 'with'

The boxed words are called relative pronouns because they *relate* a subordinate clause to a noun in the main clause and because they function like a noun within the subordinate clause. (Pronouns function very much like nouns.) The subordinate clauses they introduce are called **relative clauses**. The noun in the main clause, which the relative clause refers to, is called the **antecedent** of the relative pronoun. The antecedent is so called because it often comes immediately before the relative pronoun ('ante' means 'before').

The relative pronouns 'who' and 'whom' refer to persons, 'which' refers to things and 'that' refers to both persons and things:

The book *that* you are looking for is on the table.

The man *that* you are looking for has not arrived yet.

A relative pronoun can have for its antecedent another pronoun:

He who rises early prospers in life.

Those who live in glass houses should not throw stones.

Note

The relative pronoun 'whom' is normally found only in formal written English. In spoken English people use 'who' in place of the correct 'whom':

The girl who I met the other day....

The girl who I waited with at the bus-stop...

However, in written English, it would be:

The girl whom I met the other day...
The girl with whom I waited at the bus-stop... (or)
The girl whom I waited with at the bus-stop...

Exercise 15

In the following sentences, underline the relative pronouns and box their antecedents. The first one is an example.

a. The [boy] who spoke in favour of greater representation for women in Parliament yesterday is my son.
b. I don't like movies that have an unhappy ending.
c. It was the funniest movie that Charlie Chaplin ever made.
d. The man over there looks like one whom I once knew rather well.
e. Ravi is the one person in our family for whom I have the highest respect.
f. A good thirty years went by before I visited the house in which I was born.

The relative pronoun, we said earlier, serves as subject or object in the relative clause. How do we know whether a relative pronoun is subject or object?

For this, we need to look at the original noun that the relative pronoun stands for. If the original noun functions as subject, so does the relative pronoun that has taken its place; if it functions as object, so does the relative pronoun. Compare the sentences on the left with their split-up parts on the right:

a. The woman who lives next door is very friendly. (subject)	The woman is very friendly. The woman lives next door. (subject)
b. The book that you see on the table is mine. (object of the verb 'see')	The book is mine. You see the book on the table. (object of the verb 'see')
c. The house which is opposite the park is his. (subject)	The house is his. The house is opposite the park. (subject)
d. The girl with whom you waited at the bus-stop is my sister. (object of the preposition 'with')	The girl is my sister. You waited with the girl at the bus-stop. (object of the preposition 'with')

Note that when the relative pronoun functions as object in the relative clause, the normal word order(subject-verb-object) is changed, the object coming before the subject:

a. The book that you see on the table is mine. (object of verb)

b. You see the book on the table (subject plus verb plus object)	that you see on the table (object plus subject plus verb)

c. The girl with whom you waited at the bus-stop is my sister. (object of preposition)

d. You waited with the girl (subject plus verb plus preposition plus object)	with whom you waited (preposition plus object plus subject plus verb)

Exercise 16

Identify the relative pronouns in the following sentences and say whether they function as subject or object (of a verb or a preposition).

a. She is the girl who sang the solo at the school concert.
b. The food that you eat is first mixed with the saliva in your mouth.
c. I will do all that I can to help you out of your present troubles.
d. I admire people who have innate talent.
e. It is a novel that people will be talking about for a long time.

As was mentioned earlier, the relative pronouns 'who' and 'whom' refer to persons, 'which' refers to things, and 'that' refers to persons and things. However, sometimes we may have to choose between 'who' and 'that' when referring to persons, and between 'which' and 'that' when referring to things.

a. *who/that*

If the antecedent is a generalised noun, either 'who' or 'that' will do: He is the sort of man <u>who/that</u> sticks at nothing to get what he wants. She doesn't care much for people <u>who/that</u> tend to monopolise the conversation at a party.

But if the antecedent is more particularised, it is better to use 'who':

The uncle <u>who</u> came to see me the other day is my mother's brother.

b. *which/that*

When the antecedent stands for a thing, either 'which' or 'that' will do, but in the following cases 'that' is preferred to 'which':

1. when the antecedent is an indefinite pronoun:

   'I'll do <u>all that</u> I can to help you out of your present troubles.'

   'Thank you. <u>Anything that</u> you do will help.'
2. when the antecedent is a complement of the verb 'be':

   He <u>is</u> a <u>cricketer that</u> you will be seeing more of in the years to come.
3. when the antecedent is modified by a superlative:

   'Citizen Kane', according to some, is the <u>greatest movie that</u> has ever been made.

   That is the <u>tallest story that</u> I have ever heard.
4. when the antecedent is modified by an ordinal number:

   I still remember the <u>first movie that</u> I saw as a boy of ten.

Exercise 17

Supply the missing relative pronouns in these sentences.

a. The cyclone ____________ hit the east coast caused widespread damage.
b. Yesterday I met a gentleman ____________ had worked for the chairman as his private secretary.
c. Can you tell me the name of the book about ____________ you have been talking to me for quite some time?
d. The person ____________ you met and with ____________ you had dinner in New York is my uncle, not my cousin.

e. She works for a computer software company ____________ has its headquarters in San Francisco.

f. The candidate ____________ the Board adjudged the best of the lot was finally selected for the post.

4.4 The Impersonal 'it'

'It' is said to be a personal pronoun when it stands for, and refers back to, something already stated:

Watch out! You nearly dropped my *ash-tray*. It cost me a small fortune. (personal pronoun, standing for, and referring back to, the antecedent noun '*ash-tray*')

He picked up a *brick* and placed it on the wall. (personal pronoun, antecedent noun 'brick')

They sailed down the river, looking at the *moon* as it moved across the sky. (personal pronoun, antecedent noun 'moon')

In the following examples, however, 'it' is not a personal pronoun since it does not stand for, or refer back to, anything already stated:

It is Thursday. *It* was a cold November morning.

We call the word 'it' in the above examples **the impersonal 'it'**.

The impersonal 'it' has three uses: **the introductory 'it', the emphatic 'it'**, and **the anticipatory 'it'**.

4.4.1 The Introductory 'it'

We use the introductory 'it' to begin a sentence when we speak about the day, date, time, weather, distance, place or situation:

It is Monday.
It was the 21st November.
It is 6 o'clock.
It is hot.
It is five miles.
It's rather noisy here.

The function of the introductory 'it' is merely to introduce the sentence and no more. Note the pattern of the sentences above:
You can have, in addition, an adverb or adverb phrase after the subject complement:

Impersonal 'it'	+	verb 'be'	+	subject complement (noun, noun phrase or adjective)

It is cold here.
It is hot in the plains.
It is five miles from here to the market.

4.4.2 The Emphatic 'it'

We use the emphatic 'it' to emphasise a particular piece of information. Compare the following:

She graduated in 1995.

It was in 1995 that she graduated.

The first sentence merely states the fact of her graduating in 1995. The second emphasises the year of graduation.

Here are some more examples of the use of the emphatic 'it':

It was here, at this very spot, that he proposed to her. (Compare: He proposed to her here at this very spot.)

It is the poachers that are responsible for the situation. (Compare: The poachers are responsible for the situation.)

Any one piece of information in a sentence, out of several, can be highlighted, as shown below:

George	bought	Susan	a dress	last Monday.
1		2	3	4

Of the four pieces of information in the above sentence (numbered and underlined for you), we may focus on anyone, thus:

1. It was *George* who bought Susan a dress last Monday.
2. It was *Susan* that George bought a dress for last Monday.
3. It was *a dress* that George bought Susan last Monday.
4. It was *last Monday* that George bought Susan a dress.

Exercise 18

Using the impersonal 'it' construction, emphasise the underlined bits of information in the following sentences.

a. He died ten years ago.

b. The family lived here.

c. She went abroad for the first time in 1980.

d. Rita played the violin at the concert.

e. Stanley met Dr Livingstone at Ujiji in 1872.

4.4.3 The Anticipatory 'it'

Look at the following sentences:

It is difficult *for most people to own up their mistakes.*

It seems best *to inform the police.*

The word 'it' fills the subject position in the above sentences, yet it is only the *notional subject of the sentence* (that is, subject in name only), anticipating the real subject. The real subject comes after the predicate, as we can see from the following analysis:

notional subject	predicate	real subject
it	is difficult	for most people to own up their mistakes
it	seems best	to inform the police

We may, if you like, rewrite the above sentences by deleting the notional subject and putting in its place the real subject, thus:

For most people to own up their mistakes is difficult.

To inform the police seems best.

Note that the predicate consists of a linking verb ('be', 'seem') and an adjective complement like 'difficult', 'best' etc. Other adjectives that could come after the linking verb are: important, necessary, essential, desirable, advisable, convenient, easy, possible, impossible, better. The pattern of the entire sentence may be shown thus:

1		2		3		4		5
anticipatory 'it'	+	verb 'be'	+	adjective complement	+	'for' plus noun/ pronoun	+	infinitive phrase

The anticipatory 'it' may take a gerund or gerundial phrase instead of an infinitive phrase:

It was well worth *taking up the contract.*

It was fun *working in a garage during the summer holidays.*

Exercise 19

The anticipatory 'it' may be used to suggest or recommend a course of action. Here is a set of do's and don'ts from a doctor to her patient. Rewrite these in complete sentences using the anticipatory 'it' construction. Remember to use suitable linking devices between sentences, words like 'besides', 'next', 'finally' etc.

give up smoking at once (absolutely important)
cut down on fatty foods (equally important)
avoid alcohol altogether (advisable)
take mild but regular exercise in the mornings (desirable)
take these tablets when in pain, one at a time (important)

The anticipatory 'it' may also be used to comment on an action, activity or experience; also, the 'it' construction may be used with verbs other than linking verbs:

It is easy to learn one or more foreign languages between the ages of four and fourteen.

Thereafter, *it* becomes increasingly difficult to learn a foreign language.

It always pleased him to think of his father and the times he spent with him.

During the fifties, *it* cost the company over eight hundred rupees a month to hire cars.

It takes hours of driving on a near-impassable road to reach the place.

The anticipatory construction has this advantage: it helps us to avoid having a long subject – English does not take kindly to long subjects – and at the same time to focus on what we want to say by putting it in a more prominent position like the end of a sentence. Compare:

a. (1) It was fun working in a garage during the summer holidays. (focus)
(2) Working in a garage during the summer holidays was fun.

b. (1) It is important for you to know your strengths and your weaknesses. (focus)
(2) For you to know your strengths and your weaknesses is important.

Exercise 20

Complete each of the following sentences by adding a suitable infinitive or gerund phrase. The first one is an example.

a. It is quite easy for anyone ____________________.
Ans: It is quite easy for anyone to think up excuses for not doing a job.
b. It is almost impossible ____________________.
c. It is vitally important ____________________.
d. It is necessary in case of an accident for you ____________________.
e. Is it convenient for you ____________________?
f. It is essential for people in a democracy ____________________.

The anticipatory 'it' may be followed by a linking verb, a complement and a that-clause. We use this construction particularly when we want to express an opinion about a fact, event, or situation:

It is amazing but true that a large number of people do not know their rights.

Judging from newspaper reports, it is perfectly clear that a large number of officials contributed to the border incident, through oversight.

From what I have seen of you, it seems clear that you are not cut out for a career in this company.

It is unlikely that an outsider will ever be elected from this constituency.

It is probable that we have a hung parliament again.

You can have a wh-clause, that is, a clause beginning with 'who', 'what', 'why' or 'how' instead of a that-clause with the anticipatory 'it' construction:

It is amazing what money can do to people, especially when they come by it all of a sudden.

From the reports we have read, it seems clear why the public in general distrust canned foods.

It does not matter who you are or what you are; you are not above the law.

It is odd how you make startling discoveries about people known to you for years.

Exercise 21

Complete the following sentences with a *that*-clause.

a. It was obvious ____________________________________
b. It is a wonder ____________________________________
c. It is a pity ______________________________________
d. It surprised us ___________________________________
e. It bothered the old parents __________________________

Exercise 22

Complete the following sentences with a *wh*-clause.

a. It is strange ______________________________________
b. It is extraordinary _________________________________
c. It is funny _______________________________________
d. It doesn't matter ___________________________________

5 Adjectives

In Chapters 3 and 4, we explained the use of nouns and pronouns to name and identify people and things. In this unit we deal with a class of words which describe, or give information about, people and things. These describing words are called **adjectives**.

Look at the italicised words in these sentences.

a. She is a *brilliant* student.

b. That was an *ingenious* plan but not a *practical* one.

We may, if you like, say 'She is a student' and leave it at that. We may, on the other hand, want to say what kind of a student she is, we may want to describe the student ('a *brilliant* student'). We call 'brilliant' an adjective. In the same way, we call 'ingenious' and 'practical' in example (b) adjectives since they both describe the plan. All the three words describe, or give information about, the person or thing named by the noun or pronoun that follows:

brilliant – student (noun) ingenious – plan (noun) practical – one (pronoun).

Speaking in the language of grammar, we say that the adjective modifies a noun or pronoun. What it means in plain English is this: the adjective describes, or gives information about, the person or thing named or identified by the noun or pronoun.

Exercise 1

Find an appropriate adjective from column 1 to the noun in column 2.

Column 1	Column 2	Column 1	Column 2
pretty	baby	complex	girl
pleasant	problem	rare	term
technical	metal	patient	singer
healthy	mother	close	evening
nervous	friend	popular	candidate

The adjective usually comes before the noun (or pronoun) it modifies. When it comes before the noun (or pronoun) it is said to be **attributive**, or *attributively used*. On the other hand, the adjective may be used after a linking verb as a subject complement, the noun it modifies preceding it as the subject (as in bp 6). We then say that the adjective is **predicate**, or *predicatively used*:

The girl was brilliant.

The plan was ingenious but not practical.

The baby feels hungry.

He looked tense.

Most adjectives can be used in attributive and predicative positions, as in the following pairs of sentences:

a. 1. I had a fine day.
   2. The day was fine.

b. 1. They came to a <u>reasonable</u> settlement.
   2. They weren't <u>reasonable</u> at all.

c. 1. These are <u>dangerous</u> games.
   2. These games are <u>dangerous</u>.

Some adjectives, however, can be used only in one position or the other. The underlined adjectives, for example, are used only attributively:

The workers have agreed to resume work on <u>certain</u> conditions.
On that <u>fateful</u> night the young man took off on a single-engine plane.
The cries of the <u>adoring</u> fans filled the stadium.
I agree, yours is a <u>thankless</u> job.
These two-wheeler drivers pay <u>scant</u> regard for the rules of the road.
He moved into a <u>ramshackle</u> building.
He has a <u>cardiac</u> problem.

Exercise 2

Complete the following sentences with appropriate adjectives, choosing them from the box below. Notice that these adjectives are used only attributively.

knotty	belated	flagrant	neighbouring
preconceived	lone	remedial	eventual

a. It was bad enough that he did not own responsibility for the mess he had made. What was worse, he came up with a ____________ defence of what he had done.

b. 'Stop these ____________ violations of the law,' said the judge.

c. Everyone knows that urban pollution has been on the increase of late but no one knows what ____________ measures are to be taken to contain it.

d. One of the ____________ problems facing a democracy is how best to reconcile the claims of the individual with those of society.

e. Surprisingly for a nation which has no serious problem with any of the ____________ states, this country maintains a huge army.

f. With the ____________ return of the missing husband to his wife and children, the film ends happily and all's well that ends well.

g. There was a ____________ sentry at the entrance to the housing colony who was supposedly responsible for the security of the entire place.

h. You cannot have a fair debate if you come with a closed mind and with ____________ notions of what is right and proper.

Some adjectives are normally used only predicatively or as predicate adjectives. Look at the underlined adjectives in the following sentences:

The girl is <u>unwell</u>. (We can't say 'an unwell girl')
You cannot see him now, he is fast <u>asleep</u>. I'm <u>sorry</u>.
You say there is no clear evidence of negligence. Are you <u>sure</u>?
The parents were <u>glad</u> for their son.

Some of these predicate adjectives are followed by an infinitive phrase:

He is unable to do the job single-handed.

I am sorry to say no to your request.

She is likely to win a national scholarship.

We are glad to be of some help.

They were ready to lay down their lives for the sake of their country.

More usually, the predicate adjective is followed by a prepositional phrase:

The principal is alive to the need for changes in the curriculum.

The police are well aware of the strange goings-on in this locality.

He is accustomed to having an hour's sleep after lunch.

She was allergic to the drops they administered.

The transplant organ has to be compatible with the body tissues that make contact with it.

Exercise 3

Rewrite each of the following sentences using a predicate adjective followed by an infinitive phrase. The predicate adjective is given within brackets. The first two are examples.

a. I pleaded with him but he said he would not help me. (unwilling)

Answer: I pleaded with him but he was *unwilling to help me.*

b. You will have to pay compensation for the delay in completing the project. (liable)

Answer: You are *liable to pay compensation for the delay in completing the project.*

c. The union leaders expressed their readiness to negotiate with the management. (prepared)

d. The government have no option but to honour the court verdict. (bound)

e. Unless urgent protective measures are taken, many of the world's rare species will face extinction in the foreseeable future. (doomed)

f. The police are aware of the problem but cannot do anything to tackle it. (powerless)

g. Destiny had willed that he spend his last days in jail. (destined/fated)

h. The chances are that he will pass the exams this time. (likely)

Exercise 4

Rewrite each of the following sentences using a predicate adjective followed by a prepositional phrase. The predicate adjective is given in brackets after each sentence. The first two are examples.

a. He just refuses to see reason. (impervious)

Answer: He is *impervious to reason.*

b. Smoking harms the health of the smoker as well as that of the non-smoker who happens to inhale the smoke. (injurious)

Answer: Smoking is *injurious to the health of the smoker and the non-smoker.*

c. Given their personal ambitions, the faction leaders cannot present a united front. (incapable)
d. They show no inclination to face the ground realities. (averse)
e. Our neighbour is deeply attached to her parrot, more attached to it than to her family. (fond)
f. I must warn you that the course of action you are about to embark on is dangerous. (fraught)
g. In the parliamentary system of government the minister must own responsibility for the lapses of his subordinates. (answerable)
h. Can you honestly claim that the three of you represent the student body? (representative)

Exercise 5

Complete the definitions using the following adjectives predicatively.

adjacent	devoted	resigned	prone	susceptible

a. If the Smiths are ______________ to accident, they often get involved in accidents.
b. If you are ______________ to something, you accept it without protest or complaint, however unpleasant it may be.
c. If your house is ______________ to Nathan's, you live next door to Nathan.
d. If you are ______________ to your work, you believe in it and do it conscientiously.
e. You are ______________ to beauty if you are likely to be moved by beautiful things.

5.1 Types of Adjectives

Adjectives may be divided into the following types, as shown below:

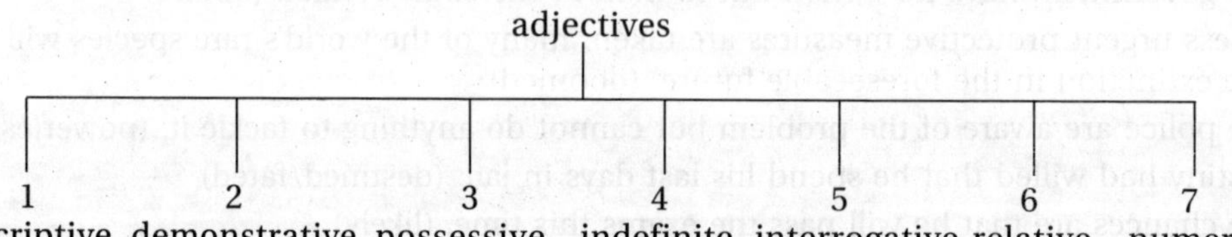

5.1.1 Descriptive Adjectives

Descriptive adjectives, sometimes called **qualitative adjectives**, usually refer to an inherent quality ('a bright boy', 'a beautiful girl') or a physical state such as:

- size ('a big house', 'a small town'),
- age ('my old aunt', 'a young nephew of hers'),
- colour ('brown paper', 'golden corn'),
- shape ('a square peg in a round hole') or
- temperature ('a hot cup of tea', 'a glass of cold water').

Some descriptive adjectives take the form of:

a. **proper adjectives:** French wine, Chinese food, a Hindu temple, a Muslim festival (By proper adjectives we mean adjectives derived from proper nouns, like 'French', or proper nouns functioning as adjectives like 'Hindu'.)

b. **participle adjectives**, that is, participles of verbs, present or past, functioning as adjectives:

1. **present participle** a boring movie, a shocking experience, an inspiring example, an enchanting view
2. **past participle** a furnished house, a broken vase, a deprived child, 'a painted ship upon a painted ocean'

Participle adjectives ending in '-ing' are active: they describe the effect produced by something on someone ('a shocking experience', 'a frightening sight', 'a disappointing performance') or a process or state that goes on over a period of time ('living creatures', 'an ageing body', 'existing laws'). Participle adjectives ending in '-ed', on the other hand, are passive in that they describe the effect passively suffered by someone ('a frightened child', 'the disappointed father', 'the alarmed residents').

To know the difference between the '-ing' form and the '-ed' form, compare:

The concert was disappointing (to the audience, obviously).

The audience were disappointed by the concert.

Like other adjectives, the participle adjectives can be:

1. used attributively:

   They had a long tiring day.

   He put forward some convincing arguments.

   They had a worried look as they sat waiting for the news.

   The alarmed children yelled and cried.

2. used predicatively:

   It is annoying the way he goes on and on.

   The situation is alarming.

   She looks troubled.

   They felt depressed by the developments at home.

Here is a list of commonly used past participle adjectives, along with the prepositions that may follow them:

amazed at amused by annoyed at (something)/with (someone)
astonished at/with/by bored by/with confused by
disappointed by (something)/in (someone) disgusted at/by/with excited by
fascinated by frightened at/by/of interested by/in
involved with (someone) / in (something) satisfied by/with shocked at/by
surprised at/by terrified by/of tired of worried by

Exercise 6

Complete the following pairs of sentences with the appropriate participle adjectives (ending in '-ing' or '-ed'). Supply the correct preposition after the past participle. The first two are examples.

a. embarrass — It was embarrassing for Ali to hear himself praised in public. Ali was embarrassed *at* hearing himself praised in public.

b. confuse — The figures given by the speaker were contradictory and confusing. The audience was confused by the contradictory figures given by the speaker.

c. annoy — She found her friend's display of temper ______________. She was ______________ her friend's display of temper.

d. fascinate — Leila is ______________ the spider as it spins its web. It is ______________ to watch a spider as it spins its web.

e. frighten — When I was child, I was ______________ thunderstorms. When I was a child, I found thunderstorms ______________.

f. shock — Hari's behaviour at the meeting was ______________. The guests at the meeting were ______________ Hari's behaviour.

g. amuse — The children were ______________ the telefilm shown yesterday. The children found the telefilm shown yesterday ______________.

h. amaze — Kumar's superior was ______________ his impudence. Kumar's superior found his impudence ______________.

Exercise 7

Complete the following pairs of sentences with the appropriate participle adjectives (ending in '-ing' or '-ed') of the verbs given in brackets.

a. 'I am ______________,' he says all the time. Such a person is usually ______________. (bore)

b. The astrologers said that the world would come to an end on 6th July, 1999. That was a ______________ thing to say. Many people felt ______________ and spent their time praying. (terrify)

c. The weather was ______________. We could not go out anywhere. We were thoroughly ______________. (depress)

d. I enjoyed reading the book. It was ______________. I recommended the book to several of my friends but they were not ______________. (interest)

e. His behaviour was ______________. No one expected a man of his age to behave so. They were all ______________.(shock)

5.1.2 Demonstrative Adjectives

Read the following conversation between a customer and a shopkeeper:

Customer:	How much does that saree cost?
Shopkeeper:	The red one with the green border?
Customer:	Not that one. The one on the lower shelf.
Shopkeeper:	This one ? It costs three hundred rupees.
Customer:	How about these sarees? I mean the sarees to your left.
Shopkeeper:	They are cheaper but the colour is not guaranteed.

The underlined words in the conversation point to a particular saree or sarees. The shelves are full of sarees and the customer shows the shopkeeper the saree or sarees she is interested in. The words 'this', 'that', 'these' and 'those' point to or demonstrate, they are therefore called demonstrative. They are followed by nouns or pronouns which they modify, they are therefore called **demonstrative adjectives.**

Demonstrative Adjectives vs Demonstrative Pronouns

Look at the table below and find out the differences between demonstrative adjectives and demonstrative pronouns.

demonstrative adjectives	demonstrative pronouns
This book is mine.	This is my book.
These books are mine.	These are my books.
That book is yours.	That is your book.
Those books are yours.	Those are your books.

Demonstrative adjectives are followed by nouns which they modify. Demonstrative pronouns stand for the things we talk about and function like nouns.

The demonstrative adjectives may well be followed by the pronouns 'one' and 'ones' :

I like this one better. How about that one?

These ones are a lot better than those ones.

The pronouns 'one' and 'ones' stand for nouns that have already been mentioned or are known both to the speaker and the listener.

Exercise 8

Complete the following sentences with demonstrative adjectives or demonstrative pronouns.

a. Mother produces a box of crayons from her shopping-bag and tells Arun, 'I bought you _______________.'
'_______________ crayons are really nice, mother. Thank you,' says Arun.

b. 'Where did you buy _______________ sewing- machine?'
'I didn't buy _______________. _______________ was a birthday present from my father.'

c. _______________ are our neighbours, Mr and Mrs Prem.

d. Do you like _______________ painting? _______________ one is by a famous artist.

e. Customer (pointing to a basket of mangoes at the far end of the shop):
Could we have a dozen of _______________ ones, please?

f. Who was the gentleman you were talking to on the phone? Was _______________ Sunil?

5.1.3 Possessive Adjectives

Possessive adjectives, like possessive pronouns, say that someone owns something. The only difference between the two is this: possessive adjectives are followed by nouns while possessive pronouns stand for nouns and function like nouns.

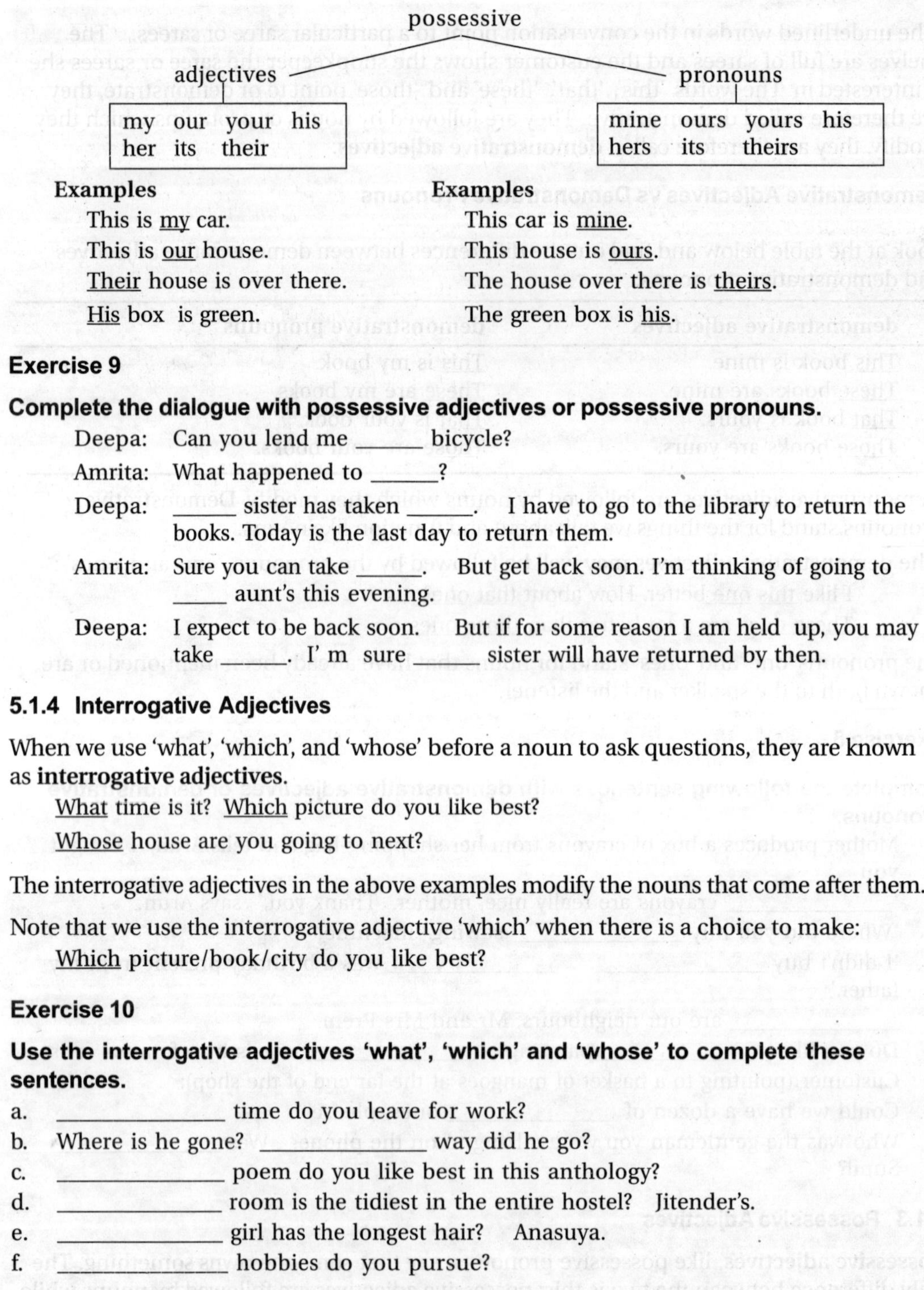

Examples	Examples
This is <u>my</u> car.	This car is <u>mine</u>.
This is <u>our</u> house.	This house is <u>ours</u>.
<u>Their</u> house is over there.	The house over there is <u>theirs</u>.
<u>His</u> box is green.	The green box is <u>his</u>.

Exercise 9

Complete the dialogue with possessive adjectives or possessive pronouns.

Deepa: Can you lend me ______ bicycle?

Amrita: What happened to ______?

Deepa: ______ sister has taken ______. I have to go to the library to return the books. Today is the last day to return them.

Amrita: Sure you can take ______. But get back soon. I'm thinking of going to ______ aunt's this evening.

Deepa: I expect to be back soon. But if for some reason I am held up, you may take ______. I' m sure ______ sister will have returned by then.

5.1.4 Interrogative Adjectives

When we use 'what', 'which', and 'whose' before a noun to ask questions, they are known as **interrogative adjectives.**

<u>What</u> time is it? <u>Which</u> picture do you like best?

<u>Whose</u> house are you going to next?

The interrogative adjectives in the above examples modify the nouns that come after them. Note that we use the interrogative adjective 'which' when there is a choice to make:

<u>Which</u> picture/book/city do you like best?

Exercise 10

Use the interrogative adjectives 'what', 'which' and 'whose' to complete these sentences.

a. ______________ time do you leave for work?
b. Where is he gone? ______________ way did he go?
c. ______________ poem do you like best in this anthology?
d. ______________ room is the tidiest in the entire hostel? Jitender's.
e. ______________ girl has the longest hair? Anasuya.
f. ______________ hobbies do you pursue?

g. ______________ detective novel did you enjoy reading most?
h. ______________ advice would you give your son as he leaves home to join school?

Interrogative Adjectives vs Interrogative Pronouns

The question words 'what', 'which' and 'whose' can be used as interrogative pronouns as well. Compare each of the following pairs of sentences:

interrogative adjective	interrogative pronoun
a. What book did you read recently?	a. What did you read recently?
b. Which school in town are you going to?	b. Which is the school you are going to?
c. Whose bicycle are you riding?	c. Whose is this bicycle?

The underlined words in column 1 are interrogative adjectives because they are followed by nouns which they modify: *what* book, *which* school, *whose* bicycle. The underlined words in column 2, on the other hand, stand alone (with no nouns following them) and function like nouns. They are therefore called interrogative pronouns.

5.1.5 Indefinite Adjectives

In Chapter 4, you studied indefinite pronouns. Some of the indefinite pronouns can also function as **indefinite adjectives**—pronouns like *any, some, each, little, less, much, many, more, most, few, enough,several, all, no* and so on.

By comparing the words in bold type in each of the following pairs of sentences in column 1 and column 2, we can learn the difference between indefinite pronouns and indefinite adjectives.

column 1 indefinite pronouns	column 2 indefinite adjectives
a. **Each** of the six boys got two slices of bread.	a. **Each** boy got two slices of bread.
b. There is very **little** of milk and even **less** of sugar	b. There is very **little** milk and even **less** sugar.
c. I know **many** of the people here.	c. I know **many** people here.
d. You can depend on **most** of the people working there.	d. You can depend on **most** people working there.

Note that the indefinite adjective is immediately followed by a noun which it modifies. The indefinite pronoun, on the other hand, functions like a noun in the sentence.

Exercise 11

Fill in the blanks with indefinite adjectives.

a. I don't care much for pop music but ______________ young people would go miles to listen to a pop concert.
b. Not ______________ members had turned up at the meeting. In fact there were not ______________ people even to form a quorum.
c. The speech was so boring that by the time the speaker finished there were ______________ people left of the audience.

d. I have ____________ time to spare for you right now. Can you see me sometime tomorrow?

e. The candidate hasn't read ____________ fiction, as you can see from his answers. As a matter of fact, he has hardly read ____________ books, fiction or non-fiction.

f. There were ____________ women in the procession. That, if you ask me, is a good sign.

g. For eighteen hours after the airplane took off, there was ____________ information about its whereabouts.

Special Usages of Indefinite Adjectives

a. *some, any*

'Some' is used in positive statements, 'any' in negative statements.

some	any
There's <u>some</u> milk in the fridge.	There isn't <u>any</u> milk in the fridge.
I'm going to buy <u>some</u> tomatoes.	I'm not going to buy <u>any</u> tomatoes.
He made some <u>useful</u> suggestions.	He didn't make <u>any</u> useful suggestions.
She has <u>some</u> money.	She doesn't have <u>any</u> money.

'Some' indicates the presence of a small quantity, and 'any' the complete absence of any quantity.

However, in questions we may use 'any' or 'some':

Does she have *some* money?

Does she have *any* money?

We normally use 'some', not 'any' when we offer things or ask for things:

Would you like *some* coffee?

No, thank you.

Can I have *some* tea, please?

Yes, of course.

Can you lend me *some* money?

No, I'm afraid not.

We can use 'any' in positive statements when it means 'it doesn't matter which', or 'any at all':

You may borrow *any* book you like.

Any citizen of India can join the club if he/she has completed 18 years of age.

Any restaurant will do as long as it serves vegetarian food.

Exercise 12

Fill in the blanks with 'some' or 'any' and say whether the words function as indefinite pronouns or adjectives.

a. I have ____________ money with me. Have you ____________?

b. I wanted to buy my friend Aisha a birthday present but I could not find ____________ worth buying.

c. The majority of patients in this hospital are men but there are ____________ women too.

d. Can you get me ______________ tomatoes on your way back home from work? There aren't ______________ at home and I need ______________ very badly.

e. ______________TV programmes are worth watching but they are very few. ______________ viewers, however, will watch ______________ programme, however uninteresting.

f. You don't stand ______________ chance of being included in the team since you haven't put in ______________ practice during the year.

b. *little, few; less, fewer; much, many*

The indefinite adjectives 'little', 'less' and 'much' are used with uncountable nouns; 'few', 'fewer' and 'many' with countable nouns in their plural form.

uncountable nouns	countable nouns (plural)
Little clothing is needed.	Few/A few clothes are needed.
Less clothing is needed at this time of the year.	Fewer clothes are needed at this time of the year.
Much clothing is needed.	Many clothes are needed.

c. *little, a little; few, a few*

'A little' and 'a few' are used in a positive sense; they stress the presence of something, although in a small quantity:

There is a little milk in the fridge, enough for making a few cups of tea.

'Little' and 'few', on the other hand, have a negative force, they suggest 'hardly any quantity or number':

There is little milk in the fridge (meaning 'hardly any').

He has few friends in the office.

d. *many, many a*

Both 'many' and 'many a' are plural in meaning but 'many a' qualifies a singular noun and is followed by a singular verb:

Many a remedy was tried but none of them worked.

'Many', however, is plural and takes a plural verb:

Many remedies were tried...

'Many a' is literary English.

e. *much, many*

In place of 'much', 'many', we may use the informal 'a lot of', 'lots of' or 'plenty of' , both with countable and uncountable nouns:

We must take with us lots of/a lot of/plenty of/milk.

We must also ensure that we have lots of/a lot of/plenty of/towels and napkins.

Exercise 13

Anil and Raju are going on a camping holiday. They tell each other what they have collected and what they still need for the holiday. Complete the dialogue between Anil and Raju with suitable indefinite adjectives or pronouns, choosing them from the list on the next page.

any	much	some	little	a lot	lots of	more	plenty of	enough	a lot of

You may have to use some of these more than once.

Anil: Let's see what we already have between us before deciding on what we have to buy. Well, I have ______________milk.

Raju: How ______________ do you have?

Anil: Three tins. That's not ______________ milk, I agree, but ______________ for the two of us for three days.

Raju: I have another three tins with me. That makes it six and that is ______________ milk for the two of us.

Anil: How about tea and sugar?

Raju: There's half a kilo of tea and nearly a kilo of sugar. That's quite ______________, if you ask me.

Anil: Candles?

Raju: We have a packet of five medium-sized candles.

Anil: I think we should have ______ candles. Let us buy another packet of five.

Raju: Fine. Have you bought ______________ bread?

Anil: Yes, I have. Three loaves. That should do.

Raju: How about jam?

Anil: I have two tins of jam, and a tin of marmalade besides. That's ample. But we have only 100 grams of butter and that's too ______________.

Raju: Let's buy another 100 grams of butter. And then we need soup, say, six tins.

Anil: Six tins of soup, I think, is too ______________. Three would do. Put that down on the list.

Raju: Soft drinks?

Anil: We have a whole crate of soft drinks. And ______________ drinking water.

5.1.6 Relative Adjectives

In Chapter 4, we learned about relative pronouns and the clauses they introduce called relative clauses. Among the relative pronouns are 'who' and 'whom'. There is, in addition to these two, the possessive form of 'who' ('whose') which can introduce a relative clause.

If we want to speak about something belonging to, or relating to, the person or thing we are talking about, we use the possessive 'whose' :

We met a gentleman <u>whose</u> car had won a prize at the Vintage Car Rally.

ABC is a triangle <u>whose</u> sides are equal.

'Whose' in the above examples takes the place of the possessive forms 'his' and 'its' :

We met a gentleman. <u>His</u> car had won a prize... Vintage Car Rally.

ABC is a triangle. <u>Its</u> sides are equal.

The clauses 'whose car had won a prize at the Vintage Car Rally' and 'whose sides are equal' are both relative clauses but the possessive 'whose' that introduces them is not a relative pronoun but a **relative adjective**.

The difference between the relative pronoun and the relative adjective lies in this: a relative pronoun, as we saw in the previous chapter, functions as subject or object in the relative clause. A relative adjective, on the other hand, modifies the noun that comes immediately after it ('car', 'sides', in the examples given above). It is the noun that comes after 'whose' which functions as subject or object:

We met a gentleman whose car had won a prize in the Vintage Car Rally.('car', subject of 'had won')

They sought the advice of people whose opinion they respected.
('opinion', object of the transitive verb 'respected')

They sought the advice of people for whose opinion they had great respect.
('opinion', object of the preposition 'for')

The relative adjective 'whose' refers to persons as well as things:

I saw a girl whose hair was very long.

India is a country whose development has not been very impressive.

5.1.7 Numeral Adjectives

Numeral adjectives tell us how many persons or things we are talking about or the order in which a particular person or thing stands. To find a numeral adjective, ask the question: 'how many?' or 'in what order?'

Numeral adjectives may be *cardinal*: words like 'one', 'two', 'three', 'twenty-five', or *ordinal*: words like 'first', 'second', 'third' , 'twenty-fifth'.

A year has twelve months and January is the first month of the year.

The nearest school was five miles away.

You may take your seat anywhere in the third row.

Words like 'next', 'last', 'following', 'subsequent', 'preceding' may also be treated like ordinal numbers since they also indicate where something comes in a series or sequence:

Last lesson we learned about nouns. Next lesson we will learn about verbs.

Speke died in 1864. The following year the Royal Geographical Society sent Dr Livingstone to Africa to resolve the dispute about the Nile.

5.2 Sequence of Adjectives

What do we do when we have a number of adjectives preceding a noun in a noun phrase? How do we arrange them before the noun being modified?

Let us say we met a number of students, a hundred of them. They were all college students from West Bengal. They were young, of course, and they were bright. How would we describe them? Would we say:

a. I met a hundred young Bengali bright college students? (or)
b. I met a hundred Bengali bright young college students? (or)
c. I met bright young a hundred Bengali college students?

None of the above three sounds quite right. This is how we should say it:

I met a hundred bright young Bengali college students.

As you can see from the above, this is how we order a sequence of adjectives:

numeral	impressionistic	descriptive	proper	material	noun adjuncts	nouns
1	2	3	4	5	6	
a hundred	bright	young	Bengali		college	students
a dozen	rare	—	Kanishka	gold	—	coins
two	wise	old	Kashmiri	—		pandits

In column 1 are numeral adjectives, both ordinal and cardinal. In column 2 are impressionistic adjectives, which suggest the impression or opinion that the speaker or writer has of someone or something, which is open to debate—adjectives like 'beautiful', 'expensive', 'bright', 'rare'. In column 3 are descriptive adjectives, which describe physical characteristics such as age, size, shape, colour, temperature. In column 4 are proper adjectives like 'Chinese' ('a Chinese restaurant') and 'African' ('an African student'). In column 5 are adjectives which tell us what materials things are made of, adjectives like 'wooden' ('a wooden horse') , 'gold' ('a gold coin'). In column 6 are noun adjuncts, that is, nouns functioning as adjectives, as in 'college students', 'kitchen utensils', 'bank manager'.

The order suggested here just gives you a general idea about the word order. If you have two or more descriptive adjectives modifying a noun, you may put them in any order you like:

a small,old, stone-cut cottage (or) an old, small, stone-cut cottage.

Also, you may vary the order of impressionistic and descriptive adjectives:

a beautiful, inexpensive, small cottage (or) a small, beautiful, inexpensive cottage.

Exercise 14

Put the following adjectives in the proper order before the underlined nouns. The first one is an example.

a. a wooden round large table
   Ans: A large round wooden table
b. a young dark handsome man
c. a residential large exclusive area
d. Maruti Suzuki five air-conditioned red cars
e. rare French old hundred several paintings
f. a small shiny plastic black bag

Exercise 15

The manager of a firm is looking for a secretary. Given on the next page are the qualities desired in the secretary and the particulars of the firm he will be working for. Help the manager to draft an advertisement for the papers.

qualities desired in the secretary	**particulars of the firm**
young, graduate, hard-working, Bengali-speaking	German, pharmaceutical, established, Calcutta-based

5.3 Markers of Adjectives

Adjectives are usually marked by adverbs of degree like 'very', 'quite', 'extremely', 'almost', 'rather':

a very clever scheme, an extremely busy day, a rather slow worker,

almost certain (as in 'Success is almost certain'), quite tall (as in 'The girl is quite tall for her age').

Note that these very same adverbs can also mark other adverbs:

very cleverly, rather slowly, almost certainly, extremely hard (as in 'He works extremely hard').

Adjectives are also marked by nouns acting as modifiers:

a film star; a tennis player; the book industry; college students.

The underlined nouns in the above examples actually function as modifiers, that is, as adjectives modifying the nouns that follow them. You may add one or more adjectives before the noun modified if you want to make the expression even more specific:

a popular South Indian film star　　a promising tennis player

the Indian book industry　　bright, young college students.

5.4 Comparison of Adjectives

Most descriptive adjectives may be compared. They may be used to express a quality(positive degree), more of a quality (comparative degree), or most of a quality (superlative degree).

When you compare X and Y, you may compare them to an *equal* or *unequal* degree. (X and Y stand for persons, places, animals, things of the same class.) We use the positive degree when we compare two things (X ,Y) to an *equal* or *unequal* degree. We use the comparative degree when we compare two things (X, Y) to an *unequal* degree. We use the superlative degree only when three (X ,Y, Z) or more things are compared to an *unequal* degree.

The normal rule for forming the comparative and superlative degree of adjectives is to add the endings '-er' and '-est' to adjectives (tall, taller, tallest) or to use the words 'more' and 'most' before adjectives (beautiful, more beautiful, most beautiful). Sometimes the words 'less' and 'least' are used before adjectives instead of 'more' and 'most'. (For details, see the next section.)

When you compare X and Y to an equal degree, this is what you say:

a. X is *as clever as* Y.　　b. X is *as beautiful as* Y.

Note that the adjectives 'clever' and 'beautiful' are in the positive degree and they are preceded and followed by 'as' : as ...as.

When you compare X and Y to an unequal degree, this is what you say:

a. X is *cleverer than* Y.　　(or)　Y is *less clever than* X.

b. X is *more beautiful than* Y.　　(or)　Y is *less beautiful than* X.

Note that the adjectives are all in the comparative degree: 'cleverer'/'less clever', 'more beautiful'/'less beautiful' and they are followed by 'than'. You may, on the other hand, keep the adjectives in the positive degree and still make an unequal comparison:

c. Y is not *so clever as* X. (or) Y is not *as clever as* X.

Exercise 16

Listed below are a number of activities. Choose your descriptive adjectives from this box and compare any two of the activities listed to an equal degree. Use all the adjectives once.

boring	interesting	exciting	dangerous	strenuous	enjoyable	relaxing

swimming
watching television
walking
stamp-collecting
cooking
learning to sing
deep-sea diving
cycling
listening to music
painting
mountain climbing
fishing
sewing
running
playing tennis
learning a foreign language
reading a novel
gardening
playing cards
trekking through the countryside

Here is an example: Swimming is *as strenuous as* playing tennis.

Exercise 17

Working in groups of three, compare the activities listed above, making each comparison sound like a statement of your opinion. Here is an example:

I think fishing is more relaxing than walking.

Well, I think it is less relaxing.

In my view, neither of them is as relaxing as reading a novel.

The superlative degree is used only when three or more things are compared to an unequal degree:

Many more people live in India than in the United States.

But China has more people than India.

China is <u>the most populous</u> of the three (countries).

The United States is <u>the least populous</u> of the three (countries).

Note that the superlative is followed by the prepositional phrase 'of the three countries'. Sometimes the prepositional phrase may begin with 'in':

Mount Everest is the highest mountain in the world. (or) You might just as well say:

Mount Everest is the world's highest mountain.

Exercise 18

What can you say about each of the items grouped together below?

Group a (mountains)	
Makalu	8421 m in height
Kanchenchunga	8529 m
Mount Everest	8796 m
Group b (rivers)	
The Congo	4640 km long
The Amazon	6712 km long
The Nile	6632 km long
Group c (planets)	
Mercury	57.6 million km
Venus	107.67 million km away from the sun
Earth	148.8 million km

The first one is an example:

Mount Everest is *the highest* mountain *in the world.*

Kanchenchunga is *higher than* Makalu but not *as high as* Mount Everest.
Makalu is *the lowest/the least high* of the three mountains.

Exercise 19

The table below gives details of size, weight, price and quality for four different brands of portable typewriters. Study the table and then complete the text that follows, filling in the blanks with suitable adjectives in the appropriate degree of comparison, one word for each blank. Choose your adjectives from the box above the text. One paragraph is done for you as an example.

name of model	country of origin	size	weight	price	quality
Concertina	Aylousia	L	3.5 kg	Rs. 4500	XXXXX
Humming Bird	Ruritania	M	2.5 kg	Rs. 3200	XXXX
Typerite	Mocassia	M	2.5 kg	Rs. 2300	XX
Ladylight	Beruvia	S	2 kg	Rs. 1700	XXX

L large M medium S small XXXXX best quality
XX worst quality

bad	cheap	elegant	expensive
good	heavy	large	light
little	small		

Four portable typewriters from four different countries were compared, with respect to size, weight, price and quality.

The Concertina from Aylousia, priced at Rs 4500, was <u>the</u> <u>most expensive</u>[1]. It was also <u>the</u> <u>largest</u>[2] and <u>the</u> <u>heaviest</u>[3] but we found it <u>the</u> <u>best</u>[4] in quality.

The Ruritanian Humming Bird was __________[5] and __________[6] the Concertina model, weighing 2.5 kg whereas the Concertina weighed 3.5 kg. It looked __________ __________[7] __________ the Concertina but its performance was not__________ __________[8].

The Typerite from Mocassia was just __________ __________[9] and __________[10] __________ __________ the Humming Bird but its performance was very much __________[11]. However, it cost only Rs 2300 while the Humming Bird cost Rs 3200.

The Ladylight from Beruvia, at Rs 1700, was __________ __________[12] of the four models. It was also __________ __________[13] and __________ __________[14], weighing 500 gm __________[15] __________ the Typerite. As far as performance was concerned, it was __________[16] quality __________ the Typerite but not __________ __________[17] __________the Humming Bird or the Concertina.

So far we have been comparing things like countries, mountains, rivers or activities like swimming and stamp-collecting. The things compared, however, can be more abstract; also, the comparison can be between a person or thing and the same person or thing at two different times:

> At fifty, Mr Shankar is *as able as* ever but *less committed* to his work *than* he was at thirty.
>
> The mango yield has been *more* this year *than* during the last ten years.
>
> The country being largely self-sufficient in food, the impact of the sanctions will be *more telling* in the field of space research *than* in agriculture.

Adjectives in their comparative degree may be used as modifiers before nouns without being followed by the 'than' construction:

> The sons asked for a *bigger share* of the property (bigger, presumably, than what they were offered).
>
> I suggest that you go in for a *cheaper/less expensive car* (than the one you are thinking of buying).
>
> A *quieter life* will help to bring down your blood pressure (quieter than the life you are living now).

The comparative adjectives may also be used predicatively, that is, as complements after a linking verb (without the 'than' construction):

> This place has grown a lot *noisier* (than it was before). With advancing age our father has become *more intolerant* of our faults and shortcomings (than he was when younger).

Note that when the comparative is not followed by the 'than' construction, the other thing in comparison should be obvious, as it is in the above examples. (The other thing in comparison is given in parentheses.)

A superlative adjective with 'most' may not always involve a comparison:

> That was a *most entertaining* movie.

The sentence means simply that the movie was highly entertaining. Compare:

(1) That was a *most entertaining* movie.

(2) Of all the movies I had seen, that was *the most entertaining.*

Sentence (2) is clearly a comparison, while sentence (1) is not. Note the presence of the definite article 'the' before the superlative and the prepositional phrase 'of all the movies…', in sentence (2).

Here is another example of a non-comparing superlative with 'most':

She was a *most extraordinary* woman (meaning 'a very extraordinary woman').

Superlatives, as we saw earlier in the chapter, are usually used with a prepositional phrase beginning with 'of' or 'in'. They can, however, be used on their own, that is, without the prepositional phrase if the context makes clear the point of comparison. You may say 'Sheila was the cleverest' if you have already identified the group to which she belonged.

Ordinal numbers may be used with the superlatives:

She is the *second* best singer in the school.

That is Russia's *third* largest city.

5.4.1 Rules for Forming the Comparative and Superlative Degree of Comparison

1. *one-syllable adjectives*

   Add '–er' and '–est' to the adjective.

   high – higher – highest   tall – taller – tallest   smart – smarter – smartest

   Other adjectives of this group: short, small, thick, young
   If the adjective ends in a single consonant preceded by a single vowel, double the final consonant.

   big – bigger – biggest   thin – thinner – thinnest   hot – hotter – hottest

2. *adjectives of three or more syllables*

   Add 'more' and 'most' (or 'less' and 'least') before the adjective: attractive – more attractive – most attractive; courageous – more courageous – most courageous; comfortable – less comfortable – least comfortable

   Other adjectives of this group:

   beautiful   incomplete   difficult   generous   enjoyable   reluctant
   revengeful   dependent   peculiar   sensible   valuable

3. *adjectives of two syllables*

   Add '-er' and '-est' to these two-syllable adjectives ending in a consonant plus '-y'. Remember to change the final '-y' to '-i' before adding the endings:

   pretty – prettier – prettiest   happy – happier – happiest   noisy – noisier – noisiest

   Other adjectives of this group:

   dirty   lucky   rocky   silly   tasty   funny

   Add '-er' and '-est' to these two-syllable adjectives ending in '-le'. Remember to drop the final '-e' before adding the endings:

   humble – humbler – humblest   simple – simpler – simplest
   noble – nobler – noblest

Other adjectives of this group:

able, ample, idle

Add 'more' and 'most' before these two-syllable adjectives:

famous – more famous – most famous   honest – more honest – most honest
recent – more recent – most recent

Other adjectives of this group:

backward   childish   exact   fruitful   hopeful   urgent   useful   useless

Add '-er' and '-est' or 'more' and 'most' to these two-syllable adjectives. These adjectives form their comparative and superlative degree either way.

common – commoner/more common – commonest/most common
handsome – handsomer/more handsome-handsomest/most handsome
pleasant – pleasanter/more pleasant – pleasantest/most pleasant

Other adjectives of this group:

bitter   clever   friendly   holy   lively   narrow   polite
remote   severe   shallow   sincere   stupid   tender

<u>Note</u>

Remember these general rules while forming the comparative and superlative degree of comparison.

1. Drop the final '-e' before adding '-er' and '-est'.

   large – larger – largest   simple – simpler – simplest

2. If the final '-y' is preceded by a consonant, change the '-y' to 'i'.

   lively – livelier – liveliest   lucky – luckier – luckiest

3. Avoid double comparatives and double superlatives like 'more happier' and 'most highest'.

4. Irregular comparison

   These adjectives are compared irregularly.

   good – better – best
   bad – worse – worst
   little – less/ lesser – least
   much/many – more – most
   old – older/elder – oldest/eldest
   far – farther/further – farthest/furthest

6 Determiners

In Chapter 2, we briefly referred to determiners and in the following chapter they were discussed in some detail.

Determiners are a whole class of structure-words which always come *before* nouns, helping to identify the persons or things referred to by the nouns that follow them.

Determiners comprise these seven grammatical categories: articles, demonstrative adjectives, possessive adjectives, indefinite adjectives, numeral adjectives, interrogative adjectives, and relative adjectives.

Broadly speaking, determiners are of two kinds: **general determiners** and **specific determiners**. The former identify the persons or things referred to by the nouns in a general way, while the latter identify them in a specific way.

Nouns in English, as we know, refer to persons and things. We may refer to these persons and things in a *general* way:

> *A* man called at our place the other day.
>
> At the end of the day there was *an* unclaimed parcel.

The indefinite article 'a' merely identifies the caller as a man; he could be any man, one out of a million or more men. Similarly, the indefinite article 'an' identifies the unclaimed thing as a parcel; it doesn't say anything specific about the parcel.

> *A few* people turned up for the meeting.
>
> There is *some* milk in the jug.

The indefinite adjectives 'a few' and 'some' merely indicate the smallness of the number of people who turned up for the meeting and of the quantity of milk in the jug. They don't tell us how small.

On the other hand, a determiner may refer to someone or something in a specific way:

> *The* woman chased *the* thief down *the* street, *the* boys cheering her along.

The definite article 'the' in the above example refers to a specific woman chasing a specific thief down a specific street, cheered by specific boys. Both speaker and listener know who the woman is that is chasing the thief, the thief who is being chased, the street down which he is being chased, and the boys who are cheering her along.

> Here was *this* man striding up to me in the middle of *the* street and putting out his hands, asking for money!

Who is *this man* that strode up to me? As the speaker, I know who he was, and I had already identified him to my listener. I wouldn't be using the demonstrative 'this' before 'man' if I had not *earlier* identified him to my listener. We both, speaker and listener, also know the very street where the encounter took place.

Among the general determiners are the indefinite articles: *a* and *an*, and indefinite adjectives like: *some, any, little, less, much, many, more, most, few, enough* etc. The specific determiners include, apart from the definite article 'the', demonstrative adjectives, possessive adjectives, numeral adjectives, interrogative adjectives, and the relative adjective 'whose'. (For more information about general and specific determiners, refer to the relevant sections in Chapter 5. For more information about the articles, 'a', 'an' and 'the', refer to the next chapter, Chapter 7.)

Boxed below for easy reference are the two types of determiners:

general determiners	specific determiners
a an all another any each every either enough few a few little a little many more much neither no other several some	the this that these those my our your his her its their; cardinal numbers—one two three etc; ordinal numbers—first second third etc; what which whose (the last, both as interrogative adjective and as relative adjective)

In English you can have only one specific determiner before a noun:

They sailed down *the* river, looking at *the* sky. (definite article)

What do you call *that* joke on wheels? A moped? (demonstrative adjective)

Her children are versatile. (possessive adjective)

A year has *twelve* months and January is the *first* month of the year. (numeral adjective)

An equilateral triangle is a triangle *whose* three sides are equal. (relative adjective)

What electives are you taking this year?
Which newspaper do you read?

Note that in the last two examples, the interrogative adjectives 'what' and 'which' ask for specific information about the electives and the newspaper.

Note also that these two determiners can be followed by specific numerals, unlike other specific determiners which are mutually exclusive:

What three reasons did you say you had?
Which three trees are to be cut down?

Exercise 1

Underline the determiners in the following sentences and box the nouns. Note that the determiner comes before the noun. The first two are examples.

a. You may apply for the job if you think you fulfil these requirements.
b. They are starting a new serial this week.
c. Our school is the oldest in the city.
d. You still talk of the time when you could get a dozen eggs for a rupee. Those days are gone.
e. Every possible suspect in the neighbourhood was rounded up by the police and detained until the investigations were over.
f. 'Can you make us some coffee?'

'Black or white?'
'White, but without too much milk.'
'With or without sugar?'
'Just a little sugar, please.'

g. Are there any mangoes in the market at this time of the year?
h. Have you enough provisions to last you a month?
i. 'What would you have? Tea or coffee?'
'Either tea or coffee.'
'Neither tea nor coffee for me. I wouldn't mind a glass of cold water, though.'
j. What programmes do you watch on TV?

6.1 Predeterminers and Postdeterminers

Apart from determiners, we have two other classes of words which we might call **predeterminers** and **postdeterminers**.

A. **Predeterminers**: As the name suggests, predeterminers come before determiners in a sentence.

Look at the underlined words in the following sentences:

All [his] sons turned against him.

Both [their] statements were verified and found true.

Planning is only half [the] job.

Notice that the underlined words, 'all', 'both' and 'half' come before determiners (the boxed words). Hence they are called predeterminers.

'All', 'both' and 'half' may be followed by articles, possessives or demonstratives:
all the sons   all his sons   all those sons of his
both the statements   both their statements   both these statements
half the share   half my share   half this share

'All' may be used with plural countable nouns and with uncountable nouns:
Not all the students showed up for the morning parade.
We gave all the help that we as neighbours could.

'Both', used with countable plural nouns, refers only to two people or things, not more:
Both the houses are nearing completion.
Both the ladies were from the same university.

Words like 'once', 'twice', 'three times', 'many times', 'double', 'triple' can also be used as predeterminers:
We go to the hills once a year.
'How much did you pay for it?'
'Fifty rupees.'
'Just fifty? Then I'm afraid I paid three times the amount'.
Doctor to patient: You are now double your weight.

The following words are also used as predeterminers: 'quite', 'such', 'what', 'rather'.

'How did the story end?'

'Well, it was quite a sad ending.'

It was on such a day that the terrible thing happened.

She has such a fine temperament.

'Pleased to meet you. What a pleasant surprise!'

It was rather a calamity.

Boxed below is a list of words or expressions that may be used as predeterminers:

all	both	double	triple	half	many	twice
thrice	quite	such	what	rather	three times	

Exercise 2

Underline the predeterminers and box the determiners in the following sentences. The first one is an example.

a. The priest spends half his time meeting people and listening to their grievances.
b. Have you read 'All My Sons' by Arthur Miller?
c. Both the candidates were equally well-qualified and it was difficult choosing between the two.
d. 'How often do you go to the library?'
'Twice a week.'
e. The manager has such a pleasant personality that his subordinates speak of him in glowing terms.
f. Your getting into a medical school was quite a surprise and a most pleasant one too.
g. See what a mess you have made. You must clean it up.
h. Many a young person would give his or her right arm for a job like this.
i. She used to give half her pay to a dependent relative of hers.

B. **Postdeterminers:** As the name suggests, postdeterminers come *after* determiners in a sentence. Cardinal numbers (one, two, three, thirty etc) and ordinal numbers (first, second, third, thirtieth etc) are used as postdeterminers:

Chicago's O'Hare Airport is one of the busiest in the world. A flight takes off or lands once every thirty seconds.

We don't work on second Saturdays. Every second Saturday of the month is a day off for us.

The first man, they say, was born in Africa.

She was the first person to arrive and the last (person) to leave.

Note that the underlined words come *after* the determiners, which are boxed.

If cardinals and ordinals figure in the same phrase, the ordinals come *first*:

I read the first three chapters of the book and the last two (chapters). I skipped the rest.

7 Articles

The **articles** are 'a', 'an' and 'the'. Strictly speaking, the articles are two only, 'a' and 'the'. They both undergo a change before a word beginning with a vowel sound: 'the' changes in pronunciation, while 'a' changes in both pronunciation and spelling.
'The' is pronounced:

1. with the ə sound (the sound as in the last sound of 'China') before words beginning with a consonant sound:

   the boy the big boy the magazine

2. with the 'i' sound (the sound as in 'sit') before words beginning with a vowel sound:

   the omnibus the elephant the ink bottle

3. with the 'i:' sound (the sound as in 'seat') when it is emphasized:

   That was the man I had wanted to meet.
   That was the place to go for a quiet, restful holiday.

The article 'a' becomes 'an' before words beginning with a vowel sound:

an apple an untidy room an octopus

We say 'a pen' but 'an ice-cream', 'a book' but 'an orange'. Note that it is the sound of the initial letter, not the letter itself that decides whether we use 'a' or 'an' before it. For instance, we say:

a university but an umbrella
a European but an Eskimo.

Both 'university' and 'umbrella' begin with the vowel 'u' but only 'umbrella' has the vowel sound; 'university', on the other hand, like 'European', has a consonant sound — they both have a sound like the first sound in 'you'. The 'e' in 'Eskimo' has a vowel sound unlike the 'e' in 'European'; hence 'an Eskimo'.

The chief structural function of articles is as determiners that precede nouns. 'The' may be used with a singular or plural noun, 'a' / 'an' is used with a *singular countable noun.*

Articles contribute to meaning by marking nouns as definite or indefinite. 'The' refers to a particular person or thing: 'the gentleman sitting next to the Prime Minister', 'the tall coconut palm in my backyard'. 'A' / 'an' refers to an unspecified one: 'a gentleman sitting in the third row' meaning 'one of the many gentlemen sitting in the third row'. For this reason, 'the' is called the *definite article,* 'a' / 'an' an *indefinite article.*

However, nouns marked as indefinite can be made definite by replacing 'a' / 'an' by 'the' and making suitable additions to the noun:

a bus but the bus to Mumbai Central

a speaker but the guest speaker of the evening

Exercise 1

In column A are a number of nouns with 'a'/'an' before them. In column B replace 'a'/'an' by 'the' and make suitable additions to the nouns so that they refer to particular persons or things. The first one is an example.

A	B
a lady	the lady in white
a tree	
a country	
an exam	
a house	
a language	
an article	
a book	

7.1 Generic Use of Articles

When we make a general statement, we may use 'a'/'an' or 'the'.

a/an — A dog is man's best friend.
the — The dog is man's best friend.

We may dispense with all articles and say:

Dogs are man's best friends.

All the three statements refer to a whole class of animals called dogs. They speak of a quality or attribute shared by all dogs. Used this way, 'a'/'an' and 'the' are said to be used generically. A generic statement about the rose may be phrased in one of these three ways:

The rose smells sweet.
A rose smells sweet.
Roses smell sweet.

Note that all these three choices are open to us only when the nouns stand for actual species of plants or animals, as in the examples above, and in the case of humans, a clearly identifiable class or group of people, as in this example:

An athlete should be encouraged to interact with the trainers.
The athlete should be encouraged to interact with the trainers.
Athletes should be encouraged to interact with the trainers.

However, with other types of concrete countable nouns, these three choices may not be available. For instance, we may say:

The computer has changed our way of life (or)
Computers have changed our way of life (but not)
A computer has changed our way of life.

Similarly, we may say:

A worker must be treated well (or)
Workers must be treated well (but not)
The worker must be treated well. ('The' in this example does not have the generic sense, it refers to a particular worker the speaker has in mind.)

In any case, the generic use of 'the' is relatively rare. The article-less plural is more common:

Workers must be treated well.

Athletes should be encouraged to interact with the trainers.

The article-less plural noun has an advantage over the 'articled' singular noun. It can be easily replaced by 'they' (as subject), 'them' (as object) and 'their' (as possessive) when the noun is referred to again:

Workers should be treated well. Otherwise, they may not give of their best.

The singular article, on the other hand, would need a somewhat awkward construction:

A worker should be treated well. Otherwise he or she may not give of his or her best.

7.1.1 Uses of 'a'/'an'

a. As mentioned earlier, we use 'a'/'an' before singular countable nouns when we do not know which particular thing we are talking about:

   A team of scientists has thought up a new technique of recycling old rubber tyres. (We do not know which particular team of scientists the sentence refers to or what particular technique they have thought up.)

b. We use 'a'/'an' to represent the number one:

   a thousand rupees   a hundred kilometers   a kilo of butter

c. 'A' and 'an' are very commonly used with nouns and noun phrases functioning as subject complements:

   Dr Mohan is a specialist in chest diseases.

   I am an engineer but my father is a businessman.

Exercise 2

Read the following dialogue:

Q: Would you like to be a teacher or a student?

A: I think I would rather be a teacher.

Q: Why?

A: Because teachers do not have to write exams.

Write short dialogues on the lines above answering the question: What would you prefer to be?

cricketer/footballer   actor/writer   journalist/photographer
corporate executive/army officer.

7.1. 2 Uses of 'the'

a. As mentioned earlier, we use the article 'the' when we refer to a particular person or thing:

   the book on the top shelf

   the girl in the middle of the third row;

   also, when we refer to a person or thing already mentioned:

   One autumn evening a man and a woman were walking along a dusty road. The man was holding a sheet in front of him, the woman was carrying a child.

   Note that 'man' and 'woman' become particular or definite when referred to a second time.

b. Another way of specifying a noun is to include it in a prepositional or participle phrase:

It is roughly three miles from the centre of the city to the airport.

The girl wearing a blue frock is my younger sister.

c. A third way of specifying a noun is through context, local or global:

Suman, will you shut the door and bring me the duster? (From local context we know the door is the door of the classroom and the duster is the duster in the classroom.)

People before Galileo believed that the sun went round the earth. (The context here is global. There is only one sun and one earth in the global context. They both are only one of their kind.)

7.1.3 More Uses of 'the'

We use 'the':

a. before the names of rivers, seas, oceans, mountain ranges, and groups of islands:

the Ganga the Arabian Sea the Himalayas the Andamans the Philippines

(We do not use 'the' before the names of single mountains or single islands:

Mount Everest Mount Blanc Long Island Coney Island)

b. before the names of trains, boats, aeroplanes:

the Tamil Nadu Express the Vikrant the Kanishka

c. before the names of Holy Books:

the Gita the Koran the Bible

d. before the names of well-known buildings:

the Parliament House the Rashtrapati Bhavan the Empire State Building

e. before the names of newspapers:

the Hindu the Statesman the Deccan Herald

f. before the names of familiar objects found in nature or made by man:

They were sailing down the river watching the clouds and the sky.

He went up the street, climbed the steps and entered the house. He then went into the bathroom for a wash.

g. before the superlatives of adjectives and adverbs:

Shyam is the most talented student I had in my undergraduate classes.

Meenu works the hardest of all.

h. before adjectives that rank nouns:

the principal reason for the discontent among the office staff

the chief difficulty in the way of imparting religious instruction in schools

the only child of his parents

i. before points on the globe:

the North Pole the South Pole the Equator the 37th Parallel

j. before points of the compass used as names for geographic areas:

the Far East the Near East the Middle West the Orient

k. before names of colleges and universities when the proper noun occurs as part of an 'of' phrase:

the University of Madras the University of Michigan

Note that 'the' is not used in the absence of the 'of' phrase:

Oxford University Harvard University Pune University

l. in certain special grammatical constructions:

1. with gerunds or abstract nouns followed by the 'of' phrase:

The inducting of teenagers into the militia is a novel feature of life today. (the + gerund + 'of' phrase)

The induction of teenagers into the militia is a novel feature of life today. (the + abstract noun + 'of' phrase)

Note that we can use the gerund phrase without 'the' and 'of':

Inducting teenagers into the militia is a novel feature of life today.

2. in 'of' phrases after words expressing quantity or number:

Most Many All The majority Several Ten One-third	+	of the candidates did not have the requisite qualifications.

3. with adjectives to form plural nouns:

The poor will always be with us. (poor people)

The British and the French are two peoples divided by a channel.

4. with adjectives and adverbs in the comparative degree:

The more, the merrier. (The more people you have, the merrier it is.)

The harder you practise, the better you perform.

The higher you go, the lower you fall.

(This construction is somewhat old but by no means outdated; it is very much in use even now.)

7.1.4 The Omission of 'the'

a. We normally do not use 'the' before plural nouns:

I love apples but I hate bananas.

Urban workers are better off than before.

Young people as a rule do not want to work in villages.

But if we specify the nouns, we must use 'the':

I love apples but the apples that grow here are not tasty.

The young people who work in villages must be admired for their commitment.

b. We do not as a rule use 'the' before proper nouns, that is, before the particular names of persons, places, cities, countries, continents:

Ravi is a chartered accountant. He is married to Shobha.

The future of the world will hinge upon the future of Europe and and Asia.

Paris, they say, is more impressive than London and Vienna is even more impressive than Paris.

Exercise 3

Insert 'the' in the following sentences, where necessary:

a. Mediterranean Sea separates Europe from Africa.

b. Alps, Europe's greatest mountain range, is over 1000 km long.

c. Lion is king of forest.

d. Indian Ocean links three continents: Asia, Africa and Australia.

e. No unexplored region in our times, neither heights of Himalayas nor Antarctic, has excited as much interest as question of where Nile rose.

f. By middle of last century, missionaries working in Africa came forward with reports that they themselves had seen Mount Kilimanjaro and Mount Kenya, somewhat to north of Kilimanjaro.

7.1.5 Zero Article

No article is used:

a. before proper nouns:

I met Roger at Kwality last night. He was with Rajesh and Rima. Rajesh is now working for a big company in Calcutta.

b. before abstract nouns which indicate:

1. a concept or quality: Honesty is the best policy.
   Punctuality is a virtue not everyone has.
2. a recreational activity: Football is not as popular in India as cricket.
   My hobbies are photography and stamp-collecting.
3. a subject of study: I tried hard but I couldn't learn to like history while at school.
   Ramesh scored a centum in mathematics.

c. before mass nouns (singular uncountable nouns) like 'water', 'milk', 'rice', when used in general statements:

Water is essential for all life.
Milk is a must for all growing children.

However, if we want to specify a particular kind or sample of 'water' or 'milk', we use 'the':

The water from this well is not potable.
The milk that we get locally is pasteurized and is therefore safe to drink.

d. before the names of most diseases and illnesses:

Polio is a disease that cripples children.
Malaria at one time killed millions of people.
Exceptions: I have a headache/cold/fever.
Sunil has the measles.

e. before the following nouns when they are preceded by prepositions like 'in', 'at', 'to' etc:

She goes <u>to church</u> every Sunday.
The man is <u>in prison</u>, so his family is destitute.
Manu has pneumonia and is now <u>in hospital</u>.
The matter is now <u>in court</u>.
He is <u>at home</u>, his children are <u>at school</u>.
Children, it is time for you to go <u>to bed</u>.
We are going <u>to town</u> this afternoon.

We do not use any article before the nouns listed above when we are thinking of the idea behind these places (church, prison, school etc), or the purpose they are associated with. But if we think of them as places or buildings, we need to use an article. Compare:

i. Children go <u>to school</u>. (to study)
   Mother goes <u>to the school</u> every day. (to pick up her child)
ii. He is <u>in prison</u>. (for some crime he committed)
   His wife goes <u>to the prison</u> every month to see him. (the place where the prison is located)
iii. We are going <u>to town</u>. (to do some shopping)
   We drove around <u>the town</u>. (the town stands for an area)

Exercise 4

Choose the correct form with or without 'the'. Cross out the incorrect form.

a. The President of India lives in Rashtrapati Bhavan/the Rashtrapati Bhavan.
b. Scrooge had not gone to church/to the church for many Christmases.
c. Our grandmother is in hospital/in the hospital, following a fall.
d. We have been to hospital/to the hospital to see her.
e. Have you seen Buckingham Palace/the Buckingham Palace?
f. I did not go to university/to the university, it was hard enough for my parents to see me through school.
g. What will you do after you finish school/the school? Will you apply for a job in town/in the town?
h. She graduated from Pune University/the Pune University.
i. The minister flew from Dumdum Airport/the Dumdum Airport to Bangalore on his annual vacation.

Exercise 5

In the following pairs of sentences, insert articles ('a'/'an', 'the'), where necessary. Write X if no article is required. The first one is an example.

a. ____X____ Bread is still cheap. <u>The</u> bread in our bakery tastes good.
b. We are for ______________ peace but we want ______________peace of the brave.
c. Is ______________ life worth living? ______________ answer to ______________ question would depend on ______________ liver. (pun intended)
d. ______________ equator is ______________ imaginary line drawn round ______________ world halfway between ______________ North Pole and

_____________ South Pole.

e. _____________ life of _____________ queen bee is very short but shorter still is _____________ life of _____________ drone.

Exercise 6

Complete this piece on Charles Darwin, inserting 'the' before the nouns/noun phrases, wherever necessary. The nouns/noun phrases are given in parentheses. Write 'X' in the blanks where the article is not required.

Charles Darwin was one of _____________ (greatest scientists) of _____________ (nineteenth century). He was born in 1809 in _____________ (England). He spent his childhood in _____________ (Shrewsbury). He went to _____________ (school) in this town. He was a slow learner. _____________ (Robert Darwin), Charles' father, was a doctor and a rich man.

As a student Charles was interested in _____________ (chemistry), _____________ (mathematics) and _____________ (natural science) rather than _____________ (Latin grammar). After finishing _____________ (school), he went to _____________ (university) and studied _____________ (medicine).

In 1831 Darwin set out on a sea voyage round the world on _____________ (Beagle). After saiiing past _____________ (France) and _____________ (Spain), the ship went to _____________ (Tenerife) in _____________ (Canary Islands), to _____________ (Cape Verde) and other islands. After four years around _____________ (South America), they reached _____________ (Galapagos Islands). _____________ giant tortoises and _____________ iguanas on these islands seemed to confirm Darwin's theory of _____________ evolution.

Charles Darwin returned to _____________ (England) in 1836. He wrote and published many books on _____________ (biology). His most famous book is 'On the Origin of Species'.

Exercise 7

Insert articles ('a'/'an' or 'the'), wherever necessary, in the following passage.

Search for sources of Nile was in fact more than ordinary field of exploration. Nile was lifeline of Egypt and of deserts it passed through. If it had failed to flow, even for one season, all Egypt would have perished. It was vitally important to know where river came from and whether it would continue to flow. No wonder Nile excited degree of interest hardly equalled in any other field of exploration.

But river remained mystery all the same. Every explorer who went up Nile from Egypt returned defeated. It was possible to go up river to distance of some 500 miles south of Khartoum but beyond that point river lost itself in swamp that no one could get through.

There was vague idea dating from 1st century A.D. that Nile had its origin in two great lakes south of equator, fed by snowy range of mountains. 1700 years later, in 1848 to be exact, missionary by name Johann Rebmann came forward with report that he himself had journeyed inland from East African coast and had seen vast mountain called Kilimanjaro with snow on its top. In following year another missionary claimed that he had seen from distance another mountain peak covered with snow. By early fifties there was also evidence of lakes in region: Arab slave traders returning to Zanzibar from far interior spoke of two great lakes there. In addition there were reports of third lake, farther to south.

All this led to renewal of interest in sources of Nile and at same time gave rise to number of questions. Were all these lakes in reality one lake? And how were lakes and mountains connected with Nile?

8 Noun Phrases

Think of English grammar as a hierarchy. A hierarchy, as we know, is a system of organisation in which things have their allotted ranks depending on how important they are, the most important being at the top and the least important at the bottom.

At the bottom of the hierarchy that is English grammar is the word, and at the top is the sentence. In between these two are the intermediate ranks, the phrase and the clause, as shown below:

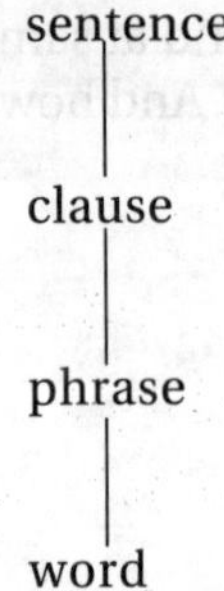

The sentence, as was said earlier, is the basic unit of communication in English. A sentence in English in normally made up of one or more clauses.

A **clause** is a word-group having a subject and a predicate of its own:

The people living upstairs/are moving to the suburbs.
(subject) (predicate)

The above word-group has a subject and a predicate, it is therefore a clause. Since it makes complete sense, it is also a sentence at the same time. We may call it a one-clause sentence.

Clauses are of two kinds: **main** and **subordinate**. A **main clause** is a clause that can stand alone. It makes complete sense. A subordinate clause, on the other hand, cannot stand alone; it makes some sense but not complete sense. Look at the following sentence:

The people who are living upstairs are moving to the suburbs.

The above sentence consists of two clauses corresponding to the two finite verbs in the sentence ('are living', 'are moving'):

The people are moving to the suburbs (clause 1), who are living upstairs (clause 2).

(Remember there are as many clauses in a sentence as there are finite verbs.)

Clause 2 contributes vital information to the sentence as a whole, it tells us which people are moving to the suburbs. Without it, clause 1 'The people are moving to the suburbs' does not make complete sense. All the same clause 2 cannot stand alone, unlike clause 1, which can. Clause 2 depends on clause 1, it modifies the subject noun of clause 1 ('people'), and we call it a **subordinate** or **dependent** clause. We call clause 1 a main clause. However, all clauses must have a subject-predicate structure, **no matter whether they are main or subordinate.**

A clause in turn may be made up of one or more **phrases**. In the clause:

The people living upstairs are moving to the suburbs

we have two phrases (underlined). The first begins with a participle followed by an adverb, the second with a preposition followed by a noun. They both are cohesive units within the clause contributing their share of meaning but they have no subject-predicate structure of their own. 'Living upstairs' has a participle verb in 'living' but it is a non-finite verb and therefore cannot make a predicate; also, it contains no noun or pronoun which can function as subject. As for the other phrase 'to the suburbs', it has neither a subject nor a predicate. *A phrase is a cohesive meaningful word-group in a clause having no subject-predicate of its own.* A clause, on the other hand, is a cohesive word-group with a subject-predicate structure. For a clearer understanding of the difference between phrase and clause, compare the underlined word-groups in these sentences:

The people living upstairs are moving to the suburbs.
The people who are living upstairs are moving to the suburbs.

Both the underlined word-groups mean the same and both modify the same noun ('people') but *formally* they are different. 'Living upstairs' is a phrase, while 'who are living upstairs' is a clause complete with a subject ('who') and a predicate ('are living upstairs').

Here are some more examples of phrases. The phrases are underlined.

We eat to live a healthy life.

After listening to the news, we sat down to dinner.

I hate driving on a rainy day.

Not having the right connections is a handicap in business.

The tall, thin, young man is here to see you.

The mysterious dead animal washed ashore has been identified.

Exercise 1

Underline all the phrases in the following sentences. The first one is an example.

a. A huge comet is on course to collide with the earth on August 14, 2116.
1 2 3
b. The collision could kill most forms of life on earth, said an expert on asteroids.
c. The five-kilometre-wide ball of ice and rock is travelling at 60 km per second.
d. The International Astronomical Union noted the comet's discovery on October 15.
e. Asteroids are spinning pieces of space rock.
f. There are millions of these space rocks circling the sun between the orbits of Mars and Jupiter.

Phrases may be classified on the basis of their *form* or *function*. Judged on the basis of function, a phrase may be a **noun phrase**, an **adjective phrase** or an **adverb phrase**. In this unit we take up the first of these three.

A **noun phrase** is a phrase which functions like a noun. A noun, as we saw earlier (Chapter 3), can perform any one of the following functions: it can function as subject of verb, object of verb, object of preposition, subject complement, object complement or appositive (that is, in apposition to another noun). If any of these functions is done by a phrase, we call it a noun phrase. Look at the underlined phrases in the following sentences:

a. The big, black dog barked.
b. Dogs in the country generally bark.
c. Two dozen boxes were stolen in transit.
d. Most of the candidates called for interview were found suitable.
e. A free, fearless, highly developed national press is a must in a democracy.
f. The principal's references to the school's achievements in sports won her a round of applause.

The underlined phrases above are all noun phrases functioning, as they do, as subjects of their respective sentences.

The noun phrase is very versatile. It can do a whole range of functions like a noun, as we can see by replacing the noun in the basic sentence patterns (N) by a noun phrase (NP):

bp 1 The big, black dog barked. (NP as subject)
bp 2 She was driving a long, low-slung, off-white car. (NP as direct object of verb)
bp 3 The groom handed the beautiful bride a garland of roses. (NP as indirect object)
bp 4 The coach nominated Michael of class X (NP as object of verb) captain of the cricket team for the academic year. (NP as object complement)
bp 5 The king was a just ruler very popular with his subjects. (NP as subject complement)

Besides, a noun phrase can function as an appositive to another noun or noun phrase:

Stanley, one of the greatest of East African explorers, was different from the general run of explorers who were drawn to Africa in the nineteenth century.

On his very first visit, Vivek fell in love with Calcutta, the largest and the most vibrant city of India.

Notice that the most important word in the noun phrase is the noun or pronoun. We call the noun or pronoun the headword; the rest of the phrase acts as modifier, modifying the headword, as shown below:

	noun phrase			noun phrase	
	headword 1	**modifier** 2		**headword** 1	**modifier** 2
a.	dog	the, big, black	d.	most (pronoun)	of the candidates, called for interview
b.	dogs	in the country	e.	press	a free, fearless, highly developed, national
c.	boxes	two dozen	f.	references	the principal's, to the school's achievements in sports

The headword in column 1 is a noun or pronoun; the modifier in column 2 consists of a determiner ('the', 'the principal's', 'two dozen') followed by one or more adjectives or adjective phrases, as you can see from the following analysis:

	determiner 1	adjective 2	headword 3	adjective pharase 4
a.	the (article)	big, black	dog	------------
b.	-----	-----	dogs	in the country
c.	two dozen (numeral adj.)	-----	boxes	
d.	-----	-----	most	of the candidates, called for interview
e.	a	free, fearless, highly developed, national	press	
f.	the principal's	references		to the school's achievements in sports

Notice that the adjectives in column 2 and the adjective phrases in column 4 modify their respective headwords (noun or pronoun) in column 3. An adjective and an adjective phrase, both do the same function: they modify a noun or pronoun. The only difference is the word order: the adjective *precedes* the noun while the adjective phrase *follows* it.

Notice that the phrases in column 4 are different *in form*: three of them begin with a preposition while the fourth begins with a participle. *Functionally*, however, all four of them are the same: adjective phrases, modifying a noun or pronoun.

Exercise 2

Each of the following sentences contains one or more noun phrases, italicised for you. Box the headword in each of the phrases and write in parentheses its noun-function. The first two are done for you.

a. *Most* [*students*] run out of their pocket money by the middle of the month. (subject of verb)
b. She was *the first Indian* [*woman*] *to swim across the Channel.* (subject complement)
c. *All his sons* respected him.
d. *Many a person in your place* would just grab the offer.
e. *The pollution of our environment* comes in many different forms.
f. I bought *my younger sister a lovely birthday present.*
g. There are *three kinds of book owners.*
h. You had better state *the central theme of your paragraph* right at the beginning.

Exercise 3

The sentences on the next page conform to the basic sentence patterns but they are incomplete for want of one or more noun phrases. Complete them with appropriate

noun phrases. The first two are examples.

a. ______________ bought ______________. (N-V-N; bp 2)
Answer: Our next-door neighbour bought a vacuum cleaner with six attachments.

b. ______________ broke down. (N-V; bp 1)
Answer: Uncle's Baby Austin, a vintage car of the thirties, broke down.

c. ______________ gave her ______________. (N-V-N-N; bp 3)

d. ______________ appointed ______________. (N-V-N-N; bp 4)

e. ______________ considers ______________ reliable. (N-V-N-Adj., bp 4)

f. ______________ is ______________. (N-LV-N; bp 5)

g. ______________ looks handsome. (N-LV-Adj., bp 6)

h. ______________ sounds false. (N-LV-Adj., bp 6)

Final Note on Noun Phrases

A noun phrase may consist of:

1. predeterminer + determiner + noun:
   all his books, both her parents, such a man
2. determiner + postdeterminer+noun:
   the first woman, every third man
3. determiner + one or more adjectives + noun:
   a small, dark, dingy room those fine Italian paintings imported German cars
4. determiner + adjective + noun + adjective phrase:
   the British gentleman just arrived from London those tall, sturdy girls from the village

A noun phrase may, in addition, take the form of an **infinitive** or **gerund** phrase:

a. *infinitive phrase as noun phrase*
To make mistakes and be able to learn from them is the mark of the wise man and the wise woman. (subject of verb)
I do not like to borrow money from strangers. (object of verb)
To know her is to like her. (subject, subject complement)

b *gerund phrase as noun phrase*
Making mistakes and learning from them may not be a bad way of learning. (subject)
I do not like borrowing money from strangers. (object of verb)
His hobby is collecting stamps. (subject complement)
I call that cheating the public. (object complement)

Exercise 4

Underline the noun phrases in the following sentences and write within parentheses what noun-function each one of them does in the sentence. The first is an example.

a. The kitten likes to play with the wool. (object of the verb 'likes')
b. The main difficulty was getting past the sentry at the gate.
c. She loves to listen to classical music; she never tires of listening to Bhimsen Joshi.
d. She cannot endure watching a sad movie.
e. You must learn to live within your income. Learning to live within your income must be your first concern.

9 Verbs: 1

The English verb – and by verb we mean the finite verb – is central to the sentence in more than one sense. Physically, it occurs in the middle of the sentence. More importantly, it is in many ways the very heart of the sentence. All other functions in the sentence such as subject, object, complement are defined in relation to the finite verb. Thus, in the sentence:

The child chased the dog (basic sentence pattern 2)

both the subject ('child') and the object ('dog') are defined in relation to the verb 'chased'. 'Who chased the dog?' we ask, to find the subject. 'What did the child chase?' we ask, to find the object. Similarly, in the sentences:

The king was a tyrant (basic sentence pattern 5)

The crowd seems restless (basic sentence pattern 6)

it is the linking verb ('was', 'seems') that selects the subject complements ('tyrant', 'restless'). Notionaliy, formally, syntactically, the English verb is so complicated that it takes up more space in pedagogic grammar books than any other part of speech.

9.1 Definition

It is all but impossible to define the verb, or at any rate to formulate a definition that will cover all the verbs in the language. Notionally, a verb may be defined as a word that expresses *action, being* or *a state of being*:

He fought like a wounded tiger. (action)

These additions to the house are all new. (being)

The medicine tastes bitter. (state of being)

Syntactically, a verb may be defined as a word that makes a statement about a subject. Thus, in the sentence:

Dogs in the country **bark**

the finite verb 'bark' makes a statement about the subject 'dogs in the country'. Formally, a verb may be defined as a word marked by the ending '-s' in the third person singular present simple tense ('He goes', 'she sings') and by the ending '-d', '-ed', '-t' in its simple past tense form ('jump – jumped', 'send – sent').

Each of these definitions is open to objection on one or more grounds. At the present moment, a perfect or more acceptable definition of the verb is not available. Hence we must make do with the definitions we have, however imperfect, to recognise the verb in the sentence.

Fortunately, it is not difficult to recognise the verb. It is like recognising glowing good health in someone. We recognise a healthy person when we see one, although we would be hard put to define good health. We recognise the verb by looking at its position in the sentence, sometimes by trying to understand what it means, and sometimes by looking at its endings.

Verbs may be classified in a number of ways: as finite and non-finite, as verbs of being and verbs of doing, as transitive and intransitive. We have already dealt with these divisions of verbs in the unit on the sentence (Chapter 2). We will now consider in some detail how these divisions help us to express ourselves and to communicate.

9.2 Finite and Non-Finite Verbs

We use finite verbs, as we said earlier, to make statements about persons or things referred to by the subject. We can no doubt communicate for short durations of time without a finite verb or with a non-finite verb:

'A cold?'/'Having a cold?'
'Yes.'
'Since when?'
'Since last week.'
'Been to the doctor?'
'Not yet.'/'Whatever for?'

But even in the spoken language we would find it difficult to sustain a conversation for long without finite verbs. And even when we do not actually express them, as in the above dialogue, we feel they are present:

'Do you suffer from a cold?'/'Are you having a cold?'

'Yes.' (I do/I am)

Exercise 1

Each of the following word-groups falls short of making a statement for want of a finite verb. Complete each word-group with a finite verb so that it makes a statement. The first one is an example.

a. He being the only son of his parents
   Ans: He *is*/*was* the only son of his parents.
b. The children going home after school
c. I done you no harm
d. They resting after walking five miles
e. The wind having dropped
f. The old people at home surprised at the young man's rudeness
g. The judge not satisfied with the answers given by the prisoner
h. The Prime Minister having gone on a goodwill visit to Russia

Exercise 2

Given below is an interview of a person not very comfortable in English. You can see that none of Mr Kumar's answers make statements because they consist of only non-finite verbs. Rewrite his answers using finite verbs so that they make statements (and at the same time correct sentences).

Interviewer: Where do you live, Mr Kumar?
Mr Kumar: I living in Anand Nagar, near Sonepur.
Interviewer: Do you come from Karnal?

Mr Kumar:	No, I coming from Hissar.
Interviewer:	Our viewers would like to know how you found the gold coins. Did you find them while digging?
Mr Kumar:	Yes, yes. Early in the morning, I to go to the field. I digging the field. I finding the gold coins in a small box.
Interviewer:	What do you want to do with the money the government has given you?
Mr Kumar:	I wanting to buy my own farm in Hissar.

9.3 Verbs of Being and Verbs of Doing

Finite verbs may be divided into *verbs of being* and *verbs of doing*. Compare the basic sentence patterns in column A with those in column B:

A	B
The king *was* a tyrant. (bp 5)	Dogs *bark*. (bp 1)
The crowd *seems* restless. (bp 6)	The child *chased* the dog. (bp 2)
The man *is* at home. (bp 7)	John *gave* Mary a letter. (bp 3)
	The Menons *named* their baby Sudha. (bp 4)

In the sentences in column A, the subject is said to **be** something; in those in column B, the subject is said to **do** something. We call the finite verbs in column A **verbs of being**, those in column B **verbs of doing**.

Verbs of being belong to a larger group called **linking verbs**. The most common linking verb is the verb '*be*' (*am is are was were will be shall be can be would be should be*) but many others are used as linking verbs. Some of these are commonly used with noun phrases as subject complements (as in basic sentence pattern 5) and some with adjectives as subject complements (as in basic sentence pattern 6).

These are the linking verbs that go with noun phrases:

appear	be	become	comprise	feel	form	look	make	remain	seem

These are the linking verbs that go with adjectives:

be	become	feel	get	go	grow	keep	look
prove	remain	see	smell	sound	stay	taste	turn

We use the linking verbs with noun phrases as complements (as in bp 5) or with adjectives as complements (as in bp 6) *to describe someone or something.* No wonder *basic sentence patterns 5 and 6 are among the most commonly used sentence patterns.*

9.3.1 With Noun Phrases as Complements

Malaria was once *a killer disease.*
The man over there looks *a stranger to the city.*
Mr Pai was *the new club's first honorary secretary.*

Notice that the linking verb merely joins what comes before it (the subject) to what comes after it (the noun phrase used as subject complement).

My father is a chemical engineer.
Abdul is a leader in the making.
He will make a good leader.
The other man looked a bit of a hoax.
The approver's evidence will form the basis of a more detailed investigation.
The class comprises fifteen boys and an equal number of girls.

Note that all the above examples conform to basic sentence pattern 5.

9.3.2 With Adjectives as Complements

The witness remained cool through the gruelling cross-examination.
Not a hair of his has turned grey although he is past seventy.
You must keep cool despite the provocation.
Food kept in this container stays hot for hours.
Your suggestion sounds good enough to merit discussion by the committee.
The days are getting warm with the advance of summer.

Notice that the above examples conform to basic sentence pattern 6, with an adverbial added on:

The witness	remained	cool	through the gruelling cross-examination.
N	LV	Adj.	Adverbial
You	must keep	cool	despite the provocation.
N	LV	Adj.	Adverbial

As a matter of fact, the subject complements are often followed by an infinitive or prepositional phrase:

- **infinitive phrase**

He is clever enough **to think up a story like that.**
She is quite competent **to assume control of the organisation.**
That was not a nice thing **to say about an old man.**
He was silly **to think of a crazy project like that.**

- **prepositional phrase**

He is good enough **for unskilled jobs.**
She is the ideal person **for housekeeping.**
I think he will make a good manager, **your fears notwithstanding.**
The weather on the mountain continued calm and sunny **through the morning.**

Note that we use the infinitive phrase and the prepositional phrase to express an opinion about someone or something.

Exercise 3

Use a suitable linking verb to complete these sentences. Choose the linking verb from the box below. Use it in a form appropriate to the sentence. Some of the verbs may have to be used more than once. The first one is an example.

a. Fermentation is what happens when milk turns sour and butter goes bad.

b. Tenzing Norgay went up the mountain as a simple man but ____________ a hero.

c. He ___________ terribly upset. Whatever has happened to him?
d. Many of the suggestions made by the committee ___________ very useful.
e. The medicine ___________ awful and ___________ nasty but it ___________ efficacious.
f. You ___________ run-down. Do you ___________ all right?
g. Have you heard the latest? Mr Sibal has been made principal. Do you think he ___________ a good principal?
h. Do you want to ___________ single all your life?

look	prove	turn	smell	taste
feel	make	remain	return	go

9.3.3 Object Complements

The object complement describes the object even as the subject complement describes the subject. The following transitive verbs take an object plus an object complement after them:

appoint	believe	burn	call	certify	consider	cut	declare
drive	elect	find	label	like	make	name	nickname
paint	prefer	proclaim	pronounce	render	think	want	wipe

These verbs which take an object plus object complement after them occur in basic sentence pattern 4:

The Menons	named	their baby	Sudha.
N(subject)	V(trans.)	N(object)	N(obj. compl.)
Parents	consider	their children	bright.
N(sub.)	V(trans.)	N(object)	Adj. (obj. compl.)

The object complement could be a noun as in the first example, or an adjective, as in the second.

9.4 Verbs Transitive and Intransitive

We may want to say something about an action or event that involves only one person or thing (represented by the subject). We then use the intransitive verb, as in basic sentence pattern 1:

The baby <u>cried</u>. The girl <u>smiled</u>. My tooth <u>aches</u>. Trouble <u>broke out</u>.

Many of these intransitive verbs are used with an adverbial (an adverb or adverb phrase) and/or a prepositional phrase:

<u>Eventually</u> the missing ticket <u>turned up</u>.
It <u>was lying</u> <u>all along</u> <u>in my trouser-pocket</u>.
<u>Weeks later</u>, he <u>appeared</u> <u>out of the blue</u>.
All <u>ended</u> <u>well</u> <u>with the return home of the prodigal son</u>.
The city <u>abounds</u> <u>in gardens</u>.

Notice that in all the above examples, the action of the verb affects or concerns only the person or thing referred to by the subject. That is the reason why these verbs are called

intransitive, they do not 'transit'or move across from the subject to someone or something other than the subject.

We use the **transitive** verb, on the other hand, to describe an action that does not stop with the subject. In the sentence:

The child chased the dog (basic sentence pattern 2)

the action of chasing involves both the person chasing ('child') and the person or thing being chased ('the dog'). It transits or moves across from the subject to someone or something outside the child—'the dog', which we call the object of the verb. Here are some more examples of transitive verbs:

We surrounded the enemy at dawn.

Even ants take long rests.

How do you pronounce pthisis?

The object affected by the verb may be human or non-human:

My behaviour angered my father.

Nothing interests Shobha any more.

The reporter's probing questions clearly annoyed the interviewee.

He decisively influenced the course of events.

The cyclonic storm devastated the countryside.

They discussed the problem for hours but found no solution.

Some transitive verbs may be used intransitively:

He married in haste only to repent at leisure. (Compare: He married his neighbour whom he had known for years.)

I am a trader, I buy and sell.

He says the usual things. He seldom or never surprises or shocks.

The guests left early.

There is another class of verbs which can be used transitively and intransitively. When used transitively, they mean one thing and quite another thing when used intransitively:

He was driving at 90 km an hour when the accident happened. (IT)

He drives his team hard. (T)

They escaped from prison but didn't know where to go. (IT)

You are a clever accountant. How did these irregularities escape your notice? (T)

He ran as though his life depended on it. (IT)

She is too young and inexperienced to run a business. (T)

My needs are few, I can manage with very little. (IT)

She managed the organisation very competently. (T)

Exercise 4

Underline the finite verbs in the following sentences and mark them T for transitive and IT for intransitive. The first two are done for you.

a. Some tourist spots in the world *have become* rather dangerous of late. (IT)

b. They *attract* all kinds of undesirable persons. (T)
c. Some of these people are no different from common criminals.
d. They swindle the tourists quite ruthlessly.
e. The metre reader calls on the tenth of every month.
f. My legs hurt a lot.
g. I cannot walk any more.
h. My cashier often works late into the night.
i. He has been working for me for the last twenty-five years.
j. I trust him completely.

Exercise 5

Look at each pair of sentences below. One of them has a transitive verb and the other an intransitive verb. Underline the finite verb and mark it T for transitive and IT for intransitive. In the sentences which have a transitive verb, box the object. The first one is an example.

a. 1. We must all hang together or hang separately. (IT)
   2. They hanged [him] for murder. (T)
b. 1. News of their leader's death spread rapidly among the villagers.
   2. Let us spread the good news among the people.
c. 1. He cheated at cards.
   2. The fly-by-night operators cheated the small investors.
d. 1. Today all sports are competitive. The players play to win.
   2. She plays the piano like a professional.
e. 1. Most of the taps in this house leak.
   2. A junior official in the ministry had leaked the information to the press.
f. 1. The old man exercises regularly.
   2. The problem of teenage fashions has much exercised the minds of parents and teachers.
g. 1. People don't change easily.
   2. The new technology has changed people's lives beyond recognition.
h. 1. She moved gingerly across the hanging bridge.
   2. They moved their furniture to the new house.
i. 1. The sun was sinking in the west.
   2. She sank all her savings into a new company attracted by the high rate of interest offered.
j. 1. He reflected for a while before turning down the offer.
   2. His manners clearly reflected his birth and upbringing.

Among transitive verbs are a class of verbs like say, believe, think, feel, which are used as reporting verbs to tell what some people say or think. These reporting verbs are followed by a that-clause, which functions as object of the verb:

He admitted that he had behaved rashly and irresponsibly.
(object of 'admitted')

He claimed that he had been a keen mountaineer in his young days.

She believes that the man has been wronged.

9.4.1 Ditransitive Verbs

There is a class of transitive verbs which take two objects. We call these **ditransitive verbs.** Ditransitive verbs occur in basic sentence pattern 3: N-V(trans.) –N (indirect object)-N(direct object). (See the chapter on the sentence, Chapter 2 for more information.)

Sita gave Hari a letter.
(IO) (DO)

We bought our daughter a story-book.

I sold him the antiques.

The usher found me a seat.

In all these examples, the action referred to by the verb involves a third person ('Hari', 'our daughter', 'him', 'me'), who is a sort of beneficiary of the action. We call the third person an indirect object (IO). The indirect object usually comes first after the verb, followed by the direct object (DO).

Notice that the indirect object is not essential to the sentence, while the direct object is. For instance, you can say:

Sita gave a letter (but not)
Sita gave Hari.

An indirect object can, however, come after a direct object with the preposition 'to' or 'for' added. Thus, the above examples can be rewritten thus:

Sita gave a letter to Hari.
We bought a story-book for our daughter.
I sold the antiques to him.
The usher found a seat for me.

The choice of the proposition will depend on the verb. These verbs take the preposition 'to' :

award	bring	give	grant	hand	leave	lend - loan
offer	owe	pass (meaning 'give by handing')			pay	post promise
read	sell	send	show	sing	teach	tell

These verbs take the preposition 'for':

bake	build	buy	cook	fetch	find	fix	get	guarantee	keep
leave	make	mix	pour	save	set	spare	win	write	

Exercise 6

Rewrite these sentences using 'to' or 'for'. The first two are examples.

a. Can you buy me a pound of butter on your way back home?
Ans: Can you buy a pound of butter for me on your way back home?

b. He offered me a fair price for my car.
Ans: He offered a fair price to me for my car.

c. They came without notice but they saved us trouble by bringing their food with them.
d. Will you please pass her the mashed potatoes?
e. Can you lend me five rupees?
f. She showed me her album.
g. The teacher read the children the story of the 'Titanic'.
h. Shall I mix you a cup of coffee?
i. Can you spare me an hour?

Exercise 7

Rewrite these sentences so that the new sentences conform to the basic sentence pattern 3: N-V-N(IO)-N(DO). The first two are examples.

a. I had loaned a hundred rupees to my friend.
   Ans: I had loaned my friend a hundred rupees.
b. He built a house for himself brick by brick.
   Ans: He built himself a house brick by brick.
c. I wrote a note for her saying I would like to see her at once.
d. The support and encouragement he received from his school won the championship for him.
e. The old man left his entire property to his youngest son.
f. The government guaranteed safe passage for the rebel leaders.
g. The mother set a series of tasks for her son to keep him occupied and out of mischief.
h. We shall post the cheque to you as soon as it is ready.

9.5 Complementation through Adverbials

We can use a linking verb with an adverbial (i.e., an adverb or adverb phrase), the adverbial acting like a complement, as in basic sentence pattern 7:

The man <u>is</u> <u>here</u>/<u>at home</u>/<u>in a foreign country</u>.

The adverbial usually takes the form of a prepositional phrase. We use this pattern to describe the circumstances someone or something is in:

My brother <u>is</u> <u>in London</u> <u>at the moment.</u>

You <u>must stay in bed for another fortnight</u>.

They <u>seemed</u> <u>in excellent spirits</u>.

They <u>remained</u> <u>indoors</u> <u>out of fear</u>.

The conference <u>will be</u> <u>on the second Saturday of the month</u>.

10 Verbs: 2

We saw in the previous chapter that for a clause to happen, there must be a subject and a predicate, and for a predicate to happen, there must be a finite verb. The finite verb is so central to the sentence that all other functions in the sentence such as subject, object and complement are determined in relation to it.

10.1 Basic Parts of the Verb

All verbs have three basic parts. The first basic part is the simple form of the verb or the **stem**. The other two are the **past tense** and the **past participle**. Thus, the three basic parts of the verb 'do' are :

'do' (stem) 'did' (past tense) 'done' (past participle).

We may add a fourth 'doing', the present participle of the verb, formed by adding '-ing' to the stem.

We call these the basic parts of the verb because without them we cannot make up the various tense forms of the verb. While the simple present and the simple past tense forms of the verb are derived from the stem ('do', 'does', 'did'), all other tense forms require the present participle or the past participle. Thus, all continuous tense forms require the present participle and all perfect tense forms require the past participle:

continuous tense forms			perfect tense forms		
present	past	future	present	past	future
am doing is doing are doing	was doing were doing	will be doing shall be doing	has done have done	had done	will have done shall have done

The past participle is required besides to form the passive forms of verbs:

tense	active voice	passive voice
present simple	do, does	am/is/are/+done
past simple	did	was/were/+done
future simple	shall/will do	shall/will+ be+ done

10.2 Regular and Irregular Verbs

Verbs may be classified in a number of ways, which shows how complex the English verb is. We have already seen verbs being classified as finite and non-finite, as verbs of being and verbs of doing, as transitive and intransitive. We may further divide them into regular and irregular verbs.

Regular verbs are verbs that form their past tense by the addition of a 'd', 't' or 'ed' sound (represented in written language by the letters '-ed') without any other change:

walk – walked thin – thinned advise – advised state – stated

Irregular verbs, on the other hand, are verbs that form their past tense irregularly, that is, otherwise than by the simple addition of '-ed' in the written language, of a 'd', 't' or 'ed' sound in the spoken language:

tell – told   sing – sang   catch – caught   read – read

Verbs which have the same form for the past tense as for the present are also called irregular verbs:

put – put   cut – cut   shut – shut   let – let

(A complete list of the most commonly used irregular verbs is given in one of the appendices.)

Newspaper headlines generally use the simple present tense form when reporting recent events, but in the story that follows the reporter uses the past tense. Thus, the headline:

HERMIT LOSES BET

becomes in the accompanying story:

A hermit who claimed he could hypnotise and tame a marauding jaguar lost his bet with the villagers near Caracas, Venezuela.

(marauding : going about in search of prey   jaguar : fierce animal of Central and South America belonging, like the tiger and the panther, to the family of wild cats)

Exercise 1

Rewrite the following headlines using the simple past tense. Remember to use the articles, where necessary. Make any further changes that may be required. The first one is done for you.

a. Police arrest Runaway Robot in Beverley Hills, California (the other day)
   Ans: The other day the police arrested a runaway robot in Beverley Hills, California.
b. It rains frogs in the Moroccan Sahara — scientists blame freak whirlwinds
c. Man bursts into flames in bathroom at Coudersport, Pennsylvania
d. Chandigarh man snores 69 decibels driving neighbours crazy
e. 15-year-old girl in Purnea yawns non-stop for five weeks
f. Sadhu in Himachal levitates before 10,000 crowd
g. Loony Leaper in Hertfordshire jumps 125 feet and lands safely

10.3 Lexical and Auxiliary Verbs

Verbs may be classified in yet another way into **lexical** and **auxiliary**. **Lexical verbs** are meaning-bearing verbs. They carry the meaning of the action or the description.

The monkey played on the harmonica.

The children screamed in delight.

The other child looked unhealthy .

Motor racing seems a dangerous sport.

The underlined verbs in the above examples are all lexical verbs. They carry meaning. But while 'played' and 'screamed' as verbs of doing carry the meaning of the action, 'looked' and 'seems' carry the meaning of the description as verbs of being. **Every sentence must have a lexical verb**.

Some verbs act as helpers. They help the lexical verbs to express tense, voice, interrogation and negation:

a. The children were screaming in delight while the monkey was playing on the harmonica.

b. Sundar has found a job at last.

c. The man was asked to account for his movements, and on his failing to do so, was arrested by the police.

d. Are you singing us another song?

e. What does he do for a living?

f. We don't have a television set at home.

The underlined verbs in a-f do not have any meaning themselves but because of them we are able to know:

1. what aspect of time we are talking about—that the actions in example (a) are continuous because the verbs are in continuous tense and the action in example (b) is complete because the verb is in perfect tense;
2. whether we are asking a question (examples d,e) or are expressing a negation (example f), and also when we are using the passive voice (example c).

The underlined verbs in examples a-f are called **auxiliary verbs.**

Auxiliary verbs are of three types:

tense auxiliaries

'do' auxiliaries

modal auxiliaries

Tense auxiliaries are used to form tenses while the **'do' auxiliaries** are used to express interrogation and negation, as we saw in examples a-f above. **Modal auxiliaries** combine with the lexical verbs to modify their meaning. This they do by adding to the lexical verb an idea such as permission, possibility, obligation or necessity:

May I borrow your bicycle? Yes, you may. (permission)

You should do what the doctor tells you. (obligation)

We must eat to live. (necessity)

The commonly used modal auxiliaries are: *may, might, can , could, shall, should, will, would, ought* and *must.*

To sum up, verbs may be broadly divided into two types—lexical verbs and auxiliary verbs. Lexical verbs may be subdivided into action verbs and linking verbs, while auxiliary verbs may be subdivided into tense auxiliaries, 'do' auxiliaries and modal auxiliaries, as shown in the diagram below:

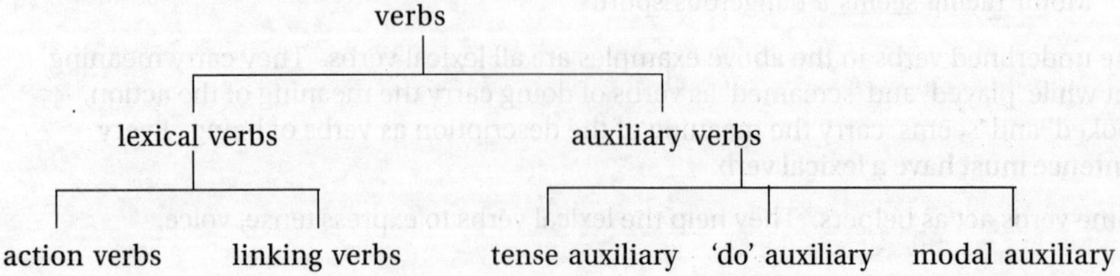

10.3.1 Tense Auxiliaries

Tense auxiliaries are chiefly two: 'be' and 'have'. These help to form tenses.

a. **auxiliary verb 'be'**

The verb 'be' has the following tense forms:

	present tense		**past tense**		**future tense**	
	singular	plural	singular	plural	singular	plural
first person	I am	we are	I was	we were	I shall be	we shall be
second person	You are	You are	You were	You were	You will be	You will be
third person	He/she/it is	They are	He/she/ it was	They were	He/She/ It will be	They will be

present participle: 'being' past participle: 'been'

The auxiliary verb 'be' is used to form the continuous tense of lexical verbs:

present continuous **past continuous** **future continuous**

am/ is/ are/ doing *was/ were* doing *shall/ will be* doing

Note that the change of tense from present to past to future is reflected only in the auxiliary verb and not in the lexical verb.

b. The verb 'have' has only two forms in the present tense: 'has' and 'have':

I/We/You/They have He/She/It has

It has only one past tense form for all persons and numbers: 'had'. It has two other basic forms: 'having' (present participle) and 'had' (past participle).

The verb 'have' helps to form the perfect tense of lexical verbs:

present perfect **past perfect** **future perfect**

has/ have done *had* done *shall/ will have* done

As you can see from the examples given above of the future continuous and the future perfect tense forms of the lexical verb 'do', a tense auxiliary may at times consist of more than one part:

Anand **will be** speaking next, opposing the motion.

By this time tomorrow he **will have** gone home.

Exercise 2

Fill in the blanks below with the correct forms of the auxiliary verbs 'be' and 'have'. The first one is an example.

a. The situation is still tense and it <u>is</u> getting worse.

b. Sridhar ___________ at last passed his finals in accountancy. Soon he ___________ joining a company as an accountant.

c. They disconnected his telephone. He ___________ not paid his bills for three months.

d. After months of recession the economy ___________ picking up.
e. Manisha ___________ finished her work at last.
f. She ___________ getting ready to go home.
g. She ___________ feeling very tired.
h. O dear! She ___________ missed the bus.
i. Tomorrow being Saturday is a half-day for everyone but not for Manisha. She ___________ working the whole day tomorrow.
j. She ___________ opted to work overtime.

10.3.2 The 'Do' Auxiliary

The 'do' auxiliary is accompanied by the simple form of the verb. It is used only in the simple present tense ('do go' and 'does go') and in the simple past tense ('did go'). As an auxiliary verb, 'do' does a number of things:

a. It serves to ask questions. Look at the statements in column 1 and the corresponding questions in column 2 below:

1	2
He goes to school.	Does he go to school?
I go to school.	Do I go to school?
They went to school.	Did they go to school?

When a statement consists of a lexical verb in the simple present tense or past tense, this is what we do to change the statement into a question. We rewrite the single-word verbs as two-word verb phrases:

goes – does go   go – do go   went – did go

We then shift the first part of the new verb phrase (that is, the 'do' auxiliary) to the front of the sentence to get a question—Does he go to school? Do I go to school? Did they go to school? Questions like the above admit of a simple 'yes' or 'no' response. For a more detailed response, we may add before the 'do' auxiliary question words like <u>when</u>, <u>where</u>, <u>why</u> and <u>how</u>:

When does he go to school?
Why did they go to school?
How do they go to school?

b. The 'do' auxiliary helps to form negatives:

affirmative	**negative**
He goes to school.	He does not (doesn't) go to school.
I go to school.	I do not (don't) go to school.
They went to school.	They did not (didn't) go to school.

In forming negatives we follow the same procedure as we followed in making questions. 'Doesn't', 'don't' and 'didn't' are the shortened forms of 'does not', 'do not', 'did not'. We normally use the shortened forms when we speak. An apostrophe (')is used after 'n' to mark the omission of the letter 'o' in 'not'.

c. The 'do' auxiliary is used to make a statement stronger or more emphatic:

1. When we want to express an outright contrast:

   You think, Mother, that I didn't go to school today, but I **did** go.
   People think that he is a recluse. That's not true. He **does** enjoy meeting people.

2. When we want to express a concessive type of contrast:

   Although I am not very fond of films, I **do** occasionally see a film.
   Shopkeeper to customer: We **do** have in stock the thing you're asking for but it is in the warehouse.

3. When we want to express a request or entreaty:

   Do please come to my birthday party. You'll enjoy it.

4. When we wish to make an invitation more welcoming and friendly:

   Do come in. **Do** make yourself comfortable.

5. with emphatic adverbs like *certainly, definitely, positively*:

   'Do you remember the time when our geography teacher told the whole school that you located the Andamans in the Arabian Sea?'

   'Yes, I **do** certainly remember.'

10.3.3 'Be', 'Have' and 'Do' as Lexical Verbs

The verbs 'be', 'have', and 'do' normally function as auxiliaries but they can function as lexical verbs in their own right.

'Be' is used as a lexical verb:

1. with a predicate noun or adjective:

   I **am** Asha.
   You **are** lazy.

2. in sentences beginning with 'there' and 'it':

   'There **is** someone knocking on the door.'
   'It could **be** the postman.'

   Doctor to patient: There **is** nothing seriously wrong with you. It **is** just a case of indigestion.

'Have' is used as a lexical verb:

1. to mean 'own' or 'possess':

   Our neighbours **have** six sons and six daughters, a round dozen.

2. to mean 'take', 'enjoy' , 'receive':
   Come and **have** lunch with me.
   Did you **have** a good holiday in Agra?

'Do' is used as a lexical verb in the sense of 'study', 'arrange', 'behave' and so on:

Are you **doing** computer science at school? (studying)

Will you please **do** the flowers while I change? (arrange them in vases)

You must **do** as the others **do**, it's much safer so. (behave)

Exercise 3

Here is a set of questions and answers. The questions are not properly framed. Write out the questions in full, making sure that they make sense with the answers given. The first one is an example.

a. Q. (you/ recognise) the man in the picture?/Do you recognise the man in the picture?
   A. Yes, I do. He is Srinivasa Ramanujan.
b. Q. How (Indians/regard) him today?
   A. Indians regard him as the greatest mathematician of the 20th century.
c. Q. What (young Ramanujan/do) for a living?
   A. He worked as a clerk in the Port Trust office, Madras.
d. Q. How (Ramanujan/spend) time in the office?
   A. By working for the most part on his mathematical papers.
e. Q. When (Ramanujan/leave) for England?
   A. He left for England in 1914.
f. Q. Why (Ramanujan/leave) for England?
   A. He went to England to join Professor G.H. Hardy at Cambridge University.
g. Q. How (Professor Hardy/come to know) Ramanujan?
   A. After reading an article by Professor Hardy, Ramanujan wrote to him introducing himself and sending along with the letter his mathematical papers.
h. Q. What (Hardy/think) of Ramanujan's mathematical papers?
   A. The papers left a deep impression on Hardy.
i. Q. What (Professor Hardy/do) after reading Ramanujan's papers?
   A. He invited him to come and join him at Cambridge.
j. Q. (Ramanujan/hesitate) to accept Hardy's offer?
   A. Yes, he did.
k. Q. Why (he/hesitate)?
   A. Out of concern for his parents and his own fears about life in a strange country.
l. Q. How long (Ramanujan/stay) in England?
   A. Until 1919.
m. Q. When (he/die)?
   A. He died in April, 1920.

10.3.4 Modal Auxiliary

Modal auxiliaries are different from tense and 'do' auxiliaries in that they combine with the lexical verbs to modify their meaning. They do this by adding to the lexical verb an idea such as ability, permission, possibility, obligation, necessity, and so on.

There are only twelve modal auxiliary verbs but they cover a wide range of meanings. The set of twelve verbs consists of:

four paired forms	**four single forms**
can, could	must

may, might	ought
shall, should	need
will, would	dare

How do modal auxiliaries help to modify or change the meaning of the main or lexical verbs?

Let us take, for an example, the modal 'can'. Compare these two sentences:

1. I **am singing** a song.
2. I **can sing** a song.

In the first sentence of the pair, the verb 'sing' carries all the meaning; the tense auxiliary 'am' merely tells us that the singing is going on at the moment of speaking. The tense auxiliary does not modify the meaning of the lexical verb by adding anything to it. The modal auxiliary 'can' in the second sentence, on the other hand, says that the speaker has the ability to sing. He is not singing now but he can, if he wants to, now or in the future. By expressing the idea of present or future ability, the modal auxiliary 'can' changes the meaning of the lexical verb 'sing'.

Here is another pair of sentences:

3. He **does go** home on Saturdays.
4. He **may go** home on Saturdays.

Notice how the addition of 'may' in sentence 4 changes the meaning of the lexical verb 'go' by adding to it the idea of permission or possibility. The addition of the 'do' auxiliary in sentence 3 merely helps to make the statement more emphatic.

Modal auxiliary verbs, or modal verbs as they are commonly known, are different from lexical verbs in a number of ways:

1. Modal verbs have no non-finite forms like:

   maying mayed to may

   musting musted to must

They have only one form.

2. They are followed by the infinitive of the lexical verb without, however, the sign of the infinitive 'to' (except in the case of 'ought'):

   Driving <u>can be</u> dangerous. ('can' + infinitive 'to be')

   We <u>must obey</u> traffic rules. ('must' + infinitive 'to obey')

   We <u>ought to obey</u> traffic rules.

3. Negative sentences are formed by adding 'not' after the modal verb:

   You <u>cannot</u> be serious.

   We <u>may not</u> go after all.

4. Interrogative sentences (that is, questions) are formed simply by inverting the subject and the modal verb:

   <u>Can</u> driving be dangerous?

   <u>Must</u> we obey traffic rules?

5. There is no '-s' ending in the third person singular in the present tense, as there is with lexical verbs (he obeys, she sings but not he mays, she musts).
6. Unlike lexical verbs, modal verbs have only two tenses, present and past. Two of them, 'must' and 'ought' have in fact only one form. The verbs 'dare' (meaning 'have the courage to') and 'need' (meaning 'have to') present special problems. While they function in all respects like lexical verbs, they also form negatives and questions in the same way as modal verbs do, as you can see from the following chart:

	need to	**dare to**
affirmative	He needs to go there.	He dares (to) go there.
negative (like modals)	He need not go there.	He dare not go there.
(like lexical verbs)	He doesn't need to go there.	He doesn't dare (to) go there.
questions (like modals)	Need he go there?	Dare he (to) go there?
(like lexical verbs)	Does he need to go there?	Does he dare (to) go there?

For this reason, 'dare' and 'need' are sometimes called **marginal modals** to distinguish them from the other ten (*can, could, may, might, shall, should, will, would, must, ought*), which may be called **central modals**.

Note

'Dare' in the sense of 'challenge' and 'need' in the sense of 'require' are regular lexical verbs with the usual forms for all the six tenses.

In addition to these two groups of modals, central and marginal, we have a third group of **modal equivalents**. Two of these need special mention: 'be able to' and 'have to'. These two, though they do not exhibit the formal characteristics of the modals, serve as auxiliaries to express similar meanings.

Be able to

He is able to (can) support a family of his own.

He was able to (could) elude the police who were after him.

Have to

We have to (must) inform the police.

Do you have to beg for your bread? (Must you beg for your bread?)

To this group of modal equivalents belong 'had rather' and 'had better'. 'Had rather' is used to express preference, like the modal 'would rather':

I had rather have a cup of tea. (I would rather have a cup of tea)

'Had better' is used, like the modals 'should' and 'ought', to suggest that a certain course of action is advisable:

We had better send for a proper mechanic. (We should...)

You had better have those loose teeth of yours pulled out. (You ought to...)

10.3.5 The Modal is the Message

Speaking is a social act. That is readily understood. We cannot speak unless there is someone to listen to us. What is more, in a normal speaking–listening situation, the speaker and the listener interchange roles all the time. When the speaker's meaning doesn't come through, the listener temporarily takes on the role of the speaker—he interrupts, questions, seeks clarification. There is thus a close relationship between speaker and listener.

What is not readily understood is that writing too is a social act. We write because there is someone to read what we have written. We write for someone and because of someone, although that someone – the reader in this case – does not physically confront the writer. When we speak or write, we naturally think of our audience. What we say or write is inevitably influenced or modified by our audience, more specifically by how we as speakers/writers relate to our audience. Thus if we are asking a favour of someone, the way we phrase our request will depend on how close to, or distant from, our audience we are, and whether the situation is formal or informal—in short, *our attitude to our audience.*

To a friend we would say:

Can/May I borrow your pen for a minute?

The request is polite enough for a friend. To an acquaintance or a mere stranger, we would say:

Could/Might I borrow your pen for a minute?

The acquaintance or stranger addressed might refuse our request, so we take care to be more polite by using the modal 'could' or 'might'. We might make it even more polite by saying:

Would you mind if I borrow your pen for a minute? (or)

I wonder/was wondering if I could borrow your pen for a minute.

It would not be proper to say to a stranger:

Lend me your pen please.

That would normally be considered rude, even with the addition of the placatory 'please'.

That is one aspect to communication—*our attitude to the person or persons we are communicating with.*

There is a second aspect, and that is *our attitude to the information* we are giving. If we say, for instance:

The doctors are wrong about the long-term effects of the drug

we are making a statement, a statement of our opinion. We are sure the doctors are wrong, and we say it directly, even bluntly. If, on the other hand, we are not sure of the doctors' being wrong, we would use the modal 'may' and say:

The doctors may be wrong about the long-term effects of the drug.

The modal 'may' at once suggests the possibility of the doctors' being wrong. 'May' at the same time implies the negative possibility of 'may not'. Thus, 'the doctors may be wrong...' implies the possibility that 'the doctors may not be wrong'. There is, in other words, a fifty-fifty chance of the doctors' being wrong, or not being wrong, which is very different from saying:

The doctors are wrong... drug.

You would use the modal 'can' if you thought the chances of the doctors' being wrong were more than fifty per cent. 'Can' suggests greater certainty than 'may'.

There is a third, and a final aspect to communication, and that is *our attitude to our own intentions or to the suggestions made by others.* Study the following dialogue between husband and wife:

Wife:	Come start of the school year, and we are up against the problem of how best to reach our daughter to school in the morning ...
Husband:	... and get her back home in the evening. The question has become a hardy annual with us.
Wife:	Couldn't you, Mohan, drop her on your way to the office? That seems best to me.
Husband:	I can't. Priya has to be at the school by 8.30 and that's too early for me.
Wife:	Can't you ask your chauffeur to drop her and come back for you?
Husband:	I won't, I definitely won't.
Wife:	Why not, Mohan?
Husband:	You forget it's the office car, given to me for official use.
Wife:	Lots of people use their office cars to ferry their children to school and back.
Husband:	Lots of people may but I can't.
Wife:	Surely you can ask our neighbour Vasu to help us out. He drops his children every day, and Priya might as well tag along with his Sowmya and Soundarya.
Husband:	I couldn't, I couldn't possibly, ask Vasu to do something that I don't want to do myself. He will probably ask us whatever has happened to our car.
Wife:	What do we do then?
Husband:	We might as well stick with the autorickshaw driver that we had last year. Neither of us is happy with the arrangement, I know, but I see no alternative... unless you decide to escort the child yourself. You might like an early morning walk to school and back.
Wife:	I would like nothing better if only I could find someone to make your breakfast and see you off to work.

Notice the wife's first suggestion to her husband: 'Couldn't you, Mohan, ...to the office?' The modal 'couldn't' indicates the wife's own attitude to the suggestion she makes: she is being very tentative because she herself is not sure that her suggestion is a feasible one. If she thought her suggestion feasible, she would use the modal 'can't', the very modal she uses when she makes her second suggestion: 'Can't you ask your chauffeur... for you?' She obviously thinks the idea a workable one but the husband responds by saying he won't, definitely won't. The modal 'won't, repeated a second time with the adverbial 'definitely' indicates his outright rejection of the wife's suggestion. When the wife persists with her suggestion saying that lots of people use their office cars for taking their children to school, the husband concedes the possibility by saying: 'Lots of people may' but as for himself, he can't. The modal 'can't' is even more emphatic than 'won't'. To the wife's third suggestion ('Surely you can ask our neighbour to help us out?') the husband's response is an anguished no. The modal 'couldn't', 'couldn't possibly' suggests that it would be morally wrong to ask another person to do something that one doesn't want to do oneself. It is now the turn of the husband to come up with a suggestion of his own—'How about escorting the child yourself? You might like an early morning walk.'

The wife's response is a conditional yes. Notice the modal 'would like' in the main clause and 'could find' in the if-clause.

Notice that the wife's suggestions move from 'couldn't you' (tentative suggestion) to 'can't you' (confident suggestion) to 'surely you can' (strong suggestion). The husband's responses to these range from 'can't' (inability) to 'won't' (unwillingness) to 'couldn't, couldn't possibly' (anguished refusal). The suggestions and the responses reveal the range of possibilities of communication that the English modals open up for us. Such is the power of the modals.

We now take up the central modals.

10.3.6 'Can' / 'could' to express the notion of ability

The modal 'can' expresses the notion of ability. It can express different kinds of ability:

I can run a mile. (physical ability)

I can drive a lorry. (learnt or acquired ability)

The factory can produce 20,000 lathes a day. (capacity to do something)

While the first two sentences apply to human beings, the third one applies to things only.

In all the three examples above, 'can' may be replaced by the modal equivalent 'be able to':

I am able to run a mile.

I am able to drive a lorry.

The factory is able to produce 20,000 lathes a day.

While 'can' refers to present and future ability, 'could' refers to past ability only:

While I was young, I could/was able to run a mile in four minutes.

The police could/were able to restore order within an hour.

The factory could not/was not able to produce even 2000 lathes a day.

'Can' and 'could' are also used to express the notion of capability to say that someone or something is capable of producing a particular effect or behaving in a particular way:

The most docile of cows can at times be intransigent.

Music can calm nerves.

Our father, one of the most thoughtful and considerate of men, could at times be insensitive.

Even the best of friends could on occasion be boring.

(intransigent: stubborn; obstinate)

Exercise 4

Here is a chart showing the proficiency of Ramesh, a tenth class student, in English, Tamil and French, as assessed by his respective teachers:

	English	Tamil	French
listening comprehension	xx	xxxx	xx
speaking	xx	xxxx	x
reading comprehension	xxxx	xxx	xxx
writing	xxxx	xx	xx

X - hardly at all XX - not very well XXX - quite well XXXX - very well

Fill in the blanks below to make the meaning of this chart clear. The first one is an example.

a. Ramesh <u>can</u> read and write English very well but he <u>cannot</u> understand it very well when it is spoken nor <u>can</u> he speak it very well.

b. He __________ speak Tamil very well and he __________ understand it equally well when it is spoken but he __________ write it very well, although he __________ read it quite well.

c. Ramesh __________ read French quite well but he __________ write French very well, nor __________ he understand French very well when it is spoken. He __________ hardly speak it at all.

d. He __________ understand French just as well as he __________ understand English in their spoken form but he __________ speak English a little better than he __________ speak French.

e. He __________ write English very well, much better than he __________ write French or Tamil. He __________ write French as well as he __________ write Tamil, but that is not saying much since he __________ write French or Tamil very well.

Exercise 5

A farmer who cannot read or write decides to join an adult education class in the village school. What would he say before joining the class? Fill in the blanks with 'can,' 'could,' or 'be able to'.

a. I __________ not read or write.

b. It would be nice to __________ read and write.

c. It would be nicer still to __________ teach others to read and write.

A few weeks after joining, the farmer says:

d. I __________ now understand what the teacher is saying.

e. In a few months I will __________read and write.

f. I __________then teach my wife to read and write.

After a few months, the farmer proudly tells his wife.

g. Now I __________ read and write.

h. A few months ago, I __________ not write a letter to my son but now I __________ not only write letters myself but read them without help.

i. I __________ now teach you to read and write.

10.3.7 'Can', 'could', 'may', 'might' to express the notion of permission

'Can', 'could', 'may', and 'might' are used to express the notion of permission. We use them, for example, to ask permission and to grant (or refuse) permission:

1. 'Can/May I borrow your bicycle?'
   'Yes, you can/may.'
   (request for permission in the first person)
2. 'Can/May he come with me to the cinema?'
   'Yes, he can/may.'
   (request for permission for a third person)

In asking permission, we may use the past forms of 'can' and 'may'. The answers, however, are generally in the present:

3. 'Could/Might I borrow your bicycle?'
   'Yes, you can/may.'
4. 'Could/Might he come with me to the cinema?'
   'Yes, he can/may.' 'No, he cannot/may not.'

'Can' and 'may' are informal and confident; 'could' and 'might' more formal, polite and tentative. We use 'can' and 'may' with friends and relatives, that is, in situations where we expect our requests to be favourably answered. We use 'could' and 'might' with strangers and with people in authority who may or may not grant our request. For example, if we ask our principal for permission to leave school earlier, we should say:

Could/Might I leave school fifteen minutes earlier, Mrs John?

Or if you are asking an acquaintance for a loan, you had better put your request this way:

Could you possibly do me a favour? Could you lend me twenty rupees, please?

Exercise 6

How would you phrase the following requests for permission? The first two are examples.

a. Your friend and colleague wants to borrow your computer. You refuse.
   Friend: May I borrow your computer for three days?
   You: Sorry, you may not. I'm using it myself.
b. You are buying a cardigan in a shop. You want to see if it fits you before you buy it.
   You: Excuse me, could I try this one on? (or) Do you think I could try this one on?
   Shopkeeper: Yes. There's a fitting room over there.
c. You are going on holiday and have discovered that your camera is not in working order. You remember your friend Abhilasha has an old camera that she is probably not using. You telephone her and ask. Abhilasha agrees.
d. You are watching a race. The gentleman next to you has a pair of binoculars. You have no more than a nodding acquaintance with him. You want to borrow his binoculars for a moment. You ask and he refuses.
e. An employee of yours wants you to change his working hours. You refuse.

'Can' and 'may' are also used to announce, for the benefit of the general public, that something is permitted or prohibited:

Anyone can/may use the swimming pool by paying a fee.
You cannot/may not smoke here.

The time referred to in the above examples is present or future time. But when we use 'could' and 'might' in the sense of 'be permitted', it refers to past time only:

You can/may use the swimming pool by paying a fee. (now and in the future)
In those days you could/might use the swimming pool by paying a fee. (but now you cannot)

Exercise 7

What do the following signs mean? The meaning of the first sign is given as an example.

a. 'No smoking'.
b.
c.
d.

'May' is used in formal written regulations:

Club members may bring not more than four guests during a calendar month.
Depositors may withdraw their fixed deposits before the date of maturity but at a price.

Exercise 8

'The Teenager Collection' is a lending library and it has the following regulations. Rephrase each of the regulations using 'may'. The first one has been rephrased for you.

a. Membership of the library is open to boys and girls of over 12 years of age.
   Ans: Only boys and girls of over 12 years may become members of the library.
b. Membership is open only to school-goers among boys and girls.
c. Students coming to the city for short stays are free to take up a temporary membership valid for a maximum period of ten weeks.
d. Members are entitled to borrow upto three books at a time.
e. Books borrowed are to be returned within fifteen days.
f. They can, however, be renewed for a further period of fifteen days.
g. It is open to members to ask for a refund of their initial deposit when they cease to be members.

10.3.8 'Can', 'could', 'may' to express requests

'Can' and 'may' are used in simple requests requiring no permission:

Can/May I have a glass of water?
Can/May I ask you a question?

We may use 'could' instead of 'can' but not 'might'. We can say:

Could I have a glass of water?

Could I interrupt you for a minute?

but not

Might I have a glass of water?

Might I interrupt you for a minute?

'Could' is more polite than 'can'.

We can make a request more persuasive by using 'can't' or 'couldn't' instead of 'can' and 'could':

Can't we watch television, Mother?

Can't we go for a swim, Dad?

Couldn't we go out for an hour?

However, for a simple request with 'you' as subject, we can use only 'can' and 'could' but not 'may' and 'might':

Can/Could you post this letter for me?

Can/Could you take this message to my son?

Note

'Can' and 'could' are generally used to make a request. 'May' with the first person (I, we) may be used for the same purpose but 'may' is more formal than 'can' and 'could'.

We can make our requests sound more polite by adding 'please' or the name of the person addressed at the beginning or the end of the question:

Can I speak to Amala please?

Could you please tell me what time the Rajadhani Express arrives?

Please may I have a glass of water?

Can I have a word with you, Kishen?

John, could you make us some coffee?

Yet, another way of making a request sound more polite is to add an adverb such as 'perhaps' or 'possibly':

'Thanks a lot for the invitation to lunch, Austin. I would love to come but could I possibly bring with me a friend of mine currently staying with us?'

Exercise 9

Practise making requests by completing the following sentences with 'can', 'may' or 'could'.

a. (to a friend) ________ you lend me a fiver?

b. (to a bank clerk at the counter) ________ I borrow your pen?

c. (to a stranger) Excuse me, ________ you tell me the way to the nearest post office?

d. (to a waiter) ________ I have some more coffee please?

e. (to your sister) ________ you turn down the radio?

f. (to your teacher) ________ I submit my assignment a day later?

g. (to the man at the enquiries) ________ you tell me when the flight from Bombay is due to arrive?

h. (clerk to manager) _________ I use the office car for my personal work just for today?

Exercise 10

Sekhar, who has just joined the college hostel, is trying to find out from Jatin, a final year student at college, all about the hostel dos and don'ts. Complete the dialogue between Sekhar and Jatin with 'can', 'may' or 'could' and their negative forms.

Sekhar: ____________ you tell me, Jatin, what we residents of the hostel ____________ do and ____________ do? ____________ I, for instance, go for a late-night film on Saturdays?

Jatin: You ____________ until last year but not any more. You ____________, however, go to a matinee on Saturdays.

Sekhar: How often ____________ I go and spend a weekend with my local guardian?

Jatin: Once a term only. Earlier, you ____________ spend a weekend with your local guardian or your friends in town once a month.

Sekhar: ____________ we entertain our visitors in our rooms?

Jatin: You ____________. You ____________, however, meet them in the anteroom between 4 and 6 p.m. on Sundays.

Sekhar: What's the lights-out time on Saturdays?

Jatin: Until some months ago, you ____________ keep the lights on for as long as you wanted. But now you have to switch them off at 11 p.m., and that's one hour longer than usual.

Sekhar: Thank you, Jatin. You've been most helpful.

10.3.9 'Shall', 'should', 'may', 'might', 'could', 'ought', 'must' to make suggestions

We can make a suggestion by using 'shall' with 'we' in an interrogative sentence:

Shall we dine out tomorrow? (meaning 'I suggest we dine out...')

Shall we change the topic of discussion?

We can also make suggestions by using 'may' or 'might' with 'as well':

You may as well drop the idea.

We may as well take her into confidence.

We might as well call the whole thing off. (meaning 'that's the most sensible thing to do in the circumstances')

He might as well go back to the States and complete the course.

We may use the modal 'might' with a verb meaning 'like' or 'want' to make a suggestion in a very polite way:

I thought you might like to go out for a drive.

You might want to eat out for a change.

We may also use the construction 'It might be...':

I thought it might be a good idea to postpone taking a decision.

When we make a strong suggestion, a suggestion that you believe in strongly, you use 'should' or 'ought':

You <u>should</u> avoid fatty foods and give up smoking at once.

You <u>ought to</u> take her more seriously.

A more polite way of making a strong suggestion is to use the negative form ('shouldn't' or 'ought not') in an interrogative sentence:

<u>Shouldn't</u> we give him another warning before we decide to suspend him?

Oughtn't we to put up the house for sale now that the market is looking up?

If we are trying to persuade someone you know well to adopt a course of action, you use the modal 'must':

You <u>must</u> forget what happened and welcome him with open arms.

You <u>must</u> avoid fatty foods and give up smoking at once.

We can also make a suggestion by using 'could' in a declarative sentence and 'couldn't' in an interrogative sentence:

You <u>could</u> open an STD booth here.

We <u>could</u> build a nice little house with the money we have come by.

<u>Couldn't</u> you open an STD booth here?

<u>Couldn't</u> some public-spirited citizen move the court and stop these encroachments?

Exercise 11

Rewrite the following suggestions using 'shall'.

a. I suggest we go for a long walk.
b. I suggest we go and see a film.
c. I suggest we stay indoors and watch the one-day match on TV.
d. I suggest we go for a swim.
e. I suggest we go for a picnic.
f. I suggest that we adjourn the meeting.

Exercise 12

Rewrite the following imperatives as strong suggestions from a doctor to a patient using 'should' and 'ought'. The first one is an example.

a. Avoid coffee altogether.

   Ans: You should avoid coffee altogether.
b. Go slow on butter and eggs.
c. Go for a long morning walk on an empty stomach.
d. Eat plenty of fresh fruit and vegetables.
e. Stop smoking at once.

Exercise 13

Rewrite these suggestions with the words given.

a. Let's invest our money in this scheme./We could ________
b. How about going to the zoo with the children? /We may as well _____

c. How about fish and chips for dinner?/ I thought you might ________
d. Please give him a second chance./ Couldn't you ________
e. What about asking your father to help with the money? / You could ________
f. Why don't we book the tickets in advance?/ Shouldn't we ________
g. How about buying an apartment?/ It might be a good idea ________
h. Why not wait for a month before we decide? / We might as well ________

Exercise 14

Use the boxed phrases to complete the following sentences. Note that the sentences make suggestions.

to come with me to curl up with a book like to join us settle for a game of cards attend it go and see it

a. We are going for a picnic tomorrow. I thought you might ________
b. 'The Titanic' is on in town. We might as well ________
c. I'm driving to the airport to meet my son. I thought you might want ________
d. It is doing to be a wet day. We might as well ________
e. If you are feeling tired, it might be a good idea ________
f. The Marcos are having a meeting in their house. I thought you might want to ________

10.3.10 'Will', 'shall', 'should', 'must', 'may' in their negative forms to express a prohibition

Both 'will not' and 'shall not' are used to express a prohibition. 'Shall not', however, is more formal and is used in written rules, agreements etc:

You will not step into this house without my permission.
You won't be watching TV until you have completed all your assignments.
Persons under 21 shall not be members of the club.
Goods once bought and paid for shall not be returned or exchanged.
Angry father to teenage daughter: You shan't stay out this late at night.

'Cannot' is also used to say that something is forbidden by law:

Children above 12 cannot travel on half-tickets.
This swimming pool is for women only. We can't let you in.

We may, as we saw earlier in the chapter, use 'may not' in place of 'cannot' but 'may not' is more formal.

You may use 'should not' and 'must not' to say that something is unacceptable but 'must not' is more forceful than 'should not':

You shouldn't take anyone for granted.
You should not be rude to strangers.
You mustn't neglect your parents in their old age.
You mustn't violate the law of the land.

'10.3.11 Will', 'would', 'shall', 'should', 'may', 'must' for making an offer or an invitation

We use 'will' or 'would' with 'you' as the subject to make an offer or an invitation:

Will you have a glass of fresh lime?
Will you come with me to a late-night movie?

What would you like, tea or coffee?

Would you care to have dinner with us?

'Would' is more polite than 'will', particularly with a verb meaning 'like'.
If we want to sound more persuasive, we may use the negative form:

Wouldn't you like to join us for dinner?

We may use 'won't' in place of 'wouldn't':

Won't you come with us for a picnic?

When we make an offer of help, we use 'may' or 'shall':

May I help you with your washing?

Shall I open the window? It's so warm here.

We use 'shall' and 'may' only when we are fairly certain that our offer of help will be accepted. If we are not certain, we use 'should':

Should I ask her to a matinee show?

If we want our invitation to sound warm and friendly, we use 'must':

You must come and visit us again.

You must spend a weekend with us.

10.3.12 'May', 'can', 'might', 'could' to express possibility

We use 'may', 'can', 'might' and 'could' to say that there is a possibility of something happening or something being the case. Look at these examples:

He may be wrong. He can be wrong.

Both 'may' and 'can' mean that it is possible that he is wrong but 'can' suggests greater certainty. You see the difference between 'may' and 'can' more clearly in their negative forms:

He may not accept the job that has been offered him. (He may not accept; on the other hand, he may.)

He cannot accept the job that has been offered him. (It is impossible for him to accept the job...)

You may use 'might' and 'could' in place of 'may':

Don't go out in this weather. You could catch a cold.

If you don't observe the rules of the road, you might end up on a stretcher.

Take an umbrella with you. You might need it.

There is hardly any difference in meaning between the modals 'may', 'might' and 'could' except that 'may' is slightly more formal than 'could' and 'might'. In all the examples given above, 'may' and 'might' and 'could' indicate present or future possibility. They say that something is possible *now or in the future*.

When we express the idea of possibility, we may mean one of these degrees of possibility. Possibility is a cline or continuum ranging from possible to probable to certain. (A cline or continuum is something that changes gradually like a slope.)

a. **possible**: may might could
She may pass this time.
She might pass this time.
She could pass this time.

b. **probable or very likely**: may well might well could well will probably

She may well pass this time.
She might well pass this time.
She could well pass this time.
She will probably pass this time.

c. **certain**: shall will must cannot

She shall/will pass this time.
She must pass this time.
She cannot fail this time.

To say that something is impossible, you use 'could not' and 'cannot':

'He says he was not at home when you called.'
'I don't believe it. That cannot be true.'
The murderer could not have obtained the weapon any other way.
You cannot foresee what is going to happen.

Exercise 15

How would you rate the chances of the following things happening by the year 2020? Answer with three choices: one that says it is possible, the second that it is probable and the third that it is certain. The first one is an example.

a. Humans settling in Mars by the year 2020

Answer: Humans *may/ might/ could* settle in Mars by the year 2020. (possible)
Humans *could well* settle/ *will probably* settle in Mars by 2020. (probable)
Humans *must/ will* settle in Mars by 2020. (certain)

b. India having a reliable telephone service
c. The world becoming free of polio
d. There being no school bags to carry and no examinations to write
e. Computers teaching children in schools

Exercise 16

Here is an extract from a mid-year progress report on Avinash, a final year student at school, giving a forecast of his probable performance in the coming exam. Complete the report with suitable modals, choosing them from the box below.

may might could must should could well will probably (all these with or without the negative 'not')

Avinash is doing reasonably well in English and he __________ pass. Maths has always been his strong point and he __________ pass with distinction. He __________ even get full marks if he tries hard. He is not very good at physics but he has never failed in the subject and he __________ __________ pass. He needn't worry about chemistry, although he __________ __________ get a distinction. His Hindi teacher has never been happy with him, nor he with Hindi having all along failed to make the grade. He has, however, shown some improvement of late and he __________ pass in the final.

10.3.13 'Would', 'should', 'would rather', 'would sooner' to express wishes

We use 'would' and 'should' with a lexical verb meaning 'to like' to say what someone wants or doesn't want:

I would like to continue in my present job.
I wouldn't like to comment on the latest developments.
I would love to be in Europe at this time of the year.
She would prefer to remain silent.
We should like to extend the lease for another year.
I should not like to see my grandson sitting glued to the television.

'Would' and 'should' both express wishes. 'Should' is more formal and less common.

We use 'would rather', 'would sooner' to express a preference, that is, to say that someone likes one thing better than the other:

I would sooner go on holiday to Britain than to the U.S.
He would rather be honest than (be) rich.
I would sooner have you than him for a friend.
She would rather like to be left alone.

Exercise 17

Three boys and three girls, all in their teens, were asked what they would like to be or what they hate to be. Here are the answers:

	likes to be	hates to be
Nitin	a doctor	an accountant
Vinita	a pilot	a model
Yasmin	a pop singer	a housewife
Manju	a business executive	a doctor

Write sentences stating the teenagers' likes and dislikes, using the modals 'should' and 'would' with appropriate verbs like 'like', 'love', 'loathe', 'hate'. Alternatively, you may use the 'would rather/sooner' construction. The first one is done for you.

a. Nitin *would like* to be a doctor but he *would hate* to be an accountant. (or) Nitin *would rather* be a doctor *than* an accountant.

Exercise 18

What would you do:

a. If you caught your best friend stealing? Would you report him to the police or shield him?
b. If you found a wallet containing a lot of money? Would you be honest and return the wallet to the owner or be greedy and take the money?
c. If in a crowded bus you saw an old man standing? Would you offer your seat to the old man?

10.3.14 'Could' to express impossible wishes

We use the modal 'could' to express impossible wishes or to indulge in wishful thinking:

1. A man earning Rs 1000 a month: I wish I could live like a matinee idol (but I cannot).
2. A woman put on a strict diet by the doctor: I wish I could eat cakes and pastries by the dozen (but I cannot).

3. An overweight person: How I wish I could have the body of an athlete!
4. A twelve-year-old: I wish I could fly like a bird.
   Note that the wishing is being done right now.

Exercise 19

Complete the following using 'could' to express impossible wishes. The first one is done for you.

a. Someone who missed the last bus: *I wish I could get a lift home.*
b. A young man dreaming of winning a lottery: I wish ____
c. Students taking an exam: We wish____
d. A young boy wanting to play for the country cricket team: I wish ____
e. A manager with too many problems: How I wish ____

Exercise 20

Match the observations in column 1 with the wishes in column 2.

1	2
a. I have no ear for music.	i. I wish I had kept a diary.
b. I didn't know you were out of work.	ii. I wish I had not given him cash.
c. I cannot recall many of the things that happened to me.	iii. I wish I were a jockey.
d. He denies having borrowed the money from me.	iv. I wish I could become a famous singer.
e. I am a tall, heavy man and I love horses.	v. I wish I had known that you were out of work.

10.3.15 'Should', 'ought' to express obligation and advisability

We use 'should' and 'ought' to offer advice and criticism; to say, in other words, what you *should* do and *shouldn't* do.

Doctor to patient:	You ought to go slow on potatoes and you shouldn't eat candies.
Teacher to student:	You ought to obey traffic rules. Otherwise there could be an accident.
Aunt Radha to niece:	Really, Rani! You shouldn't feed your dog cakes! And you should bath him regularly.

The doctor, the teacher and Aunt Radha are offering advice or criticism. They are suggesting what is advisable and what is not, what is the right and proper thing to do. The advice or the criticism may or may not be well taken, that would depend on the listener. Therefore they use 'should' and 'ought'. The modal equivalent of 'had better' also expresses the notion of advisability and may be used in place of 'should' and 'ought':

You had better eat less butter.

You had better inform the police.

Exercise 21

Here are a few things that people often say to you by way of advice. Complete the sentences below using 'should' and 'ought' with the help of the cues given within brackets.

a. You ______________________ (early to bed and early to rise)

b. You ______________________ (neither borrow nor lend)

c. You ______________________ (speak your mind but don't hurt the feelings of others)

d. You ______________________ (check your facts before drawing any conclusions)

e. You ______________________ (be tolerant of common human foibles)

Exercise 22

Think of five things that people may say to you by way of criticism of your habits or ways. The first one is done for you.

a. You ought to cut down on sweets.

b. You ______________________ (not lose your temper on flimsy pretexts)

c. You ______________________ (no snacks between meals)

d. You ______________________ (remember that other people have the same rights as you do)

e. You ______________________ (less of television)

The modals 'should' and 'ought' are at times used to make a recommendation:

This is a good book. You should/ought to read it.

This is a good film. You should/ought to see it.

10.3.16 'Must' and 'have to' to express necessity

The difference between obligation and advisability on one side and necessity on the other is one of degree only. While 'should' and 'ought' suggest a desirable course of action which may or may not be acted upon, the modal 'must' and the modal equivalent 'have to' suggest a more compelling course of action which does not allow for the possibility of rejection.

Policeman to car owner:	All drivers must carry their licence and insurance papers. I'm sorry, sir, you will have to come with me to the station.
Librarian:	You mustn't eat in the library.
Zoo keeper:	You mustn't feed the animals. And you mustn't tease them either.

The policeman, the librarian and the zoo keeper can make sure that people obey them. If they don't obey, they will be punished. Therefore they use 'must' and 'have to', which are stronger than 'should' and 'ought'. They suggest compulsion of some kind. The compulsion may be forced on us by life itself ('We must eat to live', 'We have to save for a rainy day'), or by others in authority like the government, our parents, teachers, employers, and so on ('You mustn't eat in the library', 'Everyone has to complete his or her tax return', 'You must submit your assignment on time'), or by ourselves through a strong sense of duty ('We must keep our promise at all costs', 'You have to spare a thought for the deprived and the disadvantaged among us').

Exercise 23

Complete the following sentences with 'must' and 'have to', the latter in the present, past or future tense. Sometimes both 'must' and 'have to' are possible.

a. You ____________ show much better progress if you want to pass the examination.

b. Our house was burgled last night. We ____________ call the police.

c. I'm afraid I can't come with you to the movie. I ____________ finish my homework.

d. Our know-all neighbour finally gave up and said he could not repair our TV set. We ____________ take it to the repair shop.

e. I ____________ come and see you when I am in Delhi next. I really ____________.

f. All of you ____________ be here by 5 o'clock for the rehearsal.

g. Everyone of you here who has come for the interview ____________ fill in this form to claim your travelling allowance.

Like 'should' and 'ought', 'must' and 'have to' are also used to make a recommendation but there is a difference. Compare:

This is a good film. You should/ought to see it.

This is a good film. You must/have to see it.

The first one is a moderate recommendation, the second a strong one.

The negative of 'must' does not mean the same as the negative of 'have to'. Compare:

He mustn't go there alone. It is dangerous.

He doesn't have to go there alone. Someone will go with him.
(It is not necessary for him to go alone.)

Note

'Have to' being only a modal equivalent and not a modal proper, forms its negative like any lexical verb.

Exercise 24

Here is a list of things, some necessary, some forbidden, and some unnecessary, according to the laws and customs of our country. Complete the blanks below with 'must', 'mustn't', or 'don't have to'. The first one is an example.

a. If you go to a government hospital in this country, you don't have to pay for your treatment.

b. You ____________ have plenty of money if you go to a private hospital or nursing home.

c. I can sleep till 8 o'clock tomorrow because I ____________ go to school.

d. If a guest comes to your house, you ____________ entertain him as best you can.

e. Voting at an election is not mandatory by law. That means you ____________ vote if you don't feel like it.

f. You ____________ travel on Indian rail without a valid ticket.

g. You ____________ forget to call on Grandmother when you go to Nagpur next.

h. You ____________ speak ill of the dead.

11 Verbs: 3 Tenses

Tense means time; it comes from a Latin word meaning time. The English tenses, therefore, should, logically and etymologically speaking, refer to time, that is, to time as we think of it in our everyday life.

We think of time as having three parts—past, present and future. We live in the present, behind the present is the past, and ahead of the present is the future. In other words, we compartmentalise time into the present, the past and the future, the present acting as a dividing line between the past and the future.

If the present is a dividing line, the line is so thin as to be almost imperceptible. The present slips into the past and before we know it, the future is already upon us and the present has vanished irretrievably into the past. 'Ramesh went that very moment to telephone his father,' we say very casually but most illogically. The reference is to a moment in Ramesh's life when he hears, let us say, of something sad, bad or significant happening at home and he goes to telephone his father for further information. But he couldn't have telephoned 'that very moment'. 'That very moment' of his hearing whatever he heard is well past by the time he picks up the telephone. However, we still stick to our rigid but crude and simplistic three-fold division of time into present, past and future and think of a three-tense verb system to correspond to the three-fold division so that present tense represents present time, past tense past time and future tense future time. Unfortunately for the learner and the teacher of English, there is no such strict correspondence between tense and time in English. Tense in English *does not always* mean time. For example, what we call the present simple tense does not always point to present time. The sentence:

Water freezes into ice at 0 degree centigrade

refers not to a present truth but to a general truth which, while including the present moment, stretches indefinitely into the past and the future: water froze into ice at 0 degree centigrade in the past, it does so now, and it will do so in the future.

Again, when we say 'She leaves tomorrow', the present simple 'leaves' has nothing to do with present time. In our discussion of modals in the preceding chapter, we often saw the past tense referring to present time, as for instance:

a. when we express the idea of possibility: She *might* pass next March; She *could* pass next March.

b. when we express a wish: I *would* like to continue in my present job; She *would* prefer to remain single.

c. when we make a suggestion: I *thought* you *might* want to go out for a walk; We *might* as well settle for a game of cards.

The point to note is this—the suggestions are being made now, the wishes are being expressed now, the possibilities are being explored now, and yet we use the past and not the present tense, as in fact we should if there were a strict correspondence between time and tense. What is even more significant is the fact that the past tense modals refer to either present time or future time. Thus, in the example:

She *might/could* pass next March

the verb clearly refers to the future ('next March'), while in the examples:

I *would* like to continue in my present job
I *thought* you *might* want to go out for a walk

the past tense verbs refer to present time stretching into the future.

This is not to suggest that tense doesn't refer to time at all in English. It does in some places, it doesn't in other places. If tense doesn't refer to time in some places, what, then, does it refer to? Let us see by looking at English tenses one by one.

English has six tenses—**present, past, future, present perfect, past perfect and future perfect**. We begin with the present simple tense.

11.1 Present Simple Tense

The present simple tense has the following forms:

Positive	I/We/You/They *take.* He/She/It *takes.*
Question	*Do* I/we/you/they *take*? *Does* he/she/it *take*?
Negative	I/We/You/They *do not* (*don't*) *take.* He/She/It/ *does not* (*doesn't*) *take.*
Passive Voice	I *am taken.* We/You/They *are taken.* He/She/It *is taken.*

We use the simple present tense when we talk of habitual actions or actions happening regularly:

He *gets up* at 6 o'clock and *goes* for a long walk.
Every day, after lunch, grandfather *goes* to sleep.

The present simple tense is also used to express:

a. a present truth: Hassan *is* a tailor.
(was yesterday, is today, will be tomorrow)

b. a general truth: Water *boils* at 100 degrees centigrade.
(did in the past, does now, and will do in the future)

Note that all the three functions of the present simple tense (habitual action, present truth, general truth) not only include the present moment but extend indefinitely into the past and the future.

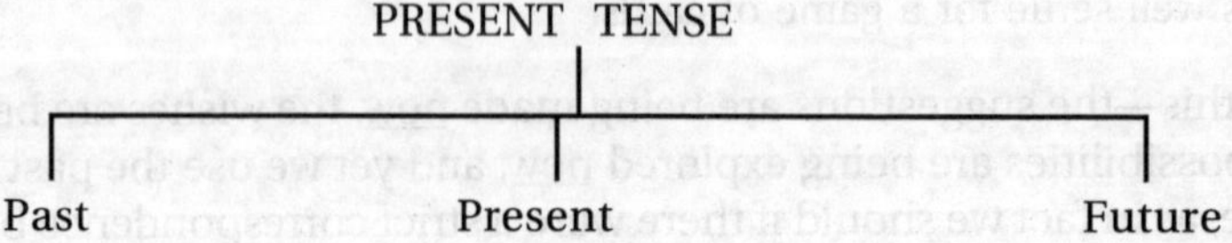

Two kinds of adverbs are used with verbs in the present simple tense. When the tense refers to a habitual or regular action, it is often accompanied by an *adverb of frequency* like: *sometimes occasionally rarely often never hardly ever* and so on.

I don't much care for cricket but I *do occasionally watch* a one-day match on television.

They *hardly ever speak* to each other.

If the simple present tense refers to a general truth, we sometimes use one of these adverbs to strengthen or weaken our statement:

always generally chiefly usually normally traditionally.

Children *normally respond* to praise and encouragement.

He *is usually* late for an appointment but not *always.*

Exercise 1

Answer the following questions, using the correct form of the verb with the adverb suggested within brackets.

a. What do you do in the evenings on getting back home from work? (generally)
b. How often do you watch television? (daily)
c. What sort of TV programmes do you watch? (serials usually)
d. What sort of serials do you prefer? (mythological mostly)
e. Do you read books? (occasionally)
f. Do you go to parties? (seldom)

Exercise 2

A coffee retailing firm sent round a questionnaire asking people of a locality about their coffee-drinking habits. Here is part of the questionnaire.
Answer the questions using the tips given in brackets.

a. What do you drink, coffee or tea? (coffee)
b. In a day how often do you drink coffee? (four to five times)
c. What time in the morning do you have your first cup of coffee? (6 o'clock on working days, 7 o'clock on Sundays)
d. Do you drink coffee before going to bed? (never)
e. When do you have your last cup of coffee? (5 o'clock in the evening or thereabouts)
f. What do you offer your guests at home? (coffee generally)
g. What kind of coffee do you drink, strong or weak? (not too strong)
h. Do you ever drink instant coffee? (never)

We use the present simple tense to express our thoughts, feelings, opinions, or our immediate reactions to persons or things:

He *thinks* games are a waste of time.
I *feel* tired. My head *aches.*

You *look* gorgeous in that saree of yours.

He *does not like* dogs but his wife *adores* them.

We use the present simple tense when we are talking about what happens in a book, play or film:

Spielberg's film 'Schindler's List' *is* about a German who *saves* hundreds of Jews from death.

Lawrence Olivier *plays* the title role in this film version of 'Hamlet'.

In his new novel, Rohinton Mistry *depicts* the heroic struggle of a widow during the emergency era in India in the mid-seventies.

We use the present simple tense in sports commentaries as well:

Sachin *drives* that one off the back foot and the ball *races* to the fence.

Exercise 3

Complete the following passage, using the verbs in the boxes in the present simple tense. The passage is divided into two paragraphs, and for each paragraph there is a box of verbs for you to choose from. A few of these verbs have to be used more than once.

Paragraph 1 avoid (twice), be (four times)

Paragraph 2 be (four times).

Paragraph 1

avoid	be	become	breed	call	do	drive
gain	keep	know	need	store	try	

There ____1____ in all of us a tendency to be attracted by novelty. We ____2____ this 'neophilia' (love of the new). This ____3____ the opposite of 'neophobia' (fear of the new). Everything unfamiliar ____4____ potentially dangerous. We ____5____ to approach it with caution, or perhaps ____6____ it altogether. But if we ____7____ it altogether, how do we ____8____ anything about it? The neophilia urge ____9____ us on and ____10____ us interested until the unknown ____11____ the known, until familiarity ____12____ contempt, and in the process, we ____13____ valuable experience which we ____14____ away for future use. The child ____15____ it all the time. So strong ____16____ his urge that parents ____17____ to restrain it. But although parents may succeed in guiding curiosity, they can never suppress it.

Paragraph 2

bang	be	begin	develop	do	drop
fascinate	fall	grow	invent	lack	lift
look	strike	take	twist		

When we ______18______ at young chimpanzees at play, what ______19______ us immediately ______20______ the similarity between their behaviour and that of our own children. Both ______21______ (passive voice) by new toys. They ______22______ on them eagerly, ______23______ them, ______24______ them, ______25______ them, ______26______ them, and ______27______ them to pieces. They both ______28______ simple games. The young chimpanzees in fact ______29______ as inventive as our own children, and during the first few years of life, they ______30______ just as well – better in fact because their muscle system ______31______ quicker. But after a while they ______32______ to lose ground. Their brains ______33______ not complex enough to build on this good beginning. Their powers of concentration ______34______ weak and ______35______ (negative form) with their bodies. Above all, they ______36______ the ability to communicate with their parents about the inventive techniques they are discovering.

(freely adapted from *The Naked Ape*, Desmond Morris, McGraw-Hill, New York)

We also use the simple present tense, when we demonstrate, as in an experiment, how something happens or is done.

(Chemistry lecturer (demonstrating the principle of solubility): I take a beaker filled with water. I put some salt in it. What happens to the salt? It dissolves in water. I add more and more salt until a stage is reached when the water takes no more salt. You see the undissolved salt at the bottom of the beaker. The water in the beaker is now saturated with salt but only with respect to salt. I now add sugar...

Exercise 4

Here is a recipe for making banana stem khich khach. The recipe consists of instructions in the form of imperative sentences. Imagine you are giving a demonstration to a cookery class. Change the verbs from the imperative form into the present simple tense using 'I' or 'we' as subject. Put in appropriate adverbs of sequence like 'next', 'then', 'finally'.

Banana Stem Khich Khach

1 ½ banana stems cut into discs after you have peeled or cut away the outer layers of the skin

1 cup tuvar dal	1 tablespoon urad dal
a pinch of turmeric	1 tablespoon rice
3 or 4 red chillies	½ coconut, grated
½ tablespoon jeera (cumin seeds)	a little mustard

Finely chop the banana stems. Pay attention to the lengths of string that unwind as you cut. Remove these and discard. Pressure-cook the banana stem with one cup of tuvar dal, a pinch of turmeric and some salt.

Take a tablespoon of rice, three or four red chillies, and fry in oil till just before the rice begins to redden. Grind to a paste with half a coconut grated and three or four red chillies and cumin seeds.

Add this paste to the boiled banana stem and a little water if the result feels too thick, and then let the khich khach come to the boil over a slow fire. Garnish with a tablespoon of urad dal and a little black mustard.

(Begin your demonstration thus: Now here is a recipe for banana stem khich khach for four persons. We need the following...)

Here is a somewhat rare use of the present simple tense. It is used at times to report an action that occurred in the past. This is done with a view to making the narration more lively and vivid:

> Well, here I am, sprawled on a huge four-poster in the railway station's only retiring room, and before you can say Jack Robinson or its Indian equivalent, I am fast asleep. The next thing I know is this: I wake up with a start. I look at my watch, the time is 2 a.m. I then switch on the reading lamp and look around. I see nothing.
> I then turn my head by 45 degrees to the right and what do I see? A Royal Bengal tiger breathing down my neck!

When the present simple tense is thus used for events in the past, it is called the historic present.

Exercise 5

Use the following verbs in the present simple tense and complete the following passage. You may have to use one of these verbs twice.

build	light	live	lurch	rig up
ring	seek	set up	tape	

Taxis in Delhi ____1____ in small herds under the shelter of roadside trees, and their nonchalant drivers, many of them Punjabis, ____2____ an awning, ____3____ their charpoys, ____4____ a fire and ____5____ a hut for the telephone. They ____6____ like the front-line fighter pilots they ____7____ to emulate, in and around their machines, tinkering and dozing, waiting to scramble... The telephone ____8____ and a taxi ____9____ like a crocodile from the kerb, into the stream of traffic, its driver intent on his prey, looking neither left, right or behind, leaving his safety in the hands of supernatural forces. His insurance policy, a picture postcard of a god, ____10____ (passive voice) to the dashboard.

Trevot Fishlock, *A Tale of Three Cities*

nonchalant: unconcerned about how or where they live

awning: canvas shelter emulate: imitate

11.1.1 Present Continuous Tense

The present continuous tense has the following forms:

Positive	I *am taking*. We/You/They *are taking*. He/She/It *is taking*.
Question	*Am* I *taking*? *Are* we/you/they *taking*? *Is* he/she/it *taking*?
Negative	I *am not taking*. We/You/They *are not* (*aren't*) *taking*. He/She/It *is not* (*isn't*) *taking*.
Passive Voice	I *am being taken*. We/You/They *are being taken*. He/She/It *is being taken*.

Unlike the present simple tense, the present continuous tense refers to present time. We use the present continuous tense to refer to actions or situations that are going on at the moment of speaking. Present time may mean either the moment of speaking or the present moment:

She *is practising* the piano.

My brother *is helping* mother in the kitchen.

I *am working* as the company's Chief Area Sales Manager.

It *is raining* now.

We use the present continuous tense to refer to a period of limited duration between two points of time, as in the example:

She *is living* in Delhi. (meaning, 'She went to Delhi some time ago and will presumably leave Delhi some time later')

The most striking characteristic of this tense is that it is used to express the idea that an event is of limited duration:

We in Hindustan Synthetics *are looking* for a dynamic salesman. (meaning, 'the search for the salesman has already begun and it will stop after some time, when the company will offer the job to one of the applicants')

The computer *is not working* properly.

Exercise 6

Complete the following sentences with the present continuous tense of the verbs. Choose the verbs from this list.

change	die	get	go up
return	run	wait	work

a. 'Can I watch television for a while? I don't want to miss my favourite serial.'
'No, you cannot. Our television set is not ___________.'

b. The waiting passengers are grumbling. The train, it looks, ___________ late.

c. I haven't seen you for ages. Do sit down. I ___________ to know all about you.

d. The situation is still tense but ___________ to normal slowly.

e. 'I hear your father has been very ill.'
'Yes, but he ___________ better now.'

f. Go and ask your friend what he wants. He __________ downstairs.

g. The world population __________ by 2% every year.

h. Scientists believe that with the thinning of the ozone layer the world climate __________ for the worse.

Verbs of perception : 'see' 'hear' 'taste' and 'smell' (the last two when intransitive) are not normally used in the present continuous tense.

I *hear* someone crying (not 'I am hearing...'). Go and see who it is.
Do you *see* the smoke over there?
The medicine *tastes* bitter. It *smells* awful, too.

Apart from verbs of perception, the following categories of verbs are not normally used in the present continuous tense:

type of verb	examples
a. verbs expressing emotion	love hate like dislike care prefer
b. verbs indicating mental condition or activity	agree believe guess imagine know understand remember realise expect want wish consider mean feel and think (the last two when followed by a that-clause)
c. non-action verbs	be have (meaning 'possess') belong seem appear (meaning 'seem') contain consist require own possess need

Exercise 7

Complete the following dialogue using the correct present tense of the verbs in brackets (present simple or present continuous).

Mr Lobo: (on the telphone to Dr Bose's secretary) Good morning, Mr Vinod. This __________ (be) Lobo. I __________ (have) an appointment with Dr Bose at 4 o'clock this evening.

Mr Vinod: Good morning, Mr Lobo. Your appointment with the doctor, if I __________ (remember) right, __________ (be) for tomorrow.

Mr Lobo: No, Mr Vinod. It __________ (be) for this evening.

Mr Vinod: You __________ (be) sure, Mr Lobo?

Mr Lobo: Yes, I __________ (be). I __________ (have) it here, written down in my diary.

Mr Vinod: Just a minute please. Let me check... Yes, you __________(be) right, Mr Lobo. And now, what can I do for you? You __________ (want) a change of date?

Mr Lobo: I __________ (wish) to cancel the appointment, Mr Vinod. I __________ (be) terribly sorry but I simply have to cancel it.

We __________ (do up) the house, half a dozen men __________ (work) right now, and I __________ (not know) how long they will take to finish. Not until next week, I __________ (imagine). But please tell Dr Bose how sorry I __________ (be).

11. 2 Past Simple Tense

The past simple tense has the following forms for all persons and numbers:

Positive	I/We/You/He/She/It/They *took*.
Question	*Did* I/we/you/he/she/it/they *take*?
Negative	I/We/You/He/She/It/They *did not* (*didn't*) *take*.
Passive Voice	I/He/She/It *was taken*. We/You/They *were taken*.

We use the simple past tense to talk about an action or event that took place sometime in the past:

Madame Curie, together with Pierre Curie, *discovered* the radioactive elements of radium and plutonium.

The point of time indicated by the past simple tense may be in the distant or immediate past:

Alexander *invaded* India well over 2300 years ago.

She *left* home five minutes ago.

I *sold* my bicycle a month ago.

We use the past simple tense when we talk about a past habit or repeated event:

We *went* for a walk after dinner when we were holidaying in Shimla.

We *had* a good monsoon for ten years in a row.

Often the simple past tense takes on an adverbial of time, frequency or duration:

Tenzing Norgay and Edmund Hillary *climbed* Mount Everest for the first time *in 1953*.

She *worked for eight hours a day during her final year*.

The adverb 'ago' goes only with the simple past tense. It means 'from now to a point in past time' and it always comes after the time-expression, not before it:

a month ago   ages ago   three weeks ago   centuries ago

Exercise 8

Use one of the verbs in the box in the simple past tense, one verb for each blank, to complete each of the following newspaper stories.

a.

bag	get	introduce	make
present	relate	win	

Teachers Get Award

Three Bangalore teachers, two of them from Kendriya Vidyalaya, Hebbal ____1____ the NCERT award for innovative practices in school education. Headmistress of Kendriya Vidyalaya, Hebbal, Ms V. Niranjani, who has been teaching for over three decades, ____2____ (passive voice) with the award for her use of mental maths, games, puzzles and magic in teaching maths in primary classes. She ____3____ mathematics fun for children in the 5 to 6 years' age group. The other innovation she ____4____ ____5____ to the use of language games and environmental studies for enriching the English vocabulary of her pupils.

Another teacher of the same school, Ms Khamar Taj, ____6____ the NCERT award for introducing value education through rhymes.

Ms Vijaya Shah of DVV Gujarati School, the third teacher from Bangalore, ____7____ the award for her paper 'Education with fun and a smile'.

innovative: introducing changes and new ideas in the way things are done
innovation (noun): new idea or method introduced in the way things are done

b.

ambush	come	destroy	escape	fight
have	join	capture	return	serve

Hero from Shimoga

Among the soldiers who ____8____ on the northern sector and ____9____ home alive is B.V. Sadashivappa of the Madras Infantry.

Sadashivappa, who hails from Bhadravathi, ____10____ the Indian Army twelve years ago. He ____11____ for a year in Nagaland fighting the insurgents when the call from the northern sector ____12____. He ____13____ a narrow escape when his battalion ____14____ (passive voice) on 20 June. Their bunker ____15____ (passive voice) in the attack but Sadashivappa not only ____16____ unhurt but ____17____ two of the intruders.

c.

be	conduct	enjoy	find
introduce	read	say	

Sunday Story-telling Holds Children Captive

It ____18____ a trip into the magical world of story-telling for the children of Fountainhead on Lavelle Road, here on Sunday. Needless to say, the children ____19____ every minute of the story session. Ms M. Patil, who ____20____ the stories, ____21____ two fun-filled sessions for children between the ages of 4 and 12. Parents sitting around ____22____ the sessions just as absorbing as their children. 'It ____23____ us to a new approach,' ____24____ Mrs Vasudev, who had come along with her son.

11. 2.1 Past Continuous Tense

The past continuous tense has the following forms:

Positive I/He/She/It *was taking.* We/You/They *were taking.*

Question *Was* I/He/She/it *taking?* *Were* we/you/they *taking?*

Negative I/He/She/It *was not* (*wasn't*) *taking.* We/You/They *were not* (*weren't*) *taking.*

Passive Voice I/He/She/It *was being taken.* We/You/They *were being taken.*

We use the past continuous tense to express past events, actions or states:

What *were* you *doing* yesterday morning?

I *was helping* mother with the cooking.

Why *were* you *sleeping* through my lecture last week?

We use the past continuous, usually with the simple past tense, to define one action in relation to another action in the past:

I *met* him as he *was crossing* the road.

Notice that the action of crossing was still in progress when I met him. That is why the verb 'cross' takes the past continuous tense. The main action of *meeting*, being complete, takes the past simple tense. Here is another example:

a. He was *making tea* when they *arrived.*

Compare the above with:

b. He *made* tea when they *arrived.*

In (a) the tea-making was in progress when they arrived, while in (b) the tea-making began and ended after they arrived: he made tea presumably to treat his guests to a cup of tea.

We use the past continuous tense alone (that is, without the past simple tense) to indicate that an action was going on for a certain period of time in the past:

It *was raining* the whole day yesterday.

He *was working* in the garden from five to eight in the morning.

Sometimes we use two or more verbs, all in the past continuous tense, to show that two or more past actions or activities were going on at the same time.

The class *were working* on the assignment while the teacher *was going* round checking.

While I *was reading*, Sam *was watching* television.

The band *was playing* the national anthem, the flags *were fluttering* and the assembled crowd *was watching* silently as the visiting Prime Minister inspected a guard of honour presented to him.

Exercise 9

Put the verbs in brackets into the correct past tense (simple or continuous).

a. We (watch) the Sherlock Holmes serial when the lights (go) out.

b. Jim Faxx (become) an American millionaire through his books on jogging. Strangely enough, he himself (die) while he (jog). He (be) 52 when he (die).

c. The Delhi-bound Frontier Mail (run) at close to 100 km an hour. In a certain compartment of the train (sit) two men. They (face) each other. For an hour or so, they (keep) silent. Then, one of them (break) the ice by asking the other whether he (go) to Delhi.

'Yes,' (say) the other.

It was now the turn of the other man to do his share of the talking. He (say) to his companion opposite, 'I don't believe in ghosts.'

'Don't you?' (reply) the other and (vanish).

d. What you (do) when I (call) on you yesterday evening? I (ring) the bell a number of times but you (not answer) the door. I (be) so keen to see you, I (have) something very urgent to discuss with you. You probably (sleep) after a late night.

Exercise 10

In the following extract, the author gives a novel explanation, all his own, for the origin of the popular saying: Where there's a will there's a way. The extract, however, is incomplete. Complete it with the verbs in the appropriate tense (present simple, past simple, or past continuous).

When it finally (become) clear that the entertainment business (be) just the career for me, I (go) to a large cinema house in Leicester Square and (beg) them to take me on in any capacity.

'You (want) to start at the very bottom of the ladder?' (ask) the manager. I (nod). He (point) to something leaning against the wall and (say), 'There (be) the ladder for you.'

In my new job I (call—passive), somewhat grandly, Head of Display. All that I (have) to do as Head of Display (be) to climb up the ladder and fix, high on the front wall of the cinema, those large metal letters which (spell) out the name of the film on that week.

It (be) not an exciting or even interesting job. In a high wind, it (be) difficult and – artistically – it (be) less than satisfying. Unlike the painter or the sculptor, I (be) in no position to step back and take a look at my finished work. This (lead) in the first few weeks to certain errors of judgement, like WEST SIDE SORTY (for *West Side Story*) and THE SNOUD OF MUSIC (for *The Sound of Music*). All the same, I (feel) happy I (get) a little bit nearer to the heart of the show business.

But it (be) only the moment of emergency which really (prove) a man's worth. My moment (come) when the telephone (ring) at three o'clock in the morning. It (be) the manager. 'I have just passed the cinema on my way home,' he (say), 'Your Y has dropped off.'

Though I (be) very sleepy, I (understand) at once why he (be) so concerned. The film we (show) that week (be) MY FAIR LADY. The cinema now appeared to be showing a film called MY FAIR LAD.

When I (reach) the cinema, I (find) the letter Y lying broken on the pavement. I (hurry) to the storeroom for a spare Y but there (be) none. There (be) a spare X, however. I (change) the X into a Y by sawing off the south-east leg of the letter but it wouldn't stay up on the wall.

It (be) four in the morning by then and I (get) desperate. Where, in London, at that odd hour, could I get a 1.25-meter-tall Y?

To my good luck, the cinema on the opposite side of Leicester Square (show) a film whose title (contain) the letter I (want). I (climb) up and (remove) the Y, and nobody even (pause) to stare at me, let alone ask what I (do). The only nasty moment (come) when I (carry) it across Coventry Street. A policeman (stop) me and (ask) what on earth I (do) at 4.30 a.m. carrying a four-foot letter Y.

'This (be) not a letter Y, officer,' I (say) coolly. 'It (be) a water-divining rod.' My luck (hold); the policeman (go) on his way.

By 5 a.m. the fair name of MY FAIR LADY had been restored. All (be) well except that the cinema opposite now (appear) to be showing a film called MOB DICK, with Gregory Peck and Orson Welles in the lead roles.

I have had warm feelings towards the screen version of Herman Melville's great novel ever since. It (show) me a way out of the emergency I (face) early on in my career, as Head of Display. I therefore (say): 'Where there's a whale, there's a Y.'

Note

> Herman Melville, a 19th century American novelist, is the author of *Moby Dick*. The novel tells the story of Capt. Ahab setting out on a whaler, seeking revenge on the white whale that has bitten off his leg. The novel is named after the whale.

11.3 Present Perfect Tense

The present perfect tense has the following forms:

Positive	I/We/You/They *have taken*. He/She/It *has taken*.
Question	*Have* I/we/you/they *taken*? *Has* he/she/it *taken*?
Negative	I/We/You/They *have not* (*haven't*) *taken*. He/She/It *has not* (*hasn't*) *taken*.
Passive Voice	I/We/You/They *have been taken*. He/She/It *has been taken*.

The word 'perfect' means 'completed' or 'finished' and must therefore refer to an action or event in the past. The past simple tense too refers to an action or event in the past. What, then, is the difference between the present perfect tense and the past simple tense? Secondly, how can an action or event be present and perfect at the same time?

Look at these two sentences:

a. We lived in Delhi for ten years.

b. We have lived in Delhi for ten years.

Sentence (a) speaks of our living in Delhi simply as a past event. We lived in Delhi once, we don't live there at present. Sentence (b), on the other hand, means the following:

1. We moved to Delhi ten years ago.
2. We lived in Delhi for ten years. (action completed to date)
3. We are living in Delhi now. (The action continues into the present and is connected to the present)
4. We are not new to Delhi; we know the city well. (the effect of the past action on the present)

The emphasis is on the result at the present time of an action already completed in the past. The present perfect tense is not concerned with the pastness of the past action as the simple past tense is.

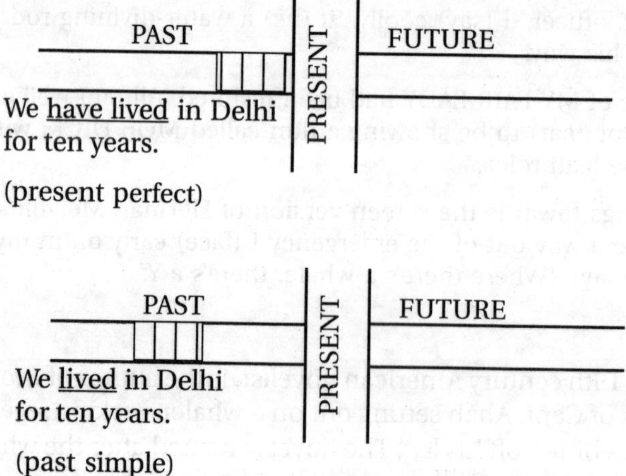

Here are some more examples of the use of the present perfect tense. Compare each of the following pairs of sentences:

1. I *read* the *Panchatantra* when I was ten. (emphasis on past action)
   I *have read* the *Panchatantra*. (I *now* know what it is about.)
2. He *went* to Calcutta last month. (report of a past action)
   He *has gone* to Calcutta. (He is not here *now*.)
3. He *was* in hospital for a few days. (He is no longer in hospital.)
   He *has been* in hospital for a week. (He was admitted a week ago and he is still in hospital.)
4. He *passed* his finals in accountancy last year.
   He *has passed* his finals in accountancy. (He can now practise as an accountant.)

The present perfect tense can also refer to a recurrent event during a period leading up to the present time:

Global warming and pollution *have* over the years *changed* the world's climate for the worse.

Exercise 11

Change the verbs in brackets into either the past simple tense or the present perfect tense and complete the sentences.

a. George (meet) Susan at a party on New Year's Eve and (fall) in love with her. He (be) in love with her since.

b. 'Is Dad in?'
'No, he isn't. He (leave) home an hour ago. He (not return) yet.'

c. 'Would you like some coffee? I just (make) some.'
'No, thank you. I (have) a cup some ten minutes ago.'

d. 'You ever (meet) Mr William Sharp?'
'No, never. But I (meet) Mr Wilfrid Blunt.'

e. 'You ever (see) a U.F.O.?'
'What is a U.F.O.?'
'An Unidentified Flying Object.'
'No, I (not see) one yet. And I don't think there are such things.'

f. 'Lovely meeting you here. What a surprise! When you (come) here?'
'Three months ago.'
'I (come) here about the same time. I (not know) that you (be) here. How I (miss) running into you all these days?'

g. 'You (be) to the Rail Museum?'
'Yes, I (go) there last Monday.'

h. 'You ever (be) abroad?'
'Yes, several times.'
'When you (be) abroad last?'
'Three months ago I (be) in Germany.'

i. 'I (lose) my purse. You (see) it anywhere?'
'No, I'm afraid I (not see) it. When you last (see) it?'
'I (have) it with me when I (go) to the movie last night.'
'Perhaps you (leave) it at the theatre.'
'Not likely. I now remember I (take) money out of it to pay the auto fare on reaching home.'

j. 'I just (be) to the film TESS. You (see) it?'
'No, I (not see) it. Is it like the novel?'
'I (not read) the book. I must confess I (not read) any of Hardy's novels.'
'What a shame! I (read) it when I (be) in college. It (be) one of three novels that we had to read as undergraduates in those days.'
'When Hardy (write) it?'
'I think he (write) it in 1891. I'm not sure.'
'You (read) any other novel of Hardy?'
'Yes, I (read) all his major novels including the very last one he (write), *Jude the Obscure.*'

'Since' and 'for'

The present perfect tense, we have seen, refers to an action that began in the past and has continued into the present, right up to the moment of speaking. It refers, in other words, to an action that covers a past-to-present time span.

Two prepositions, 'since' and 'for', express this past-to-present time span and these are used very often with the present perfect tense. 'Since' indicates the beginning point in the past while 'for' indicates the entire period of time from the past to the present.

How long have you worked at Asafally's? (the question asked in 2000)

I <u>have worked</u> at Asafally's <u>since 1990</u> / <u>for ten years</u>.

since
x...x

1990 Now (2000)

(beginning point in the past) for (entire period of time)

Given below are some commonly used time expressions that go with 'since' and 'for':

since	for
Monday 1985 last year the year before last Christmas yesterday	a long time three days six hours a week several months a decade ages

Exercise 12

Answer these questions quickly using 'since' or 'for' with the words in parentheses. The first one is done for you.

a. How long have you waited for me? (7 a.m.)

Answer: I have waited for you since 7 a.m.

b. How long have you worked in your present school? (five years)

c. How long have you lived in this city? (last year)

d. How long have they been married? (three years)

e. How long have these roads been closed? (last Monday)

f. How long have they lived in France? (1980)

g. How long have the workers been on strike? (six months)

h. How long has she been Minister for Health? (the last cabinet reshuffle)

<u>*Note*</u>

The preposition 'for' can be used with the past simple tense to indicate a period of time in the past:

I became a chartered accountant in 1985. Then, *for* five years (that is, from 1985 to 1990), I *worked* for a firm of auditors. I then set up my own practice.

Apart from the prepositions 'since' and 'for', the following adverbs are used with the present perfect tense:

Ever : Have you *ever* been to Timbuctoo?
I don't think I have *ever* seen my father get so angry.

'Ever' is used with questions and negatives only.

Never : I have *never* been to Timbuctoo. In fact I have *never* travelled outside India.

'Never', however, can be used with the past simple tense also:

When I was a boy, stamp collecting was the rage with my friends but I *never* liked the idea of collecting stamps.

Recently: He has *recently* changed his job.

So far: I wrote to him a month ago and I have not received a reply *so far*.

Just, yet: Have you met the minister?
I have *just* met him. No, I haven't met him *yet*.

11.3.1 Present Perfect Continuous

The present perfect continuous tense has the following forms:

Positive	I/We/You/They *have been taking*.	He/She/It *has been taking*.
Question	*Have* I/we/you/they *been taking*?	*Has* he/she/it *been taking*?
Negative	I/We/You/They *have not* (*haven't*) *been taking*.	
	He/She/It *has not* (*hasn't*) *been taking*.	
Passive	The present perfect continuous has no passive form in use.	

The present perfect continuous tense is even more closely related to the present than the present perfect simple tense. It shows that an action that began in the past has continued into the present and is in all likelihood still going on. Compare:

I *have telephoned* all your friends. (completed upto now)

I *have been telephoning* your friends since 8 o'clock. (I'm still telephoning)

However, there is a subtle difference, a difference in emphasis, between the two. In the first example, the emphasis is on what the speaker has actually done, on her achievement. In the second, the emphasis is on the length of time the action of telephoning has gone on continuously. The first example stresses the achievement ('I've telephoned all your friends and I'm rather pleased with what I have done. Don't you think it an achievement?') while the second stresses the activity, the fact of her telephoning his friends since 8 o'clock ('Look, this is what I've been doing since 8 o'clock').

For a clearer understanding of the difference between the present perfect tense and the present perfect continuous tense, compare these two sentences:

I *have taught* English for twenty years.

I *have been teaching* English for twenty years.

What would you say? The first, or the second? That would depend on what you think of your work as an English teacher.

The prepositions 'since' and 'for' are used with the continuous tense as well:

The gardener *has been working* in the garden *since* 3 o'clock.

The gardener *has been working* in the garden *for* three hours.

Exercise 13

Put the verbs in parentheses into the correct tense (present perfect simple or present perfect continuous) and insert 'since' or 'for' in the blanks, if any. The first one is an example.

a. I (not read) a single novel __________ last year.
Answer: I <u>have not read</u> a single novel <u>since last year</u>.

b. The minister (be) unusually busy __________ early this morning. Look at these two gentlemen. They (wait) to see him __________ ten o'clock.

c. I (know) her __________ a long time, __________ she was a child. Her father and I (be) friends and colleagues __________ a little over twenty years.

d. 'I (make) chapathies all the evening. There's a dinner on.'

'How many you (make)?'

'I (made) a hundred.'

'What else you (do)?'

'I (cook) __________ two o'clock in the afternoon.'

'You (not finish) yet?'

'I just (finish).'

e. 'I (not feel) well __________ last Sunday.'

'You (see) a doctor?'

'No, not yet.'

'Why you (not make) an appointment with him?'

'__________ the last three days, I (not have) a minute to spare from my work. I (be) so terribly busy.'

Like the present perfect tense, the continuous tense too can be used to refer to actions that happened in the recent past but have consequences or results for the present:

You're looking very tired. *Have* you *been working* very hard of late? Or *have* you not *been sleeping* well?

Arun, there is a glint of mischief in your eyes. *Have* you *been raiding* the storeroom again?

11.4 Past Perfect Tense

The past perfect tense has the following forms:

<u>Positive</u> I/We/You/He/She/It/They *had taken*.

<u>Question</u> *Had* I/we/you/he/she/it/they *taken*?

Negative I/We/You/He/She/It/They *had not (hadn't) taken.*

Passive Voice I/We/You/He/She/It/They *had been taken.*

The past perfect is sometimes called the past in the past. It is used to refer to events or states at a time before a point of time which is already in the past. Look at this example:

Yesterday we were to leave for Delhi. We arrived at the station at 5.30 p.m. The train had already left. (The train was scheduled to leave at 5.20 p.m. and it left on time.)

before then (time before a time in the past)	then (time at a point in the past)	now (time now)
5.20 p.m. yesterday	5.30 p.m. yesterday	statement made today

The past perfect tense is generally used with the past simple tense to indicate that one past event or action is earlier than some other past event or action. The earlier event or action is put in the past perfect tense while the later one is put in the past simple tense:

When we *arrived* at the station, the train *had* already *left.* (We missed the train.)

Compare:

When we *arrived* at the station, the train *left.*

When we *arrived* at the station, the train *had left.*

The first sentence suggests that our arrival at the station coincided with the train's leaving; we might have caught the train or missed it. Notice that both the finite verbs are in the past simple tense. The second sentence clearly means we missed the train; the train left first and then, minutes later, we arrived at the station.

The purpose of the past perfect tense is to put events or actions in a chronological order and to make it clear which event or action happened first. Here are two more examples:

He called for a taxi after he *had finished* the packing.

I went for a swim after I *had finished* with the cooking.

The past perfect tense in addition can express not just the chronological sequence, but also the relevance of the earlier happening:

He didn't attend the wedding, the invitation *had not reached* him in time.

Exercise 14

Complete the following, putting the verbs in brackets into the past perfect tense.

a. They disconnected my electricity. I (not pay) the bill for two months.

b. Huge trees lay uprooted all over the countryside. There (be) a cyclonic storm.

c. I'm sorry I wasn't at home when you called. I (go) to look up my mother. She suddenly (fall) ill.

d. They withheld his results. He (not furnish) proof of his age.

e. I did not recognise my old schoolfellow Ravi. He (put on) a lot of weight and he (grow) a bushy beard besides.

Exercise 15

Put the verbs in brackets into the correct past tense (past simple or past perfect).

a. The accident victim (die) by the time they (rush) him to the hospital.

b. A vast crowd (gather) at the stadium hours before the Prime Minister (arrive).

c. They (lock) the stable door after the horses (bolt).

d. I (not watch) the film on TV last night because I (see) it before.

e. By the time the fire engine (arrive) on the scene, the building already (burn down – passive).

f. The mob (do) enough damage to property before the police (reach) the spot.

11. 4.1 Past Perfect Continuous Tense

The past perfect continuous tense has the following forms:

Positive I/We/You/He/She/It/They *had been taking.*

Question *Had* I/we/you/he/she/it/they *been taking*?

Negative I/We/You/He/She/It/They *had not* (*hadn't*) *been taking.*

The tense has no passive form in use. The past perfect continuous tense, like the past perfect tense, refers to actions, events or states at a time before a particular time in the past but unlike the past perfect tense, the continuous tense stresses the duration of the action and for this reason the tense usually goes with a time-expression beginning with 'since' or 'for':

He *had been working for* twenty-two years when he asked for retirement.

The boy was a prodigy. He *had been singing* in concerts *since* his fifth year.

Exercise 16

Do this exercise with your colleague. Your colleague tells you of things that happened some time ago or a long time ago and you respond by telling her what had been happening before the things mentioned by your colleague. Here is an example to guide you.

Colleague: My brother passed his B.Sc. with a brilliant first class.

You: I am not surprised. He *had been working* very hard.

a. Colleague: You looked tired and groggy with sleep when you arrived at 9 p.m. yesterday.

You: I... (drive non-stop for ten hours)

b. Colleague: Last month the entire State of Mizoram was completely cut off from the rest of the country.

You: No wonder. It ... (rain heavily)

c.	Colleague:	You looked rather depressed when I met you in the park yesterday.
	You:	Yes, I... (worry over a personal problem)
d.	Colleague:	With the discovery of nitrous oxide or laughing gas, the problem of finding a pain-killer was nearer a solution and surgeons in the 19th century heaved a sign of relief.
	You:	As a matter of fact, surgeons down the ages ... (desperately look for a pain-killer)
e.	Colleague:	Last month scientists announced a new discovery which could cure cancer.
	You:	They ... (work on it for the last ten years)

Exercise 17

Here is a newspaper story which once hit the headlines all over the world. Rewrite the story putting the verbs in parentheses into the correct past tense (past simple or past perfect).

Charlie Chaplin, 20th century's greatest comedian, (die [1]) on Christmas Day 1977 and (bury – passive [2]) two days later in a little cemetery overlooking Lake Geneva in Switzerland. He (spend[3]) twenty-five years in a nearby village, where the comedian (maintain [4]) a mansion. Throughout the world, newspapers (publish[5]) tributes to Chaplin's career both as actor and film director.

And then, in the spring of 1978, while the tributes (continue[6]) to flood in, a quite fantastic story (break[7]). On March 2, press reports (announce [8]) that the body of Sir Charles Chaplin (vanish[9]) overnight from its grave.

The cemetery (be[10]) small and square, surrounded by a low stone wall. It (contain [11]) some 400 tombs mostly belonging to local people and marked by modest headstones and simple wooden crosses.

The Swiss police (institute[12]) a search. Local people (offer[13]) details. One man (say [14]) that shortly after midnight he (hear [15]) a noise like that of a pickaxe from the cemetery.

But who would want to steal the comedian's body? A number of theories (advance – passive [16]) in the days that (follow [17]). Since there apparently (be [18]) no ransom demand, one possibility (be [19]) that the body (take – passive [20]) by a group of fanatical admirers. Frederick Sands, the author, (write [21]) a book about the Chaplins which (say[22]) that the comedian once (express [23]) a wish to be buried in England, the country of his birth. Other theories (concentrate [24]) on the fact that Chaplin (be [25]) Jewish, and one report (allege [26]) that the body (remove – passive [27]) because Chaplin (bury – passive [28]) in a cemetery meant for Christians.

Then, on May 7, (come [29]) the news that the kidnappers (find – passive [30]) and the body recovered. The culprits (turn out [31]) to be two East European motor mechanics who (obtain[32]) political asylum in Switzerland some time earlier. And the motive? It (be [33]) ransom after all.

institute: formally set up ransom demand: demand for ransom; ransom is money that kidnappers ask for in exchange (in this case) for the dead body.

11. 5 The Future Tense

There are two forms of the future in English—**pure** future and **coloured** future. An action or event taking place in the future may be a pure future or a coloured future. A pure future is an action or event that happens because it cannot help happening; there is nothing that we can do to make it happen or to stop it from happening. Look at these examples of the pure future:

I *shall be* seventeen next April.

Tomorrow *will be* a rainy day.

Night *will fall* soon.

The floods *will subside* in a day or two.

Actions or events of this kind which are totally independent of human control are, however, rare. This is because the element of wish, will, intention or obligation is nearly always present in human actions. The purest futures are those that have the least to do with people or persons (as in the examples above) or the kind of future actions which are made to depend on external factors, as in these examples:

I *shall let* you watch a cartoon if you behave yourself.

He *will get* you a tape-recorder when he visits India next.

Exercise 17

Complete the following weather forecasts putting the verbs in parantheses in the pure future.

a. Rainfall ________ (occur) at almost all places in the Andaman and Nicobar islands, at many places in Arunachal Pradesh, Assam, Meghalaya, West Bengal and Sikkim. There ________ (be) heavy rain at one or two places in the Andaman and Nicobar islands, Arunachal Pradesh and Assam during the next twenty-four hours. The western disturbance over Jammu and Kashmir in all probability ________ (move) north-eastwards.

b. There is a depression forming off coastal Andhra. It most probably ________ (move) in a north-easterly direction during the next eighteen hours and ________ (hit) parts of West Bengal and Chittagong in Bangladesh. The weather for the next forty-eight hours ________ (be) wet and stormy. Heavy rain accompanied by gusty winds ________ (occur) in coastal Orissa, parts of West Bengal and Chittagong. The rest of the country ________ (have) dry weather.

A coloured future, unlike a pure future, is an action or event that happens because someone wants it to happen:

We *will go* for a picnic tomorrow. (Why? Because we want to go)

You *will wait* here until I return. (It is my order that you wait here.)

He *shall not go* unpunished. (I'll see to it that he is punished.)

We use the same auxiliary verbs for both forms of the future:

'will'/'shall' followed by the infinitive of the lexical verb without, however, the sign of the infinitive; 'shall go', 'will go'.

'Shall' and 'will' function as tense auxiliaries when they express pure future and as modal auxiliaries when they express coloured future.

'Will' as pure future

'Will' as a sign of the pure future can be used with all persons: first, second, third, singular and plural. You may, if you like, replace it with 'shall' when the subject is 'I' or 'we'.

I/We + shall/will + go to town tomorrow. (positive)

You/He/She/It/They + will + go to town tomorrow. (positive)

I/We + shall not (shan't)/will not (won't) + go to town tomorrow. (negative)

You/He/She/It/They + will not (won't) + go to town tomorrow. (negative)

Exercise 18

Read the following sentences quickly, using the verbs in brackets with 'shall' or 'will' in its pure future form.

a. What the weather (be) like tomorrow?

b. Do you think it (rain) tomorrow?

c. I don't think so. Going by the weather forecast, it (be) dry weather tomorrow.

d. The cold weather (start) in the north soon after the rains are over.

e. Do you think it (get) dark by six in the evening?

f. The Prime Minister (speak) to the nation on television tonight.

g. The men (work) on Sundays if they are paid overtime.

Exercise 19

The following are questions put to you by a stranger to your city. Answer them for him with the help of the suggested cues.

a. How early in the morning will the shops be open? (8 a.m.)

b. Will they be open throughout the day, or will there be a break for lunch? (break for lunch)

c. How long will the lunch break be? (12 to 2 p.m.)

d. Will the shops be open on Sundays? (some of them)

e. Will there be anything interesting to buy? (plenty)

Exercise 20

Just as newspaper headlines use the simple present while reporting recent events, they use the infinitive to report future events or events to come. Thus, the headline:

Smokers to Challenge the New Ban on Smoking in Public Places means: Smokers will challenge in court the new government ban on smoking in public places.

Rewrite the following headlines using 'shall' or 'will' in its pure future form. Use articles where necessary. You may add details of your own to make the message in the headlines clearer. Here is an example to guide you.

Monkeys in Southern Thailand to Go out of Work Following Drop in Coconut Price

Several thousand monkeys in Southern Thailand will go out of work following a drop in the price of coconuts which they had been trained to pick.

a. Man in Ankola to Spend Six Months in Jail for Posing as Policeman
b. Flying Yogi to Face Trial for Trespass of Air Space
c. Cigarettes to be Priced out of Smoker's Reach, Says Govt Official

'Will' as coloured future in statements

'Will' as coloured future (modal 'will', in other words) expresses:

1. determination on the part of the speaker (first person) or a third party (third person):

   I *will choose* the fabrics I want. (meaning 'I won't let others choose them for me')
   She *will not* (*won't*) *be dictated to.*

2. a promise:

   We *will see* you next Monday.
   You *will have* your book tomorrow.

3. an order:

   You *will stay* at home and *do* the washing up.
   All students *will assemble* in the auditorium by 9 a.m.

('Will' as coloured future in questions has already been covered in the section on modals – Chapter 10.)

'Shall' as coloured future in statements

'Shall' as coloured future expresses:

1. determination or a decision on the part of someone to prevent or restrain someone else from doing something:

   You *shan't* ever *drive my car again.* (I'll see to it that you don't.)

   Angry father to daughter: You *shan't* come back home this late at night.

2. a promise:

   You *shall have* your money back tomorrow.

   Father to son: You have made us proud, son. Ask for anything you want and you *shall have* it.

('Shall' as coloured future in questions has already been covered in the section on modals – Chapter 10.)

Exercise 21

Insert 'shall' or 'will' in the following sentences.

a. Mother to son: You ____________ have a bicycle on your next birthday. That's for sure.

b. You ____________ not leave office without my permission.

c. I ____________ do what I please, no matter what you think of it.

d. Our representative ____________ meet you to discuss the terms of the sale next Monday.

e. She ____________ not come to the meeting. I know the reason.

f. Persons without valid passes ____________ not enter the premises. The sentries at the gate ensure that they don't.

g. 'What ____________ our metropolitan cities look like in twenty years' time?'

'They ____________ look like beehives but without the order and cleanliness of beehives.'

'No one can say for certain what they ____________ look like.'

11.5.1 Future Continuous Tense

The future continuous tense has the following forms:

Positive I/We/You/He/She/It/They *will be taking.*

Question *Will* I/we/you/he/she/it/they *be taking*?

Negative I/We/You/He/She/It/They *will not* (*won't*) *be taking.*

The future continuous has no passive form in use.

The future continuous is more of a pure future. We use it to refer to a future event or experience happening as a matter of course without its being intended or planned:

Mr Agarwal *will be retiring* by the end of the month, when he *will be moving* to his home-town, Lucknow.

'So, Ranjit, You're off to Calcutta for the Puja holidays?'

'Yes, Mohan. I'm leaving on the 9 o'clock flight.'

'It's eight o'clock now and I wonder what you *will be doing* at this time tomorrow.'

'I *will* probably *be having* breakfast with my aunt or *will be walking* down Chowringhee Lane.'

'I bet you *will be doing* neither. You *will be sleeping* soundly at this hour tomorrow.'

The future signalled may be the near or immediate future, as in the examples above, or it may be the distant future, as in this example:

I wonder what I *will be doing* ten years from now.

The future signalled may, on the other hand, be very close to the present if the tense is used with an appropriate time-expression:

The walls and ceilings are ready and *soon* the workmen *will be plastering* them.

The procession has just left the town hall. It *will be passing* our house *in ten minutes.*

Compare:

The school is short of space and we *are going to build* another block soon.

The school is short of space and soon we *will be building* another block.

Although the two sentences mean roughly the same, there is a fine difference in emphasis. The first sentence is coloured future, it focusses on the present intentions of the school authorities. The second sentence ignores the intentions and focusses on what is going to happen at a future date, it is more of a pure future.

Exercise 22

Put the following into the future continuous tense.

a. The family is shortly moving to the suburbs.

b. You will hear from us soon. Wait until then.

c. Are you singing us another song?

d. We will go shopping in the afternoon if the weather stays fine.

e. Will you visit us again?

f. After supper we will either go for a stroll or watch television, depending on our mood.

Sometimes we use the future continuous as a roundabout way of making a request:

Will you *be using* your typewriter today?

The question is not an innocent query made out of curiosity or interest, and the person to whom the question is put knows that too. He will say something like this in reply:

No, do you want to borrow it?

Yes, I do.

Sorry, but you can borrow it tomorrow.

Exercise 23

Learn to make indirect requests by asking someone to do something for you. Use the future continuous tense. Here's an example to guide you.

Your colleague is going to the public library in the afternoon.

You: Will you be going to the public library in the afternoon?

Colleague: Yes, do you want me to return your books?

You: Yes, please,. if you don't mind.

a. Your friend is going to town. You want her to get your clothes from the dry cleaner's.

b. Your neighbour has a lawn mower, which you would like to borrow for a day.

c. Your colleague is going to the post office. Ask her to get you a couple of aerogrammes and a dozen inland letters.

Which of these would you say to a departing guest?

1. *Are* you *visiting* us again?
2. *Will* you *visit* us again?
3. *Will* you *be visiting* us again?

The three questions do not mean the same. The first one is a query about the guest's intentions: Do you intend to visit us again? (coloured future) The second one amounts to a request: Do visit us again. We have enjoyed your present visit. (coloured future)

The last question is more of a pure future, it is like asking the guest—Will such a thing as a second visit happen? The speaker is being polite to the departing guest. The question doesn't mean anything much.

11.6 Future Perfect Tense

The future perfect tense has the following forms:

I/We/You/He/She/It/They *will have taken.*

Question *Will* I/we/you/he/she/it/they *have taken*?

Negative I/We/You/He/She/It/They *will not* (*won't*) *have taken.*

Passive Voice I/We/You/He/She/It/They *will not* (*won't*) *have been taken.*

We use the future perfect tense to say that a certain event or action will have happened by or before a certain time in the future:

> Grandpa *will have completed* a century by the end of the year if he is alive.
> If I stop smoking from today, in six months' time I *will have saved* enough money to buy myself a tennis racket.

The future perfect is often used to make predictions:

> Economists say that by the end of the year the rate of inflation *will have come* down by 1 per cent.
>
> According to real estate agents, the prices of houses in the city *will have risen* by a further 10 per cent by the middle of next year.

Exercise 24

Complete the following sentences, using the future perfect tense of the verbs in brackets.

a. If I save Rs 500 a month, in a year's time I ___________ (save)

b. If you walk 5 km every day, in a month of thirty days you ___________ (walk)

c. My car travels 50 km a day on an average. In a year's time it ___________ (travel)

d. Some studies show that an average American spends eight hours a day watching television. In a lifetime spanning sixty years, he ___________ (spend)

Exercise 25

Here are some predictions. Put them in the form of statements, using the future perfect form of the verbs in brackets.

a. World population (increase) by more than ten billion by the year 2005.

b. By the middle of the twenty-first century, India (become) a world power.

c. By 2020 A.D. the world's reserves of non-renewable fuel (dwindle) by one-third.

d. According to demographers, the population of India (peak) by 2030 A.D.

(demographer: one who studies human population in terms of numbers)

Exercise 26

Replace the underlined words in each of the following sentences, using the future perfect tense of the verbs in brackets. The first one is done for you.

a. By the end of next April, you will be out of school. (pass)
Answer: By the end of next April, you will have passed out of school.

b. By the time the ambulance reaches the accident victims to the hospital, quite a few will be dead. (die)

c. By the time I retire from service two years hence, my son will be a qualified doctor. (qualify)

d. The smugglers will be safely across the border before the police catch up with them. (cross)

11.7 Other ways of expressing the future

1. Present Simple Tense

We use the present simple tense with verbs like *come, go, arrive, depart, leave* to express future time. The verbs are usually followed by an expression indicating future time:

The Rajadhani Express *leaves* at 6.45 a.m.

She *leaves* for Mumbai this evening.

A new serial *starts* on television next Saturday.

Verbs used for making short announcements of future events already planned take the simple present tense. These verbs, again, are followed by a future time expression:

Our school *celebrates* its diamond jubilee next month.

The new train timings *come into force* on the 1st of October.

Note that the future signalled by the simple present tense is always the near or immediate future.

Exercise 27

Say whether the verbs in the following sentences refer to the habitual present or the future. Write at the end of the sentence HP for habitual present and F for the future.

a. I wake up at 6 o'clock, brush my teeth and go for a long walk. I get back home usually by 8 o'clock.

b. She arrives tomorrow morning and leaves the same evening for Mumbai.

c. The last plane to Mumbai leaves at 8 p.m. and reaches Mumbai at 9.20 p.m.

d. I catch the first train tomorrow. I have an important appointment to keep at 3 in the afternoon.

e. The Prime Minister leaves on a chartered flight in the morning, spends a few hours surveying the cyclone-devastated areas, and returns to Delhi the same afternoon.

f. I take the 8.10 suburban to reach my place of work. I always take the train rather than the bus.

We use the present simple tense to express the future in dependent clauses: in adverb clauses of condition and adverb clauses of time. Look at these examples:

We *will go* for a picnic if the weather *is* fine.

We *will cancel* the picnic if it *rains*.

Notice that the verb in the main clause has the 'shall'/'will' form while the verb in the dependent clause has the simple present tense form. Both the verbs, the verb in the main clause and the verb in the subordinate clause, refer to the future – the state of the weather for 'tomorrow' is as much a matter for the future as the 'going for the picnic' – but only the verb in the main clause takes the future form in English. Here are some more examples:

I *shall head* straight for home when I *am* through with my work.

The management *will negotiate* with the men as soon as they *return* to work.

Exercise 28

Complete the following sentences using the verbs in brackets in the appropriate tense (present simple or future). The first one is an example.

a. If you (work) to a plan, you (complete) the project in time, nay, ahead of time.

Answer: If you *work* to a plan, you *will complete* the project in time, nay, ahead of time.

b. You (be) late if you (not hurry).

c. I must leave at once. I have had a long day and I'm feeling very tired. I think I (go) straight to bed when I (get) home.

d. The summit party (make) a try for the top if there (be) a break in the weather.

e. I (telephone) you as soon as I (arrive) at New Delhi station.

f. If you (telephone) me as soon as you (arrive) at New Delhi station, I (come) and pick you up.

g. Suresh will surely make it to the top ten this time. I for one (be) very surprised if he (not make) it.

h. Once the monsoon (set) in, the roads in this area (become) impassable.

i. We (wait) until we (hear) from you.

2. Present Continuous Tense

We use the present continuous tense with a future time expression to signal future time:

We *are going* to the concert *tomorrow*.

I *am writing* my finals *next week*.

The present continuous tense usually denotes coloured future. When we use the present continuous tense to signal a future action, we indicate that the action is an intended one and is possibly part of a plan:

My niece *is getting* married next April.

Where *are* they *going* for the holidays?

Note

You can use the present continuous tense to signal future time only with verbs of doing, not verbs of being. Thus, you can say:

Spencers *are opening* a new departmental store in the city;
but not: It *is raining* tomorrow.

With verbs of being, you must use 'shall' or 'will':

It *will rain* tomorrow.

There *will be* no evening classes next week.

The future time expression must be used or understood from the context, only then will the present continuous signal the future. Also, the future signalled need not necessarily be near or immediate, as it is with the simple present tense.

Exercise 29

Put each of the verbs in brackets into the present continuous tense and say whether it signals present or future time.

a. 'What you (do) on Saturday evening?'
'We (have) a party.'

b. The gardener (cut) the grass, he (not water) the plants.

c. I (go) for a swim after I've had a game of tennis.

d. The President (visit) France next May.

e. 'What Kamala (do)?'
'She (cut) vegetables for dinner.'

f. Mr Swaroop will be sixty next month. His children (plan) to celebrate the occasion.

g. The delegation (meet) the minister in three weeks' time.

h. She (see) him next Monday.

3. 'Be going' plus infinitive

One of the most frequently used forms of the future is 'be going' followed by the infinitive of the lexical verb:

She *is going to take up* her new assignment in January.

They *are going to resign* their membership of the club as a group.

Like the present continuous tense, the 'going to' form signals coloured future. But unlike the present continuous tense, the 'going to' form can be used with persons as well as things.

When used with persons, it strongly suggests intention on the part of the person or persons concerned:

They *are going to redo* the kitchen.

I *am going to do* some serious reading during the holidays.

In other places, it may suggest expectation or certainty rather than intention:

I think I *am going to catch* a cold.

Watch out! You *are going to fall* off that stool.

Notice that the expectation or certainty is in the mind of the speaker.

That bus *is going to overturn.*

It *is going to be* a fine day.

There *is going to be* widespread famine in these parts.

Note

The 'going to' form, as well as the present continuous tense form as a signal of the future, is more often used in informal speech than in writing.

Exercise 30

Repeat each of the following sentences, using the 'going to' and the present continuous form of the future. The first one is an example.

a. She has made up her mind. She will get married next April.
Answer: She has made up her mind. She is going to get married next April.
She...mind. She is getting married next April.

b. He will quit his job by the end of the month.

c. When will you write to her?

d. We will go to the zoo tomorrow.

e. I will not visit that place again.

f. Won't you come to my party?

g. They will have a charity show next week in aid of the flood victims.

h. They will arrive in a day or two.
i. We will leave for Delhi tomorrow by the Rajadhani Express.

Exercise 31

Put the verbs in brackets into the 'going to' form with things in the following sentences.

a. Look at those clouds. It (rain).
b. Going by what the weathermen say, it (be) a hot sultry day.
c. I'm sorry for you. It (be) rather hard on you.
d. The winter this year, they say, (be) a severe one.
e. Sugar (cost) us more from next month.
f. Take my word. Those low-cost houses (collapse) next monsoon.
g. Look at those mango blossoms. Most of them (fall) off, only a few will ripen into fruit.
h. That rickety old car (break down) soon.

Notice the difference in meaning between these two sentences:

She is going to get married. (stress on present intentions; coloured future)

She will get married if she finds/can find the right man. (the future action dependent on an external factor introduced by the if-clause; pure future)

Exercise 32

Change the verbs in each of the following sentences from coloured to pure future by adding an 'if-clause' or a 'when-clause'. The first one is an example.

a. He is going abroad for higher studies. (coloured future)

Answer: He will go abroad for higher studies if he finds/can find someone to sponsor him. (pure future)

b. There is going to be a drought in this part of the country.
c. They are leaving by an earlier train.
d. They are going to move into a new apartment.
e. He is going to build himself a house.
f. He is coming to see you tomorrow.

12 Adverbs

Notionally we may define adverbs as words which answer the questions 'when?', 'where?', 'how?', and 'how much?'. We may expand this notional definition and say an **adverb** is a word that indicates, in regard to an action or event, time, place, reason, result, purpose, manner, degree etc.

The 'etc.' includes any other circumstance that may attend on an action or event.

Formally we may define adverbs as words ending with the suffix '-ly':
beautifully lawfully warmly

The suffix, you may notice, is added to descriptive or qualitative adjectives: beautiful – beautifully; lawful – lawfully; warm – warmly

This is not to suggest that all adverbs are marked by the suffix '-ly'. There are a number of adverbs which do not end in '-ly'—adverbs like *here, there, now, then, often, sometimes, always, never,* and so on. Also, there are words ending in '-ly' which function as adjectives only—words like *manly, kingly, portly.*

Granted that all adverbs do not end in '-ly' and that all words ending in '-ly' are not adverbs, the formal definition is still valid. Adverbs like *here, there, now* and *then* have a distribution similar to adverbs ending in '-ly'. We may say, for instance, 'come *quickly*' or 'come *here*', 'send him *urgently*' or 'send him *there*', 'she welcomed us *warmly*' or 'she welcomes us *always*'. In other words, the adverbs (without '-ly') *here, there,* and *always* occur in the same place as the adverbs (with '-ly') *quickly, urgently, warmly;* the one group of words can be replaced by the other group in the sentence.

In the same way, the adjectives ending in '-ly' have a distribution similar to the adjectives like *beautiful, lawful, warm.* We may speak of 'a manly voice' or 'a beautiful voice', 'a kingly reception' or 'a warm reception', 'the portly husband of Tina' or 'the lawful husband of Tina', which just shows that *manly, kingly* and *portly* are not in the same class as *beautifully, lawfully* and *warmly,* despite both the groups being marked by the same '-ly' ending.

Even in the case of words like *early, late, hard, fast, near, straight,* which have the same form, whether they are used as adjectives or as adverbs, the context of occurrence will make it clear whether a given word is an adjective or an adverb. Look at these sentences, for instance, in which the italicised words in column 1 are adjectives and the same words in column 2 are adverbs:

column 1	column 2
He is an *early/late riser.*	He rises *early/late.*
She is a *hard/fast* worker.	She works *hard/fast.*
He is a *near* relation of the minister.	He came *near.*
It was a *straight* fight between two political parties.	She went *straight* to the point.

Most pedagogic grammars, however, define an adverb syntactically.

An adverb is a word that modifies a verb, an adjective or another adverb:

She ran *fast.* (adverb, modifying the verb 'ran')

She was a *very* fast runner. (adverb, modifying the adjective 'fast')

She ran *very* fast. (adverb, modifying the other adverb 'fast')

The above is a useful definition but it does not go far enough. An adverb may modify, apart from verbs, adjectives and other adverbs, phrases, clauses, or even whole sentences:

Phrase: They live *close* to the temple. (adverb, modifying the phrase 'to the temple')
He hit the ball *clear* over the goal-post. (adverb, modifying the phrase 'over the goal-post')

Clause: The police knew *exactly* where the murder weapon had been hidden. (adverb, modifying the clause 'where the murder weapon had been hidden')
The parents told the boy *just* what he needed to know.(adverb, modifying 'what he needed to know')

Sentence: *Fortunately,* I had cancelled my air booking at the last moment.
Never in the annals of human endeavour did so many owe so much to so few.

The adverbs 'fortunately' and 'never' modifying, as they do, whole sentences are sometimes referred to as **sentence adverbs.** We shall return to the subject of sentence adverbs later in the chapter.

None of the three definitions of an adverb – notional, formal, or syntactic – is a complete or comprehensive one. We use one or the other as the circumstances demand. We may, for instance, identify an adverb on the basis of its formal characteristic and then go on to examine its function. We may even use the notional definition, if it helps, by asking whether the given word is an answer to the question 'when?' 'where?' 'how?' or 'how much?'

Many adverbs are related to adjectives both in form and meaning. Adverbs of manner are mostly formed by adding '-ly' to descriptive or qualitative adjectives:

bad – badly clear – clearly fluent – fluently rapid – rapidly slow – slowly

You behaved *badly.* She spoke *clearly/fluently/rapidly.*

However, not all adverbs ending in '-ly' are adverbs of manner. Some are adverbs of degree and some adverbs of frequency:

- adverbs of degree

  The chairman's remarks were *extremely* provocative.

  He trusted his staff *absolutely.*

  She has done *fairly* well in the practicals.

  She was *immensely* proud of her children.

- adverbs of frequency

  They *usually* send us a Christmas card every year.

  We *rarely* go out visiting friends.

  Although I am not a movie addict, I do *occasionally* go and see a movie.

  The power supply was *frequently* interrupted.

Most adverbs formed from adjectives with the addition of '-ly' have the same meaning, or a similar meaning, to the related adjective. A few adverbs ending in '-ly' have, however, a different meaning.

hard – hardly

He came up the *hard* way. (facing many difficulties)

I *hardly* know him. (He is almost a stranger to me.)

late – lately

She is a *late* riser.

She has not been feeling well *lately.* (recently)

present – presently

Mr Johnson, the *present* headmaster of the school, is retiring soon. (headmaster at present)

Wait a while. I have a telephone call to make. I'll join you *presently.* (soon)

(However, in American English, 'presently' is related to 'present' in meaning; it means 'at present'.)

bare – barely

These people live without even the *bare* necessities of life. (the minimum essential)

This room can *barely* accommodate two people. (hardly)

short – shortly

The groom replied to the toast with a *short* speech.

We will *shortly* be moving house. (soon; in a little time)

Some adverbs ending in '-ly' are not formed from adjectives at all, they are formed from nouns:

day – daily	body – bodily	month – monthly
year – yearly	purpose – purposely	week – weekly

12.1 Kinds of Adverbs

Classified on the basis of their meaning, adverbs fall into four groups: adverbs of manner, of place, of time and of degree.

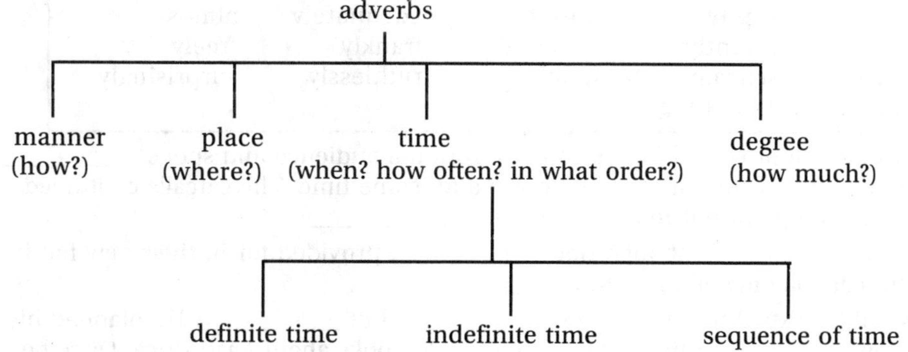

a. Adverbs of manner answer the question 'how?':
He recovered *slowly.* We faced the enemy *boldly.*

b. Adverbs of place answer the question 'where'? or 'in which direction?':

They arrived *here* yesterday. Turn *left* and go *straight* for another two hundred yards, and you'll see on your right the 'Golden Enclave Apartments'.

c. Adverbs of time answer the question 'when?', 'how often?' or 'in what order?':

Definite time:	They came here *yesterday.* He will come *tomorrow.*
Indefinite time:	They were *late* for the concert. My husband *often* helps me with the housework. *Sometimes* I do the work by myself.
Sequence of time:	*First,* we do nouns. *Next,* we do verbs.

d. Adverbs of degree answer the question 'how much?':
He works *too* slowly but his progress is *fairly* satisfactory.

She worked *extremely* hard to come out on top.

Exercise 1

Underline the adverbs in the following sentences and say what kind each one is. The first two are examples.

a. He speaks fluently but not correctly. (adverbs of manner)
b. You are partly right and partly wrong. (adverbs of degree)
c. Work on the project was slow initially but picked up momentum later.
d. I agree with you absolutely.
e. The parents waited anxiously for news of their missing son.
f. Whatever help came, it came voluntarily and it was gratefully accepted.
g. She had to work very hard to achieve what little she did.
h. He seldom comes on time and sometimes he forgets to show up.
i. They met accidentally in London.
j. The buildings were extensively damaged during the cyclonic storm.

Exercise 2

Fill in the blanks with suitable adverbs. Choose the adverbs from this box.

ably	abruptly	absolutely	adequately	almost
amply	differently	eventually	frankly	freely
meticulously	practically	quickly	ruthlessly	surprisingly
thoroughly	unhesitatingly			

a. He refused to be provoked by the catcalls from the audience and spoke ________ coolly hoping the disturbance would cease after some time. The catcalls continued and he had no option but to end his speech ________.

b. They were ________, though not ________, provided for in their new flat but they kept complaining all the time.

c. Stanley led his expedition to East Africa ________ but ________. He planned his expedition ________; he read as many as 130 books about East Africa. Once he set off towards his chosen objective, he advanced ___________ through the bush, shooting down any African tribes that opposed him on the way and _________ reached the objective. He felt, thought, and acted ____________ from the explorers who had preceded him. He was a new man in Africa.

d. The minister answered the questions put to her by the press corps ___________, ____________, and ____________. It looked as though she had prepared herself ____________for the press conference.

e. The party secretary was ____________, though not ____________, certain that the riot was sparked off by one of the political parties opposed to his own. However, the committee set up to inquire into the causes of the riot found ___________ no evidence to support the secretary's assertion.

12.2 Position of Adverbs

The adverb is probably the only part of speech that can take more than one position in a sentence:

initial position: *Often* they went wrong with their calculations.
mid-position: They *often* went wrong with their calculations.
final position: They went wrong with their calculations *often*.

Some adverbs may occupy all three of the possible positions; others only one or two of these positions. The following chart summarises the most usual positions for the different classes of adverbs as well as their less common positions:

type of adverb	most usual position	other possible positions
1. adverbs of manner	final position: The army marched towards its objective *slowly* and *steadily*.	mid-position: The army *slowly* and *steadily* marched towards its objective.
2. adverbs of place	final position: The boys went *home*. Go *left* and then turn *right*.	
3. adverbs of time a. definite time	final position: We sent off all the invitations *yesterday*.	initial position: *Yesterday* we sent off all the invitations.
b. indefinite time (adverbs like 'soon', 'recently')	mid-position: He *recently* changed his job.	initial position: *Recently* he changed his job. final position: He changed his job *recently*.
c. adverbs of frequency	mid-position: His parents *often/ sometimes* helped him with his homework.	initial position: *Often/Sometimes* his parents helped him with his homework. final position: His parents helped him with his homework *often/sometimes*.

	My parents *always/never* help me with my homework. 'Never' is not used in the final position but 'always' sometimes appears in that position:	My parents help me with my homework *always.*
	'Never' is occasionally used in the initial position, with the sentence order reversed:	*Never* do my parents help me with my homework.
d. adverbs of sequence	initial position always: *First,* we do nouns. *Next,* we do verbs.	
4. adverbs of degree	position: just before the word that is being intensified : She sings *extremely* well. The days are *very* warm. I *entirely* agree with you.	final position for only adverbs of degree used with verbs: I agree with you *entirely.* She misunderstood him *wholly.*

Exercise 3

Insert in the following sentences the adverbs given in parentheses. Indicate where more than one position is possible. The first one is done for you.

a. He aimed well but missed the wastepaper basket. (entirely)

Answer: He aimed well but *entirely* missed... / He aimed well but missed ... *entirely.*

b. Look where you are going. You collided with the woman going in the opposite direction. (nearly)

c. We will be sending out all the New Year greeting cards. (tomorrow)

d. Our parents were overprotective towards us. (always)

e. As a little girl I was allowed to go out alone, not even to visit our immediate neighbours. (never)

f. There was someone accompanying us. (always)

g. Even as a college-going girl, I was allowed to go out alone. (seldom)

h. Things have changed for the better. (fortunately, now)

i. My teenage daughter believes me when I tell her of the kind of sheltered life I lived in those days. (hardly)

j. She thinks I am making up although she openly says so. (probably, never)

12.3 Sentence Adverbs

Sentence adverbs are adverbs which modify whole sentences, as we saw earlier:

Fortunately, I had cancelled my air booking at the last minute.

Surprisingly, none of the passengers was hurt, although the car turned turtle.

The adverbs 'fortunately' and 'surprisingly' modify the entire sentence. What was fortunate? The fact that I had cancelled my air booking at the last minute. In fact we may rewrite the above sentences, thus:

It was fortunate that I had cancelled my air booking at the last minute.

It was surprising that none of the passengers was hurt, ... turtle.

We use the sentence adverbs for a variety of communicative purposes. One group of sentence adverbs helps us to indicate our reaction to, and our opinion of, a fact or event, as in the above examples. Here are more examples of the same type of sentence adverbs:

Luckily, there was a doctor on board the flight to attend to the passenger who had collapsed on boarding the aircraft.

Predictably, Mr Clean gave a long lecture on probity in public life.

Coincidentally, Ram and Shyam arrived in London on the same day. One was on his way to Frankfurt, and the other was on his way home from New York.

Some of these sentence adverbs are often followed by 'enough':

Strangely enough, even those who called themselves rationalists were not above watching mythological serials on television.

If you have a job that you want done urgently, give it to a busy person. *Paradoxically enough,* it is the busy person who finds time to do others' jobs as well.

Adverbs like *luckily, unluckily, fortunately, unfortunately, happily, unhappily* are sometimes followed by a prepositional phrase beginning with 'for':

Fortunately for Peter, he didn't have to work for a living.

Luckily for Sheila, the children were very supportive. They did their share of household chores.

Another group of sentence adverbs helps us to offer a comment on what someone did:

Kamala *rightly* refused to sign on the dotted line. (I feel it was right on the part of Kamala to have refused... on the dotted line.)

Rightly or *wrongly,* I agreed to finance his project.

The *New York Herald* and the London *Daily Telegraph generously* helped Stanley with money, without which he could not have launched his East African expedition.

My host very *considerately* put me up in the only airy bedroom in the house. (It was very considerate of my host to have put me up... in the house)

Some sentence adverbs help us to make a statement based on what we have seen, heard, or known:

'How did you come to know what was discussed only at the cabinet level?'

'*Apparently,* there had been a leak.'

The company's offer of unconditional talks was *obviously* a ploy to create a split among the striking workers.

He was *visibly* moved by the laudatory references made to him.

(laudatory: expressing praise or admiration)

Evidently, there was no truth in the rumour.

If, however, we are not sure of what we are saying, we use the adverbs *allegedy, possibly, probably, presumably* or *hopefully*:

Bribes were *allegedly* paid by the contracting firm. (It was alleged that bribes were paid by the contracting firm.)

Could you *possibly* help us out of this crisis?

He is *probably* abroad.

'What's stopping Guru from going abroad? I should think he has got admission in several universities.'

'*Presumably* he has not got a scholarship yet. I'm not sure.' (I presume he has not got a scholarship yet.)

Hopefully, the new measures announced by the Finance Minister will bring down the rate of inflation. (We hope and are fairly confident that the new measures... the rate of inflation.)

(Some say that the use of 'hopefully' in this sense is incorrect but the word is being increasingly used in this sense, purists' objections notwithstanding.)

Exercise 4

Rewrite the following sentences using sentence adverbs. The first one is an example.

a. I don't know whether it was right or wrong on my part to have taken a rigid stand on the question of reservation.
Answer: *Rightly or wrongly*, I took a rigid stand on the question of reservation.

b. It was a head-on collision between a car and a tempo but the passengers in both the vehicles escaped with nothing worse than bruises. It was a miracle.

c. They asked me at the interview to name the bilabial plosives. As luck would have it, I had done a course in phonetics and had no difficulty answering the question.
phonetics: the study of speech sounds

d. My neighbour, who is well over sixty, has the most extraordinary taste in clothes. I think it odd.

e. It is ironic that a country like India known for its cuisine all the world over should go crazy over the Italian pizza.
cuisine: style of cooking

Exercise 5

Choose one of the sentence adverbs in the box and complete each sentence below. Note that the box contains some extra items.

actually	admittedly	curiously enough	interestingly enough
mercifully	mysteriously	officially	rightly
theoretically	typically	unofficially	

a. ____________ the shops are closed between 12 noon and 2 p.m. but ____________ they are open throughout the day.

b. ____________, 'Alice in Wonderland' has been down the years as much a draw with adults as with children.

c. ____________ the man had his share of weaknesses, perhaps more than his share, but he did far more good to the country than any of his predecessors in office.

d. ___________ I was thinking the same thing.
e. The doctors were of the view that the tumour might turn malignant. ___________ it didn't.
f. Chennai, as the city of Madras is now known, is ___________ famed for its beach.
g. ___________ there is no limit to the length of an English sentence but in practice it consists of no more than four of five clauses.

12.4 Other Types of Adverbs

Some adverbs not only modify verbs or sentences but also connect clauses. Some of them have other functions like introducing a question. These adverbs are of three kinds—**interrogative adverbs, relative adverbs,** and **conjunctive adverbs.**

12.4.1 Interrogative Adverbs

Adverbs which are used to ask questions are called **interrogative adverbs**:
a. When did you arrive? (interrogative adverb of time)
b. Where were you hiding all these days? (interrogative adverb of place)
c. Why is he always late? (interrogative adverb of reason)
d. How did he manage to dodge the police? (interrogative adverb of manner)
e. How high is Mount Everest? (interrogative adverb of degree)

Notice that the underlined words in the above examples are adverbs (they modify a verb or an entire predicate) and at the same time introduce a question. Hence they are called interrogative adverbs.

Compare the questions above with the two classes of questions below.

1	2
Who is at the door?	*Whose* pen is this?
Whom do you want?	*Which* tie shall I wear for the party,
Which of these do you like better?	the blue one or the red one?
What is your father?	*What* colour are your socks?

The question words in column 1 above are interrogative pronouns, while those in column 2 are interrogative adjectives. The former function like pronouns (as subject, object of verb, subject complement – See Chapter 4, 4.3.5); the latter function like adjectives, modifying the nouns that follow them (see Chapter 5.1.4).

Exercise 6

Given below are some questions and answers. Supply the missing interrogative adverbs – *when, where, why* or *how* – and then match the questions with the answers.

Questions	Answers
a.________ did no one speak the King's English between 1714 and 1727 in England?	1. in Peru
b.________ are the islets of Langerhans?	2. in the human pancreas

c. ________ did the Red Sea gets its name?	3. because of a type of algae or water plant which gives a reddish tinge to the surface
d. ________ tall was the world's tallest man?	4. 2001 A.D.
e. ________ is the world's highest railway?	5. Robert P. Wadlow, who was 7'5" tall at the age of 22
f. _______ does the third millenium start?	6. because King George I, the then King of England, did not speak English

12.4.2 Relative Adverbs

Relative adverbs are like relative pronouns (See Chapter 4, Section 4.3.8) in that they refer to a noun antecedent in the main clause. At the same time they function like adverbs in the relative clause. Look at the underlined words in the following sentences:

Do you know the time when the Shatabdi Express leaves Bangalore for Chennai?

I still remember the house where I spent my childhood.

This is the main reason why the Indian cricketers fare badly overseas.

'When', 'where' and 'why' in the above examples refer back to their antecedents ('time', 'house', 'reason') just like relative pronouns. They also function like adverbs in that they modify the verbs in the relative clause ('leaves', 'spent', 'fare'). The modification is typically adverbial: time, place, reason.

Relative adverbs modify the verbs in the relative clause, unlike relative pronouns which function like pronouns serving as subject or object in the relative clause. Compare:

a. This is the house *where* I was born. (relative adverb, modifying 'was born')
b. This is the house in *which* I was born. (relative pronoun, object of the preposition 'in')

Both 'where' and 'which' refer to the antecedent 'house' in the main clause and both behave somewhat like subordinate conjunctions connecting the subordinate clause to the main clause. But within the subordinate (i.e., relative) clause, 'where' modifies the verb 'was born', while 'which' functions as object of the preposition 'in'. In other words, 'where' is a relative adverb and 'which' a relative pronoun.

Exercise 7

Say whether the underlined relatives are relative adverbs or relative pronouns.

a. That was the year when Halley's comet appeared.
b. That was the year in which Halley's comet appeared.
c. With all his preoccupations, the Prime Minister never forgot to visit the village in which his old parents lived.
d. I often think fondly of the village where I spent my childhood.
e. No one knows the reason why he gave up a lucrative career and took to living like a monk.
f. This is the spot where Gandhiji fell to an assassin's bullet.

Exercise 8

Supply the missing relative adverb or pronoun in the following sentences.

a. Japan is a country ____________ everybody works hard.

b. There was a reason ____________ an armed sentry was posted at the entrance to the wedding reception.
c. There were days ____________ he had to go without food.
d. Can you suggest a restaurant ____________ we can get good vegetarian food?
e. Can you give me one good reason ____________ I should take you back?
f. It was the time ____________ thousands were thrown out of work following a global recession.

12.4.3 Conjunctive Adverbs

Conjunctive adverbs, as the term itself suggests, are both adverbs and conjunctions at the same time. Look at the underlined words in the following sentences:

a. The surgeon was suddenly taken ill; therefore the operation had to be postponed.
b. He is very able; moreover he works hard.
c. He had no hope of being selected for the post advertised; nevertheless he applied.
d. You have to be ambitious and hard-working; otherwise you will never do well in life.

As conjunctions, the underlined words above connect two main clauses:

main clause 1	main clause 2
The surgeon was suddenly taken ill	the operation had to be postponed
He is very able	he works hard
He had no hope of being selected for the post advertised	he applied
You have to be ambitious and hard working	you will never do well in life

As adverbs, they modify the clauses that come after them or the verbs in those clauses.

We use conjunctive adverbs to express the relationship between two ideas. Ideas may be related together in one of several ways. The relationship may be one of similarity, contrast (or concession), cause and effect, condition and effect, and so on. The following sentences illustrate the ways in which conjunctive adverbs demonstrate the relationship between two ideas.

Similarity

He is very able; *moreover* he works hard.
He is very able; he works hard *besides.*
He is very able; *what is more,* he works hard.
He is incompetent; *what is worse,* he shirks work.

Contrast / concession

The visiting team hardly exerted themselves; *however,* at no point was the result of the match ever in doubt.
She had no reason to hope for a favourable answer from her father; *all the same/just the same* she decided to ask him.
I didn't support the motion; *on the contrary,* I opposed it.

Food in the U.S. is cheap; clothing, *on the other hand*, is more expensive.

Cause and effect

It rained continuously for three days; *consequently/as a consequence/in consequence/ as a result* the dam gave way.

Condition and effect

We must have a good monsoon this year; *otherwise* we would have a drought on our hands.

Tabulated below for easy reference are the commonest conjunctive adverbs, arranged according to the relationship they indicate:

relation between ideas	conjunctive adverb
similarity	moreover; besides; further; furthermore; likewise; also; again; in addition; what is more; what is worse
contrast/concession	however; even so; all the same; just the same; still; on the other hand; on the contrary
cause and effect	consequently; therefore; thus; hence; accordingly; as a result; for this reason; in consequence
condition and effect	or else; otherwise

Note

Some of the items listed in the second column (like 'on the other hand', 'on the contrary') are phrases rather than words. However, it is best to treat them as conjunctive adverbs since they function like them.

Exercise 9

Choose a suitable sentence from column 2 to link with a sentence in column 1. Select an appropriate conjunctive adverb from column 3 to join the two sentences.

column 1	column 2	column 3
a. He took an umbrella with him	The road to the temple is very rough	or else
b. He has taken up jogging	He has given up fatty foods	however
c. He will miss the last bus home	The doctor told Mr Chopra that he should get more exercise	on the contrary
d. It gives greater mileage than the rival brands	The weather was fine and it looked like staying fine	what is more
e. The majority want the monarchy to continue	I have never been in favour of conscription	accordingly
f. He has lost a lot of weight	A vocal minority in Britain is opposed to the monarchy	what is worse
g. It is impassable during the rains	The car is competitively priced	besides
h. I believe conscription has no place in a democracy	He must hurry up	all the same

12.5 Markers of Adverbs

Adverbs are marked by adverbs of degree like 'quite', 'rather', 'too', 'very':

He conducted himself *very* properly at the party.

You are walking *too* fast for me to keep pace with you.

She has done *quite* well in the last sessional exams.

He behaved *rather* childishly at the meeting.

Note

These very same adverbs can also mark adjectives, as we learnt in Chapter 5:

very clever *too* impatient *quite* tall *rather* silly

12.6 Comparison of Adverbs

We may compare adverbs of manner in the same way as we compare descriptive adjectives. Most adverbs of manner are derived from descriptive adjectives:
quick – quickly neat – neatly intelligent – intelligently.

Apart from adverbs of manner, the following adverbs can be compared:

adverbs of time: early late often soon long

adverbs of distance and direction: far near low high close

The rules of comparison for adverbs are the same as for adjectives and are summarised below:

- **Comparing two things to an equal degree**

  X works as hard as Y.

- **Comparing two things to an unequal degree**

  X works harder than Y. Y works less hard than X.
  Y does not work so hard as X. Y does not work as hard as X.

- **Comparing three (X,Y,Z) or more things to an unequal degree**

  X works harder than Y. X works harder than Z. X works the hardest of the three.

  Of all the teachers in our school, Mr Bose wears the most expensively tailored clothes. (adverb, modifying the adjective 'tailored')

  He spoke the least eloquently of all the debaters. (adverb, modifying the verb 'spoke')

Rules for forming the comparative and superlative degrees of comparison

1. short adverbs, mostly of one syllable
   Add '-er' and '-est' to the adverb.

	positive	comparative	superlative
adverbs of manner	hard	harder	hardest
	fast	faster	fastest
adverbs of time	early	earlier	earliest
	late	later	latest
	soon	sooner	soonest
	often	oftener	oftenest
	long	longer	longest

adverbs of distance and direction	high	higher	highest
	low	lower	lowest
	near	nearer	nearest
	close	closer	closest

2. adverbs of manner ending in '-ly'
   Add 'more' and 'most' before the adverb.

beautifully	more beautifully	most beautifully
intelligently	more intelligently	most intelligently
efficiently	more efficiently	most efficiently

3. irregular comparison
   A few short adverbs are compared irregularly.

well	better	best
badly	worse	worst
much	more	most
little	less	least
far	farther/further	farthest/furthest

Exercise 10

Complete the following progress report of Ashok Dhawan with suitable adverbs in the appropriate degree of comparison. Choose the adverbs from this box. You may use an adverb more than once. Use one word for each blank.

atrociously	badly	fast	fluently	hard	regularly	well

The good news about Ashok Dhawan is his reading. He has been attending the speed reading classes __________ __________ __________ before, and he now reads __________ and __________ __________ he did last year. As a matter of fact, he reads __________ __________ in the class, with optimum comprehension. His speaking, strangely enough, has suffered. He doesn't speak __________ __________ __________ before. His writing has improved but only marginally. He needs to work a lot __________ at his writing. As for his spelling, he spells __________ __________ __________ ever. His English teacher keeps wondering how Ashok could read __________ __________ __________ he does and yet spell __________ __________ __________ he does. Maybe there is no necessary correlation between reading and spelling.

Note

1. The following words ending in '-ly' function both as adjectives and as adverbs:
   daily fortnightly hourly monthly quarterly weekly yearly
2. The following words ending in '-ly' function only as adjectives:
   brotherly cowardly deadly elderly fatherly friendly kingly leisurely lively lonely lovely manly motherly portly.

13 Prepositions and Prepositional Phrases

Prepositions are different from other parts of speech like nouns, verbs, adjectives in that they form a small class of words and they have no formal characteristic endings by which they can be identified—words like *in, on, at, to, from, above, below, over, under, near, beside, between* etc. Another distinguishing feature of prepositions is that they signal or announce structures which function as one of the other parts of speech, that is, as adjectives or adverbs. For these reasons, modern grammarians prefer to call them **structure words** rather than parts of speech.

Prepositions are so called because they are 'positioned' **before** nouns or noun phrases ('pre-' means 'before'). The noun/noun phrase is called the object of the preposition or prepositional object. The preposition and the noun/noun phrase following it form an integral part called a **prepositional phrase**:

The watchman is standing *at* the gate.

The nurse is standing *beside* the doctor.

The patient is lying *on* the bed.

The italicised words are the prepositions. Each one of them initiates a phrase, which we call a prepositional phrase (underlined for you).

The function of a preposition is to show the relationship between a noun/noun phrase and some other word, usually a noun/noun phrase, in the sentence:

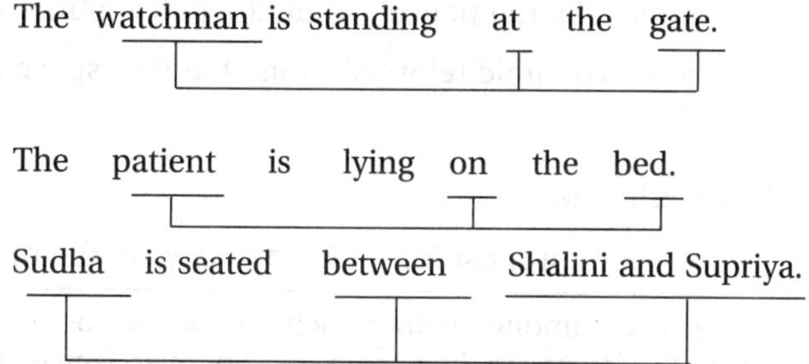

The preposition 'at' indicates the relationship between the watchman and the gate; rather it defines his position in relation to the gate: He is standing at the gate, not near or away from the gate. Similarly, the preposition 'on' relates the patient to the bed, even as the preposition 'between' defines the position of Sudha in relation to Shalini and Supriya.

Notice that the prepositions 'at', 'on' and 'between' signal structures that are adverbial in function. The prepositional phrases 'at the gate', 'on the bed', 'between Shalini and Supriya' are adverbial phrases: they answer the question 'where?' Where is the watchman standing? At the gate.

Prepositional phrases might signal structures that are adjectival in function as well, as in the following examples:

The man at the gate is the watchman. (modifying the noun 'man')

The girls in uniform are nurses under training. (modifying the noun 'girls'; modifying the noun 'nurses')

Prepositions and prepositional phrases are arguably the most difficult single item in English grammar, difficult to learn and difficult to teach. They express a whole complex of meanings, ranging from such simple, easily understood semantic notions as time, place, duration, reason, purpose, means and manner to such abstract, purely structural meanings as those derived from the elements making up a basic sentence pattern. This is because they operate on two levels. On one level the prepositional phrases represent the purely physical arrangement of phrases beginning with a preposition, modifying a headword (noun or verb). On this level they function as modifiers, adjectival or adverbial:

The man at the gate is the watchman. (adjectival, modifying the noun 'man')

The girls in uniform are nurses under training. (adjectival, modifying the headwords 'girls' and 'nurses')

The watchman is standing at the gate. (adverbial, modifying the verb 'is standing')

The road ran between two rows of tall buildings. (adverbial, modifying the headword 'ran')

When they function as adverbial modifiers, they express such relatively simple semantic notions as time, place, direction, reason, purpose, means and manner.

On the other level, the prepositional phrases express a deeper, abstract kind of relationship, the relationship of elements in a basic sentence pattern like N-V(transitive) - N or N-V(intransitive) plus an adverbial:

'Her love for the man' (from 'she loved the man')

'The pursuit of the robbers by the police' (from 'the police pursued the robbers')

'The P.M.'s speech about economic reforms' (from 'the P.M. spoke about economic reforms')

13.1 Types of Prepositions

Most prepositions are one-word prepositions. Listed below are the most commonly used:

about across after against among before behind below beside between despite during down for from in like near of on over since through throughout till to under until up into upon within (the last three made up of two prepositions)

The rest are **phrasal prepositions,** prepositions made up of two or more words. Listed below are the most commonly used of these phrasal prepositions.

Two-word phrasal prepositions:

ahead of because of instead of irrespective of regardless of according to contrary to due to east/west/north/south of owing to next to subject to subsequent to thanks to up to along with together with as for but for apart from away from aside from up against inclusive of exclusive of

Phrasal prepositions consisting of three or more words:

by dint of	by force of	by means of	by virtue of	by reason of	by way of
at the cost of	at the expense of	at the risk of	at the hands of	at the end of	
at the head of	with a view to	with the exception of	for fear/lack/want of		
on account/behalf/pain of	on the face/part/occasion/verge of	in accordance with			
in front of	in spite of	in the course of	in the event of	in the face of	
in the name of	in the process of	in the middle of	in the light of		

We have in addition a few **participle prepositions** like *concerning, considering, during, excepting, including, excluding, notwithstanding, regarding, pending.*

Prepositions and prepositional phrases, as was said earlier, operate on two levels and express a great number of meanings, from the simpler to the more complex. We begin with the simpler meanings.

13.1.1 Position Prepositions

We use the position prepositions to indicate the place, or locate the position, where someone or something is.

at	aboard	above	among	below	behind	beside
between	in	in front of	inside	near	next to	on
outside	opposite	over	round	through	under	underneath

Note that the preposition 'aboard' is used only with a noun referring to a form of transport, such as 'ship', 'plane', 'train', 'bus' etc.

They boarded the bus and sat *on* the top deck.

A storm *at* sea is a most frightening experience.

The restaurant is *above* the supermarket.

The minister is wearing a bullet-proof vest *under* his shirt.

The plane is flying *over* the mountain.

She sat *next to* the Prime Minister *in* the V.I.P. enclosure.

13.1.2 Prepositions Expressing Movement and Direction

We use these prepositions to indicate the place someone or something is moving towards, or the direction that someone or something is moving in.

across	along	from-to	into-out of	
past	round	through	towards-away from	up-down

The children kept climbing *up* the stairs and coming *down* the stairs.

She went *to* the mall to do her weekend shopping.

From the mall she went *to* the zoo.

The cadets ran *round* the parade ground.

A river ran *through* the city dividing it into two halves.

Exercise 1

Complete the following sentences with suitable prepositions, choosing them from the box. Some of the prepositions may have to be used more than once.

across	away from	behind	from	into	in	next to	out of
outside	on	over	opposite to	towards	under		

a. Can you tell me the way ___________ the MIT Housing Colony? They said it is ___________ the bus station.

b. Rosie and her friend sat way back ___________ the twelfth row, far ___________ the front of the stage. What was worse, the petite Rosie had to sit ___________ a man so huge that she could hardly see the stage.

c. You see the multi-storied building right ___________ the road? Your friend lives there, ___________ a two-bedroom flat ___________ the third floor.

d. 'The lady sitting _________ the cubicle is the secretary to the manager.'

'Where's the cubicle?'

'Just six feet _________the manager's cabin, _________ there.'

e. He thought the library book was lost but he found it _________ the pillow.

f. 'Who is the gentleman that keeps getting _________, and _________, the minister's chamber?'

'That is his private secretary.'

g. You see the man going _________ the restaurant _________ the supermarket? That's my cousin. And the man there standing _________ a queue _________ the cinema? That's his brother. One is a gourmet, the other is a movie addict.

Exercise 2

Use the nouns/noun phrases in the box to complete these sentences.

class	corner	door	end	head	house	office	row	trouser-pocket	years

a. There, in his _________, was the ring he had been looking for the whole day.

b. They live in a single-storied _________ standing at the _________ of the road.

c. There's someone knocking at the _________. Is it the postman?

d. The boy sitting in the last _________ seems uninterested in what is happening in the_________ but at the _________of the lesson he is the one who asks the most intelligent questions.

e. I was standing at the _________ of the queue, so I had no problem getting my reservation done.

f. He has been working in this _________ for the last twenty _________ and he has never taken a day off.

13.1.3 Time Prepositions

Time prepositions are used to indicate time. The time indicated could be one point of time or extended time.

at	during	for	from-to	in	on	since	till	until

1. *one point of time* (at, in, on)

   She arrived *at* 4 o'clock. (at + an hour of the day)

   They left *at* noon/night/midnight. (at + a part of the day)

   I shall see you *on* Sunday. (on + a day of the week)

   He was born *on* the 21st of November. (on + a day of the month)

   We met *in* July. (in + a month)

   They met *in* 1994. (in + a year)

   The two chief ministers met *in* the morning/afternoon/evening. (in + a part of the day)

2. *extended time* (for, from-to, since, during, till, until)

   He has been ill *for* several weeks/a long time.

   We waited *for* an hour. (for + an expression indicating a quantity of time)

   It rained *from* six o'clock *to* half past eight.

   He has been ill *since* last week. (from last week to now)

   I have not been abroad *since* 1990. (from 1990 to now)

   Prices of vegetables go up *during* the summer.

   The minister cannot see you *till/until* Monday next.

13.1.4 Prepositions Expressing Other Adverbial Relationships

1. *reason/purpose*

   They went to the baker's *for* a loaf of bread. (for buying a loaf)
   He went to the chemist's *for* cough syrup.
   He was dismissed *for* incompetence.

2. *means*

   Most textiles are made *by* machines.
   You can get there *by* bus or *by* train.

3. *concession*

   Despite his illness, the minister spoke for an hour.
   Notwithstanding the erratic monsoon, we had a good harvest.

'Despite' and 'notwithstanding' are normally found in formal usage.

4. *comparison*

   The men accepted her *as* an equal.
   He looks pleased, *like* a cat that has got the cream.

5. *in the capacity of*

   As a teacher, he was enormously popular; *as* a headmaster, much less so.
   An infinitive phrase can sometimes function *as* a noun.

6. *source*

   We get butter *from* milk.

7. *manner*

   She does whatever she is asked to do *with* skill and enthusiasm.
   He spoke *in* an offensive way.
   With a defiant look, she said 'no' to her employer.

Exercise 3

Fill the blank spaces in the following passage with appropriate time and position prepositions. The first three spaces have been completed as examples.

Late *in* the morning of May 29, 1953, two mountaineers, named Edmund Hillary and Tenzing Norgay, stood *for* fifteen minutes *on* the summit of Mount Everest. They did what all climbers do when they have reached their goal: shook hands, took pictures, looked at the view, and started to come down. For Tenzing, in particular, it was a new world, a world he had never known. He went ________ the mountain as a simple man, but came ________ it a hero.

Tenzing was probably born ________ the year 1914. He was born a Sherpa. The Sherpas are a people, a tribe. Their ancestors belonged to Tibet. ________ Tibet they came south, many years ago, and settled ________ their present-day homeland, Solo Khumbu, ________ north-eastern Nepal.

Life ________ Solo Khumbu was very hard and many were forced to move out in search of a living. ________ years Sherpas had gone ________ Solo Khumbu ________ Darjeeling ________ India, where they worked ________ the tea plantations or as porters. Then, ________ the nineteen twenties, expeditions ________ Mount Everest came to be organized, and many Sherpas, both ________ Darjeeling and Solo Khumbu, were engaged as porters.

None of Tenzing's own family went on these early Everest expeditions. Tenzing himself was too young to go. ________ some years, word went round that there was to be another expedition ________ Everest. Tenzing wanted to go with it and he left home ________ Darjeeling. That was ________ the year 1932 and Tenzing was eighteen then.

________ the next twenty years Tenzing was a porter and a mountain man, living ________ most of the time ________ Darjeeling, which became his home.

Tenzing's very first expedition ________ Everest was ________ 1935. ________ the next seventeen years, he went with five other expeditions. Quite early on he made his mark as a climber. He won the Tiger Medal ________ 1938 for going up ________ a height of 8242 m. (The Tiger Medal is an award given to all sherpas with an outstanding climbing record.) Then ________ the spring of 1952, he along with Lambert, climbed ________ a height of 8560 m, setting up a new world record in Himalayan climbing. ________ 1953, with such outstanding achievement behind him, all that was left for Tenzing to do was to get ________ the top, which he did with Hillary.

Exercise 4

Complete the following passage with appropriate prepositions of time.

The Indian Museum, Calcutta, is the oldest in India. It was opened ___________ 1879. Specimens of Indian art ___________ the second century B.C. ___________ the fifth century A.D. can be seen here. The Geological Section is considered to be the largest in the world. The Museum is open daily ___________ 10 a.m.___________ 5 p.m. ___________ nine months of the year (___________ March___________ November) and ___________ 10 a.m.___________ 4.30 p.m.___________ three months (___________ December ___________ February). Admission is free___________ Fridays. The Museum has drawn thousands of people ___________ the year of its opening.

13.1.5 Phrasal Prepositions

Phrasal prepositions (prepositions consisting of two or more words) like *because of, owing to, on account of, as a result of, in the event of, in spite of* etc express a wide range of relationships but most of them are purely adverbial—like reason, result, concession, condition, purpose etc. Consider these phrases, for example:

prepositional phrase	meaning/ relationship	illustrative example
because of owing to on account of as a result of	reason/result	Because of/On account of his arrogance and high-handed manner, he became most unpopular with the staff. Whole villages were cut off from the rest of the country owing to heavy floods. As a result of the pointsman's mistake, the train was derailed.
for want of for lack of	negative reason	The army lost the battle for want of/for lack of timely supplies.

Because the prepositional phrases in the above examples function as adverb phrases, they may be replaced by adverb clauses:

prepositional phrase	equivalent adverb clause
because of his arrogance and high-handed manner	because he was arrogant and high-handed in manner
owing to heavy floods	because they were heavily flooded
for want of timely supplies	because it did not receive timely supplies
as a result of the pointsman's mistake	because the pointsman made a mistake

Since reason is usually followed by result, the above prepositional phrases in effect express a reason-and-result relationship:

reason	result
because of his arrogance and high-handed manner	he became most unpopular with the staff
owing to heavy floods	whole villages were cut off
for want of timely supplies	the army lost the battle
as a result of the pointsman's mistake	the train was derailed

Exercise 5

Listed below, side by side, are some of the things happening today and their causes. Match each happening with its cause using appropriate prepositional phrases. The first one is done for you.

a. Parts of Asia and Africa are periodically afflicted with drought/widespread destruction of rain forests

Ans: Parts of Asia and Africa are periodically afflicted with drought because of/on account of widespread destruction of rain forests.

b. Our environment is being increasingly polluted/large-scale use of pesticides

c. Our cities suffer from an acute shortage of housing/large-scale migration from villages

d. Millions of villagers suffer from all manner of illnesses/no hospitals or doctors

e. The air in our metropolitan cities is highly polluted/the burning of fossil fuels like coal and oil

Here are some more phrasal prepositions of the same kind:

prepositional phrase	meaning/ relationship	illustrative example
a. in spite of regardless of	concession	He succeeded in life in spite of his physical disabilities. They went ahead with their plan regardless of warnings by friends.
b. in case of in the event of (formal)	condition	In case of rain we will cancel the picnic. In the event of the Prime Minister's ill health his deputy will take his place.
c. but for	negative condition	But for your help, I would never have gone to college.
d. for the purpose of	purpose	He is saving his pocket money for the purpose of buying himself a pocket calculator.

The prepositional phrases in the last column may be replaced by appropriate adverb clauses:

prepositional phrase	equivalent adverb clause
in spite of his physical disabilities	although he was physically disabled (clause of concession)
regardless of warnings by friends	though friends warned them against going ahead (clause of concession)
in case of rain	if it rains (clause of condition)
in the event of the Prime Minister's ill health	if the Prime Minister falls ill (clause of condition)
but for your help	if you had not helped me (clause of condition)
for the purpose of buying himself a pocket calculator	so that he may buy himself a pocket calculator (clause of purpose)

Exercise 6

Write a sentence joining each set of items below by means of appropriate phrasal prepositions. The first one is an example.

a. A rash man acts/with no thought given to the consequences of his actions
Ans: A rash man acts regardless of the consequences of his actions.
b. The people adored their leader/his many faults and weaknesses
c. Keep a stock of candles/electrical failure
d. There would have been a serious water shortage/timely rains
e. President's rule would be imposed on the state/constitutional breakdown
f. The Chief Minister made an aerial survey of the flood-affected areas/assess the damage caused

Many other phrasal prepositions like: *according to, at the hands of, contrary to, thanks to, apart from, by dint of, by virtue of, by way of, on the occasion of, in accordance with, in return for, in the course of* introduce structures that are plainly adverbial in function:

Contrary to the expectations of his supporters, the man never rose to anything beyond the rank of a junior minister. (concession)

Thanks to Alexander Fleming's discovery of penicillin, millions of lives have been saved since. (reason)

Apart from getting an A in botany, he never did anything much in his final year at school. (concession)

She started life with no advantage whatever but by dint of hard work she rose to the very top. (means)

By virtue of his political connections, the young man managed to get himself out of trouble. (means)

The court awarded him a handsome amount by way of compensation for the loss of reputation he had suffered at the hands of his opponents. (purpose; source)

In the course of the discussion on national security, many interesting suggestions came up. (duration)

The family organised a big party on the occasion of the father's sixtieth birthday. (time)

The man was cremated in accordance with his last wishes. (manner)

Exercise 7

Complete the following sentences with one of these phrasal prepositions.

ahead of	along with	at the risk of	in the face of
in the light of	on pain of	with the exception of	

a. The community leaders told her not to cross the seas and that she would be excommunicated if she did. They told her that she would cross the seas only_______________ excommunication.

b. She went all the same to the United States to study medicine even _______________ being excommunicated on her return to India.

c. Luckily her fears proved unfounded. On her return she was hailed for her pioneering achievement by her countrymen _______________ a few diehard conservatives.

d. She married outside her religion _______________ stiff opposition from her family and friends.

e. Every parent does what he thinks best for his children _______________ of his own knowledge and experience.

f. The bill was no doubt flawed but on the whole a much needed one and the Opposition committed a big blunder by voting against it and defeating it. It was like throwing the baby out _______________ the bath water.

g. Those who think _______________their contemporaries run the risk of martyrdom.

13.2 Structural Meanings

We now turn to the other level on which prepositions and prepositional phrases operate, where they express a structural, abstract kind of relationship, the relationships of elements in a basic sentence pattern like N-V(transitive)-N or N-V(intransitive) plus an adverbial. Prepositional phrases of this kind occur in noun phrases of which they are a part, as shown below:

noun phrase	prepositional phrase	original basic sentence pattern from which the noun phrase is derived
her love for the man	for the man	She loved the man (N-V-N)
the pursuit of the robbers by the police	of the robbers by the police	The police pursued the robbers (N-V-N)
the Prime Minister's speech about economic reforms	about economic reforms	The Prime Minister spoke about economic reforms (N-V(intrans.) + adverbial)

Notice that the noun phrase is headed by a noun derived from the verb in the original sentence, either an abstract noun ('love' from 'loved', 'pursuit' from 'pursued', 'speech' from 'spoke', as in the above examples) or a gerund, as in the following example:

Dr Barnardo's giving up of a career in medicine for the sake of the homeless of London (from 'Dr Barnardo gave up a career in medicine...' (N-V-N)

Exercise 8

Add a suitable second sentence to the first, the second sentence beginning with a noun phrase derived from the first. The first two exercises are examples.

a. I admire the doctor. However, my admiration for the doctor does not blind me to his shortcomings as a person.

b. She disagreed with her father. Her disagreement with her father was to cost her dearly, as she soon found out.

c. The President in his speech touched upon a number of current issues. ___________

d. The police recovered the car from the thieves. ___________

e. The Prime Minister differed from the party president in nearly all matters of national importance. ___________

f. The editorial fully covered all aspects of the topic. ___________

g. The man apologised to the lady again and again. ___________

13.3 Position of Prepositions

The preposition usually occurs before a noun or noun phrase, the noun or noun phrase functioning as its object:

The boy crawled under the fence to enter the garden. ('fence', noun, object of the preposition 'under')

He stood up for his friend. ('his friend', object of 'for')

However, it is possible to end a clause with a preposition, especially in informal usage:

Houses are meant to live in, not to look on.

He cannot be saved. He is past caring for.

Which book are you talking about? (instead of 'About which book are you talking?')

No one knows which country he has fled to.

In contact relative clauses, the preposition always comes at the end of the clause:

He spoke all the time nostalgically about the house he had lived in.

The man you are looking for is on long leave.

Some phrases too end with a preposition:

This is not a matter worth thinking of or worrying about.

Note that the underlined phrases are like elliptical relative clauses of the defining kind:

This is not a matter that is worth thinking of or (that is) worth worrying about.

13.3.1 Position of Prepositional Phrases

The position of the prepositional phrase depends on its function, whether it functions as an adverbial or adjectival modifier.

Prepositional phrases functioning as adverbial modifiers are most commonly used after verbs:

The family lives in Lucknow.

They moved to Lucknow from Delhi in 1995.

Sometimes, the phrases are moved to the front of the sentence for the sake of emphasis:

At home, in the heart of the monarchy, there was peace during the rule of the Incas.

On the border of the kingdom, however, there was war.

Notice the inversion of subject–predicate in the above examples. It happens when the verb used is a linking verb (as in the above examples) or an intransitive verb, as in the following example:

On the floor lay a wide assortment of toys.

Some prepositional phrases functioning as adverbial modifiers may take one of three positions: initial, middle or final–

In view of the precarious balance of payments, the government decided on a number of austerity measures.

The government, in view of the precarious balance of payments, decided on a number of austerity measures.

The government decided on a number of austerity measures in view of the precarious balance of payments.

Not all prepositional phrases functioning as adverbial modifiers can take all the three positions.

As for the prepositional phrases functioning as adjectival modifiers, they follow the noun head:

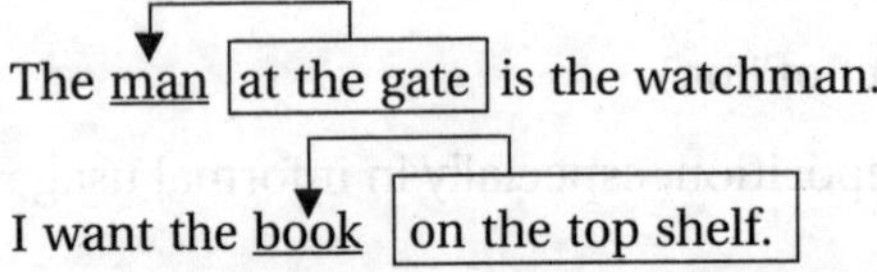

There may be more than one prepositional phrase modifying the same noun head:

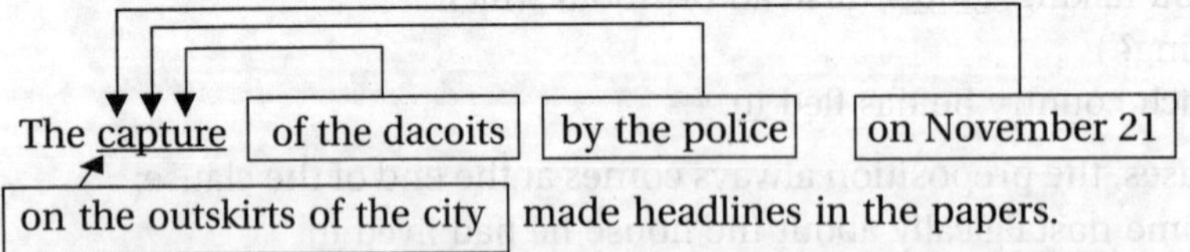

Note that each of the prepositional phrases in the above example modifies the same noun head, 'capture'. On the other hand, there may be a succession of prepositional phrases *modifying the noun in the preceding prepositional phrase*:

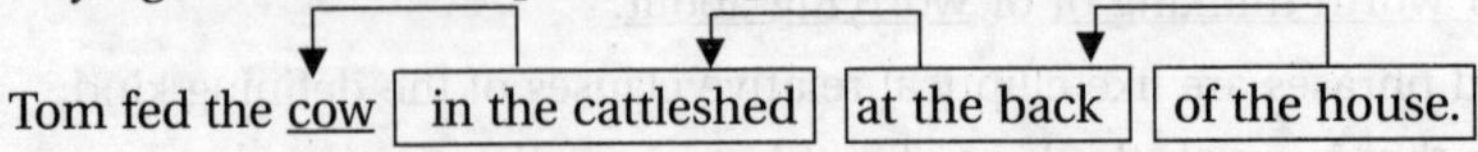

The phrase 'in the cattleshed' modifies 'cow', 'at the back' modifies 'cattledshed', and 'of the house' modifies 'back'.

There may be a third way of arranging a succession of prepositional phrases, some modifying the same noun head and some modifying the noun head in the preceding phrase:

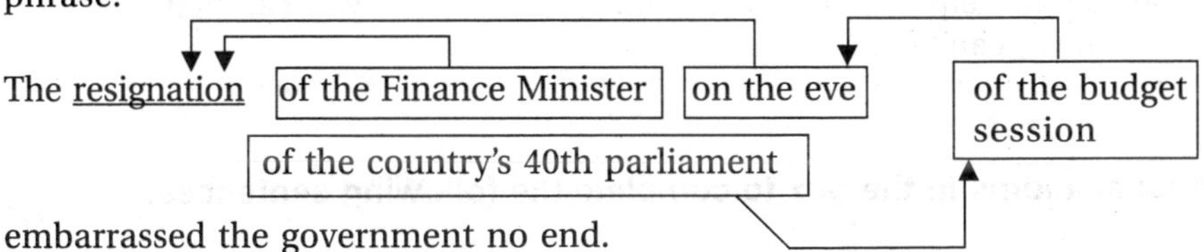

embarrassed the government no end.

13.4 Prepositional Idioms

Prepositional idioms are prepositional phrases of a distinct kind. These phrases are made up of single prepositions followed by nouns or noun phrases with which they are closely linked. They are so closely linked that they form *an indivisible unit.* Look at the underlined prepositional phrases in the following sentences:

The men were never at leisure. They were always at work.

Their children, however, were lucky, for most of the time they were at play.

The phrases 'at leisure', 'at work', 'at play' must be used as they are. We cannot change them. We cannot, for instance, say 'at the work' or 'at their work' or 'at some work'. That is why they are called prepositional idioms. Compare the underlined prepositional phrases in these two sentences:

The men were at work.

The men were at the gate.

We may, if we like, change 'at the gate' to 'at the prison gate', 'at a barred gate', 'at a little gate in the hedge', 'at the gate of an old building', and so on. But you cannot take such liberties with the phrase 'at work'.

The following exercises call for the use of some of the most commonly used prepositional idioms, arranged according to the prepositions that begin them.

Exercise 9

Complete these sentences, using the prepositional idioms in the box.

at

at best (taking the most hopeful view)	at first	at hand	at last
at least	at peace	at present (now)	at times (occasionally)
at war	at worst (taking the most unfavourable view)		

a. ____________ he made a fuss, saying that he would have nothing to do with any political office but____________ he agreed to be nominated for the post of party president.

b. She is not a film buff or movie addict but she does go to the movies____________.

c. One of the passengers collapsed soon after boarding the aircraft but luckily a doctor was____________to attend to him.

d. The two countries which have been traditionally ____________ suddenly found themselves ____________. It all began with a wordy quarrel over a disputed penalty in a match between the two countries' football teams.

e. Most people call him a fool. I wouldn't go as far as that. I would call him simple-minded ____________.

f. You may not be able to help us with money but ____________ you can help by working as a volunteer, can't you?

Exercise 10

Use the prepositional idioms in the box to complete the following sentences.

by

by accident/chance	by habit	by heart	by letter/telephone	
by mistake	by name	by no means	by oneself	by sight

a. The two Prime Ministers met____________. The meeting was accidental and not pre-planned.

b. You want to know who these people are, do you? I'm afraid I can't help you. Most of them I know ____________. Those whom I know____________, I cannot name; the few whom I know____________, I cannot introduce to you.

c. True he paid the wrong man but he didn't do it deliberately. It was done ____________.

d. Sometime ago he moved into a new flat but____________he went to his old flat yesterday as he was returning from work.

e. Do write to tell me what you have decided. You may inform me____________or ____________. You have my address already and here's the telephone number.

f. Your performance during the semester has____________ been satisfactory.

g. She did it all____________. She couldn't count on anyone for help.

Exercise 11

Fill in the blanks with the prepositional idioms in the box.

in

in hospital/bed/prison/jail	in trouble/danger/debt/difficulty				
in all ('as the total')	in general ('in most cases')	in the air ('spreading about')			
in theory/practice	in fact	in point of fact	in fun	in earnest	in private / in public

a. If I had to choose between hospital and prison, I would rather be ____________than ____________.

b. 'He said he was going to run around Connaught Circus ten times on New Year's Day.'
'He must have been joking. He must have said it ____________.'
'No, he was ____________.'

c. Don't believe what he says ____________. He often holds a different view ____________.

d. Your idea sounds all right____________ but I am not sure it will work ____________.

e. 'Kamal seems to be____________.'
'What kind of trouble is he in?'
'He seems to have borrowed large sums of money.'
'You mean he is ____________?'
'Yes, what's more, he is ____________ of being sent to prison if he doesn't pay up.'
'How did he get so heavily into debt?'

'No one knows for certain but there are all sorts of rumours ___________.'

f. 'I think men ___________ are rather vain and boastful.'

'You think so? I don't agree with you there.'

'You think that men ___________ are humble and modest?'

'No, I don't. I think all generalisations are untrue.___________ they are.'

'Including this one of yours, I suppose.'

Here are some more prepositional idioms beginning with 'in'.

in time/in no time/in good time/in the nick of time in tears/pain/love/suspense in short in the long run ('ultimately') in other words

Exercise 12

Use the prepositional idioms in the box and complete the following sentences.

on

on duty/business/holiday/tour on time/the minute ('punctually') on the radio/ air/telephone on television on loan/sale/fire on purpose ('deliberately') on an average

a. The Prime Minister will be addressing the nation today. He will be___________ at 8 p.m. An hour later, he will appear ___________.

b. The outpatient department of this hospital treats ___________ three hundred people a day.

c. 'What brings you here? Are you___________ or ___________?'

'Neither business nor holiday. I'm here in my official capacity as the Collector of the district. I am, in other words, ___________.'

d. I cannot forgive him, he wronged me___________.

e. 'Have you got John Wyndham's *The Kraken Wakes*?'

'We have the book but it is not on the shelf right now. It is ___________. You may borrow it in a week's time.'

Exercise 13

Choose a prepositional idiom from the box to replace the underlined word/words in each of the following sentences. Make any other changes that may be necessary.

out of

out of date/sight/danger/work/control/hand/ reach/stock/order/luck/breath/fashion/print

a. These men have been <u>unemployed</u> for months.

b. He was critically ill but now his illness has taken a turn for the better and <u>his life is in no danger</u>.

c. The crowd broke through the police cordon and went on a rampage and soon the situation <u>became unmanageable</u>.

d. 'May I use your telephone?'

'Sorry. It is <u>not in working order</u>.'

e. 'The book you are looking for is not available with us. You may not get it anywhere else either. I'm afraid no printed copies of the book are available with the publishers.'

Exercise 14

Complete these sentences with prepositional idioms, choosing them from the box.

under	
under age/arrest/control/repair/discussion/pressure	under someone

a. According to the police, the situation is tense but ________.

b. Most of what you said was irrelevant. It had nothing to do with the topic________.

c. She is in charge of the department. She has as many as two hundred people working ________.

d. The fact that he gave his consent should not be held against him because the consent was given ________.

e. We haven't gone out for a fairly long time. The family car is ________ and the repair work has been held up for want of some spares.

f. You can't get a driving licence because you are________.

Prepositional idioms are different from phrasal prepositions. Phrasal prepositions, as we saw earlier, consist of two or more words. Two-word prepositional phrases are made up of an adverb plus preposition ('ahead of', 'away from', 'together with'), or a participle plus preposition ('owing to', 'according to'), or an adjective plus preposition ('due to', 'subsequent to', 'inclusive of'), or, very rarely, a noun plus preposition ('east of', 'thanks to', 'south of'). As for the multi-word phrasal prepositions, they begin and end with a single preposition ('at the risk of', 'for want of', 'in spite of', 'with a view to') so that they have in effect two prepositional objects, as shown below:

at the risk/of one's life ('risk' object of the preposition 'at'; 'life', object of the preposition 'of')
with a view/to integration ('view', object of 'with'; 'integration', object of 'to').

Prepositional idioms, on the other hand, begin with a single preposition followed by a noun or noun phrase. The table given below will help us to distinguish between the three kinds of prepositional groups:

phrasal prepositions		**prepositional idioms**	**phrasal verbs**
a. two-word	**b. multi-word**		
contrary to	by dint of	at first	come by
instead of	on account of	at best	carry out
according to	for fear of	by sight	look upon
subject to	in accordance with	in debt	look down upon
along with	on the part of	in fun/earnest	put down
apart from	in front of	under arrest	set off
inclusive of	in the course of	off duty	take to

Finally, we need to consider an aspect of prepositions and prepositional phrases, which has more to do with lexis than with grammar.

Certain adjectives and certain verbs choose their own prepositions, which in turn choose their own prepositional objects. Thus, the adjective 'immune' takes the prepositions 'from', 'to' or 'against', followed by a prepositional object like 'attack', 'prosecution' etc:

> A person who has suffered from chickenpox once is believed to be immune from/to/against a second attack.
>
> The police told one of the accused that he would be immune from prosecution if he turned approver.

In the same way, the verb 'connive', meaning 'to work together secretly for some wrong or illegal purpose', is followed by the preposition 'with' or 'at', depending on the prepositional object that follows:

> The invigilators were alleged to have connived with the examinees at mass copying.

Listed below are the most commonly used adjectives, arranged alphabetically, along with the prepositions that go with them. Note that some of these adjectives can be used only predicatively, as shown by the abbreviation 'pred' in parentheses.

A–B

abreast of (pred.) absent from (pred.) acceptable/unacceptable to adequate/inadequate for adjacent to afraid of (pred.) amenable to (pred.) angry with someone/at something anxious for (meaning 'eager') anxious about (in the sense of 'worried') applicable/inapplicable to appropriate/inappropriate for an occasion attentive to averse to/from (pred.) aware/unaware of (pred) boastful of bound for a destination (pred.) beneficial to

> Even when he was in his late seventies, he kept himself abreast of political developments at home and abroad.
>
> We will not accept these conditions, these conditions are totally unacceptable to us.
>
> They had adequate funds for the journey.
>
> The workmen they had hired were adequate for the purpose.
>
> The two countries were anxious for starting a new era of good-neighbourly relations. (eager to start)
>
> Having had no news of their son, the parents were naturally anxious about his health and his whereabouts.
>
> Although not a gambler, he was not averse to having an occasional flutter.
>
> He is terribly averse to door-to-door salesmen, so averse that he put up a board on the gate forbidding their entry into the house.
>
> They boarded a flight bound for London.

C–D

capable/incapable of careful/careless of certain/unncertain of (pred.) characteristic of (pred.) comparable to/with (pred.) compatible with complete with conducive to (pred.) conscious/unconscious of consistent/inconsistent with content with (pred.) contented/discontented with critical/uncritical of deficient in dependent on desirous of (pred.) deserving/undeserving of detrimental to (pred.) devoid of (pred.) different from distinct from

She is old enough to look after herself. She is quite capable of looking after herself.

These men are hardy and capable of long hours of work.

The school provides a system of education which very few parents can afford for their children but it is comparable to the best that money can buy anywhere in the world.

The job carries a salary which is good by Indian standards but hardly comparable with what one can earn abroad.

If you are looking for blood for the purpose of transfusion, you must make sure that the donor's blood is compatible with the patient's.

In its manifesto the party pledged to achieve as fast a rate of growth as was consistent with the preservation of the environment.

You may call his life dull but he is content with it. (happy or satisfied)

Not content with confiscating Shylock's property, the court of justice in Venice forced him to become a Christian.

He is contented with his lot. (quite happy with his lot and doesn't want to change it)

Deficient in fossil fuel, the country imports large quantities of oil and natural gas.

The country is heavily dependent on oil imports.

Noise in excess of 120 decibel level is detrimental to health.

The Asian elephant is quite distinct from the African elephant.

E–G

eager for efficient in eligible for envious of essential for expert in/at/on faithful/unfaithful to familiar/unfamiliar with fatal to fearful/fearless of fit/unfit for fond of forgetful of free from friendly/unfriendly with full of generous to gentle with glad of/about (pred.) good at a skill good for a purpose grateful/ungrateful for guilty of

Life cannot be entirely painless. A certain amount of pain is necessary, nay, essential for human survival.

Fighter pilots have to be expert at making split-second decisions.

He may be an expert in financial matters but he can go wrong with his predictions.

'Expert' may be followed by 'on' when the prepositional object is the name of a subject or discipline:

She is an expert on tantric art/Eastern mysticism/Elizabethan drama.

Having passed your final exams, you now are eligible for practising accountancy.

I must admit I am rather fond of Bengali sweets.

She was generous to friends and foes alike.

I am glad about your new job, it is more in line with your qualifications.

He was glad of a chance to make amends for his past mistakes.

That he is gentle with animals is no guarantee that he will be equally gentle with his fellow-humans.

I would gladly plead guilty of cheating him if that would save you from prison.

He is grateful for favours received.

H–N

heedful/heedless of homesick for hopeful of hostile to identical to/with ignorant of illustrative of indignant with someone indignant about something indignant at + usually a gerund inferior to injurious to innocent of intent on jealous of kind/unkind to loyal/disloyal to mindful/unmindful of necessary for neglectful of negligent of

The smell of coconut oil made her homesick for her family's coconut plantation by the side of the river.

All chemicals are potentially hostile to our environment.

He was indignant with his friends, for they had played a practical joke on him and made him look a fool.

He was indignant at being cheated by the smooth operator of a salesman.

The jury thought the accused was innocent of the crime he was charged with.

The police were intent on nabbing the culprits, no matter how long it took.

He pursued his research in medicine unmindful of what his contemporaries said about him.

The family had a lot to answer for but one thing was certain: they were not negligent of the books and paintings their forefathers had garnered over the years.

The committee found the man neglectful of his duties and recommended his dismissal.

O–R

obedient/disobedient to partial/impartial to patient/impatient with peculiar to polite/impolite to preferable to present at (pred.) proficient in prone to (pred.) proud of quick at/in relevant/irrelevant to remote from responsible for rich in rude to pertinent to

They say he is partial to foreign imports, be they food, drink, clothes, or gadgets.

All of us are programmed to speak a natural language by virtue of being born human. The capacity to speak a language is peculiar to humans.

The boy is being investigated for wilful wrong doing. The fact that he is poor is hardly pertinent to the investigation.

The action of the play is set amid a primitive people with their fierce loyalties to clan and family and their black-and-white notions of right and wrong, to whom death is preferable to dishonour.

Psychologists say that certain types of people are prone to road accidents.

The child is barely five years of age but she is quick at doing complicated sums.

She is very precise and quick in her movements.

The adjective 'quick' is followed by 'on', when followed by the prepositional object 'uptake':

She is quick on the uptake. (meaning, 'she understands things quickly')

That country is immensely rich in human resources; it has close to half a billion people.

He is not being rude to people; he is merely being blunt.

S–Z

sacred to safe from separate from similar to slow at/in sorry for successful in sufficient in suitable to superior to sure of susceptible to tantamount to thoughtful/thoughtless of tolerant/intolerant of true/untrue to weary of worthy/unworthy of

The cat was sacred to the ancient Egyptians.

Through an oversight, the cheese was not kept separate from the onions, so it was smelling of onion.

He was successful in persuading the party leaders to adopt a more flexible policy vis-à-vis the Opposition.

He is terribly slow in learning even the simplest of things. (meaning 'he is slow on the uptake')

Racism is based on the implicit assumption that some people are superior to some others simply on the basis of their colour.

He was so susceptible to music that certain tunes moved him to tears.

That was a case of culpable homicide not tantamount to murder, and the accused was let off with a lighter sentence. (amounting to)

By campaigning against the consumption of milk by humans, she was being true to her long-held convictions, however bizarre they might appear to others.

As the months passed, the campaigners were growing increasingly weary of their long struggle.

It was rather thoughtless of you to have brought up the subject of partition of family property when your mother was still in mourning.

There were moments when the most decorated hero of the country wondered whether he was worthy of all the honours heaped on him.

Exercise 15

Fill in the blanks with prepositions that go with the underlined adjectives. The first two are examples.

a. Our house is opposite the park and adjacent to your cousin's. (next to)

b. We will not tolerate indiscipline in this school. Children who are not amenable to discipline will be sent out of school.

c. He is extremely careful ____________ what he wears, even to the point of being fussy. He says that one cannot be too careful ____________ what one wears.

d. I feel you're being too critical ____________ your father. He did what was best for his children according to the received wisdom of his time.

e. He was totally devoid ___________compassion. To be fair to him, he did not expect others to have any compassion for him. (without)

f. The atmosphere in the conference room certainly helped. It was conducive ___________ free, frank and friendly discussions. (helped to bring about).

g. It was evident from the lukewarm response of the community that not everyone in the village believed that the scheme was beneficial ___________them.

h. In a forthright, no-nonsense manner so characteristic ___________ him, the man told us what he thought of the new office-bearers of the Residents' Association.

i. No one grudged him the recognition that came his way in his later life. He was thoroughly deserving ___________it.

j. I am not aware ___________any such rule that would permit an out-of-turn allotment of accommodation in your case.

Exercise 16

Complete the following passages with adjectives (given in the box) appropriate to the context and the prepositions (in italics).

detrimental	envious	familiar	identical
impatient	illustrative	present	irrelevant

a. Before I give you directions, I would like to know whether you are___________ *with* the area.

b. She married early and that was her undoing. Her marriage proved___________*to* her career.

c. ___________*of* the charismatic youngster's rapid rise in the party, disgruntled old party stalwarts were busy plotting his downfall.

d. No two persons are ___________ *with* one another, not even identical twins.

e. A parable is a story with a moral, the story being ___________ *of* the underlying moral.

f. A brilliant mathematician, he tends to be___________ *with* colleagues and students not so gifted as he himself is.

g. ___________ *at* the fashion show were the city's glitterati. All those who mattered in the city made it a point to attend the show.

h. Most of the time you were going off at a tangent. Most of what you said at the meeting was ___________ *to* the discussion in hand.

*glitterati: slang for the celebrities or 'glittering stars' of fashionable society

In the chapter on adjectives (Chapter 5), mention was made of participle adjectives, that is, participles of verbs, present or past, functioning as adjectives ('a boring movie', 'a broken chair'). Chapter 5 also contains a list for easy reference of the most commonly used participle adjectives, along with the prepositions that follow the '-ed' form: amazed at, amused by, disgusted at/by/with, and so on. Here is a supplementary list of the **past participle adjectives**, together with the prepositions that follow them.

absorbed in acquainted with accustomed to adapted to afflicted with alarmed at/by associated with blessed with committed to composed of concerned about/over confined to covered with dedicated to delighted at/by deprived of endowed with gifted with impressed by infested with inhabited by known/unknown to occupied with perplexed at/by pleased/displeased with/about/at puzzled at/by satisfied/dissatisfied with suited to a person suited for an occasion

Like the adjectives listed above, certain verbs too choose their own prepositions. Listed below are some of the commonly used verbs and the prepositions that follow them.

A

abound in abstain from accede to acquiesce in act on/upon adhere to admit of agree on something agree with someone about something allude to approve/disapprove of arbitrate between aspire to assent to associate with atone for

B–C

beware of border on clamour for coincide with concur in confide in conform to cope with consent to consist of consist in count on/upon

D

deal in deal with declare for/against defer to depend on desist from deviate from discriminate between dispense with dispose of distinguish between dream of/about

E–K

embark on encroach on escape from excel in fight for/against flee from frown at/on/upon gaze at/on/upon grieve for hope for impose on indulge in insist on judge between

A teetotaller is one who abstains from alcohol in any form.

The government felt – and quite rightly too – that to accede to the highjackers' demands would set a dangerous precedent. (accept or agree to)

Such was the subtle pressure exerted on him by his parents that he finally acquiesced in the plans they had for his higher education. (unwillingly agreed to go along with)

You must act at once. The situation does not admit of any delay. (does not allow for)

They could not agree on the agenda, or on the date, for the meeting. I fully agree with you about the need for doing something, although I don't have a clue what is to be done.

The family did not approve of the girl he had chosen but he went ahead and married her. The family disapproved of his action.

His replies to the questions put to him bordered on rudeness.

She had strong reservations about his plan but not wanting to discourage him, she concurred in it.

Such is the competitive environment in which the young people of today grow up that some of them wilt under the pressure, unable to cope with it.

He deals in second-hand furniture.

She is so upright that she will not deviate an inch from the straight and narrow. (She will not do anything dishonest. 'The straight and narrow' is a biblical phrase and means 'an honest life'.)

The boys are much too young to discriminate between what is right and what is wrong.

Despite her illness, she insisted on going to work.

Exercise 17

Complete the following sentences with appropriate verbs, chosen from the list below. Use the verb in a form appropriate to the sentence.

abound	act	arbitrate	defer	desist	dispense	embark	excel	gaze

a. When it comes to the crunch, one finds one can__________ with many things that one would normally consider indispensable.

b. It is best to think through the implications of a course of action before __________ on it.

c. There was a very old man that everyone at the shrine seemed to __________ to as he laboriously walked up to the platform and stood, __________ upon the image of the saint, tears in his eyes.

d. His friends pleaded with him to give up his plan of going to Timbuctoo, to __________ from what they thought was a suicidal course of action.

e. He knew he was staking his reputation by agreeing to__________ between the two contending parties and resolve a long-standing dispute between them.

f. The boy had no aptitude for studies but he __________in games.

g. You may not__________ on my suggestions but you may at least give me a hearing.

h. The book __________ in too many purple passages but is nevertheless readable.

L–Q

long for look at marvel at meddle with object to operate on participate in persevere in persist in plot against

R

rebel against recover from refrain from (plus gerund usually) reign over rejoice at/over repent of resolve on resort to respond to result from result in

S–Z

smile at/on snap at sneer at strike for/against strive against struggle against subscribe to succeed in transform into vie with vote for/against wink at wonder at/about withdraw from yield to

Those who are willing and keen may participate in games.

He persisted in applying for membership until the club finally accepted him.

He would have liked to take another look at the girl but he refrained from doing so lest he should be thought too forward. (deliberately stopped taking another look, something he would like to do)

He resolved on one more attempt – he had already made three – at passing his finals in accountancy.

People responded to the Prime Minister's appeal for funds to rehabilitate the war-wounded.

Why do you keep snapping at me all the time? (speaking in a sharp, unfriendly manner)

I don't subscribe to your theory that men and women are biologically incapable of digesting milk.

The Israelis have managed to transform vast areas of the desert into smiling orchards.

For a good part of his life he was savagely attacked; later the same critics vied with one another to praise him to the skies.

When he knew for certain that his chances of winning were slim, he withdrew from the contest.

The best way to overcome a temptation, said Oscar Wilde, is to yield to it.

Exercise 18

Complete the following sentences with appropriate verbs, choosing them from the list below. Use the verb in a form appropriate to the sentence. One of the verbs may have to be used twice.

conform	insist	object	operate	rebel
reign	resort	result	succeed	wonder

a. The Board of Censors ________ to some of the scenes in the film as being too violent and ________ on cuts.

b. The doctors traced the pain to a ruptured appendix and decided to ________ on the patient.

c. The young are usually non-conformist. They refuse to________to a social code that has no meaning for them and ________ against it.

d. The queen ________ over her subjects, spread over several continents.

e. He is personally honest but will not hesitate to ________to any means, fair or foul, to promote the interests of his party.

f. The workers' agitation ________ from legitimate grievances nursed over a long period.

g. The agitation ________ in violence when the management tried to put it down with a heavy hand.

h. Eventually the workers ________ in forcing the management to come to the negotiating table.

i. You can't help ________ at children's capacity for learning when you realise that they learn during their first three years more about the world around them than most adults do in any three years of their life.

14 Phrasal Verbs

Formally, a phrasal verb consists of a monosyllabic verb like: *come, go, bring, look, take, set, stand, put* and a particle. By 'particle' is meant a preposition or adverb. The particles, again, are monosyllabic like *at, by, for, in, on, to, up, down,* the exceptions being *across, over* and *upon.*

Compare the italicised verbs in the following sentences:

1	2
a. They *came.*	They *came in.*
b. She *jumped.*	She *jumped out.*
c. *Bring* me a book.	*Bring up* the almirah.

The verbs in column 1 are all one-word verbs. The verbs in column 2 are made up of a verb plus a particle like 'in', 'out', 'up'. We call the verbs in column 2 **phrasal verbs.** The phrasal verbs are so called because they look like phrases. However, the verb and the accompanying particle are so closely related that together they form a single unit of meaning.

Look at this table:

Read the phrasal verbs in the last column aloud, stressing the particles.

main verb		particle		phrasal verb
go		up		go up
come		down		come down
bring	+	in	=	bring in
turn		out		turn out
switch		on		switch on
switch		off		switch off
look		on		look on

A phrasal verb is sometimes confused with a verb phrase but the two are different. A verb phrase is just a finite verb made up of more than one word (one or two auxiliaries followed by a main verb) while a phrasal verb consists of a main verb (of one syllable) and one or two particles (usually of one syllable). Compare the verb phrases in column 1 with the phrasal verbs in column 2 and note the difference:

1 (verb phrase)	2 (phrasal verb)
is looking	look for look down upon
has been taking	take on
will be going	go for go in for
has turned	turn up

A phrasal verb, as mentioned earlier, consists of a main verb and one or two particles. Thus, it may consist of a verb plus an adverb, a verb plus a preposition, or a verb plus an adverb plus a preposition. The verb may be transitive or intransitive.

Examples

1. <u>verb plus adverb</u>

   Both oil and coal are finite resources but it looks as though oil will *run out* sooner than coal. (be exhausted)

   Cross out every third name in the list.

   Darkness *set in* and we found the going difficult.

   Do you think the company can *sort out* its problems in the near future? (solve)

   The noise sank to a murmur and finally *died down.*

2. <u>verb plus preposition</u>

   Can you *count on* the new treasurer you have appointed? (depend on)

   The new Prime Minister did not have the charisma of his predecessor but the party did not *hold* that *against* him. (did not view his lack of charisma as a great disadvantage)

   She *put on* the best clothes she had for the occasion. (wore)

   Promise us that you will *stick with* us and we will *let* you *into* our secret. (share our secret with you)

   At night, after a long day in the surgical wards, Lister *pored over* many books trying to find an answer to the problem of blood-poisoning. (studied closely)

3. <u>verb plus adverb plus preposition</u>

   They *frightened* the child *out of* his wits by telling him a horror story.

   My uncle *burst in on* me one fine morning. (entered my room suddenly and quickly)

   The issue of economic reforms has *come in for* widespread criticism. (received)

   In the process of implementing the scheme, they *came up against* unexpected difficulties.

   We enjoyed your last visit and *look forward to* the next one.

Most phrasal verbs, however, consist of two words only—a main verb and a particle.

Exercise 1

Complete the second sentence with the phrasal verb given in brackets, using it in a form appropriate to the sentence.

a. Tell me how it happened. I want to know how it __________ (come about).

b. He was very, very tired. He still would not __________ (give up).

c. This is not the first time that they are promoting a junior over her head. She has been __________ several times. (pass over)

d. An opportunity of this kind may never come your way again. Don't __________ this opportunity. (pass up)

e. Martin Luther King Jr was a Southerner by birth. He __________ Atalanta, Georgia. (come from)

f. He has no job of his own. He __________ his hard-working parents. (live off)

g. The new government is quite serious about fighting corruption. They have pledged to __________ corruption during their term in office. (stamp out)

h. I cannot go on living like this. There are limits to what one can __________ in life. (put up with)

i. He has a long way to go. But he will surely __________ the rest of the class. (catch up with)

j. He now finds himself in a difficult situation. He is trying hard to __________ it. (wriggle out of)

Exercise 2

Use the phrasal verbs given in the box to complete the sentences. Use each phrasal verb in a form appropriate to the sentence. The meaning of the phrasal verb is given within parentheses.

bring out	curl up	cut across	doze off	make of
miss out on	run away with	stand back	think up	

a. When are you __________ the next issue of your journal? (publish)

b. Can you __________ a way out of the mess we are in at the moment? (devise)

c. What do you __________ his words? (understand by)

d. For twenty years the man had worked for him loyally. How could he imagine that he would __________ all the cash one fine morning? (abscond)

e. She __________ with a book and within minutes __________. (1. roll up or lie down with arms, legs and head brought in towards the stomach 2. fall into a light sleep)

f. The issue of economic reforms __________ party lines. (go beyond the usual divisions between parties.)

g. The cottage __________ from the main road. (lay some distance)

h. Millions of children start working early, __________ their childhood. (lose the chance of enjoying)

Exercise 3

Rewrite these sentences using the following phrasal verbs. The first one is done for you as an example.

build on	bump into	chip in	measure up to	stumble on	walk out on

a. My parents were disappointed in me. They had high expectations of me.

Answer: I did not measure up to the expectations my parents had of me.

b. 1. Yesterday I met an old friend of mine. The meeting was accidental.

b. 2. Yesterday ______________________________

c. 1. Here is a novel of Somerset Maugham which tells the story of a successful man who decides to desert his family all on a sudden.

c. 2. This novel of Somerset Maugham ______________________

d. 1. Cricket matches are not won by outstanding individual players. They are won by players playing as a team, each one contributing his share.

d. 2. For a cricket team to win, it is important ______________________

e. 1. These six books form a graded, progressive series.

e. 2. For instance, in Book 4, we ______________________________ what has already been covered in Books 1, 2 and 3.

f. 1. Alexander Fleming was not looking for penicillin when he discovered it; he discovered it by sheer accident.

f. 2. Alexander Fleming ____

A good many phrasal verbs can be used both transitively and intransitively. However, they have one meaning when used transitively, quite another when used intransitively.

The plane *took off* exactly at nine. (was airborne, intrans.)
He *took off* his coat. (removed, trans.)

He had tried several times and failed, but he still would not *give up*. (stop trying, intrans.)

A martyr is one who *gives up* his/her life for a particular cause. (lays down, trans.)

The car ground to a halt. We thought the engine had *cut out* but actually we had merely run out of petrol. (stopped working, intrans.)

She had *cut out* a picture of a god from an old calendar and pasted it on a cardboard. (removed by cutting, trans.)

Exercise 4

Use a phrasal verb from the box in a form appropriate to the sentence and complete each pair of sentences below. Notice that each phrasal verb is used in two different senses. Guess the meaning of the phrasal verb with the help of the context clues. The first one is done for you.

carry on	call in	draw up	get in	hang out
hold off	keep up	split up	switch off	wind down

a. She carried on with her reading undisturbed by the distractions. (continued; intrans.)
They carried on their discussion behind closed doors. (conducted; trans.)

b. They had been friends for years and then they quarrelled over something silly and __________. (   )
The class was getting unwieldy, so it __________ into three smaller groups.(   )

c. The management hiked the workers' wages to __________ with the rise in prices.(   )
He was unable to __________ the payments on the two-wheeler he had bought under an instalment plan. (   )

d. Please remember to __________ the lights and the fans before you leave the classroom. (   )
He went on and on with his hard-luck stories. Halfway through his recital, I lost interest and __________. (   )

e. After five days of hard work one needs to __________ (   )
They had on their payroll over five hundred workers at one time; now they have just about a hundred. They are in the process of __________ their family business.(   )

f. Luckily for us, the rain __________ after an hour and we didn't have to cancel the picnic. ( )

The police force deployed was small and yet they managed to ___________ a numerically superior crowd. ( )

g. When the situation got out of control, they ___________ the army.( )

I ___________ just to tell my parents that I was fine.

h. The first bus to the city ___________ exactly at 7 a.m. right in front of our house.( )

They ___________ an ambitious plan for the development of the city.( )

i. What time does the Shatabdi Express ___________? ( )

He was talking non-stop and it was a full ten minutes before I could ___________a word about what I wanted to say.( )

j. You can see him ___________ at the market place or the bus station.( )

The maid was out in the backyard ___________ the day's washing.( )

14. 1 Separable and Non-Separable Phrasal Verbs

Phrasal verbs, as mentioned right at the beginning, may be transitive or intransitive. The transitive verbs are of two types—**separable** and **non-separable**. Separable phrasal verbs are those of which the component parts (i.e., the main verb and the particle) can be separated. Compare:

1	2
separable phrasal verbs	non-separable phrasal verbs
a. He *picked up* his pen from the floor. *or* He *picked* his pen *up* from the floor.	She had to *look after* her old mother. (*not*, she had to *look* her old mother *after*.)
b. She *looked up* the word in the dictionary. *or* She *looked* the word *up* in the dictionary.	He *got over* the shock soon. (not, He *got* the shock *over*.)]
c. The demonstrators *held up* the train for several hours. *or* The demonstrators *held* the train *up* for several hours.	Stop *picking on* your little brother. (*not*, Stop *picking* your little brother *on*.)

As may be seen from the pair of sentences in column 1, the object of a separable phrasal verb may come after it or between the main verb and the particle. In the case of the non-separable phrasal verbs (see column 2), the main verb and the particle stay together and the object comes after the main verb plus particle.

Example 5

Rewrite these sentences replacing the underlined verbs by phrasal verbs, chosen from the box below. Note that the phrasal verbs in the box are all transitive, some separable, some non-separable. Write the new sentence twice over in the case of the separable phrasal verb. The first two are examples.

bring up	call for	call off	call on	go over
keep back	look after	pick on	put out	take after

a. They <u>cancelled</u> the meeting for want of a quorum.

Answer: They <u>called off</u> the meeting for want of a quorum.

They called off the meeting for want of a quorum.

b. The eldest girl is the spitting image of her mother. She resembles her mother so closely.
Answer: The eldest girl takes after her mother.

c. Did they raise the subject of the refund at the general body meeting?

d. I get the impression that you are withholding something from me.

e. Your plan is all right but it will require a lot of money.

f. Have you a live-in maid to take care of the children in your absence?

g. They managed to extinguish the fire before it spread to the neighbouring buildings.

h. Why do you treat your kid sister so unkindly? You are a real bully!

i. The play was a resounding success. The players had rehearsed the parts so well.

j. It is customary for a newcomer to the colony to pay a call on his neighbours.

When the object of a separable phrasal verb is a pronoun (me/you/him/her/us/it/them) it must always come between the main verb and the particle:

He *picked up* the pen *or* He *picked* the pen *up*
but He *picked it up*. (*not*, He *picked up it*)
The nanny *brought up* the children *or* The nanny *brought* the children *up*
but The nanny *brought them up* (*not*, the nanny *brought up* them).

Exercise 6

Each of the following exercises consists of a statement followed by a question. The question is incomplete. Complete it with a pronoun (in place of the noun in italics) as object. The first one is an example.

a. The school authorities have put off a *decision* about a new auditorium.
Why_____________?
Ans : Why have they put *it* off?

b. He tore up the *letter*. Why ___________?

c. She called up her *neighbours* one by one. Why___________?

d. I give you six months to sort out your personal *problems*. Can ___________ during that time?

e. I asked him to hand over the *keys* to you. Has he __________?

f. We want you to take up the *assignment* at the earliest. How early___________?

g. 'We intend to put up your *proposals* to the Board for a decision.'
'When are you ___________?'

h. 'They are trying out the new *drug* with selected groups.'
'How long are they going to ___________?'

Notionally, phrasal verbs may be divided into three kinds:

a. those of which the parts (i.e., the main verb and the particle) keep their separate meanings, although the two together form a single unit: *come in get up sleep out switch off cut down*

b. those of which only the main verb carries its first meaning, the particle merely acting as an intensifier: *yell out wipe away hurry up start off wash up*

c. those of which the component parts lose their first meanings and acquire new meanings: *bring up* (rear) *give in* (yield) *hold up* (rob) *make up* (invent) *run across* (meet by chance).

The majority of the phrasal verbs belong to the third category. We must be particularly careful with these phrasal verbs. We cannot easily guess the meaning of these. We may try to guess the meaning from the context but context does not always help or help enough. The only safe and reliable way is to look up the verbs as we encounter them in a good dictionary.

The following example will give us an idea of how difficult phrasal verbs of the third kind can be. Let us take the verb 'bring'. We now add various particles to it and see what radical changes in meaning these tiny particles can cause.

bring

about (cause to happen)
The new principal *brought about* many improvements in the running of the school.

in (introduce)
The state legislature has *brought in* a bill on smoking in public places.

off (do something successfully)
The bowler *brought off* a difficult catch to dismiss the batsman.

down (lower or reduce)
The government is trying to *bring down* the prices of essential commodities.

up (rear)
The parents *brought up* their only son with great care.

The above are just a few of the many phrasal verbs that we can form with just one verb ('bring') and there are quite a large number of such verbs, verbs like *come, go, run, look, set, put,* etc. Phrasal verbs, besides, can have more than one meaning. For instance, each of the phrasal verbs cited as examples above has other meanings than the one given. One of the dictionaries lists six different meanings for the phrasal verb 'bring down'!

15 Conjunctions

A conjunction is a word whose primary purpose is to join words or word-groups. Conjunctions are of two types—**coordinate conjunctions** and **subordinate conjunctions.** There is a third type called the **correlative conjunction** but it is only a variation of the coordinate conjunction.

15.1 Coordinate Conjunctions

Coordinate conjunctions are normally used to connect words and word-groups of the same class: that is, nouns with nouns, adjectives with adjectives, adverbs with adverbs, phrases with phrases, clauses with clauses.

a. single words: *bread* [and] *butter* (nouns joined)

clever [but] *lazy* (adjectives joined)

slowly [and] *steadily* (adverbs joined)

b. word-groups: *boys in shorts* [and] *girls in skirts* (word-groups joined)

The band played [and] *the crowd cheered.* (clauses joined)

The commonest coordinate conjunctions are *and, but, or, so, for* and *yet.* Of these the first three – *'and', 'but',* and *'or'* – may be used to connect words or word-groups of the same class such as nouns, verbs, adjectives, adverbs; phrases such as infinitive, prepositional and participle phrases; and clauses, both main and dependent (noun, adjective and adverb clauses).

single words:

man [or] *woman (nouns)*
cuts [and] *binds (verbs)*
dark [and] *dingy (adjectives)*
slowly [but] *surely (adverbs)*

phrases:

To be [or] *not to be,* that is the question. (infinitive phrases)

He is *out of pocket* but *in high spirits.* (prepositional phrases)

Feeling terribly sleepy but *not wanting to spoil the party,* he kept awake and sat through it. (participle phrases)

After taking a long walk [and] *eating a light meal,* he felt much better.

main clauses:

He swallowed his breakfast hurriedly [and] *ran to catch the bus.*

You may accept the job on offer [or] *you may wait for a better job.*

You had better hurry up [or] *you will miss the train.*

I believe in the equality of men and women [but] *I do not favour the idea of women making a career of soldiering.*

dependent clauses:

The accused said *that he was innocent, that he had never met the murder victim,* [and] *that he was somewhere else at the time of the murder.* (noun clauses)

He married a woman *who lived next door* and *who shared his values.* (relative clauses)

Because life in the villages is hard and *because the city affords them better opportunities for work,* people migrate from villages to the city. (adverb clauses)

The other three coordinate conjunctions – *so, for* and *yet* – are used to connect only clauses:

The Englishman knew no Russian and the Russian knew no English, so they used sign language.

The book has cost me a small fortune, so you had better read it.

He sought shelter for the night in an old men's home, for he had nowhere to go.

The manager asked her to wait after office hours, for he had something important to tell her.

The word '*nor*', when used alone, serves as a coordinate conjunction joining two negative clauses:

I have not met him, nor do I wish to meet him. (meaning, I have not met him and I do not wish to meet him)

I have not met him, nor has my wife.

The host was not happy with the arrangements made, nor were the guests.

Notice that in the above examples we put the verb 'be', 'do' or 'have' at the beginning of the second clause, as shown below:

first negative clause		**second negative clause**
I have not met him	nor	do I wish to meet him.
I haven't met him	nor	has my wife.
The host was not happy with the arrangements made	nor	were the guests.

What do the coordinate conjunctions communicate? They communicate a variety of meanings.

coordinate conjunction	**what it communicates**	**examples**
and	1. a simple addition	men *and* women (both men and women) boys in shorts *and* girls in skirts The band played *and* the crowd cheered.
	2. a relationship of similarity	The boy is clever *and* hard-working. He is dull *and* lazy.
	3. a relationship of cause and effect	He spurned the advice of his elders *and* came to grief.
but, yet	a contrast or concession	The boy is intelligent *but* lazy. The man was out of pocket *but* in high spirits. He was rich beyond the dreams of avarice, *yet* he was unhappy.

so, for	a cause-and-effect relationship	I had no money, *so* I borrowed some from my neighbour. He is sure to get elected, *for* he is a son of the soil unlike his opponent.
or	1. a choice 2. a negative condition	men *or* women (either men or women but not both) tea *or* coffee (one or the other) Agree to a cut in your salary *or* quit. You had better hurry up, *or* you will miss the train. (If you don't hurry up, you will miss the train)
nor (when used alone between two negative clauses)	a negation	I have not met him, *nor* do I wish to meet him. He hasn't reported for work, *nor* has he applied for leave.

Exercise 1

Use 'and', 'but', or 'or' in the blanks below. Note that the conjunctions join words or phrases.

a. 'What would you have: coffee ____________ tea?'
'Coffee, please.'
'Black ____________ white?'
'White.'
'With ____________ without sugar?'
'Without sugar.'

b. There was a lot of singing ____________ dancing at my neighbour's last night.

c. She is brilliant____________ erratic.

d. Get me a dozen eggs ____________ a kilo of onions.

Exercise 2

Combine the following pairs of main clauses using 'and', 'but', or 'or'.

a. Substantiate your charges ____________ apologise.

b. I must finish this piece of work, ____________I will not be paid my wages.

c. She said she was sorry ____________secretly she was pleased.

d. The bicycle is something that most people can afford, ____________it does not pollute the air.

e. He is a brilliant teacher ____________he has no great interest in theories of teaching or learning.

Exercise 3

Fill in the blanks with the coordinate conjunctions 'so', 'for', 'nor' and 'yet'.

a. These gadgets are ruinously expensive, ____________ handle them carefully.

b. Jamshed lost the debate, ___________ he managed to emerge the most popular speaker of the evening.
c. I don't like the new maths teacher, ___________ do the rest of the class.
d. Giving advice is bad. Giving good advice is in fact fatal,___________ it is bound to be rejected.
e. Fourteen is an awkward age. One is not a child, ___________is one a grown-up.

15.1.1 Correlative Conjunctions

'Correlative conjunction' is a name given to a small group of conjunctions which always go together like *either...or, neither...nor, not only...but also, both...and.* The correlative conjunction is a variation, and a stronger version, of the coordinate conjunction. Compare and note the difference between the two:

coordinate conjunction	correlative conjunction
The principal is an able teacher <u>and</u> a fine sportsman.	The principle is <u>not only</u> an able teacher <u>but also</u> a fine sportsman. The principal is <u>both</u> an able teacher <u>and</u> a fine sportsman.
The minister <u>or</u> his deputy will preside over the function.	<u>Either</u> the minister <u>or</u> his deputy will preside over the function.
Vikram doesn't collect stamps, <u>nor</u> does Naveen.	<u>Neither</u> Vikram <u>nor</u> Naveen collects stamps.

The word 'also' in 'not only...but also' may be omitted, or it may be placed at the end of the sentence:

He <u>not only</u> said that he would come <u>but</u> later confirmed it in writing.

He <u>not only</u> gave them dinner <u>but</u> put them up for the night <u>also</u>.

Sometimes we use 'as well' in place of 'also' in the final position:

He <u>not only</u> gave them dinner <u>but</u> put them up for the night <u>as well</u>.

<u>*Note*</u>

While using correlative conjunctions, take care to ensure:

1. that each initial correlative is followed by its correct complementary correlative: *neither* by *nor, both* by *and* and *not only* by *but also*, and
2. that the correlatives are correctly placed in the sentences.

Exercise 4

Join each pair of the main clauses, using correlative conjunctions, to make a more emphatic statement. The first one is an example.

a. She was stunningly beautiful. She was highly articulate.
   Ans: She was <u>not only</u> stunningly beautiful <u>but also</u> highly articulate.

Notice that in the above example, the two items correlated are 'stunningly beautiful', and 'highly articulate' and the correlatives therefore placed <u>before</u> them.

b. He is a shirker. He has a deep aversion to all work.

c. Put up with what you can't avoid. If you can't do it, at least keep quiet.
d. The police are aware of the problem. They are taking steps to tackle it.
e. 'Why doesn't the man return the money?'
'Maybe he is unable to return it. Maybe he is unwilling to return it.'

15. 2 Subordinate Conjunctions

A subordinate conjunction introduces a subordinate clause, that is, a clause that depends on a main clause. Clauses, as stated before, are word-groups which have a subject-predicate structure of their own. They are of two kinds—main and subordinate. A main clause is a clause that can stand alone; a subordinate clause, on the other hand, is a dependent clause: it depends (usually, though not always) on a main clause. Compare the clauses in column 1 and column 2 and note the difference:

1 **main clause**	2 **subordinate clause**
1. You may start	*when* you are ready.
2. He skipped his breakfast	*as* he was in a hurry.
3. You are sure to pass	*if* you work hard.
4. They went for a walk	*after* they had had their dinner.

The clauses in column 1 are main or independent clauses, for they can stand alone. The clauses in column 2, on the other hand, cannot stand alone, depending, as they do, on the main clauses in column 1. We call them subordinate clauses ('subordinate' means 'dependent') and the words that introduce these clauses (italicised in column 2) are called **subordinate conjunctions.**

Notice that the subordinate conjunctions, unlike the coordinate conjunctions, are part of the subordinate clauses they introduce. Compare:

a. He had no great hopes of being selected for the post,/yet/he applied.
Although he had no great hopes of being selected for the post,/he applied.

b. It was raining,/so/we had to cancel the picnic.
As its was raining,/we had to cancel the picnic.

The coordinate conjunctions 'yet' and 'so' are not part of either of the main clauses they join but the subordinate conjunctions 'although' and 'as' are very much part of the clauses they introduce, as we can see from the following analysis:

Subordinate clauses are of three kinds: noun clause, adverb clause and adjective (or

main clause 1	**coord. conj.**	**main clause 2**	**main clause**	**sub. clause**
He had no great hopes...post	yet	he applied	he applied	Although he had no great hopes ... for the post
It was raining	so	we had to cancel the picnic	we had to cancel the picnic	As it was raining

A subordinate conjunction does two things: it introduces the subordinate clause, and at the same time it joins the subordinate clause to the main clause.

relative) clause. Broadly speaking, all the introductory words in the three kinds of subordinate clauses (including relative pronouns and relative adverbs which introduce the relative clause) may be classified as subordinate conjunctions. However, in practice, the term is restricted to:

1. the words introducing adverb clauses: *when, until, as, since, though, although, if* etc, and
2. *that* and *whether*, introducing noun clauses.

Exercise 5

Pick out the subordinate conjunctions in the following sentences and the subordinate clauses they introduce. The first one is an example.

a. You must wait until you hear from me.
   Ans: until: sub. conj. until you hear from me: sub. cl.
b. We never saw them again after they moved to the suburbs.
c. If the weather stays fine, we will go shopping.
d. She resumed work although she had not fully recovered from her illness.
e. He will never ask for a loan unless he has compelling reasons for doing so.
f. I met her briefly as she was leaving for the airport.

So far we have been considering single-word subordinate conjunctions.

Subordinate conjunctions may consist of two or more words:

two-word conjunctions	multi-word conjunctions
as if, as though She looks *as if* she is going to faint. He is only a tenant but he behaves *as though* he owns the house.	**as long as** Keep it *as long as* you like.
now that *Now that* we have come to a parting of the ways, I must say goodbye to you.	**for fear that** For weeks before the interview, he kept to a strenuous workout *for fear that* he might be rejected by the Board for being overweight.
granted that *Granted that* he was provoked, he still shouldn't have beaten up the man.	**in the event that** *In the event that* the reigning king dies, he will be succeeded by his eldest child, son or daughter.
assuming that *Assuming that* you have a genuine grievance against the management, must you go on strike?	**in order that** The parents moved to the city *in order that* they might ensure better schooling for their children. **notwithstanding the fact that** *Notwithstanding the fact that* he started life with every advantage that he could hope for, he achieved precious little.

We thus have single-word conjunctions, two-word conjunctions and conjunctions with three or more words. However, the greatest number of subordinate conjunctions introduce adverb clauses and express an adverbial relationship such as time, place, cause, manner, condition, purpose etc. Listed below are these conjunctions and the adverbial relationships they express.

a. Single-word subordinate conjunctions

sub. conj.	relationship expressed	example
as	time cause	I met him as he was crossing the road. They left early as the airport was a good 30 km from the city.
since	time cause	We haven't heard from them since they left for the States. Since he did not get a scholarship, he discontinued his studies.
while	time contrast (total) concession (partial contrast)	You were sleeping soundly while I was working. She was crazy about cats while her husband hated them. While I don't like the man, I admire his ability.
once	time condition	Once the press gets hold of the story, there will be an uproar. Once you make a wrong choice in regard to your career, you will regret it for the rest of your life.
although, though	concession	Although she hated to go out for long walks, she went with her father just to please him. Though he had done his best, he failed to make the grade.
where, wherever	place	As a policeman, he will be where/wherever there is trouble.
lest	purpose (negative)	They talked in whispers lest they should disturb the sick man.
if, unless	condition	If you go for a walk after dinner, it may help you to sleep. You will be in serious trouble unless you inform the police.
after, before, till, until, when, whenever	time	Look before you leap. Wait until I send for you. Do drop in when you have a little time to spare.
because	cause	He is most likely to be elected because his opponent is a stranger to the constituency.

b. Two-word subordinate conjunctions

as if ; as though	manner	She looks as if she is tired. He is only a tenant but he behaves as though he owns the house.
if only; in case; only if; provided that; providing that	condition	I would read a lot more if only I had the time. We will admit you to the course only if you pay the fee in advance. Ring the police at once in case there is an accident. We will undertake to do the job provided that you co-operate with us unreservedly.
so that	purpose	He is saving up money so that he may buy a personal computer.
	result	She worked very hard so that she passed with good grades.
now (that)	time	Now that we have come to the parting of the ways, I must say goodbye to you.
	cause	Now that we have decided to part for ever, let us part friends.
granted (that); assuming that	concession	Granted that he was provoked he still shouldn't have shouted at the man. (meaning 'We grant that he was provoked into reacting but we still disapprove of the manner of his reacting.') Assuming that you have a genuine grievance against the management, must you protest by going on strike?

c. Subordinate conjunctions with three or more words

i. prepositional phrase plus 'as'		
sub. conj.	**relationship expressed**	**examples**
as far as	degree or extent	As far as I am concerned, I don't care whether he chooses to marry or remain single.
as long as; so long as	time; condition	I'll never forget the days we spent together as long as I live. So long as you keep up the monthly payments, you will have no problem.
ii. prepositional phrase plus 'that'		
in order that	purpose	The parents moved to the city in order that they might ensure better schooling for their children.
for fear that	negative purpose	For weeks before the interview, he kept to a strenuous workout for fear that he might be rejected by the Board for being overweight.

on condition that; in the event that	condition	I will do the job for you on condition that you don't disclose my identity. In the event that the reigning king dies, he will be succeeded by his eldest child, son or daughter.
on the ground/ grounds that	cause	They rejected his application outright on the ground/grounds that he had falsified his age.
iii. preposition or prepositional phrase +'the fact that'		
because of the fact that; in view of the fact that; owing to the fact that; on account of the fact that		Owing to the fact that/ Because of the fact that/ On account of the fact that the military operation under his command had suffered excessive casualties, he had to face a court-martial. In view of the fact that the marks sheets were received late, I request that the delay in the submission of the application be condoned.
despite the fact that; in spite of the fact that; notwithstanding the fact that; regardless of the fact that; but for the fact that	concession	In spite of the fact that/Despite the fact that his life was crowded with achievement, Louis Pasteur continued to work without resting on his laurels. Notwithstanding the fact that he started life with every advantage that one could hope for, he achieved precious little. She insisted on attending the function regardless of the fact that she had not been formally invited.
but/except for the fact that	condition (exception)	But for the fact that two large newspapers had helped him generously with funds, Stanley would not have undertaken his East African expedition. He is a very nice person except for the fact that he talks a little too much.

You will learn more about these subordinate conjunctions when you come to the chapter on subordinate clauses.

Exercise 6

Fill in the blanks below with appropriate one-word subordinate conjunctions. Choose your conjunctions from the box.

although	as	since	unless	whenever

a. I was brought up by my uncle. He treated me __________ his own son.

b. Feel free to stop with us __________ you visit the city.

c. __________ he was not to blame for the accident, he was charged with rash driving.

d. Please remember that I am a busy man and don't call me __________ you really need me.

e. We have not heard from the Wilsons __________ they emigrated to Australia.

Exercise 7

Complete the following sentences with appropriate two-word subordinate conjunctions. Choose the conjunctions from the box.

assuming that	granted that	in case	now that	so that

a. __________ you have decided on a career in management, I suggest that you take the first step by writing for the application form for the exam.

b. __________your certificates were lost in transit and that you had to write to the university asking for duplicate certificates, that still does not fully account for the delay in sending in the application.

c. __________ he is innocent, he still has to explain why he did not say so earlier.

d. He went into hiding and grew a bushy beard __________ the police might not identify him.

e. __________ there is an emergency of some kind, you can always get in touch with me on this number.

Exercise 8

Complete the following sentences with appropriate multi-word subordinate conjunctions, choosing them from the box.

but for the fact that	in view of the fact that	in the event that
on the grounds that	notwithstanding the fact that	

a. __________ you intervened in time, the situation would have taken a nasty turn.

b. The woman filed for a divorce __________ her husband had deserted her and their children.

c. __________ my telephone has been dead for a month, would you please allow me a proportionate reduction in the rental charged?

d. __________the Board of Examiners awarded ten marks as grace, the pass percentage was no more than thirty-three.

e. __________ there is a tie, the chairman will use his casting vote.

16 Types of Simple Sentences

English sentences are generally classified either on the basis of their meaning and word order or on the basis of their clause structure. In this chapter we take up the first of these two classifications.

Sentences are classified, on the basis of their meaning and word order, as:

1. declarative sentences (statements)
2. interrogative sentences (questions) and
3. imperative sentences (commands and requests).

This division corresponds to the use to which we put the sentences. For example, the **declarative sentence** is most commonly used to give information:

Chotu comes from Bihar.

None of my children went to university.

Sometimes we use a sentence to ask for information rather than give it:

Has the post arrived?

Who were you talking to last night at the party?

When are our guests expected?

At other times we make a request, come up with a suggestion or ask someone to do something:

Lend me your pen, please.

Drink up the milk.

Go for a walk by all means.

Often it is the word order which indicates what type a sentence is or the use to which it is being put. For example, if we say 'Chotu comes from Bihar', the word order (subject followed by the predicate) makes it clear that the sentence is a statement. If, on the other hand, we say, 'Has the post arrived?' or 'Who were you talking to last night at the party?' we are asking for information and the sentence obviously is a question. The word order confirms our conclusion. In both sentences, an auxiliary verb precedes the subject and in the second sentence there is a question word besides introducing the sentence.

Another way of indicating what type a sentence is is to begin with a verb rather than the subject:

Lend me your pen, please.

Drink up the milk.

We use the first sentence to make a request, the second to give an order. The three uses of the language (giving information, asking for information, making a request/giving out an order) correspond to the three main moods in English: the <u>indicative</u> (or <u>declarative</u>) mood, the <u>interrogative</u> mood and the <u>imperative</u> mood.

Exercise 1

Say what type each of the following sentences is.

a. The newly appointed clerk hasn't reported for work.
b. What was London like?
c. Eat your dinner without making a fuss.
d. Do you enjoy your exalted status?
e. He cannot read yet.
f. Must you leave so soon?
g. She spends an hour doing yoga.
h. Shut up.

16.1 The Declarative Sentence

We use the declarative sentence most commonly to give information:

The post office is about a mile away.

We play football in the evenings.

Ravi has gone to the library.

Often we use the declarative sentence to express an opinion, or to make a promise:

Civil servants should not take part in politics.

She is a professional pianist in the making.

You will have your money back in a week's time.

I'll have the letter couriered by tomorrow morning.

Sometimes we make an emphatic statement by using the 'do' auxiliary in front of the main verb:

He *did go* to Oxford.

It *does look* as though the new cashier has absconded with the money.

Notice that the declarative sentence conforms to the normal word order: the subject followed by the predicate.

16.2 The Interrogative Sentence

We use the interrogative mood to ask a question:

Do you go home for the weekends?

Where is your father?

Questions are of two types: **'yes-no'** questions and **'wh-'** questions.

16.2.1 Yes – No Questions

'Yes-no' questions are questions which are answered simply with 'yes' or 'no':

Is your father a doctor?

Do you come from Haryana?

Are you planning to go abroad?

May I leave an hour early, sir?

These questions admit of only one answer: 'yes' or 'no'. Sometimes the answers may not be so simple or straightforward. If we ask someone, 'Do you smoke?' they may say, 'sometimes' or 'never'. If we ask a colleague 'Do you like our new boss?' he/she might reply: 'I think he is just wonderful' or 'He is plain horrible'. The answers may not contain 'yes' or 'no' but all the same they are 'yes-no' questions. 'Sometimes' means 'yes, sometimes', and as for 'never', it is an emphatic way of saying 'no'.

A 'yes–no' question always begins with an auxiliary verb (tense auxiliary, 'do' auxiliary, or modal auxiliary):

Has he gone home? (tense auxiliary)

Do you smoke? ('do' auxiliary)

May I go home early? (modal auxiliary)

If the verb consists of more than one auxiliary, the first auxiliary is put at the very beginning of the question, followed by the subject, followed by the other auxiliary and the main verb:

Has	he	been	shirking	work of late?
(1st aux.)		(2nd aux.)	(main verb)	

Will you be going to the library by any chance?

Have all the invitations been sent out?

If the main verb of the sentence is 'be', we simply transpose it to the front of the sentence:

Are you happy? (compare: 'You are happy')

Is it all right with you?

Was she at home?

Am I rude to people? (compare: 'I am rude to people')

If the main verb is 'have' in the sense of 'own' or 'possess', we move it to the front of the sentence:

'Has he a two-wheeler?' 'No.'

'Has he a bicycle?' 'Yes.'

The verb 'have' used in other senses attracts the 'do' auxiliary:

Do animals have a soul? (compare: 'Animals have a soul')

Do you have regrets about joining the army?

Did she have dinner with him last night? (compare: 'She had dinner with him last night')

Note

Even where 'have' is used in the sense of 'own' or 'possess', the Americans tend to use the 'do' auxiliary. Thus, they say 'Do you have any money?' instead of 'Have you any money?', the preferred form in British English. (There is the story, probably apocryphal, of an American lady on a visit to Britain asking her British hostess 'Do you have children?', to which the hostess replied: 'Yes, sometimes.')

Tabulated in the chart below are the ways in which 'yes–no' questions are framed:

statements	questions
1. verbs with no auxiliary (simple present and simple past only)	
be	
Arun is ill.	Is Arun ill?
They are foreigners.	Are they foreigners?
The children were alone.	Were the children alone?
have (meaning 'possess')	
Arun has a bicycle.	Has Arun a bicycle?
They had a car.	Had they a car?
with all other verbs	
They go to school.	Do they go to school?
They went to school.	Did they go to school?
She goes to school.	Does she go to school?
2. verbs with one or more auxiliary	
Sheila has gone home.	Has Sheila gone home?
She has been coming late.	Has she been coming late?
She could have gone home.	Could she have gone home?

'Yes–no' questions usually call for short answers and these contain only a personal pronoun as subject, followed by the same verb that initiated the question. In the case of negative answers, we add the word 'not'.

Is Arun ill? Yes, he is. No, he isn't.

Are they foreigners? Yes, they are. No, they aren't.

Has Arun a bicycle? Yes, he has. No, he hasn't.

Had they a car? Yes, they had. No, they hadn't.

Do they go to school? Yes, they do. No, they don't.

Does she go to school? Yes, she does. No, she doesn't.

Did they go to school? Yes, they did. No, they didn't.

Has Sheila gone home? Yes, she has. No, she hasn't.

Sometimes the first two auxiliaries of the verb in question are included in the short answer:

Has she been coming late? Yes, she has been.

Could she have gone home? Yes, she could have.

Apart from personal pronouns, the words 'there' and 'it' may appear in a short answer to a 'yes-no' question:

Are there enough plates and glasses? Yes, there are. No, there aren't.

Is it raining out there? Yes it is. No, it isn't.

We can have a positive 'yes–no' question, as in:

Is your father a doctor?

or a negative 'yes–no' question, as in:

Isn't your father a doctor?

In the case of the negative 'yes–no' questions, 'not' is contracted with the auxiliary that introduces the question:

Isn't Arun ill? Aren't they foreigners? Don't they go to school? Didn't they go to school? Doesn't she go to school? Hasn't she been coming late?

In formal usage, like in serious writing, 'not' is placed immediately after the reversed auxiliary and subject:

Is Arun not ill? *Do they not* go to school? *Did they not* go to school?

Has Sheila not gone home? *Has she not* been coming late?

There is a subtle difference in emphasis, however, when you place 'not' after the reversed auxiliary and subject. Compare:

Don't they go to school?

Do they *not* go to school?

In the second question more emphasis is placed on the negative. 'Do they not go to school?' carries an undertone of surprise and irritation on the part of the speaker. The speaker is surprised that they don't go to school and possibly annoyed.

Negative 'yes–no' questions as a rule attract the 'yes' answer:

Isn't he a genius? Yes, he is.

Haven't the invitations been sent out? Yes, they have.

In highly informal conversation, the auxiliary and the subject of a 'yes-no' question are often omitted:

Just arrived from Mumbai? (Have you just arrived from Mumbai?)

Going to bed so early? (Are you going to bed so early?)

Exercise 2

Change the following statements into 'yes–no' questions.

a. It is nearly a mile from here to the railway station.
b. People here trudge miles for a bucket of water.
c. That man is the only literate in the village.
d. I have had my breakfast. (use the appropriate pronouns)
e. They did it deliberately.

Exercise 3

Give short answers to these 'yes–no' questions. The first two are done for you.

a. Have you done your homework?

   Yes, I have. No, I haven't.

b. Wasn't there a large crowd at the airport?

   Yes, there was. No, there wasn't.

c. Didn't he apologise to her?

d. Do you go for a walk in the morning?
e. Did you have a pleasant journey?
f. Is there enough accommodation for all?
g. Hasn't he been ill for some months now?

Tag Questions

There is a type of 'yes–no' question called the tag question. The tag question is a two-part question. In the first part we make a statement; in the second we ask a question that expects agreement with the statement:

Arun is ill,	isn't he?
(1st part statement)	(2nd part question)

Notice that the second part contains the regular question auxiliary plus the personal pronoun that stands for the subject.

If the first part is a positive statement, the question that follows in the second part is negative; if the statement part is negative, the question part is positive.

Arun is ill,	isn't he?
(positive statement)	(negative question)
Arun isn't ill,	is he?
(negative statement)	(positive question)

As in the regular 'yes–no' questions, you may use the words 'there' and 'it' (in place of the personal pronouns) in the second part of the tag question:

There is still some milk left in the jug, isn't *there*? Yes, *there* is.

It's not very cold, is *it*? No, *it* isn't.

Tabulated below are the ways in which the tag questions are framed:

the two-part tag question

	1st part (statement)	2nd part (question)	expected answer
1. verbs with no auxiliary (simple present and simple past only)			
be	Arun is ill,	isn't he?	Yes, he is.
	Arun isn't ill,	is he?	No, he isn't.
	They are foreigners,	aren't they?	Yes, they are.
	They aren't foreigners,	are they?	No, they aren't.
have (meaning 'possess')	Arun has a bicycle,	hasn't he?	Yes, he has.
	Arun hasn't bicycle,	has he?	No, he hasn't.
with all other verbs	They go to school,	don't they?	Yes, they do.
	They don't go to school,	do they?	No, they don't.
	They went to school,	didn't they?	Yes, they did.
	They didn't go to school,	did they?	No, they didn't.

2. verbs with one or more auxiliaries	Sheila has gone home,	hasn't she?	Yes, she has.
	Sheila hasn't gone home,	has she?	No, she hasn't.
	She has been coming late,	hasn't she?	Yes, she has.
	She hasn't been coming late,	has she?	No, she hasn't.

Note that the negative tag with 'I' is 'aren't I?' when 'am' is the auxiliary or main verb in the main clause:

I *am* in charge here, *aren't I?*

I *am* managing the show here, *aren't I?*

Note that 'aren't' is pronounced like 'aunt'.

Exercise 4

Use question tags to complete the following sentences. The first one is an example.

a. They have been living in Agra for twenty years, ___________
   Ans: They have been living in Agra for twenty years, haven't they?

b. They haven't yet seen the Taj, ___________

c. They hope to see it one day, ___________

d. There really is no time to be lost, ___________

e. They had anticipated the attack, ___________

f. It is summer now in Australia, ___________

g. You will stay for lunch, ___________

h. I am the one to decide, ___________

We use tag questions when we want confirmation that something is true. That is the reason why we add a negative tag to a positive statement, part 1 of the tag question:

He *has* a car, *hasn't* he?

and a positive tag to a negative statement:

He *hasn't* a car, *has* he?

Other Uses of Tag Questions

When we make a statement about ourselves and want to check if the person we are talking to thinks or feels the same way as we do, we then put a tag with 'you' after your statement:

I *love* thrillers, *don't* you?

I *think* Lawrence Olivier the greatest actor ever, *don't* you?

Sometimes, we use an affirmative tag after an affirmative statement. We do this when we want to indicate our reaction to something that someone has said or suggested, to indicate, for instance, our anger, surprise or interest:

He *threatens* to sue me, *does* he?

So you *hit* the jackpot, *did* you?

The man *woke* up to find himself a pauper, *did* he?

If we make a suggestion to someone with 'let's' (as in 'Let's go for a walk'), we may use the tag 'shall we' to find out if he/she agrees with you:

Let's close the old chapter of distrust once for all, *shall we*?

'Either–or' Questions

Sometimes we ask an 'either–or' question:

'Was it a boy *or* a girl?' 'A girl.' 'Will you have tea *or* coffee?' 'Tea, if you don't mind.'

Included in this type of question are two alternative answers. The alternatives joined by 'or' may be words (as in the examples above), word-groups or even clauses:

'Will you have your tea with sugar *or* without sugar?'

'With sugar, please.'

Would you like to rest now, *or* do you want your shopping done right away?

Will you eat your lunch right here, *or* shall we pack it for you?

16.2.2 Wh-Questions

Unlike a 'yes–no' question, a wh-question calls for a detailed, specific answer:

Where do you come from?

What time did you arrive?

Why are you late?

Wh-questions begin with a wh-word *who, whom, whose, when, where, why, which, how.*

Basically, this is what we do when we make a wh-question: we add a wh-word to an 'yes–no' question:

Whom (do you want)?

Why (are you late for work)?

Whose pen (did you borrow)?

When (is he reporting for work)?

What time (should I pick you up)?

Exercise 5

Match each wh-question in column 1 and its answer in column 2.

Column 1	Column 2
a. Who was the US astronaut who circled the globe over twenty times?	1. Gordon Cooper
b. What nationality was Cleopatra, Queen of Egypt?	2. a secret
c. Which is the least contagious of all contagious diseases?	3. leprosy
d. What is the one thing alchohol doesn't preserve?	4. Greek
e. Where are the Pyramids?	5. in Egypt

Wh-questions are of three kinds:

a. questions beginning with an interrogative adverb (see Chapter 12);
b. questions beginning with an interrogative pronoun (see Chapter 4); and
c. questions beginning with an interrogative adjective (see Chapter 5).

a. Questions Beginning with an Interrogative Adverb

Given below are the ways in which we make a wh-question with an interrogative adverb:

statement	inter. adverb	question
1. verbs with no auxiliary (simple present and simple past only)		
Arun is late for work.	Why?	Why is Arun late for work?
Arun was late for work.	Why?	Why was Arun late for work?
2. with all other verbs		
They go to school.	How?	How do they go to school?
They went to school.	When?	When did they go to school?
3. verbs with one or more auxiliaries		
Arun has come late for work.	Why?	Why has Arun come late for work?
Arun has been coming late.	Why?	Why has Arun been coming late?

Notice carefully the word order in the questions:

- in the case of verbs with no auxiliary

  interrogative adverb + verb + subject + rest of the predicate
  Why is Arun late for work?

- in the case of verbs with one auxiliary

  interrogative adverb + auxiliary + subject + main verb + rest of the predicate
  Why has Arun come late for work?

- in the case of verbs with two or more auxiliaries

inter. adv. + 1st aux. + subject + the other aux./auxs. + main verb
Why has Arun been coming
+ rest of the predicate (late for work)?

The interrogative adverb may combine with an adjective or adverb:

How easy were the questions?
How soon can you complete the job?
How early must I come?

Exercise 6

Each of the following exercises contains a statement plus an interrogative adverb. Combine the two to form a wh-question. The first one is an example.

a. I met a man from Timbuctoo. Where?
 Ans: Where did you meet the man from Timbuctoo?
b. She will be moved to the general ward. When?
c. He is looking worried. Why?
d. We will find a solution to the problem. How?
e. We will soon nab the culprits? How soon?

Exercise 7

Form wh-questions with interrogative adverbs to which the underlined phrases/ clauses are the answers. The first one is an example.

a. Stanley met Dr Livingstone at Ujiji.
   Ans: Where did Stanley meet Dr Livingstone?

b. Stanley met Dr Livingstone at Ujiji in 1872.

c. Ujiji is located on the shore of Lake Tanganyika.

d. Stanley was very different from the general run of explorers who were drawn to Africa during the 19th century. He was a new kind of man—brash, ruthless and unscrupulous.

e. The search for the sources of the Nile was more than an ordinary field of exploration. The Nile was the lifeline of Egypt.

f. Two years later Speke went to Africa, this time as leader of the expedition.

b. Questions Beginning with an Interrogative Pronoun

who, whom, whose	for persons
what	for things
which	for persons or things, when a choice is involved

interrogative pronoun as subject of verb	interrogative pronoun as object of verb	interrogative pronoun as object of preposition
Who discovered America?	*Whom* do you want?	To *whom* were you talking last night?
Who has been talking about me in this fashion?	*Who* do you want? (informal)	*Who* were you talking to last night? (informal)
Which came first, the egg or the chicken?	*What* do you want?	On *what* is he basing his defence?
What caused the downfall of the Delhi sultanate?		*What* is he basing his defence on? (informal)
What is causing urban pollution?		
Whose is this book?		

As may be seen from the above chart,

1. When you use the interrogative pronoun as subject of verb, you do not reverse the word order.
2. When 'whom' as object introduces a question, it may be replaced by 'who' in informal English.
3. When 'whom' or 'what' as object of preposition introduces a question, the preposition may be placed at the end of the question rather than at the beginning. The wh-question with the end-preposition is in fact more idiomatic.

Exercise 8

Fill in the blanks with suitable interrogative pronouns to form questions.

a. ____________ do you want to see? (formal usage)

b. ____________ are you looking for? (informal usage)

c. ___________ does he rest his case on? (informal usage)
d. For ___________ are you saving up all this money?
e. ___________ were the causes of the decline and fall of the Roman Empire?

c. Questions Beginning with Interrogative Adjectives: What, Which, Whose

What time did he return home last night?

What books on the subject should I consult?

Which journal should I read for the purpose?

The interrogative adjective may be part of a prepositional phrase:

In *which* sense is Thomas Hardy a pessimist?

At *what* time should I report?

From *which* college did you graduate?

For *what* purpose are you making all this sacrifice?

For an emphatic wh-question, we use 'whatever' instead of 'what', 'whoever' instead of 'who' and 'wherever' instead of 'where':

Whoever heard of a wolf advocating vegetarianism?

Whatever has happened to you?

Wherever did you find this?

Exercise 9

Complete the following wh-questions with suitable interrogative adjectives.

a. ___________ street are we in?
b. ___________ doctor do you have an appointment with?
c. For ___________ benefit are you doing all this?
d. In ___________ direction should I go to reach the airport?
e. ___________ day is today?
f. ___________ restaurant in the city would you recommend to us?

16.3 The Imperative Sentence

The imperative sentence begins with a verb, with 'you' as implicit subject:

Double up.

Change into your pyjamas at once.

Be quiet.

Sometimes the subject 'you' is made explicit in order to make the order more forceful:

You double up.

You be quiet.

We use the imperative sentence:

a. to make a request or to appeal to someone for help:

Give me a hand, please.

Switch off the mains at once.

Hurry up and *ring* for the ambulance.

b. to give orders or instructions:

Keep reading silently.

Go straight and *turn* left.

Grate some coconut and *spread* it over the curry.

c. to give advice:

Be patient. *Don't rush* into a decision. *Don't lend* or *borrow.*

Sometimes we use the imperative with certain verbs like 'take', 'imagine', 'suppose', 'consider' when we are explaining something:

Suppose for a moment that you are on Mars.

Take, for example, the government's new taxation proposals.

Sentences starting with 'let' are also imperative sentences.

Let me fix the plug for you. (offering help)

Let us sit together and discuss the matter threadbare. (making a suggestion)

Let the electrician attend to it. (giving an order or instruction)

16.4 Forming Negative Statements

We use a negative statement to say that something is not true or is not the case.

We change a positive declarative sentence into a negative one simply by adding 'not' to the verb as shown below.

	negative
1. verbs with no auxiliary (simple present and simple past only)	
Arun *is* ill.	Arun *is not* (*isn't*) ill.
	negative
They *are* foreigners.	They *are not* (*aren't*) foreigners.
Arun *has* a bicycle	Arun *has not* (*hasn't*) a bicycle.
with all other verbs	
They *go* to school.	They *do not* (*don't*) *go* to school.
She *goes* to school.	She *does not* (*doesn't*) *go* to school.
They *went* to school.	They *did not* (*didn't*) *go* to school.
2. verbs with one or more auxiliaries	
Sheila *has gone* home.	Sheila *has not* (*hasn't*) *gone* home.
They *have gone* home.	They *have not* (*haven't*) *gone* home.
She *has been coming* late.	She *has not* (*hasn't*) *been coming* late.
They *could have been punished.*	They *could not* (*couldn't*) *have been punished.*

The simple present tense and the simple past tense of 'have' (meaning 'own' or 'possess') form their negative either way:

I *have* some money.	I *haven't* any money. (or) I *don't have* any money.
I *had* some money.	I *hadn't* any money. (or) I *didn't have* any money.
We *have* the latest figures.	We *haven't* the latest figures. (or) We *don't have* the latest figures.

As you can see from the chart,

1. in the case of verbs with no auxiliaries, the negative 'not' comes after the verb:
   Arun *is not* ill. I *have not* (*haven't*) any money.
2. When the verb consists of an auxiliary verb followed by a main verb, the negative word 'not' comes *after* the auxiliary verb and *before* the main verb:
   She *has not gone* yet. They *will not say* no.
   You *may not see* him now. He *was not authorised* to sign any papers.
3. If the verb consists of more than one auxiliary plus a main verb, the negative 'not' comes between the first and the second auxiliary:
   They *have not been attending* classes of late.
   She *should not have been* so reckless.
   He *should not have been rushed* into marriage by his parents.
4. If the verb is a verb of doing occurring in the simple present or the simple past tense, we bring in the 'do' auxiliary. In that case, the negative word 'not' comes <u>after</u> the 'do' auxiliary and <u>before</u> the main verb:
   He *does not need* to work for a living.
   They *do not know* what they are going in for.
   He *did not criticise* her, as has been alleged by his enemies.

Exercise 10

Turn the following positive declarative statements into negatives.

a. Finding excuses is the easiest thing to do.
b. He has plenty of time to decide.
c. He took a first from Oxford.
d. The new millennium began badly for Indian cricket.
e. If you had come to me, I would have helped you.

Apart from 'not', we use the negative word 'never' to make negative statements:

It is <u>never</u> too late to learn.
There <u>never</u> was enough food to go round.
I <u>never</u> had enough money when I was at college.
My children <u>never</u> went to university.
I <u>never</u> want to see you again.
She has <u>never</u> visited her stepmother to this day.
She may <u>never</u> visit her.

'Never' (meaning 'not ever') is a stronger form of 'not'. With imperative sentences, we use 'never' at the beginning:

Never sign a contract without reading the small print.

Never go alone into New York's Central Park.

If the main verb is the simple present or simple past of 'be', 'never' usually comes after the verb:

It is never too late to learn.

However, for the sake of emphasis, 'never' may be put in front of the verb 'be':

There never was enough food to go round.

With the verb 'have' (meaning 'own' or 'possess'), 'never' usually comes before the verb 'have':

I never had enough money when I was at college.

With other verbs occurring in the simple present or simple past, 'never' comes in front of the verb:

I never want to see you again.

My children never went to university.

When the verb is made up of an auxiliary and a main verb, 'never', like 'not', comes between the auxiliary and the main verb:

She has never visited her stepmother to this day.

She may never visit her.

The other negative words that are used to make negative statements are the indefinite pronouns: 'no one/none', 'nothing'; the indefinite adjective 'no'; and the indefinite place adverb 'nowhere'.

No one was to blame for the accident.

None of the reasons given was credible or convincing.

None of the girls volunteered for the job of usher.

This is no place for old people.

We had no time to go round the city.

They could do nothing to help us.

On the last day we went nowhere.

Final note on simple sentences

Apart from the declarative, the interrogative and the imperative sentences, there is a fourth kind known as **exclamatory sentences** or, simply, as **exclamations**.

Such sentences begin with an exclamatory phrase consisting of 'what' or 'how' followed by a part of the predicate:

What a memorable performance that was!

How bright that star is!

Sometimes the exclamatory phrase stands alone without the rest of the predicate following it:

What a memorable performance!

How beautiful!

What lovely sights!

'How'(but not 'what') may be followed by an adverb:

How <u>gracefully</u> she moves!

Exclamatory sentences are seldom negative but they can take the passive form:

What lovely sights <u>were seen</u> that day!

What a memorable performance <u>was witnessed</u> last night!

Sometimes an infinitive figures in an exclamation:

What a penalty <u>to pay</u> for such a small offence!

How nice of you <u>to remember</u> me after all these years!

Exclamations are an emphatic way of expressing our reaction to someone or something we are experiencing:

What a pleasant surprise!

What a lovely time we had!

How nice of you to have come at such short notice!

How meticulously the whole show had been planned!

17 The Passive Voice

In the previous chapter we learned the ways in which a declarative sentence may be changed into an interrogative sentence and an affirmative declarative sentence may be changed into a negative declarative sentence. We call these changes **transformations.** Interrogation and negation are among the simpler transformations permitted in English. In the simpler transformations the subject–predicate structures of the sentences are kept intact or changed very little.

We now come to a more complex kind of transformation called **passivisation.** When we passivise, we change the verb from **active voice** to **passive voice.** A verb is said to be in active voice when the subject is thought of as the doer, rather than the receiver, of the action:

The farmer *chased* the dog.

In the above example, the farmer, the agent or doer of the action indicated by the verb (the farmer is the person chasing) is the subject of the verb 'chase', while the dog, the receiver of the action, the animal affected by the action, is the object of the verb.

We may change the verb in the above sentence into its passive form, thus:

The dog *was chased* by the farmer.

Notice that in the passive form the subject is 'dog'. The dog, however, is not the doer, but the receiver, of the action. The farmer is still the doer but it is now the object of the preposition 'by'. The verb 'was chased' in the sentence is said to be in passive voice.

A verb – by that we mean a transitive verb – is said to be in active voice when the subject of the verb is the agent or doer of the action indicated by the verb. It is said to be in passive voice when the subject of the verb is the receiver of the action indicated by the verb.

The sentence, 'The farmer chased the dog', you may recall, conforms to basic sentence pattern 2 (see Chapter 2). Two other basic sentence patterns contain a transitive verb:

The *children gave* the *elephant peanuts.* (bp 3)
(subject) (verb trans.) object 1 object 2

The *trainers named* the *elephant Hima.* (bp 4)
(subject) (verb-trans.) (object) (object complement)

In all those three basic sentence patterns, the verb is used in active voice. Intransitive verbs have only one form:

He <u>came</u> home tired. (active voice only)

The children <u>looked</u> sad.

Transitive verbs, on the other hand, may be in the active or the passive form.

When the verb takes two objects (as in bp 3), either of the objects may be made the subject of the passive construction. Thus, the sentence:

The children gave the elephant peanuts

may be transformed into the passive form in two ways:

The elephant *was given* peanuts by the children.

Peanuts *were given* (to) the elephant by the children.

Notice, however, that the verb 'named' in:

The trainers named the elephant Hima (bp 4) has only one passive form:

The elephant was named Hima by the trainers.

This is because there is only one object of the verb in the sentence. The noun 'Hima' is the object complement, not an object of the verb.

The action referred to by a transitive verb, as you know, involves two people or things. It 'transits' or moves across from the subject to the object, that is, from the doer of the action to the receiver of the action. If you want to say that India won a cricket match against Sri Lanka, you may say:

India beat Sri Lanka.

The focus in the sentence is on India, the doer, and 'India' is also the subject of the verb. You may, however, want to focus on Sri Lanka, the team affected by the action of beating. In that case, you make 'Sri Lanka' the subject of the verb and say:

Sri Lanka was beaten by India.

The two forms, the active and the passive, mean roughly the same but only roughly. There is a difference in emphasis, as we will see presently. First, let us look at the forms of the passive.

The table below summarises the active and the passive tenses for ready reference:

tense	**active form**	**passive form**
present simple	take, takes	am/is/are + taken
	We take steps.	Steps are taken.
present continuous	am/is/are + taking	am/is/are + being taken
	We are taking steps.	Steps are being taken.
present perfect	has/have + taken	has/have + been taken
	We have taken steps.	Steps have been taken.
past simple	took	was/were + taken
	We took steps.	Steps were taken.
past continuous	was/were + taking	was/were + being taken
	We were taking steps.	Steps were being taken.
past perfect	had taken	had + been taken
	We had taken steps.	Steps had been taken.
future	will/shall + take	will/shall + be taken
	We will take steps.	Steps will be taken.
future perfect	will/shall + have taken	will/shall + have been taken
	We will have taken steps.	Steps will have been taken.

verbs with modals	can/may/must/ought to + take	can/may/must/ought to + be taken
	We can take steps.	Steps can be taken.
	We must take steps.	Steps must be taken.
	We ought to take steps.	Steps ought to be taken.
	could/might/should/ would + take	could/might/should/ would + be taken
	We could take steps.	Steps could be taken.
	We should take steps.	Step should be taken.
	We might take steps.	Steps might be taken.

Exercise 1

Change the following into the passive.

a. Columbus discovered America.

b. Tenzing and Hillary climbed Mount Everest for the first time in 1953.

c. We will inform the selected candidates in due course.

d. Last June they elected him mayor of the city.

e. They had informed her of our arrival.

17.1 The Use of the Passive

The active and the passive forms are not freely interchangeable. It is necessary to learn to change active to passive and vice versa. However, it is not correct to equate the active with the passive as though we could use one form or the other freely.

Basically, the choice of the form, active or passive, would depend on what we wish to communicate. If we wish to say that it was Columbus who discovered America, we should focus on Columbus and make 'Columbus' the subject of the sentence and say:

Columbus *discovered* America. (active voice)

If, on the other hand, we want to focus on the discovery of America, the event of the discovery rather than the identity of the discoverer, we should say:

America *was discovered* by Columbus. (passive voice)

Notice that in the above sentence 'America' is the subject while 'Columbus' has been relegated to the status of an object of a preposition. In the same way, when we say:

Mount Everest *was climbed* in 1953 by Hillary and Tenzing

we are focussing on a historic event in Himalayan climbing, the conquest of Mount Everest, the conquerors themselves taking a back seat, as it were. But if we say:

Hillary and Tenzing *climbed* Mount Everest in 1953

the focus clearly is on the climbers.

We use the passive voice:

1. when we wish to draw attention to the receiver, rather than the doer, of the action:

The superstar *was greeted* at the airport by a large hysterical crowd. (stress on the superstar, the receiver of the greetings and not on the crowd which did the greeting)

2. when the doer of the action is unimportant, is not known, or is too well known to require mention:

All the invitations *were sent* out yesterday. (the doer, the sender, unimportant)

Our house *was burgled* last night. (the doer, the burglar, not known)

The escaped convict *was arrested* two days later. (the doer, the police, too well known to be mentioned)

He *is being treated* for hypertension. (by the doctor, obviously)

In all the four examples above, the emphasis is on the event (the invitations being sent out, our house being burgled, the escaped convict being arrested and the 'he' being treated for hypertension).

3. The passive construction occurs quite frequently in newspaper stories, since the emphasis in such stories is usually on the newsy event, on what happened to X rather than on what Y did. Here are some excerpts from newspaper stories:

In 1981, a New Jersey man *was charged* with deserting his family. The title of Britain's Most Optimistic Burglar *was awarded* by **The Sunday Times** to a Yorkshireman with a withered hand, an artificial leg and one eye missing. He *was advised* by magistrates to take up a more rewarding occupation after his seventh conviction, in 1977.

4. The passive construction is fairly common in scientific/technical writing in which the emphasis is on the event, the thing, or the process being described:

The first thermonuclear weapon, or hydrogen bomb, as it *is* often *called, was exploded* in a test by the United States in 1952.

Because they come from the ground, most iron ores *are associated* with gangue, worthless earthy material which *must* subsequently *be removed.* This *may be done* by washing, or it *may be done* magnetically. Often the ore *is roasted* to drive off water and, in the case of carbonate ores, carbon dioxide. The ore *is* usually *crushed* during preparation, resulting in a fine dust ...

Exercise 2

Expand each of the following newspaper headlines into a complete sentence, adding appropriate articles ('a', 'an', 'the').

a. Kanishka coins found in Kathmandu valley

b. Three men trapped in mine freed at last

c. Delhi man fined Rs. 500 for threatening to jump off Qutub Minar

d. New record in non-stop talking by 57-year-old from Chennai

e. German airliner hijacked mid-way between London and Frankfurt

f. Man found with medical equipment worth Rs 40,000 stolen from hospitals

Exercise 3

Sentences conforming to basic sentence pattern 3 have two passive forms. Given below is one form, write the other. The first one is an example.

a. My sister was bought a birthday present by our parents.

   Answer: A birthday present was bought (for) my sister by our parents.

b. Full details of the courses were sent to the candidates on receipt of a request.

c. A cash prize was awarded to the most successful salesman of the year by the president of thc company.

d. We were found seats by the usher.

e. Drinks and snacks were given to all the waiting passengers.

f. We were shown the original document.

Exercise 4

Add a second sentence to each of the sentences below, using the words in brackets and making the word or words in italics the focus of the sentence. The first one is an example.

a. It was the worst air accident in years. (*all the 263 on board,* kill)

   Answer: It was the worst air accident in years. All the 263 passengers on board were killed.

b. Unlike viruses, microbes are living creatures. (*they,* can see, only through a microscope)

c. Alexander Fleming's discovery of penicillin was just a laboratory discovery. (Dr Florey and Dr Chain, *the laboratory discovery,* turn into a powerful drug, many years later)

d. No unexplored region in our times, neither the heights of the Himalayas nor the Antarctic, has excited quite the same interest as the question of where the Nile rose. (*the question,* debate, for 2000 years at least)

e. Galileo died a prisoner at the age of seventy-eight. (today, *he,* as the greatest scientist of his time, remember)

f. The Renaissance was a time of 're-awakening' in both the arts and the sciences. (*medieval idcas,* challenged and rejected, which had reigned supreme for centuries)

Exercise 5

Turn the following into the passive. Mention the doer only if you have to. Note that the passive is the more natural way of expressing the idea. The first one is done for you.

a. Workmen are painting our house.

   Answer: Our house is being painted.

b. We shall in due course inform the candidates selected for interview.

c. By the time we arrived at the cinema, they had sold all the tickets.

d. The government is introducing a new bill to ban smoking in public places.

e. If the judge finds the prisoner guilty, he will sentence him to three years' hard labour.
f. The government has done something to save our forests. It must do a lot more. It must not allow our forests to die for want of timely action.

The passive form has other uses as well.

5. Sometimes we wish to make a statement sound impersonal for reasons of modesty or because the statement we are going to make is unpleasant. We then use the passive.

Manufacturer to defaulting client: There will be no more supplies until all arrears of payment *are cleared* by next Monday. (The passive is much less unpleasant than the active: '... until you *clear* all arrears of payment by next Monday')

6. The passive form is the obvious choice when we talk about natural calamities like floods, storms and earthquakes:

The town *was hit* by an earthquake.

7. Sometimes we wish to conceal the identity of the agent or distance ourselves from the agent:

All papers relating to the purchase of the aircraft *had been destroyed.*
Senior officials who could provide incriminating evidence *had been transferred* or *retired.*
Don't be harsh on the poor man. He *has been forced* to tell lies.

8. We use the passive when the people in general are the agents:

A lot of junk food *is consumed* today, thanks to high-pressure advertising on television.
Information about bookings *can be had* by dialling 123.

Exercise 6

Rewrite the following sentences in the passive, omitting the words in brackets. The first one is done for you.

a. (Everyone) knows the facts of the case very well.
Answer: The facts of the case are very well known.
b. (They) have advertised the posts and called for applications.
c. (They) declared all the old houses in town unsafe.
d. (They) have since demolished all of them.
e. (They) will soon make cryogenic engines in India.
f. How does (one) operate the machine?

Exercise 7

Complete the following story using appropriate passive forms of the verbs in brackets.

Believing that his seniority __________ (ignore), a senior teacher went to the principal demanding to know why a younger man __________ (promote) to a position to which he __________ (entitle) and he himself, a senior man, __________ (pass over). He complained that it was most unfair, as his own twenty years of experience __________ (ignore).

'No injustice ____________ (do) to you,' said the principal, 'you really cannot boast of twenty years of experience. All that you have is one year's experience repeated twenty times. You must thank your stars that you ____________ (keep) on the school's payroll for so long.'

9. In theory all transitive verbs have an active and a passive form but in practice certain transitive verbs are seldom used in the passive:

Anees *resembles* her mother (but not 'her mother is resembled by Anees')

They *have* a son and a daughter.

The day and the time *suit* me.

He *got* her a basket of mangoes.

The assassins *fled* the city after committing the crime.

10. Some transitive verbs are usually used only in the passive:

His thesis *was acclaimed* as a pioneering piece of research.

The official *was alleged* to have amassed wealth disproportionate to his known sources of income.

The former President *was cremated* with state honours.

Lister *was horrified* by what he saw when he went round the surgical wards of Glasgow Infirmary for the first time.

The President of Ruritania *is rumoured* to be suffering from terminal cancer.

11. Reflexive verbs are never used in the passive:

He *hurt* himself.

They *blamed* themselves for the accident.

12. Transitive phrasal verbs may be used in the passive:

A number of proposals *have been put forward* by citizen groups for the improvement of the city.

The metre reader *was mistaken* for a burglar and *(was) beaten up by* the tenant.

After days of protracted discussion, a solution acceptable to all *was hammered out.*

All old buildings *were knocked down* and flats (were) put up in their place.

All objections to the proposal *were set aside* by the chairman and the proposal was carried by a voice vote.

The Prime Minister's visit to the city is *being looked forward to.*

13. The Impersonal Passive

Look at these sentences:

It is known that ultraviolet light kills bacteria.

In the days before Galileo, *it was believed* that the sun went round the earth.

We call the italicised clauses in the above sentences the *impersonal passive.* The verbs 'is known' and 'was believed' are obviously passive and they have for their subject the impersonal pronoun 'it'. Hence the name.

We use the impersonal passive when we want to say something with authority without having to name the authority. Note that the impersonal 'it' is the nominal subject. We may, if we so wish, replace the nominal by the real subject:

That ultraviolet light kills bacteria is known.

Such a construction, though possible, is somewhat unusual and often clumsy. The impersonal passive sounds more natural.

We use the impersonal passive for a contrary reason, that is, when we want to distance ourselves from the statements we are making.

It is claimed that yoga has the answer to nearly every killer disease that afflicts mankind.

It is said that the lowly carrot prevents cancer.

What we are saying in effect when we make such statements is this: we are not certain about the claims that are being made for yoga and the carrot.

Exercise 8

Here are some impersonal passive sentence openings. Complete them. The first one is an example.

a. It is generally agreed .....

Answer: It is generally agreed <u>that most people act from selfish motives.</u>

b. It has now been proved .....

c. It is hoped .....

d. It is widely assumed .....

e. It was established beyond doubt .....

f. It is universally believed .....

It is possible to put the impersonal passive in the middle of the sentence:

Yoga, *it is claimed,* has the answer to nearly every killer disease that afflicts mankind.

The lowly carrot, *it is said,* prevents cancer.

This often creates a dramatic effect, as in the above examples—the sentence begins with the theme or the topic (yoga, the lowly carrot), then comes the impersonal passive interrupting the promised information about the topic and thereby building up some kind of suspense or expectancy in the listener/reader.

Exercise 9

Rewrite the following in the passive, using the impersonal passive construction. The first two are examples.

a. They say that he is related to a senior member of the cabinet.

Answer: It is said that he is related to a senior member of the cabinet.

b. People feel that the teachers of today are not getting their due.

Answer: It is felt that the teachers of today are not getting their due.

c. Everyone thought that the government had not handled the problem in the right manner.

d. The manufacturers have in fact claimed that the drug is entirely safe and that it produces no undesirable side-effects.

e. People felt that the traders had created an artificial scarcity.

f. The teacher alleged that the seven students caught copying at the examination were not first-time offenders.

18 Introduction to Complex Syntactic Structures

Syntactically, a sentence may be defined as a group of words with a subject and a predicate. Notionally, a sentence may be defined as a group of words expressing a complete thought. (That was how we defined the sentence in Chapter 2, syntactically as well as notionally.)

Neither of these definitions is foolproof. The syntactic definition would exclude out of its scope utterances like these:

The cheek of these young people! (for 'The cheek of these young people is amazing')

Goodbye from me until Christmas. (for 'It is goodbye from me until Christmas')

Nonsense! (for 'You are talking nonsense')

Jogging at six in the morning? Not my cup of tea. (for 'Jogging at an unearthly hour is not my cup of tea')

Utterances like these are verbless – and without a finite verb you cannot have a predicate – and sometimes subjectless too. They occur most commonly in spoken English and less commonly in formal English.

The notional definition, on the other hand, brings up the question 'What is a complete thought?' or 'When is a thought said to be complete?', to which there is no easy answer, or even a possible one.

Granted that both the syntactic and the notional definitions of the sentence are not without pitfalls, it is still best, and pedagogically most useful, to continue with these definitions in the classroom. We may not be able to come up with an unexceptionable, universally applicable definition of an English sentence but most of us can, after a few years' exposure to the language, know a sentence from a non-sentence. We develop over the years a 'sentence sense', as it were, and have no difficulty in accepting verbless utterances like 'The cheek of these young people!' as complete utterances, and therefore as sentences, supplying the missing verb and the complement ourselves. As for the notion of a 'complete thought', here is a rule-of-thumb definition: Any thought perceived to be an independent unit, expressed by a word or word-group beginning with a capital letter and ending with a period or full stop.

Given below is a short summary of what was said earlier (in Chapter 8) on the subject of clauses and sentences, before we start on a study of complex syntactic structures.

The sentence is the basic unit of communication in English grammar. It is normally made up of one or more clauses. A clause is a group of words with a subject and a predicate. Clauses are of two kinds, main and subordinate. A main clause is a clause that can stand alone, it expresses a thought perceived to be an independent unit. It begins with a capital letter and ends with a period. A subordinate clause, on the other hand, cannot stand alone; we cannot put a period at the end of the clause except when it comes at the end of the sentence. Look at this sentence, for example:

People *who live in glass houses* must not throw stones.

The sentence contains two clauses corresponding to the two finite verbs in it, 'live' and 'must (not) throw'. Of these two clauses, one is a main clause: People must not throw stones; the other clause (italicised) is a subordinate clause: who live in glass houses.

Exercise 1

Underline the subordinate clauses <u>if any</u> in the following sentences. The first is done for you.

a. I heard the telephone ring <u>as I was sitting down to dinner.</u>

b. If you miss the train, you can always take the bus home.

c. The children waved to the soldiers marching by.

d. She spent hours looking for the missing bunch of keys.

e. He has not written to me since he left the country.

18.1 Main Clause

An English sentence must have <u>at least</u> one main clause. It may have two or more main clauses with or without subordinate clauses. A sentence therefore may be:

a. one main clause:
He has a car.
(A sentence like 'He has a car' may be called a main clause, a sentence, or better still, a one-clause sentence.)

b. two main clauses joined by a coordinate conjunction:
He has a car/and/he looks after it lovingly.
main cl. 1 main c1. 2

c. three main clauses joined by two coordinate conjunctions:
He has a car/and/he looks after it lovingly/but/he seldom uses it.
main cl. 1 main cl. 2 main cl. 3

d. one main clause and one subordinate clause:
Although he has a car/he seldom uses it.
sub. cl. 1 main cl. 1

e. one main clause and two subordinate clauses:
Although he has a car,/
sub. cl. 1
which he looks after lovingly,/he seldom uses it.
sub. cl. 2 main cl. 1

f. two main clauses plus a subordinate clause:
He has a car,/ which he looks after lovingly,/but/he seldom uses it.
main cl. 1 sub. cl. 1 main cl. 2

g. two main clauses plus two subordinate clauses:
He has a car,/which he looks after lovingly,/ but/he seldom uses it/
main cl. 1 sub. cl. 1 main cl. 2
except when he takes his wife and children for a drive.
sub. cl. 2.

The above are just a few of the many possibilities of sentence construction that the language makes available to us.

Exercise 2

Count the number of finite verbs in each sentence and write within parentheses after each sentence the number of clauses it has. Remember that there are as many clauses as there are finite verbs in a sentence. The first one is an example.

a. She told him bluntly that she couldn't help him. (2)

b. He knew he was rude to her and he apologised handsomely.

c. While I concede that freedom of speech is important, I wouldn't go so far as to say that I approve of your free use of my telephone.

d. Whenever a friend of yours rings you up and leaves a message that he has some very important business to discuss with you, you may be sure that the business is far more important to him than it is to you.

e. The priest was of the opinion that the honest man who married and brought up a large family did more service to society than the man who stayed single and only talked of population.

Exercise 3

Pick out the main and subordinate clauses in the following sentences. Draw two columns, as shown below, and enter each clause in the appropriate column. The first one is an example.

a. Could I ask you a question before you leave?

Column. 1 (main clause)	Column. 2 (subordinate clause)
Could I ask you a question	before you leave

b. If you are a prestidigitator, you are a magician who makes a living by pulling rabbits out of your hat and by other similar tricks.

c. He was wearing a new wrist watch which had cost him a small fortune, so he was busy waving to all and sundry all day.

d. Proponents of capital punishment say that there would be many more murders if capital punishment were abolished.

e. He sold the house that he had lived in for twenty years and moved to a flat because he said that houses had become prohibitively expensive to maintain.

f. She is in no hurry to get married and she won't marry until she finds a man who treats her as an equal, respects her as a person and shares at least some of her values.

As mentioned in the chapter on conjunctions (Chapter 15), a subordinate clause is <u>always</u> introduced by a subordinate conjunction, which forms part of the subordinate clause. A coordinate conjunction, on the other hand, is not part of either of the main clauses it joins.

18.2 Subordinate Clauses

A subordinate clause usually depends on a main clause even when you have more than one of its kind, as in the following example:

Although he tried hard,/he could not find a steady job/until he was well past forty.

Both the subordinate clauses in the sentence separately modify the main clause:

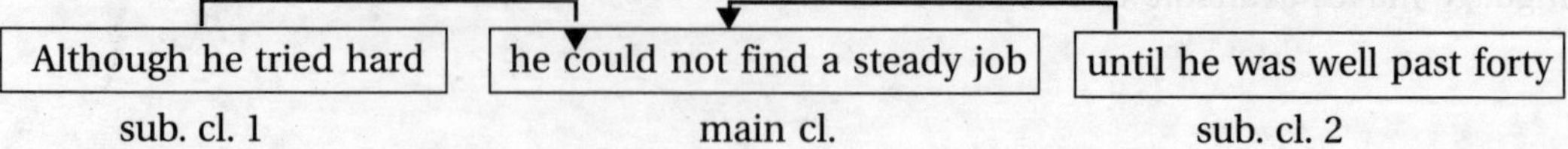

sub. cl. 1 main cl. sub. cl. 2

A subordinate clause, on the other hand, may depend on another subordinate clause, as in the following sentence:

Everyone knows/ that he is a criminal/who has been convicted a number of times.
sub. cl. 1 sub. cl. 2

Note that the second subordinate clause depends on the first subordinate clause: it modifies the noun 'criminal' in subordinate clause 1.

Here are a few more examples of a subordinate clause depending on another subordinate clause:

The man who lives in the house *that you see across the street* is a millionaire. (the italicised subordinate clause depends on the subordinate clause 'who lives in the house' modifying, as it does, the noun 'house')

He arrived late because he missed the bus *that he was hoping to catch.*

Although I try as hard *as I can,* I never seem to please my employer.

18.2.1 Types of Subordinate Clauses

A subordinate clause may be a noun clause, an adjective (or relative) clause, or an adverb clause, depending on the function it does in the sentence.

He said that he wanted to be a tea taster. (subordinate clause, object of the verb 'said'; noun clause)

I met a man who knew my great-grandfather. (subordinate clause, modifying the noun 'man' in the main clause; adjective clause)

When news of his death was flashed on the television screen, I could not believe it. (subordinate clause, modifying the verb 'could (not) believe' in the main clause; adverb clause)

18.3 Types of Sentences

Sentences are of four types, depending on the number of clauses and the kind of clauses they contain, as shown below:

sentences

simple	**complex**	**compound**	**complex-compound**
only one main clause and no subordinate clause	one main clause and one or more subordinate clauses	two or more main clauses and no subordinate clause	two or more main clauses with one or more subordinate clauses

Examples

simple sentence

The man hid the stolen camera in his home. (one main clause and no subordinate clause)

complex sentence

The man *who stole the camera* hid it in his home. (one main clause and one subordinate clause).

The man *who stole the camera* hid it in his home *until he could safely get it out of town.* (one main clause and two subordinate clauses)

compound sentence	The man stole the camera/and/(he) hid it in his home. (two main clauses and no subordinate clause). The man stole the camera/and/hid it in his home/and/waited for an opportunity to get it safely out of town. (three main clauses and no subordinate clause) The man was not a thief/but/he needed money badly,/so/he stole the camera,/hid it in his home,/and/ waited for an opportunity to get it safely out of town. (five main clauses and no subordinate clause)
complex-compound sentence	The man *who stole the camera* hid it in his home *until he could safely get it out of town*/ but/*just as he was getting out*, the police arrested him. (two main clauses and three subordinate clauses)

A simple sentence need not necessarily be a short one. The length of a sentence has nothing to do with its classification. Consider these two sentences:

1. For want of work to do or anything else to engage their minds and bodies, these young men are roaming the streets from morning till late in the evening, trying to find ways of spending time and generally making themselves a nuisance to their parents and the public at large. (50 words)
2. They say that he who pays the piper calls the tune. (11 words)

Sentence 1 is more than four times as long as sentence 2, yet it is a simple sentence. Sentence 2, on the other hand, is a complex sentence with three clauses, the entire sentence taking up just eleven words.

Exercise 4

Say what type of sentence each of the following is. The first two are examples.

a. Of all the bodily pains, the dental is the transcendental. (simple)

b. A person is presumed innocent until he is proved guilty. (complex)

c. If the young people of today pose a problem, which I doubt, it may be the older people who create it, not the young themselves.

d. Almost all Hollywood pictures are characterised by an inner emptiness, which is compensated for by glitter and glitz.

e. Whenever a literary German dives into a sentence, it is the last you are going to see of him till he emerges on the other side of the Atlantic with his verb in his mouth. (Mark Twain)

f. It is not really understood how the spoken language operates but to most speakers it simply does not matter how it operates so long as it does.

g. Democracy, like liberty or science or progress, is the kind of word with which we are all so familiar that we rarely take the trouble to ask what we mean by it.

The English sentence is extremely plastic—you can stretch it as much as you can, or want to, to accommodate your idea in all its many-sidedness and complexity. As a matter of fact, there is no limit <u>in theory</u> to the number of clauses, main and subordinate, that a sentence can have, but <u>in practice</u> sentences in present-day English seldom have more than four or five clauses, at least one of which must be a main clause.

19 The Adverb Clause

The adverb clause is a subordinate clause that does the work of an adverb. Like an adverb, it usually modifies a verb and sometimes a whole predicate.

He retired *when he became incapacitated by an accident.* (adverb clause, modifying the verb 'retired' in the main clause)

The Prime Minister decided not to seek a second term *so that he might find time to write his memoirs.* (adverb clause, modifying the predicate 'decided not to seek a second term')

Again, like an adverb, the adverb clause can take an initial position, a mid-position or a final position in a sentence.

While he was watching television, he heard someone knock on the door of his bedroom.

He heard, *while he was watching television,* someone knock on the door of his bedroom.

He heard someone knock on the door of his bedroom *while he was watching television.*

However, the more usual position for an adverb clause is just after the main clause or in front of the main clause. Some types of adverb clause, like the adverb clause of result, the adverb clause of purpose and the adverb clause of manner, come only after the main clause. There are several ways in which a verb may be modified. In plain English, this statement means that there are several ways of adding information to an action or happening. If someone said, 'A car collided with a lorry', the reporter would at once be besieged with a volley of questions seeking information about the accident like 'Where?', 'When?', 'How?' and 'Why?'. With certain actions and happenings, additional questions like 'With what result?', 'To what purpose?', etc would be perfectly in order. Thus, we find that there are as many as eight types of adverb clause corresponding to the eight ways of modifying a verb:

time clause	place clause	reason clause	result clause
concessive clause	conditional clause	purpose clause	manner clause

19.1 Adverb Clause of Time

Adverb clauses of time are usually introduced by one of the following single-word subordinate conjunctions:

sub. conj.	**example**
when, whenever	Drop in *when* (*whenever*) *you are free.*
while	*While he was taking a walk,* he saw a man jump over the neighbour's wall.
before	He promised to keep in touch *before he left.*
after	It was a case of closing the stable door *after the horse had bolted.*
since	I have never been to my home-town *since I moved out of it twenty years ago.*
till, until	Wait outside *until I call for you.*
as	I met him briefly *as he was leaving for the city.*

The following multi-word subordinate conjunctions also introduce adverb clauses of time:

Let me know as soon as you hear from them.

You may keep it as long as you like.

Exercise 1

Join each of the clauses in column 1 to the appropriate clause in column 2 using one of the subordinate conjunctions in column 3.

1	2	3
There was a virtual stampede at the airport	it was pouring outside	until
Fermentation happens	the day's chores were done	as soon as
The husband and wife sat down to watch television	the superstar arrived	while
He will not decide on the course of action	milk turns sour	when
We were having a quiet game of Scrabble	the time is right	after

Certain adverbial expressions of time may serve as subordinate conjunctions, with or without 'that':

The moment (that) the man left the room, the officer called for the police. (as soon as the man left the room)

By the time(that) we reached the airport, the plane had taken off.

She got married during the time (that) you were studying abroad. (while you were studying abroad)

19.1.1 Correlative Subordinate Conjunctions of Time

no sooner ... than	No sooner had I done one assignment than I was set another. (or)
	I had no sooner done one assignment than I was set another.
scarcely/hardly ... when	Scarcely had she started the car when she realised that there was no petrol.
	He had hardly been out of hospital when he slipped and fractured his arm.

Note

The future tense is never used after the subordinate conjunctions of time even when the subordinate clause refers to future time. Thus, in the sentence 'We will wait until we hear from you', both the verbs 'wait' and 'hear' clearly refer to future time but only the verb in the main clause takes the future tense form. Here are some more examples of the same kind:

I shall leave for the airport as soon as I have finished/finish (not 'will have finished' or 'will finish') my packing.

The band will play the National Anthem when the President arrives (not 'will arrive').

19.1.2 Elliptical Clause of Time

We may use an elliptical clause of time instead of the regular adverb clause of time. An elliptical clause is an adverb clause (any type of adverb clause) from which parts of the clause are omitted. The omitted parts could be the subject, the subject and part of the verb, or even the entire subject and verb. In the following examples, the omitted parts are enclosed in brackets.

I saw the sea for the first time *when* (I was) *a boy of twelve.*

When (you are) *in Rome,* do as the Romans do.

I do most of my reading *while* (I am) *travelling by train.*

The dam, *when* (it is) *completed,* will generate a hundred megawatts of power.

Note

We can use an elliptical clause only when the clause is about the same person or thing as the main clause.

Notice, for instance, in the expanded time clause the subject is the same as in the main clause. If the subject of the elliptical clause is different, you will be left with a 'dangling' time clause, as in this example:

While still a boy of twelve, his ambition was to become a fighter pilot.

The main clause has for its subject 'his ambition', while the elliptical clause has for its subject 'he': while (he was) still a boy of twelve.

The sentence should be corrected to:

While still a boy of twelve, he had the ambition to become a fighter pilot.

19.2 Adverb Clause of Place

Adverb clauses of place are introduced by one of these two subordinate conjunctions—'where' and 'wherever':

Leave the books *where you found them.*

The lamb followed Mary *wherever she went.*

The italicised clauses are adverb clauses of place. They are so called because they refer to the place of action.

Leave the books. Where must I leave them? Where you found them.

We can have an elliptical clause of place by leaving out the subject and a form of the verb 'be':

As part of drought relief, work for food will be provided for *where* (it is) *necessary.*

Rural works will be undertaken *wherever* (they are) *possible.*

19.3 Adverb Clause of Reason

An adverb clause of reason supplies the reason for an action or happening referred to in the main clause, and it is usually introduced by the following subordinate conjunctions:

sub. conj.	example
as	*As her husband was away,* she invited a friend of hers to come and stay with her.
since	I thought her unmarried *since she never talked about herself or her family.*
because	He accepted the offer *because there was nothing better coming his way.*

'Because' may be preceded by an intensifier like 'only' or 'just':

He was selected for the post *only because he was the best of a mediocre lot.*

The subordinate conjunction 'as' may follow part of the predicate of the reason clause instead of introducing it:

The farmhouse was vulnerable to attacks by dacoits, *situated as it was on the outskirts of the city.*

Bully as he was, he ran away when confronted by a stronger man. *Knowing her as I do,* I can tell you that she will never bend the rules to accommodate anyone. (instead of 'As I know her......')

In informal speech, we use the two-word subordinate conjunctions 'now that' and 'seeing that' to introduce a clause of reason:

There is no point putting any more questions to the candidate *seeing that he has not read the book at all.*

Now that he has come into a fortune, there is no need for him to work for a living.

'Now that' is generally used to suggest a new situation as the reason for something: There is no need for him to work for a living. The reason?

He has come into a fortune, which is the new situation as well.

'In that', 'inasmuch as', insofar as' are also used to introduce a clause of reason but these phrasal conjunctions are formal expressions usually found only in formal English. Clauses introduced by these conjunctions follow the main clause. The main clause makes a statement for which a reason is assigned in the subordinate clause that follows:

He is like his father *in that he is very impulsive.*

We are a conservative family *insofar as we cherish certain traditional values* but we are by no means opposed to change.

Capital punishment does not work *inasmuch as it does not deter people from committing a capital offence.*

Yet another formal conjunction that introduces a clause of reason is 'whereas':

Whereas the stone crusher supplied by you crushes far below its guaranteed capacity, we regret we are unable to keep it but holding it entirely at your own risk.

19.4 Adverb Clause of Result

An adverb clause of result always follows the main clause.

It is introduced by one of the following two-word subordinate conjunctions:

sub. conj.	example
a. so.... that	
1. so + adjective + that	The crowd was *so* large *that it overflowed the concert hall.*
	The doorkeeper was *so* surprised to see the reporter making for the door with half a dozen urchins in tow *that he didn't try to stop him.*
2. so + adverb + that	She spoke *so* eloquently *that the audience gave her a standing ovation* when she finished.
b. such... that	
1. such + countable noun + that	It was *such* a hot day *that even the airconditioner didn't make much of a difference.*

2. such + uncountable noun + that	The evening was *such* fun *that the participants asked for more.*
c. so that	She worked hard *so that she passed with good grades.* It rained heavily in the catchment area *so that the dam gave way.*
d. such that	The extent of the disaster caused by the cyclone was *such that the state government was unable to cope.*

The two words of the conjunctions sometimes come together, as in the last two examples above. More usually, they are kept apart, as in examples a and b above, the first word occurring in the main clause and the second in the result clause.

Exercise 2

Each of the following sentences contains an adverb clause which is in italics. Say what type of clause it is: time, place, reason or result. The first one is an example.

a. Don't be in a hurry; wait *until you get your chance.* (time)
b. He is likely to win the election *because he enjoys great support at the grass-roots level.*
c. As a policeman, he has to be *where there is trouble or a likelihood of trouble.*
d. Things have only marginally improved for the poor of the country *since the country became independent.*
e. *As news of the Prime Minister's resignation spread,* his admirers gathered in front of his residence pleading with him to withdraw his resignation.
f. He stood there before his boss looking sheepish *since he didn't have anything to say in defence of his outrageous action.*

Exercise 3

Complete these sentences with adverb clauses of the type indicated in brackets. The first one is an example.

a. He waited for her______________________________ (place)
   Ans. He waited for her <u>where he usually did</u>.
b. The children had rehearsed the play so well __________________ (result)
c. ______________________________, I shall expect to see more of you. (reason clause beginning with 'now that')
d. He suffered such a loss in trade __________________________ (result)
e. The guests had brought their dinner with them ________________ (reason)

Exercise 4

Here are sentences in pairs. Complete one sentence with 'so' and the other with 'such' or 'such a'. The first one is an example.

a. He was ________ a miser that even his children had a hard time wheedling a rupee out of him. (Ans: such)

He was ________ miserly that even his children had a hard time wheedling a rupee out of him. (Ans: so)

b. He took ________ long to tell the story that his listeners got bored midway through his narration.
   He took________ long time to tell the story that his listeners got bored midway through his narration.
c. The man was________ hurt and pained by the accusation that he broke down in front of the TV camera.
   The hurt and the pain were ________ that the man broke down in front of the TV camera.
d. The house was ________ untidy that it took us three days to make it habitable again.
   The house was in ______ mess that it took us three days to make it habitable again.
e. He was ________ shaken that he didn't know what to say.
   He was in ________ state that he didn't know what to say.
f. The salesman canvassed ________ persuasively that nearly everyone who watched the demonstration went in for the expensive mop.
   The salesman canvassed in ________ persuasive manner that nearly everyone who watched the demonstration went in for the expensive mop.

19.5 Adverb Clause of Concession

Adverb clauses of concession are usually introduced by the following subordinate conjunctions:

sub. conj.	example
although	Although he tried hard, he didn't get through his finals.
though	Though it rained for most of the time, we enjoyed our holiday on the hills.
even though	Even though she was not an outdoor type, she used to go for long walks.

An adverb clause of concession implies a contrast, or opposition in idea:

He worked hard (and should therefore have got through his finals) *but* he did not.

It rained for most of the time (and the rains should have spoilt our holiday on the hills) *but* they didn't and we enjoyed the holiday.

She was not an outdoor type (and was not expected to go for long walks) *but* she did.

The three subordinate conjunctions mean roughly the same. 'Though' is less formal than 'although', and 'even though' is a strong form of 'though'/'although'.

When a 'though'-clause ends with a subject complement, the complement can be brought forward to the beginning of the clause. Thus, instead of saying 'Though she was disappointed in her son, she still was very fond of him', we can say: Disappointed though she was in her son, she still was very fond of him.

Experienced manager though he was, he could not cope with this crisis.

Competent doctor though she was, her bedside manner was far from reassuring.

When the complement is an adjective, we can use 'as' instead of 'though':

Disappointed as she was in her son, ...

Simple as the test may appear, I would caution you against being over-confident.
Unconvincing as his explanation was, I had no option but to accept it.

When the 'though'-clause ends with an adverb, we may use the adverb to begin the clause:

Hard though he tried, he could not get through his finals.

Much as she admired him, she had no wish to marry him.

An adverb clause of concession may also be introduced by one of these subordinate conjunctions.

sub. conj.	example
'however' + adverb	However hard you try, you cannot please some people. (Although you try very hard ...)
'however' + adjective	However brilliant he may be, he has no right to despise others not so gifted.
'no matter' + wh-word (what where who how)	No matter who you are, you are not above the law. We look for the best person we can get, no matter where he comes from. No matter what you say, they won't believe you. You must go and find your missing brother, no matter how you do it.

The contrast expressed by an adverb clause of concession may be partial or total:

Although I don't like the man, I admire his ability. (or)
Although I admire the man's ability, I don't like the man. (partial contrast)
She is crazy about the Great Khan, whom she calls the actor of the millennium, while her husband considers him an amateur of all time. (total contrast)

Clauses expressing total contrast are commonly introduced by 'while' or 'whereas':

While Tom is happy curling up with a book, his brother Dick is fond of the great outdoors. (or)
While Dick is fond of the great outdoors, his brother Tom is happy curling up with a book.
Cricket is the most popular spectator sport in India, whereas in France it is football that draws huge crowds.

Note that 'while' can also express a partial contrast:

While I don't like the man, I admire his ability (or) While I admire the man's ability, I don't like the man.

Exercise 5

Join each of the clauses in column A to the appropriate clause in column B after turning either of the clauses into a clause of concession by adding 'though', 'although' or 'even though'.

A	B
1. we didn't understand a word of what the visiting dignitary was saying	a. I don't go to the gym now

2. you are the spitting image of your father
3. he still continued with his researches and did not want to rest on his laurels
4. I made it a point of speaking English all the time
5. I used to exercise regularly before I became a minister

b. my English was not very good
c. you are not half as talented as he was
d. we kept smiling and nodding our heads
e. he was well past sixty and the most famous scientist of his time

Exercise 6

Complete the following sentences, using 'no matter' + wh-word. The first one is an example.

a. No matter how hard he begs, don't give him any money.

b. I think I will make a better union president but ___________ wins the election, we will still be friends.

c. She is so involved in the subject that she is determined to continue with her research ___________ long it takes her to become a Ph.D.

d. You must forgive him. Remember he is your brother ___________ he has done to you.

e. ___________ bad the situation is, we must not give up hope.

19.6 Adverb Clause of Purpose

Like the adverb clause of result, the clause of purpose follows the main clause:

He gave up all fatty foods so that/in order that he might not put on weight.

Speak up so that/in order that the boy in the last row may hear you.

Make a note of the date so that you do not/shall not forget to show up for the function.

The underlined clauses express purpose. In each of the above sentences, the main clause expresses a statement or a directive and the subordinate clause supplies the purpose.

The purpose expressed may be negative:

They left very early for the station *for fear that they might be held up by the traffic on the way.* (purpose: they did *not* want to be held up by the traffic on the way)

The thieves undid the bolt and tiptoed into the house *for fear that they might wake up the inmates.*

The subordinate conjunction 'lest', once used to introduce a negative clause of purpose, is formal and archaic.

When the verb in the main clause is in the past tense, we use 'might', 'could', 'should', or 'would' in the purpose clause. When the verb in the main clause is in the present (or when the main clause is an imperative sentence) we use in the purpose clause the corresponding present tense forms: 'may', 'can', 'shall' or 'will'.

An adverb clause of purpose is relatively easy to identify. It is introduced by 'so that' or 'in order that'. However, a clause of purpose, especially one introduced by 'so that', may be confused with a clause of result. Compare:

He worked hard *so that he might win a scholarship.* (purpose)

He worked hard *so that he won a scholarship.* (result)

One way of telling a purpose clause from a result clause is to look at the verb in the subordinate clause. The purpose clause usually has the modal auxiliary 'may', 'can', 'shall' or 'will' or its corresponding past tense form 'might', 'could', 'should', or 'would':

She is saving up money *so that she may buy herself a personal computer.* (purpose)

She was saving up money *so that she might buy herself a personal computer.* (purpose)

There is yet another way of distinguishing the two types. If 'so that' can be replaced by 'in order that', then the clause is an adverb clause of purpose.

Exercise 7

Say which of these sentences contain purpose clauses and which result clauses. Underline the subordinate clause and identify.

a. They had planned meticulously so that the function was a great success.
b. They planned meticulously so that the function might be a success.
c. He revised his work thoroughly so that no one could fault it.
d. He revised his work thoroughly so that it was not possible for anyone to fault it.
e. The teacher wrote in block capitals on the blackboard so that everyone in the class could read and understand.

Exercise 8

Complete each of these sentences with a suitable clause of purpose.

a. The dacoits went into hiding and grew beards_______________. (negative purpose)
b. She gave up her job ____________________________________.
c. He went to Mumbai ____________________________________.
d. People all over the world learn English _________________________.
e. I sold my house ____.

19.7 Adverb Clause of Manner

The adverb clause of manner is usually introduced by one of these subordinate conjunctions:

sub. conj.	example
as	My uncle treats me as he treats his own son. I always do as my parents tell me.
as if	He behaves as if he owns the house. (He is not the owner of the house but he behaves like the owner.)
as though	You look as though you have been in a pigsty.

As we can see from the above examples, you use an adverb clause of manner to make a comparison.

We may for emphasis use 'exactly', 'precisely' or 'just' in front of 'as':

He planned his holiday exactly as he wanted to.

He behaved just as I thought he would.

In conversational English, though not in formal writing, we may use 'like' as a conjunction to make a comparison.

Are you going to misbehave again like you did yesterday?

Speak like I do if you want to improve your diction.

You may use expressions like 'the way', 'in a way', 'in the way' to talk about someone's manner of behaving or doing things:

I was never allowed to live the way I wanted to. (as I wanted to) She lived in the way she wanted to, despite her orthodox upbringing. (just as she wanted to)

He spoke to me in a way I didn't quite understand.

Exercise 9

Rewrite these sentences using 'as if' or 'as though'. The first one is an example.

a. The butter smells awful. I think it has gone rancid.

Ans. The butter smells as though it has gone rancid.

b. His eyes are red and his nose is running. I think he is suffering from a bad cold. (He looks...................).

c. The baby looks pale and thin. I think it is undernourished.

d. The children kept yawning through the lesson. I think they were bored.

e. I rang the bell several times but no one answered the door. I think the house is untenanted. (The house looks......)

19.8 Adverb Clause of Condition

Adverb clauses of condition, or conditional clauses as they are sometimes called, begin with 'if' or 'unless':

If the weather is fine, I shall meet you this evening.

If you invite him in person, he will come to the party.

Unless you invite him in person, he won't come to the party.

The italicised conditional clause in the above sentences stipulates a condition ('the weather must be fine', 'you must invite him in person') and the main clause states what will happen if the condition is realised ('I shall meet you in the evening', 'he will come to the party'). Compare:

I shall meet you this evening.

I shall meet you this evening *if the weather is fine.*

The first sentence is a straightforward, unconditional promise. In the second sentence, a condition is attached to the promise—the promised meeting is subject to the weather being fine. The weather this evening may or may not be fine, but if it is fine, I shall meet you.

The entire sentence 'If the weather is fine, I shall meet you this evening' is called a conditional sentence, or simply, a conditional.

The conditions stipulated may be real or unreal. Compare the conditional clauses in columns A and B:

A	B
If he works hard, he will pass.	If he worked hard, he would pass.
If the roads are motorable, we shall drive.	If I were you, I would think no more about it.

The underlined clauses in A express real conditions, that is, conditions that can be realised, that in all probability will be realised. The underlined clauses in B, on the other hand, express unreal conditions, conditions that are unlikely or impossible to realise at any time in the present or future.

If he worked hard, he would pass.

The statement makes it clear that he is not working hard *now* and that he is unlikely to work hard *in the future.*

If I were you, I would think no more about it.

The speaker of the above cannot be the other person now or in the future.

The condition stipulated is even more unreal than in 'If he worked hard'. Sometimes the unreal condition relates to the past:

If I had had enough money last year, I would have gone on a long holiday.

The speaker says now that he did not have enough money last year and therefore he did not go on a long holiday. The condition specified was not realised, and the result stated in the main clause did not happen.

It is customary, while teaching the conditional clause, especially in an ESL situation, to talk of the three kinds of conditional sentences:

the first conditional :	If you work hard, you will pass. If they call me, I shall go.
the second conditional:	If you worked hard, you would pass. If they called me, I should go.
the third conditional :	If you had worked hard, you would have passed. If they had called me, I should have gone.

The three conditional sentences have their own distinctive forms, tabulated below for ready reference:

kind of conditional sentence	**if-clause verb**	**main clause verb**
the first conditional	present simple (if you work hard)	future tense 'shall'/'will' plus main verb (you will pass)
the second conditional	past simple (if you worked hard)	'should'/'would' plus main verb (you would pass)
the third conditional	past perfect (if you had worked)	'would have'/'should have' plus main verb (you would have passed)

This three-fold division of conditional sentences is largely true but there is a certain over-simplification in that the three conditionals do not exhaust all possibilities of conditional sentences.

19.8.1 The First Conditional

The first conditional refers to the future. We use the first conditional when there is a real possibility of the if-event happening:

If you *help* me with my marking, I *shall help* you with your shopping. (You may or may not help me with my marking but there is a good chance of your agreeing to help, and if you do, I shall in turn surely help you with your shopping)

You may use 'unless' to mean 'if not':

Unless you *help* me with my marking, I *shan't help* you with your shopping.

Note that the verb 'help' in both the clauses refers to the future. 'If you help me' implies 'you are not helping me now, you are yet to help me, your helping me with my marking is a matter for the future'. In the same way, 'I shall help you with your shopping' implies 'I am not helping you now, I am yet to help you'. But only one of the verbs, the verb in the main clause, takes the future tense form in the first conditional. The verb in the if-clause is in the simple present only.

The clauses are reversible, that is, either of the clauses can come first. We may say 'If you help me with my marking, I shall help you with your shopping' or 'I shall help you with your shopping if you help me with my marking'.

Exercise 10

Complete the following first conditionals by putting the verbs in brackets in the right tenses. Do this exercise orally but rapidly.

a. If the sun (shine), we (go) for a picnic.

b. If it (rain), we(stay) indoors watching television.

c. I (go) if he (invite) me.

d. I (buy) you a present if you (behave) yourself.

e. What you (do) if you (hear) a knock on the door at midnight?

You may have an imperative sentence as the main clause instead of the more usual statement with 'shall'/'will':

Give us the weapons if you want us to throw the enemy out.

Go for a walk by all means if it helps you to sleep.

Exercise 11

Complete these first conditionals. The first one is an example.

a. If ever you visit a safari park, you will see lions roaming free.

b. Do phone me ________________ but please remember that I am a busy man and don't phone me________________.

c. If I do well in my job,____________ but if I don't, ____________.

d. I shall lend you the money you need________________.

e. Just lie down and relax________________. If that doesn't help,________________ but don't take these tablets________________.

19.8.2 The Second Conditional

The second conditional refers to the future like the first conditional but the if-event in the second conditional is

a. unlikely:	If he *worked* hard, he *would pass.*
(or) b. extremely unlikely, almost impossible:	If I *went* to London, I *would seek* an audience with the Queen.

(or) c. hypothetical : If they *made* me the principal of the school, I *would change* a good many things.

The speaker of the sentence in (b) is, let us say, a not so well-to-do person with a large family and his going to London is as unlikely as his seeking an audience with the Queen. As for the speaker of the sentence in (c), he is, let us assume, a peon in the school, so the question of his being made principal does not arise. But if by some miracle it happened, he would then change a good many things in the school. The conditions expressed in the second conditional are thus unreal, they are unlikely to be realised. The conditions can become even more unreal, as in the following examples:

If I *were* a bird, I *would fly*.

If money *grew* on trees, we *would* all *be* rich.

The degree of probability expressed by the second conditional may range from:

a. improbable but not impossible (If he worked hard, he would pass): through
b. extremely improbable, almost impossible (If I went to London, I would seek an audience with the Queen): to
c. downright impossible (If money grew on trees, we would all be rich) and may be represented by a cline rather than a flight of stairs. At stage b, even more definitely at stage c of the cline, the second conditional expresses wishful thinking. Wishful thinking refers to a hope or wish that cannot come true. It is wishful thinking, for instance, to assume that wolves will sit in a body and legislate for vegetarianism.

The clauses in the second conditional are reversible.

Exercise 12

Here is a little story that illustrates tellingly, as only a story can, the use of the second conditional. The story tells of three men who meet somewhere and indulge in a bit of wishful thinking. The story is incomplete. Complete it.

Once an American, a Spaniard and a Scotsman met. In the course of a rambling conversation, the Scotsman turned to the other two and said: 'Hey? What you(do) if you (wake) up one fine morning and (find) yourself a millionaire?' Pat came the answer from the Spaniard: 'If I (find) myself with a million dollars, I (go) home and (build) a bullring.' (Bullfights are as popular in Spain as football is in Italy.) The American throught for a while and said, 'If I (wake) up and (find) myself a millionaire one fine morning, I (take) the next flight to Paris and (have) a good time.' He then turned to the Scotsman and said, 'What you(do)?' The Scotsman replied without a moment's hesitation, 'I (go) to sleep again and (make) another million.'

Exercise 13

In the above story, the American's question to the Scotsman and the Scotsman's answer contain hidden conditions. What are they?

The American: 'What you(do) if ____________?'

The Scotsman: 'I (go) to sleep again and (make) another million if ____________

Exercise 14

Ask and answer yourself how life would be different for you:

a. if you were a matinee idol

b. if you were an Eskimo

c. if you were a kangaroo

19.8.3 The Third Conditional

The third conditional, unlike the first and the second, refers to the past, as you can see from these examples:

If I *had worked* hard, I *would have passed.* (but I didn't work hard, so I didn't pass)

If he *had invited* me, I *would have gone.* (but the didn't invite me, so I didn't go)

The third conditional refers to the past, but a past that never was, an unreal past. (The real past is as expressed in parentheses.)

The third conditional therefore refers to an unreal condition. The clauses are reversible.

Exercise 15

In column 1 below are sentences you hear. Explain in column 2, against each sentence, what you understand by it. The first one is an example.

1(you hear)	2 (you understand)
a. If the beleagured troops had received timely reinforcements, they would not have surrendered.	The beleagured troops did not receive timely reinforcements, so they surrendered.
b. If it had not rained so heavily in the catchment area, the dam would not have given way.	
c. If the train had arrived on time that day, we would have missed it.	
d. If Dad had known about it, he would have been very upset.	
e. If you had not booked a room for us, we would have had nowhere to stay.	

Exercise 16

Rewrite these sentences as third conditionals.

a. Fortunately for him, he missed the flight or he would have been killed in the crash.

b. Luckily he didn't notice what you were doing behind his back or he would have punished you.

c. You didn't take the usual precautions, so your travel programme was a fiasco.

Exercise 17

Here is a story about a general of the US army that never was. Read it and say what is the point of the story.

James Whistler (1834-1903) was a famous American painter who moved to London when he was twenty-five and made the city his adopted home. As a boy, he had spent some time as a cadet at West Point Military Academy, training to be an officer in the American army. Whistler, however, was a bad cadet. He disobeyed orders and neglected his studies. He was finally thrown out of the Academy. The immediate cause of his expulsion was this: at a chemistry exam, he was asked the question 'What is silicon?' and he wrote: 'Silicon is a metal.'

Years after he had moved to London and become a famous painter, Whistler, it seems, used to say:

'If silicon <u>had been</u> a metal, I <u>would have been</u> a general in the American army.'

Silicon alas! was not a metal and the American army was one general short.

<u>Note</u>

In formal or literary English, it is usual to omit the subordinate conjunction 'if' and reverse the subject and verb if the first verb in the if-clause is 'were' or 'had'.

Were the charge of match-fixing true, the game would lose all its lustre. (2nd conditional)

Were I in your place, I would do exactly as you have done. (2nd conditional)

Had I known of your problems, I would have done my bit to help you. (3rd conditional)

Note that the conditionals expressed in the above examples are unreal. It is possible to omit 'if' and reverse the subject and verb when the first verb of the conditional clause is 'should', no matter whether the condition expressed is real or unreal:

Should you ever go to Timbuctoo, you would see some very strange things there. (unreal condition)

Should anyone ask for you, what shall I tell him? (If anyone happens to ask for you...)

'Should' in the above two examples is used as an equivalent of 'happen to'.

Exercise 18

This is an exercise in revision. Match the two parts of these conditional sentences and write after each conditional whether it is the first, second or third.

a. I shall beg or borrow
b. If I had known you were coming
c. Say I have gone out
d. Unless it rains in the next few days
e. Were wishes horses
f. Had she not married

1. if anyone telephones and asks for me.
2. there will be a severe drought in this area.
3. beggars would ride.
4. she would have been an outstanding astrophysicist of her time.
5. if I don't have the money.
6. I would have sent someone to receive you at the station.

Apart from 'if' and 'unless', the following subordinate conjunctions may introduce an adverb clause of condition:

sub. conj.	example
In case	<u>In case there is an accident,</u> inform the police at once. <u>In case it rains</u>, we will cancel the picnic.

even if	Even if the circular had reached me in time, I wouldn't have attended the meeting. (conditional 3) She wouldn't forgive him even if he went down on his knees and begged for forgiveness. (conditional 2)
if only	If only he repented, all would still be well between husband and wife. (conditional 2)
on condition that (formal)	The company will agree to talks with the union leaders on condition that they call off the strike at once.

In addition, you may use 'so long as', 'as long as', 'only if' and 'provided that' if you want to talk of conditions that are not only real but necessary:

The maid will work for you so long as/as long as you treat her as a fellow human being.
Competition will be fair only if there is a level playing field for all competitors.
Agro-industries can flourish only if there are abundant seasonal rains.
We will be glad to attend the concert provided that there are late-night buses plying.
He will do the right thing himself provided that you don't try to twist his arm.

Elliptical Clause of Condition

You may use an elliptical if-clause containing the verb 'be':

If (you are) in doubt, consult a dictionary.
Avoid getting provoked, If (it is) possible.
If (you are) caught stealing in the supermarket, you will be charged with a heavy fine.
If (it is) a success, the demonstration will be repeated.
We will borrow, if (it is) necessary, and complete the house.

20 The Noun Clause

A noun clause is a subordinate clause that does the work of a noun. A noun, we saw earlier in Chapter 3 and elsewhere, can serve as subject of verb, object of verb, object of preposition, subject or object complement, or as an appositive, that is, in apposition to a noun or pronoun. Grammatically, a noun clause is as much a unit as a simple noun is. Compare each of the following sets of sentences:

subject of verb

His reply was most unconvincing. (noun, subject of 'was')

What he said in reply was most unconvincing. (noun clause, subject of 'was')

object of verb

I didn't hear his reply. (noun, object of 'didn't hear')

I didn't hear what he said in reply. (noun clause, object of 'didn't hear')

object of preposition

I wasn't listening to his reply. (noun, object of 'to')

I wasn't listening to what he said in reply. (noun clause, object of 'to')

complement

That was an unconvincing reply. (noun, subject complement)

That was what he said in reply. (noun clause, subject complement)

appositive

We must note this important fact, his reply. (noun, in apposition to the noun 'fact')

We must note this important fact, that he didn't reply in time. (noun clause, in apposition to the noun 'fact')

20.1 Noun Clause as Direct Object of Verb

Although in theory a noun clause can do all the functions of a noun, in practice the commonest function of a noun clause is as direct object of verb.

This type of noun clause can be from a sentence which was originally a statement, or from a sentence which was originally a question.

20.1.1 Noun Clauses From Statements

Look at the underlined clause in the following sentence:

He said that he hadn't played first-class cricket for a long while.

The underlined clause answers the question – What did he say? He said – He hadn't played first-class cricket for a long while. The clause 'that he hadn't played first-class cricket for a long while' is direct object of the verb 'said' in the main clause. It functions, in other words, as a noun clause.

Here are some more examples of noun clauses from statements, serving as objects of verb:

She admits that she has been rather careless of late.

I understand that your father has been taken ill.

I know for a fact that he is innocent.

She thinks that people are taking her for granted.

The underlined noun clauses are all from sentences which were originally statements:

She has been rather careless of late.

Your father has been taken ill.

He is innocent.

People are taking her for granted.

Note

In a noun clause, the full subject and predicate of the original sentence are retained but the structure is changed by the addition of an introductory word 'that' in the case of statements. All noun clauses from statements are introduced by the subordinate conjunction 'that'. Sometimes the conjunction is omitted:

She admits she has been rather careless of late.

I understand your father has been taken ill.

Exercise 1

Supply a suitable noun clause to each of these main clauses. The first is an example.

a. He found to his joy that his name was on the list of selected candidates.

b. The mother found to her relief ____________________

c. I understand ____________________

d. The thief admitted ____________________

e. He pleaded in self-defence ____________________

20.1.2 Noun Clauses From Questions

Noun clauses from questions are introduced by the question word (wh-word) if the questions were originally wh-questions, as in the following examples:

No one knew who he was or where he came from.

I can't say when he will be back home.

The underlined noun clauses are all from wh-questions:

main clause	introductory word	noun clause	original question
No one knew	who where	who he was where he came from	Who was he? Where did he come from?
I can't say	when	when he will be back home	When will he be back home?

But if the questions were originally yes–no questions, the noun clauses from these questions are introduced by 'if' or 'whether':

Tell us if you are coming to the party. (original question: Are you coming to the party?)

We must know at once whether you agree to our proposal. (original question: Do you agree to our proposal?)

She asked me if she might use my telephone. (original question: Might she use my telephone?)

Exericse 2

Pick out the noun clauses in the following sentences and say whether they are from statements or questions. If they are from questions, say whether they are wh-questions or yes–no questions. The first two are examples.

a. I know for certain that he took the exam. (noun clause from statement)

b. None of the neighbours knew why the family left so suddenly.
(noun clause from wh-question: Why did the family leave so suddenly?)

c. He asked her whether she had come on official work.

d. They insisted that I should see a doctor at once.

e. They asked the visitors where they were going to stay and whether they needed hotel accommodation.

f. The little girl asked her Grandpa if his teeth were all real.

Noun clauses from sentences which were originally wh-questions begin with:

a. interrogative pronouns: who whom what which

You know very well who is in charge here. ('who', pronoun, subject of 'is')

I wonder whom he is going to blame this time for the fiasco.
('whom', pronoun, object of 'is going to blame')

Do you recall what he told you? ('what', pronoun, direct object of 'told')

They were discussing which came first, the egg or the chicken.
('which', pronoun, subject of 'came')

b. interrogative adjectives: whose what which

They asked me whose poem/which poem I liked best in the anthology.
('whose'/'which', modifying the noun 'poem')

I asked her what time she got back home.
('what', adjective, modifying the noun 'time')

c. interrogative adverbs: when where why how

Tell me when the Shatabdi Express arrives from Chennai.
('when', adverb, modifying the verb 'arrives')

She knew, but wouldn't tell me, where he came from.
('where', adverb, modifying the verb 'came from')

His fellow-members of the club wondered why on earth he behaved in that silly manner. ('why', adverb, modifying the verb 'behaved')

I should like to know how he managed to dodge the police. ('how', adverb, modifying the verb 'managed to dodge')

Notice that the interrogative words in the above examples – pronouns, adjectives and adverbs – function exactly the same way in the noun clauses as they do in the original wh-question.

noun clause	original wh-question
interrogative pronouns	
who is in charge here (subject of 'is')	Who is in charge here? (subject of 'is')
what he told you (direct object of 'told')	What did he tell you? (direct object of 'did tell')
Interrogative adjectives	
whose poem/which poem I like best in the anthology (modifying the noun 'poem')	Whose poem/which poem did you like best in the anthology? (modifying the noun 'poem')
Interrogative adverbs	
where he came from (modifying the verb 'came from')	Where did he come from? (modifying the verb 'did come from')

Notice that the interrogative words – pronouns, adjectives and adverbs – join the noun clauses they introduce to the main clauses, thereby functioning like subordinate conjunctions.

The two types of noun clauses that we have considered so far, noun clauses from statements and noun clauses from questions, function as direct objects of verbs in the main clause. The verbs in the main clause are usually verbs of speech or verbs expressing some kind of mental activity. Here is a list of the more common verbs among them:

verbs of speech	admit agree (disagree) announce argue boast claim complain confess convince declare deny explain inform persuade promise remark report say state teach tell warn
verbs expressing mental activity	believe conclude consider decide discover doubt expect feel find out forget hear hope imagine know learn mean notice pretend prove realise remember suppose think trust understand wish

20.2 Noun Clause as Subject

Look at this pair of sentences:

He has given up his bad old ways. This is most promising.

The demonstrative 'this' in the second sentence refers to, and stands for, the entire first sentence. You may therefore combine these two sentences into one by substituting for 'this' the entire first sentence and adding to it the subordinate conjunction 'that':

That he has given up his bad old ways is most promising. (noun clause, subject of 'is')

Apart from the subordinate conjunction 'that', interrogative words like 'what', 'when', 'where', 'how' may introduce a noun clause as subject:

What is most disturbing is that he didn't get in touch with the police after the accident. (noun clause, subject of 'is')

When the General Body will meet is anybody's guess. (noun clause, subject of 'is')

Where the bank robbers were heading with their booty is not known. (noun clause, subject of 'is (not) known')

How you raise the money for the project is your problem, not mine. (noun clause, subject of 'is')

You may have a 'whether'-clause as subject:

Whether the pre-university exam results will be announced next week or the week after next will be known tomorrow. (noun clause, subject of 'will be known')

Exercise 3

Fill in the introductory word in the underlined noun clauses.

a. ____________ she should have married him wasn't surprising.

b. ____________ was surprising was that she stayed in a small town for twenty long years.

c. ____________ he was called upon to act as chief guest flattered him immensely.

d. ____________ the dacoits managed to escape from police custody is a mystery.

e. ____________ the police would succeed in recapturing them is open to doubt.

20.3 Noun Clause as Subject Complement

Look at the underlined clauses in these sentences:

a. He knew that he must go abroad and further improve his qualifications. His problem was how he should go about raising the necessary funds.

b. Madness runs in his family. His chief worry is that he may turn mad in his old age like his father.

c. To me the important thing is not what you say but what you do.

d. What I wonder is whether the Board will co-operate with the police investigation.

Each of the underlined clauses comes after a linking verb ('be') and completes the sentence. The clauses therefore are subject complements. Serving as subject complement is one of the functions of the noun. The underlined clauses are noun clauses serving, as they do, as subject complements.

Exercise 4

Complete the following sentences with suitable noun clauses serving as subject complements. The first one is done for you.

a. The remarkable thing is not that they failed but that they made the attempt at all. (2 clauses)

b. His main argument against permitting smoking in public places was ____________.

c. My fear about letting children be inducted into advertising campaigns is ____________.

d. The question that we need to consider as parents is ___________.
e. The argument of the defence was ___________.
f. What should concern us as citizens is ___________.

20.4 Noun Clause as Appositive

A fairly common type of noun clause is the clause that serves as an appositive, that is, stands in apposition to a noun or pronoun:

> The [fact] that protection against smallpox could be had through inoculation was known to many Asians and Africans for centuries.

The fact was known for centuries. What fact? That protection against smallpox could be had through inoculation. The clause 'that protection against smallpox could be had through inoculation' is the same as the noun 'fact' and therefore a noun clause. Given below are more examples of the noun clause linked in apposition to a noun:

> The [announcement] that the flight was being delayed for technical reasons evoked from the waiting passengers a groan of despair.
>
> The [theory] that life could originate from dead bodies through 'spontaneous generation' was finally disproved by Louis Pasteur.

The underlined clause in each sentence above is in apposition to the boxed noun.

Sometimes a noun clause of this type stands in apposition to the impersonal pronoun 'it':

> It was clear that the hosts did not like the topic of conversation among the guests. (noun clause, in apposition to the impersonal pronoun 'it')
>
> It became clear, as the interview continued, that the candidate had not come prepared. (noun clause, in apposition to the impersonal pronoun 'it')

The impersonal 'it' in the above examples is so called because it does not stand for anything; it has no meaning of its own. Its function is merely to start the sentence as well as to act as nominal subject (that is, as subject in name only), to which the real subject, the noun clause that follows, may be linked in apposition. That the noun clause is appositive to 'it' becomes clear when you substitute for 'it' the real subject, thus:

> That the hosts did not like the topic of conversation among the guests was clear.
>
> That the candidate had not come prepared became clear as the interview continued.

It is more usual to use a noun clause linked as an appositive to the impersonal 'it' than to use the noun clause as subject. For example, instead of saying: 'When the General Body will meet is anybody's guess' one might as well say, 'It is anybody's guess when the General Body will meet'.

Exercise 5

Join the sentences below, using appositive noun clauses anticipated by the impersonal 'it'. The first one is an example.

a. You must consult a lawyer at once. This is my considered view.

Answer: It is my considered view that you must consult a lawyer at once.

b. Louis Pasteur did not discover the microbe nor did he invent the microscope. This has been pointed out again and again.
c. The star-crossed lovers killed themselves by hurling themselves into the sea from a cliff. It is so believed in these parts.
d. Mr Ambrose always talks his way out of trouble. This is most remarkable.
e. Why was I ever sent to a boarding school? This was never made clear to me.

20.5 Sequence of Tenses

If the verb in the main clause is in the past tense, the verb in the noun clause must also be in the past tense. This special requirement is known as 'sequence of tenses'. Sequence of tenses occurs mostly with noun clause objects:

He said (that):

the old lady was rich.
the old lady had always been rich.
the old lady had just come by a large fortune.
the old lady was leaving everything to her nephew.
the old lady would leave everything to her nephew.
the old lady might be leaving everything to her nephew.

Notice the sequence of tenses in the above examples. The past tense 'said' in the main clause is followed by a past form of a verb in the noun class. If, on the other had, the verb in the main clause is in the present tense, the verb in the noun clause may be present, past or future. In that case there is no sequence of tenses:

He says (that):

the old lady is rich.
the old lady has always been rich.
the old lady was once rich.
the old lady will one day be rich.
the old lady may be rich.
the old lady could be rich.

The rule about sequence of tenses does not apply if the noun clause refers to a general truth, a universal truth, or a habitual action:

He said that most people act out of selfish motives.

Galileo observed that the earth goes round the sun and not the sun round the earth.

She said that she plays tennis in the evenings.

21 Reported Speech

In the previous chapter, we learned the different types of noun clauses and ways of structuring them. In this chapter we deal with the uses of the noun clause.

We use the noun clause primarily to report **speech** and **thought**. The speech and thought can be our own or someone else's.

> I *thought* I was being over-hasty.
>
> She *told* the Board that she had but a smattering of French.

There are two ways of reporting speech:

> 'I like all kinds of music but I draw the line at Rock,' said Dad to Mum.
>
> Dad told Mum that he liked all kinds of music but that he drew the line at Rock.

The first is called **direct speech**, the second **indirect or reported speech**. 'Speech' is meant to include all forms of 'inner speech' or thought.

In direct speech we reproduce the exact words of the speaker and enclose them in quotes, single (' ') or double (" ").

In reported speech, the reporter reports in his own words instead of reproducing within quotes the speaker's exact words—Dad told Mum that he liked all kinds of music but that he drew the line at Rock.

In our day-to-day life we use reported speech more often than direct speech. This is because it is difficult, if not impossible, to remember and recall what others tell us in their own words. Direct speech is found mostly in stories.

In direct speech, there is the <u>introductory part</u>, which tells us <u>who</u> said to <u>whom</u> (Dad told Mum), and then there is the spoken part within quotes ('I like all kinds of music but I draw the line at Rock'). There is a comma at the end of the introductory part and there are the quotes enclosing the speaker's exact words. The comma and the quotes together separate the spoken part from the introductory part:

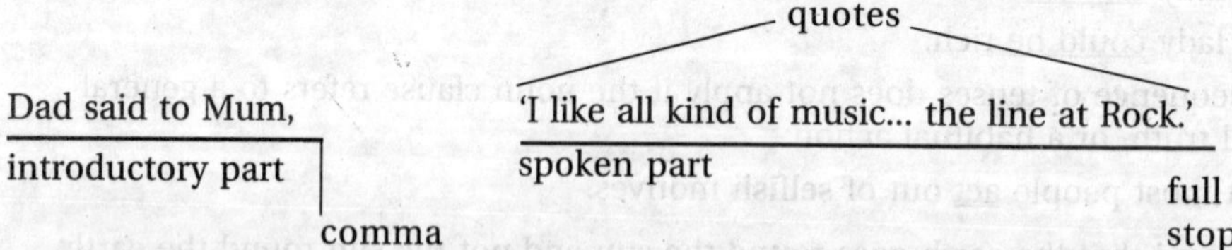

In reported speech, the two parts of direct speech are joined together in a single sentence. Rather, the spoken part is joined to the introductory part so that it is part of the introductory part and subordinated to it. As a result, the comma at the end of the introductory part and the quotes disappear.

<u>The problem in all reporting is one of incorporating the spoken part so that it is part of the introductory part</u>. The problem is one of turning the spoken part into a subordinate clause, more specifically, a noun clause acting as object of a verb in the introductory part.

Compare the two ways of reporting:

direct speech	reported speech
Dad said to Mum, 'I like all kinds of music but I draw the line at Rock.'	Dad *told* Mum *that he liked* all kinds of music but *that he drew* the line at Rock.

In changing direct speech into reported speech, we made the following changes:

1. The introductory verb 'said' was changed to the reporting verb 'told'.
2. A new word was brought in to join the spoken part to the introductory part (the subordinate conjunction 'that').
3. The first person pronoun 'I' was changed to the third person pronoun 'he'.
4. The simple present tense verbs 'like' and 'draw' were changed to the corresponding simple past tense forms 'liked' and 'drew'.

The changes listed above relate to the following in short:

1. the reporting verb;
2. the subordinate conjunction joining the spoken part to the introductory part;
3. personal pronouns, to which we may add possessive pronouns and possessive adjectives;
4. the tense of the verb or verbs within quotes, depending on the tense of the reporting verb.

Two other changes, relatively minor, may be called for, and these (not covered by the illustrative example given at the start of the chapter) relate to:

5. adverbs of time and place like 'today', 'now', 'here' and 'herein' and
6. demonstratives 'this' and 'these'.

These changes are tabulated below for easy reference:

Reporting verbs

kind of sentence	reporting verb	example
statement	say tell + personal object add admit affirm agree allege announce answer argue assert assure boast claim comment complain concede confirm declare demand deny imply insist mention observe predict proclaim propose reassure recall remark remind reply threaten urge warn	John *said* that he was going home with his sister Mary. She *claimed* that she was the champion runner of her school. He *boasted* that he came from a family of millionaires. The principal *insisted* that the teachers should set an example to the students. He *assured* me that the investment carried practically no risk.
question	ask enquire (of someone) want to know find out wonder	I *asked* him whether he went home every weekend. She *enquired* of me how I enjoyed the concert.

command	tell order demand forbid instruct direct	The captain *told* his team to assemble at the stadium by 9 a.m. The watchman *demanded* to see our identity cards.
request	ask request urge beg implore entreat plead (with someone)	I *urged* her to reconsider her decision. She *asked* him not to hurry and precipitate matters.

Connectives

kind of sentence	connective	example
statement	that	He said that he had to leave school abruptly.
question (wh-question) (yes–no question)	wh-word if/whether	They asked me who I was and where I came from. The customs official asked him if he had anything to declare.
command/request	sign of the infinitive 'to'	I told him to shut up. I begged her to lend me a fiver.

Verbs within inverted commas
(irrespective of the kind of sentence reported barring imperatives)

direct speech tense of the introducing verb	**reported speech** tense of the verb or verbs within quotes
present simple, present perfect or future	no change in tense; the rule regarding sequence of tenses does not apply.
example: John says/has said/will say, 'I am going home with my sister.'	John says/has said/will say that he *is going* home with his sister.
past simple tense	verbs changed to corresponding past tense:

examples

John said, 'I *am going* home today with my sister.'	am/is/are	—	was/were
John said that he *was going* home that day with his sister.	has/have do/does	 —	had did
John said, 'I *went* home yesterday with my sister.'	shall/will	—	should/would
John said that he *had gone* home the previous day with his sister.	can/may must	— —	could/might had to/would have to/must
John said, 'I *shall go* home tomorrow with my sister.'	ought to	—	ought to

John said that he *would go* home the next day with his sister.

John said, 'I *may go* home tomorrow with my sister.'

John said that he *might go* home the next day with his sister.

present simple (sing/sings)	—	past simple (sang)
present continuous (am/is/are singing)	—	past continuous (was/were singing)
present perfect (has/have sung)	—	past perfect (had sung)
past simple (sang)	—	past perfect (had sung)

Personal pronouns and possessives (irrespective of the kind of sentence reported)		
	direct speech	**reported speech**
subject of the sentence	I you we you	he or she they
object of verb or preposition	me you	him or her
possessive adjectives	my your our your	his or her their
possessive pronouns	mine yours ours yours	his or hers theirs

Adverbs of time and place/Demonstratives		
	direct speech	**reported speech**
adverbs of time	now	then
	ago	before
	today	that day
	tomorrow	the next day/the following day
	yesterday	the previous day/the day before
	last year	the previous year/the year before
	next Monday	the following Monday
adverbs of place	here herein	there therein
demonstratives	this these	that those

Tabulating the changes involved in conversion from direct speech to reported speech is not very difficult. The more difficult part is to know when to make the changes, for the changes are, by no means, automatic. Reporting is not a mindless, mechanical drill. An exercise in reporting is essentially an exercise in comprehension and interpretation. This means that we need to understand thoroughly what we are reporting, understand not just the content of the passage but the style and tone as well, and we need to interpret it accordingly, while remaining faithful to the spirit of the spoken text. Let us now consider the changes in detail.

21.1 The Reporting Verb

The spoken part of direct speech is usually one of the following three kinds of sentences—*statement, question, command or request.* But when reported, it becomes a statement, no matter what kind of sentence it originally was. All reported speech is rigorously restricted to one kind of sentence: the statement. It is the reporting verb that gives us an indication of the kind of sentence that is being reported. The reporting verb does more than that; it describes the nature of the remark that is being reported, whether it is a warning, a suggestion, a command or request, and so on. The description is based on the substance of the remark as well as the context in which it was originally made. For plain statements we have a variety of reporting verbs (see table on pages 273 – 74) and for statements in reply, we may use 'reply' or 'answer'. We may even use 'argue' if the remark involved some kind of logical thinking, however elementary:

Jagan said, 'The benefits of military training are vastly exaggerated.'
Jagan *argued* that the benefits of military training were vastly exaggerated.

Exercise 1

Replace the reporting verb 'said' by a more appropriate one, choosing it from this list. The first two are examples.

admit	assert	allege	complain
declare	predict	recall	suggest

a. The man known for his temperance lectures, when quizzed, finally said that he occasionally had a glass of beer.
Ans: The man known for his temperance lectures, when quizzed, finally *admitted* that he occasionally had a glass of beer.
b. I said that we should go out for a walk after dinner.
Ans: I *suggested* that we should go out for a walk after dinner.
c. The boarders said that the rooms were infested with bugs.
d. The prisoner said in court that he was innocent.
e. The punters said that some of the horses had been doped.
f. The weathermen said that we would have sunny but cool days.
g. The witness said that the car involved in the accident was a vintage Ambassador.
h. The boy was sure that the satchel was his, and said so.

Exercise 2

Complete the following reported statements with appropriate reporting verbs.

a. The principal ______ that preparation leave for the final year students would begin from the following Monday.

b. The reporter ________ that he was witness to the murder he had covered for his paper.
c. The doctor ________ the patient that he would be on his feet and out of the hospital in less than two weeks.
d. She ________ she had never told her colleague of her plans to quit the firm.
e. On the subject of radio taxis, the minister ________ that they were doing a good job.

21.1.1 Sequence of Tenses

The 'sequence of tenses' rule does not apply when the introducing verb is in the present simple tense, present perfect or future tense.

Exercise 3

Report the following. Notice that the introducing verb is in the present (simple or perfect) or future tense. The first is an example.

a. Sunita says, 'I am turning vegetarian.'
   Ans: Sunita says that she is turning vegetarian.
b. Mohan will say, 'I was not responsible for what happened.'
c. My youngest son says, 'I want to be a doctor.'
d. Ask him and he will say, 'I know nothing of the matter.'
e. He has gone public and said, 'There has been large-scale match-fixing since the eighties.'

If the introductory verb, however, is in the past tense, the verb or verbs within quotes change to their corresponding past tense forms. If the verb within quotes is already in the past tense, it may change into the past perfect tense. This rule is known as the **back-shift of tenses**.

Exercise 4

Put the following statements into reported speech, with the introducing verb in the past tense. The first two are examples.

a. Ravi: I am busy doing my homework and I can't come out now.
   Ans: Ravi said that he was busy doing his homework and that he could not come out at once. (Note that 'now' has been replaced by 'at once' and not 'then'; 'at once' is truer to the meaning intended.)
b. Doctor: You will have to stay in bed for a month.
   Ans: The doctor warned the patient that she would have to stay in bed for a month.
c. Parent to headmaster: I fear that my son may fail the finals this year.
d. Nita at the interview: I have completed the secretarial course and can type sixty words a minute.
e. Teacher to Ram: This is the third time you are slipping up and I hope there will be no fourth.
f. Person at the enquiries desk: Flight IC 105 from Calcutta to Lucknow is arriving an hour and thirty minutes late.

The changes we make in the tenses of verbs and adverbs of time enclosed within quotes also depend on the **time of reporting**, whether the reporting is done the same day, a few days later, or after a lapse of months or years.

John said to James, 'I am going home today with my sister.'

Let us say this was said on a Saturday morning. The same afternoon, Kumar, who happened to overhear what John said to James, reports to Keshav:

John told James that he is going home today with his sister.

Notice that the tense of the verb as well as the adverb of time ('today') remains unchanged in reported speech. This is because the reporting is done the same day before the event (John's going home) has taken place.

But if the reporting were done the next day, the reported version would then be:

John told James that he was going home yesterday with his sister.

The tense of the verb is changed to the past but the adverb of time is not changed to 'that day'. 'Yesterday' identifies the day of going home better than 'that day'. You use 'that day' only if the reporting takes place days or weeks later with the result that the particular Saturday is in the distant past and is not easily identifiable:

John told James that he was going home *that day* with his sister. (meaning 'the day he made the statement to James')

Exercise 5

Rewrite the following as reported speech.

a. 'I shall be in London next Saturday.' (said on Monday, as reported the same week)
b. 'I have no hopes of winning the match next week.' (reported the same day)
c. 'We'll be off on our trek tomorrow.' (said by two people, as reported the next day)
d. 'The Joint Parliamentary Committee will finish the report by the end of September.' (said by the secretary to the committee, as reported early September)

As a matter of fact, the rule in regard to the back-shift of tenses must be observed with great caution. The time of reporting, as we saw earlier, is one constraint. There are other constraints.

1. If the statement within quotes is a universal or general truth, which is as valid at the time of reporting as it was when it was originally made, the verb within quotes remains unchanged in tense:

   Galileo said, 'The earth moves round the sun.'
   Galileo observed that the earth *moves* round the sun.
   The doctor said to me, 'Your blood group is A.'
   The doctor told me that my blood group *is* A.

2. The statement within quotes may only be a local truth and not a general or universal truth but if the reporter has reason to believe the statement to be still valid at the time of reporting, the tense of the verb remains unchanged:

   Abdul said, 'My father is ill.'
   Abdul said that his father <u>is</u> ill. (as reported by a friend of Abdul who has reason to believe that Abdul's father is still ill)

3. The statement within quotes might well have been made in the past, even the distant past, but if it has still any relevance or interest for the reporter at the time of reporting, the back-shift of tenses need not happen. For example, a father reporting, months or years later, the compliment paid to his daughter by some of the people present at her dance recital might say:

Several of the invitees present said that my daughter *is* talented,

whereas one of the ushers in the hall might treat the remark about the girl simply as a past event and report it the day after the recital:

Several of the invitees present said that the danseuse *was* talented.

4. Changing the past simple tense of direct speech to the past perfect tense, again, is not automatic. Look at this example:

The speaker said, 'India *won* independence in 1947.'

The speaker observed that India *won* (not *had won*) independence in 1947.

Johnson said, 'I *met* Sunita way back in the eighties. She *was* a very vivacious girl.'

Johnson recalled that he *had met* Sunita way back in the eighties and that she *was* (not *had been*) a very vivacious girl.

Exercise 6

Rewrite the following as reported speech, using the words within parentheses as the main clause. Change the verb within quotes to the past tense only if necessary.

a. 'Most people are driven by greed.' (The preacher said)

b. 'Shakespeare was the greatest of Elizabethan playwrights and he wrote over forty plays.' (Our English tutor said)

c. 'The harvest could have been saved if the rains had not failed at the critical time.' (The farmer said to the revenue official)

d. 'Though people are important, the relations between them are not, and that in particular too much fuss has been made of marriage....' (Mrs Moore felt increasingly)

e. 'Columbus discovered America more than five hundred years ago.' (My father told me)

(Mrs Moore is a character in E.M. Forster's *A Passage To India.*)

21.1.2 Pronouns and Possessives

Changes in pronouns and possessives are strictly dependent on who is reporting to whom. It is generally assumed that the reporting is done by a third person to a fourth person, hence we have the rule that first person and second person pronouns and possessives be changed to third person pronouns and possessives. Thus,

John said to James, 'I am going home today with my sister'

becomes in reported speech:

John told James that *he* was going home that day with *his* sister.

The reporter here is a third person, neither John nor James, and he is reporting to a fourth person. This need not always be the case. Either of the participants involved in the original speech-act, John or James, may report, in which case the pronouns and possessives will have to be changed accordingly. The reported statement, as reported by John, would be:

I told James that *I* was going home that day with *my* sister.

As reported by James, the reported statement would be:

John told *me* that *he* was going home that day with *his* sister.

21.1.3 The Modal 'Must'

The modal 'must' takes three different forms in reported speech, depending on its meaning. 'Must' may mean:

1. necessity or compulsion at the moment of speaking:
   I *must* go now. (meaning 'I have to go now')
2. necessity or compulsion in the future:
   I *must* go tomorrow/next week. (meaning 'I shall have to go tomorrow/next week')
3. obligation or prohibition:
   You *must* do your duty by the country. (meaning 'You should do your duty by the country')
   You *mustn't* fail your country. (meaning 'You ought not to fail your country')

In reported speech, these three sentences become:

4. He said that he *had to go* at once.
5. He said that he *would have to go* the next day/the following week.
6. She told him that he *must do* his duty by the country.
   She told him that he *must not fail/ought not to fail* his country.

Even in the matter of changing adverbs of proximity (like 'now', 'here') and demonstratives ('this' and 'these') we must be careful. Consider these examples.

Direct speech:	We will *now* turn to the Indus Valley civilisation.
Indirect speech:	The professor said that the class would *next* turn to the Indus Valley civilisation.
Direct speech:	*Now* is the time for all broad-based political parties to unite on the basis of a common programme.
Indirect speech:	The Prime Minister said that the time had come for all broad-based political parties....a common programme.
Direct speech:	I used to know a lot of people in Bombay but I have few friends *here*, in Bangalore.
Indirect speech:	Mrs Sharma said that she used to know a lot of people in Bombay but that she had few friends in Bangalore. *Don't report: She had few friends there.*

21.2 Reporting Questions

Noun clauses from questions, we saw in the previous chapter, become statements and end with a full stop:

'What's the matter with you, child? Why are you crying?'
The policeman on the beat asked the child what the matter was with her and why she was crying.
'Can I help you?'
The policeman further asked the child if/whether he could help her.

<u>*Note*</u>

When we report a wh-question, we use the wh-word as a conjunction, and when we report a yes–no question, we bring in 'if' or 'whether' as a conjunction. Notice that in reported questions the subject comes before the verb, as in a statement.

Exercise 7

Put the following into reported speech using the verbs in parentheses with suitable changes. The first one is an example.

a. 'How old are you?' (They said at the interview)
   Ans: They asked me at the interview how old I was.
   (or) They asked her at the interview how old she was.
b. 'Why are you late for work? Can't you come on time?' (My boss said)
c. 'Did you see the manager?' (The receptionist said to the visitor)
d. 'How far is it to the General Post Office?' (The stranger said)
e. 'What do you do during the weekends? Do you spend your weekends catching up on your correspondence?' (My friend Sheila said)
f. 'What was the last movie you saw? Did you enjoy it?' (My uncle said to my sister)

21.2.1 'Shall' – Questions

Questions beginning with 'shall' followed by first person pronoun 'I' or 'we' may be:

a. pure future: Shall I ever go abroad? or
b. coloured future: Shall I lay the table?

The question in (a) is pure future; the speaker is wondering whether he will ever go abroad, whether such a thing will ever happen. In reported speech this becomes:

He wondered if he *would* ever go abroad.

We use 'would' with 'he' in the reported version in order to keep the pure future of the verb.

The question in (b), on the other hand, is coloured future; it is an offer of help. He wants to help by laying the table. In reported speech this becomes:

He asked her if he *should* lay the table.

'Should' with the third person 'he' keeps the future coloured.

Exercise 8

Turn the following 'shall' – questions into reported speech.

a. 'Shall I call Mala or Amala, Mum?' (Raju asked his mother...)
b. 'Shall I live to a hundred years?' (The octogenarian wondered...)
c. 'Shall I win a lottery?' (Mohan said to himself)
d. 'Shall I go and reserve the tickets for the concert?' (Sonali to her son)
e. 'Shall we expect a raise before Diwali?' (The workers' representative to the hotel manager)

A question like:

Will/Would you please switch off the fans as you leave the hall?

is not really a question but a request. It may be treated as a request or as a question and reported accordingly:

He asked them, politely, to switch off the fans as they left the hall (or)

He asked them if they would kindly switch off the fans as they left the hall.

'Will' may be used in exasperated commands or requests:

Will you stop playing that terrible music of yours and let me do my work in peace?

In reported speech this becomes:

He asked his daughter to stop playing her music and let him do his work in peace (or)

The father, by now thoroughly exasperated, told his daughter to stop playing her music and let him do his work in peace.

Here is another example of the same kind:

Direct speech: 'Will you, for heaven's sake, stop interrupting the speaker!'

Indirect speech: The chairman told/ordered the heckler to stop interrupting the speaker.

We can have a variation on this kind of exasperated command/request beginning with 'must':

Must you disturb me with your loud music?

Must you interrupt the speaker?

These are complaints and not questions. They may be treated as complaints and reported accordingly:

The father complained bitterly that his daughter always disturbed him with her loud music.

The chairman accused the heckler of interrupting the speaker.

Exercise 9

Report the following, with the reporting verb in the past tense.

a. Must you go so soon? Can't you spend the night with us?

b. Would you please spare your lawn mower for a day?

c. Will you, for God's sake, stop treating me as a five-year-old!

d. Will you please sing us another song?

e. Will you be singing us another song?

21.3 Reporting Requests/Instructions

Requests and instructions in English have the same grammatical forms: they are both imperatives. They may be positive or negative.

requests	instructions
Please pay cash.	Be quiet!
Will you please pay cash?	Will you please be quiet?
Turn down the radio, please.	Do your rough sketch in the space provided.
Would you please turn down the radio?	Don't write your name on the answer script. (negative)
Don't make noise. (negative)	

Note

'Will you please pay cash?' and 'Would you please turn down the radio?' are in fact requests, although they look like questions. In the same way, 'Will you please be quiet?' is an instruction.

reported requests	reported instructions
The shopkeeper asked the customer to pay cash.	The librarian told the students sitting in the library to be quiet.
He pleaded with his elder sister to turn down the radio.	The invigilator instructed the examinees to do their rough sketch in the space provided.

When reporting requests/instructions, we change the verb within quotes to an infinitive by adding the sign of the infinitive 'to' before the imperative verb:

pay, will pay ———> to pay

If the request is a negative one, we add 'not' before the infinitive:

don't make noise ——> not to make noise

Exercise 10

Change these requests into reported speech. The first one is an example.

a. Show me your ticket, please, (or) will you please show me your ticket?
   Ans: The inspector asked the passenger, politely, to show him his/her ticket.
b. Would you mind passing the mashed potatoes?
c. Pass me the salt, please.
d. Please don't keep the lights on after 10 p.m.

Exercise 11

Rewrite these instructions as reported speech. The first one is an example.

a. Stand at ease.
   Ans: The adjutant asked the cadets on parade to stand at ease.
b. Will you shut up?
c. Don't you ever be late for the rehearsal.
d. Don't feed the animals in the zoo. Don't tease them either.

21.4 Reporting Mixed Types

When we report direct speech which is a mixture of statements and questions, each sentence must be introduced by an appropriate verb:

He said, 'I'll meet you next Saturday. Does 10 o'clock suit you?'

He said that he would meet him the following Saturday and asked if 10 o'clock suited him.

Note that the first sentence is a statement and the second a question. Each sentence is appropriately introduced in the reported version. If, however, we get a question first and then a statement, we may introduce the statement with the connective device 'adding that':

Nita said to Satish, 'Where are you hiding, Satish? Father wants to see you.'

Nita asked Satish where he was hiding, adding that Father wanted to see him.

Exercise 12

Put the following into reported speech. The first one is an example.

a. Swapna: Are you going to the party, Susan?
Susan: I don't want to but mother insists that I go, and I may.
Answer: Swapna wanted to know from Susan if she was going to the party. Susan said that she did not want to go but that her mother insisted that she should, and she might therefore go. (or) Swapna asked Susan if she was going to the party. Susan replied that she did not want to go but that her mother insisted on her going and so she might go.

b. He said to her, 'Where are you off to? I have something important to tell you. Can you spare me five minutes?'

c. The tourist said, 'Can you tell me the way to the nearest hotel?'
'Yes, certainly,' said the passerby. 'Are you looking for a place where you can have a decent meal?'
'No,' replied the tourist, 'I want a place where I can stay for a few days in reasonable comfort and at an affordable price.'
'Go straight and turn left at the next intersection, and you will see on your right Hotel Annapoorna. That's just the place for you.'

d. The manager said to the new clerk, 'I am not happy with your work. Can't you do any better? If you can't, you will have to go.'

e. 'I haven't seen you for ages,' said my uncle. 'I understand you have been travelling a great deal lately.'
'Yes, uncle. I have just come back from a trip to Thiruvanthapuram.'
'How lovely! Did you visit the Kovalam Beach?'
'No, uncle. I wanted to but I didn't have the time,' I said in reply.
'What a pity! Doesn't matter. You must visit the beach when you go next. When are you likely to go again?'

<u>Note</u>

When you report sentences beginning: 'I think that...', 'I hope that...', 'I understand that....' you may make the verb within quotes the reporting verb, as shown below:
My old professor said, 'I think John Gielgud's *Hamlet* the best I've ever seen, next only to Lawrence Olivier's.'
My old professor thought John Gielgud's *Hamlet* the best he had ever seen, next only to Lawrence Olivier's.
Don't report:
My old professor said that he thought...
Here is another example:

Direct speech: He said, 'Has your father been taken seriously ill? I understand he had a mild heart attack. I hope he will soon be home, none the worse for the attack.'

Indirect speech: He asked me if my father had been taken seriously ill. He understood that he had had a mild heart attack and hoped that my father would soon be home, none the worse for the attack.

Don't report: He said that he understood... He further said that he hoped....

Exercise 13

Read the following passage from Jane Austen's *Pride and Prejudice*. Report the exchanges between Mr Bennet, Elizabeth and Mrs Bennet as you would report them, and also as Elizabeth would report them to her elder sister Jane.

Mrs Bennet rang the bell and Miss Elizabeth was summoned to the library.

'Come here, child,' cried her father as she appeared. 'I have sent for you on an affair of importance. I understand that Mr Collins has made you an offer of marriage. Is it true?' Elizabeth replied that it was.

'Very well – and this offer of marriage you have refused?'

'I have, sir.'

'Very well. We now come to the point. Your mother insists upon your accepting it. Is it not so, Mrs Bennet?'

'Yes, or I will never see her again.'

'An unhappy choice is before you, Elizabeth. From this day you must be a stranger to one of your parents. Your mother will never see you again if you do <u>not</u> marry Mr Collins, and I will never see you again if you <u>do</u>.'

'What do you mean, Mr Bennet, by talking in this way? You promised me to insist upon her marrying him.'

'My dear,' replied her husband, 'I have two small favours to request. First, that you will allow me the free use of my understanding on the present occasion; and secondly, of my room. I shall be glad to have the library to myself as soon as possible.'

A Note of Warning

1. Ignore the vocatives in the passage like 'child', 'My dear' etc. These, so natural in direct speech, have no place in reported speech.
2. Ignore the expressions 'come here' and 'very well'. Expressions like these are familiar opening gambits in conversation but they cannot easily be translated into reported speech.
3. The focus in reporting ought to be on a clear, concise, accurate account of what was said and by whom.

   (Jane Austen (1775–1817), novelist, author of *Pride and Prejudice,* her best known novel)

Given below are part proceedings of a trial in two sections. In section 1, Sergeant Mathers, witness for the defence, is being examined by the defence counsel, Mr Bairns. In section 2, the same sergeant is being cross-examined by Sir Ernest Prettiboy, counsel for the prosecution.

Section 1

(The accused: Mr Todhunter; victim: Miss Norwood; witness for defence: Detective-Sergeant Mathers; counsel for defence: Mr Bairns; counsel for the prosecution: Sir Ernest Prettiboy)

Amid an expectant hush Sergeant Mathers is recalled to the box.

Mr Bairns: 'When you accompanied the accused back to his house after his visit to Scotland Yard last November, did he show you a revolver?'

Witness: 'He did.'
Mr Bairns: 'Did you examine it?'
Witness: 'I did.'
Mr Bairns: 'What did you find?'
Witness: 'That it was a brand-new one.'
Mr Bairns: 'What do you mean by that?'
Witness: 'It has never been fired.'
Mr Bairns: 'You are sure of that?'
Witness: 'Quite sure.'
Mr Bairns: 'How could you tell it had never been fired?'
Witness: 'I examined the inside of the barrel. It was coated with oldish, dried oil. Where there was no oil the barrel showed quite smooth.'
Mr Bairns: 'How long would you estimate that the oil had been there?'
Witness: 'It had been there some months, by the look of it.'
Mr Bairns: 'What would you have expected to find if the gun had been fired recently, say, within the last few weeks?'
Witness: 'Oil not so old as that, and I should have expected to see signs of striation on the exposed portions of the barrel and possibly lead fouling.'

Section 2

Sir Ernest: 'You are the Scotland Yard expert on firearms, Sergeant Mathers?' (Sir Ernest began with a kindly smile.)
Witness: 'No, sir.'
Sir Ernest: 'You are not?' (Sir Ernest appeared surprised.) 'But you are an expert?'
Witness: 'Not an expert. I have a working knowledge of firearms.'
Sir Ernest: 'Well, most of us have that. In what way does your knowledge exceed that of the ordinary person?'
Witness: 'I've been through a course on the subject, as part of my training.'
Sir Ernest: 'And that course, though it did not make you an expert, enabled you to pronounce, after a casual examination, just how long ago a gun had been fired?'
Witness: 'It enabled me to tell when a gun had not been fired.'
Sir Ernest: 'Did you take this revolver to pieces to examine it?'
Witness: 'No.'
Sir Ernest: 'Did you examine it at all, or did you merely glance at it?'
Witness: 'I examined it as much as I thought necessary.'
Sir Ernest: 'In other words, you just glanced down the barrel?'
Witness: 'No.'
Sir Ernest: 'You didn't even glance down the barrel?'
Witness: 'I looked very carefully down the barrel.'
Sir Ernest: 'Oh, I see. So carefully and with such good eyesight that you were able to detect the absence of lead fouling and striation in the barrel, which a lens is usually required to detect?'
Witness: 'I was satisfied with my examination.'

(adapted from Anthony Berkeley, *Trial and Error*)

Report the above. Section 1 has been done as an example.

Answer (Section 1)

> Examined by Mr Bairns, counsel for defence, Detective-Sergeant Mathers, witness for defence, said that he had been shown a revolver by Mr Todhunter the accused when he had accompanied him to his house after his visit to Scotland Yard the previous November. He had examined the revolver and found it to be a brand-new one in that it had never been fired. He based his conclusion on the presence of oldish, dried oil inside the barrel and the absence of any signs of striation on the exposed portions of the barrel and of lead fouling.

Notice that in the reported examination of Sergeant Mathers by Mr Bairns, no attempt has been made to follow Mr Bairns' questions and the Sergeant's answers one by one, one after the other. To do so would be to make the report at least three times as large as the original! Considerations of space apart, there is no need in most cases to report the question and then the answer to the question. The answer presupposes the question. Do not report the way it has been reported below:

> Mr Bairns began by asking Sergeant Mathers whether he had been shown a revolver by the accused (Mr Todhunter) when he had accompanied him to his house after his visit to Scotland Yard the previous November. Sergeant Mathers replied that he had been. Mr Bairns then asked him what he had found, to which the Sergeant replied that he had found that it was a brand-new one.... and so on.

Just report the way it has been reported in the specimen answer. Notice the relevant points made by the defence witness to convince the court that the revolver shown him by Mr Todhunter could not be the murder weapon since, according to him, the gun had never been fired. Your report must be clear, concise and coherent, and if possible, elegant too.

Exercise 14

Report the cross-examination of Sergeant Mathers by Sir Ernest Prettiboy on the lines of the specimen answer.

Final Note on Reported Speech

1. Direct speech and reported speech are not freely interchangeable any more than active and passive voice. The two modes of speech presentation in writing are basically different. Direct speech is natural, spontaneous, (or spontaneous-seeming) speech; it exists in an eternal present: the speaker's present originally, which yet becomes our present as we let ourselves be transposed backward in time to listen to the dialogue of a novel or play.

   Reported speech, on the other hand, is artificial speech. When we turn direct into reported speech, we effect more than a formal change. A third person has intervened who undertakes to transmit to us the original speech. In the process a number of changes take place.

   In the first place, the original speech loses all its naturalness, its living quality. All those elements which impart to direct speech its natural flavour – like, for instance, questions, exclamations, ellipses, not to mention the fumblings and hesitancies so natural to spontaneous speech – disappear. Secondly, it no longer exists in the present; it becomes the report of something said in the past—hence the rules in regard to the shift of time and tense. This is a big loss but there are compensating gains—clarity, conciseness, coherence and (usually) elegance. A reported version can never afford to be slipshod; it has to be an absolutely clear, concise and coherent account of what has been said, by whom, and to whom. As teachers of English, we need to bring home to our learners the immense difference between direct and reported speech. One way of doing that would be to compare the examination of Sergeant Mathers, or even better, the cross-examination of the Sergeant with its reported version and discuss with the class the profit and loss involved in conversion of direct to reported speech.

2. Direct speech and indirect speech are not the only ways of reporting open to the writer. A number of interesting variations on the traditional modes of direct and indirect speech are possible, and writers from Jane Austen to Stevie Smith have tried these variations on the traditional modes. The most important of these is what is known as free indirect speech. Look at this example of reporting:

   a. Where had he gone wrong? he wondered.

Compare the above with:

b. He said, 'Where did I go wrong?' and

c. He wondered where he had gone wrong.

Example (b) is a clear case of direct speech (or thought), just as example (c) is a case of reported speech. Example (a), on the other hand, is neither the one nor the other but a blend of the two. It has the following features of reported speech:

1. the introducing verb 'said' has been changed to 'wondered';
2. the tense of the verb has been changed from past simple ('did go') to past perfect ('had gone');
3. the first person 'I' has been changed to the third person 'he'.

At the same time it has some of the features of direct speech:

1. the question form is retained;
2. there is no subordination of the spoken part to the introductory part, that is to say, the spoken part has not been made part of the main clause, as is done in reported speech proper.

Free indirect speech is stylistically different from traditional direct and indirect (or reported) speech. Much has been written about the stylistically significant effects of free indirect speech but as teachers of grammar we need not go into these nor need we teach the class to report the free indirect way. All that we might do is to get the class to notice this variation in view of its pervasiveness in fiction and non-fiction so that they are not puzzled by what might appear to them as an arbitrary departure from what they were taught in the classroom as correct modes of reproducing speech when they encounter it in their free reading.

---

* Stevie Smith (1902–1971), poet and novelist, author of three novels and several volumes of verse

22 The Adjective Clause

The adjective clause is a subordinate clause that does the work of an adjective—it modifies a noun or pronoun. The function of the adjective clause may be seen by comparison with the simple adjective construction:

a *tall* man; a man *who is tall*

a *broken* chair; a chair *which is broken*

a *haunted* house; a house *where a ghost regularly appears* (or) a house *in which a ghost lives.*

The only difference between the adjective and the adjective clause is this: the adjective <u>precedes</u> the noun it modifies, the adjective clause <u>follows</u> the noun it modifies.

The adjective clause is more commonly known as the **relative clause.** It will hereafter be referred to as the relative clause.

We use a relative clause to give further information about someone or something:

The other day I met a man *who knew Mahatma Gandhi.* (relative clause, modifying the noun 'man' in the main clause)

The tomatoes *that you bought* are all rotten. (relative clause, modifying the noun 'tomatoes' in the main clause)

The nouns 'man' and 'tomatoes' modified by the relative clauses in the above sentences are called **antecedents** to the relative pronouns 'who' and 'that'.

Relative clauses are most commonly introduced by the **relative pronouns** 'who' ('whom'), 'which' and 'that' (see Chapter 4, 4.3.8), less commonly by the **relative adjective** 'whose' (Chapter 5, 5.1.6) and by the **relative adverbs** 'when', 'where' and 'why' (Chapter 12, 12.4.2).

22.1 Relative Clauses Introduced by Relative Pronouns

Exercise 1

Pick out the relative clauses in the following sentences and the nouns/pronouns they modify. The first two are examples.

a. They selected the candidate *who was the best of the lot.* (rel. cl., modifying the noun 'candidate')

b. The candidate selected was for a post *which had remained vacant for years.* (rel. cl., modifying the noun 'post')

c. The selected candidate was a woman who had been to a very ordinary school.

d. The author whom I used to adore as a little girl was Enid Blyton.

e. Those who live in glass houses should not throw stones.

The relative class is different from the other two types of subordinate clauses, the noun clause and the adverb clause. Compare the italicised subordinate clauses in column 1 with those in column 2:

1	2
He said *that his ambition was to be a scientist.* (noun clause, object of 'said')	The children *who live in this street* are very naughty. (relative cl., modifying the noun 'children')
I met her briefly *as she was leaving for the airport.* (adverb clause of time, modifying the verb 'met')	The book *that you lent me* is very interesting. (relative cl., modifying the noun 'book')

The relative clauses in column 2 are introduced by the relative pronouns 'who' and 'that'. The relative pronoun is like a subordinate conjunction in that it introduces the relative clause and joins it to the main clause. At the same time it functions as a subject or object in the relative clause. Thus, 'who' is the subject of 'live' in the relative clause 'who live in this street', 'that' is the direct object of the verb 'lent' in the relative clause 'that you lent me'. The subordinate conjunctions that introduce the noun clause and the adverb clause in column 1 ('that', 'as') have no other function than introducing the clause and joining it to the main clause.

The relative pronoun, as you saw in the chapter on pronouns, may function as the object of a preposition in the relative clause:

The girl *with whom you went to school* is my cousin and not my sister. ('whom', object of the preposition 'with')

The house *in which we live now* is a rented one. ('which', object of the preposition 'in')

The relative clause is very much like a sentence. It becomes a relative clause when it is inserted in another sentence to become part of it. This is how we relativise a sentence. The process of relativisation is shown step by step.

Example 1

Here are two separate sentences:

The man is from Timbuctoo. *The man* arrived yesterday.

Since the subject of both sentences is the same, we may replace the second subject by a personal pronoun:

Step 1 *The man* is from Timbuctoo. *He* arrived yesterday.

We still have two separate sentences. To change the second sentence into a relative clause and make it part of the first, we go through two additional steps.

Step 2 Replace 'he' by the relative pronoun 'who':
*The man is from Timbuctoo *who arrived yesterday.*

We now have a single sentence but it is not acceptable English.

Step 3 In this step we insert the relative clause 'who arrived yesterday' immediately after the noun ('man') it modifies:
The man *who arrived yesterday* is from Timbuctoo.

Example 2

Here is another example of relativisation. Look at these two sentences:

The painting is a Turner. I showed you *the painting.*

Step 1 Replace the second noun by a personal pronoun:
The painting is a Turner. I showed you *it*.

Step 2 Replace the pronoun 'it' by the relative pronoun 'which':
*The painting is a Turner *I showed you which*.

Step 3 Move the relative pronoun to the front of the relative clause:
*The painting is a Turner *which I showed you*.

Step 4 Insert the relative clause immediately after the noun it modifies:
The painting *which I showed you* is a Turner.

Here there is an additional step: the relative pronoun is moved to the front of the relative clause before it is inserted in the first sentence. Note that the word-groups marked by an asterisk are not English sentences.

*Turner: J.M.W. Turner (1775-1851), a major English landscape painter. By 'a Turner' is meant a painting by Turner.

Example 3

The woman is my wife. You spoke to me so warmly of *the woman*.

Step 1 *The woman* is my wife. You spoke to me so warmly of *her*.

Step 2 *The woman is my wife *you spoke to me so warmly of whom*.

Step 3 *The woman is my wife *of whom you spoke to me so warmly*.

Step 4 The woman *of whom you spoke to me so warmly* is my wife.

In example 1, the relative pronoun is the subject of a verb in the relative; in example 2, it is the object of a verb in the relative clause; in example 3, it is the object of a preposition in the relative clause.

Revision of Chapter 4, 4.3.8, dealing with the relative pronoun, would be useful.

Exercise 2

Join the sentences below by turning the second sentence into a relative clause.

a. The man owns a dog. The dog walks on its hind legs.
b. Henrik Ibsen, the Norwegian playwright, wrote a play. The play was called *A Doll's House*.
c. The play created a veritable sensation in Victorian England. The play was produced in 1879.
d. I once saw a man. The man was sawing off a branch of a tree.
e. He was sawing off a branch. He was sitting on the branch.
f. The people have forgotten you. You did a great deal for the people.

22.1.1 Types of Relative Clauses

Compare the italicised relative clauses in the following sentences:

The boy *who lives next door* is a computer whiz kid.

My friend and classmate Rahim, *who lives next door*, is a computer whiz kid.

The relative clause in the first sentence gives us essential information about the boy who is a computer whiz kid. It defines or restricts the antecedent to one particular type:

The boy is a computer whiz kid.
Which boy are you talking about?
The boy who lives next door, and not any other boy.

Out of the thousands of boys the clause selects one particular boy, the boy who lives next door.

Notice that the clause 'who lives next door' cannot be omitted, since without it the sentence does not make sense. We call it a **defining** or **restrictive** relative clause.

The clause in the second sentence, on the other hand, is not an essential part of the sentence. Even without it the essential message remains: my friend and classmate Rahim is a computer whiz kid. When you say 'my friend and classmate Rahim', the person referred to is fully defined. What, then, does the relative clause do in the sentence? It gives us additional but non-essential information about Rahim. We call the clause a **non-defining** or **non-restrictive** clause.

He lectured on William Wordsworth, *who is England's greatest nature poet.*

My youngest sister, *who is barely six years old,* wants to be a software engineer.

Note that the defining relative clause is never preceded by a comma. A non-defining relative clause is set off from the main clause by a comma or a pair of commas, one comma if the clause comes at the end of the sentence or a pair of commas if the clause comes in the middle of the sentence. Note that the non-defining relative clause is a feature of written English.

Contact Clauses

Relative pronouns functioning as objects of verbs or of prepositions may be omitted from defining relative clauses:

The man (whom) *I wanted to see* was on vacation.
He found the book (which) *he was looking for.*

Such clauses are contact clauses. For making a contact clause:

a. you need to have a defining relative clause, and
b. the relative pronoun introducing the relative clause must be object of verb or preposition.

Exercise 3

What do you call a person who does not believe in the existence of God? We call him an 'atheist'. An atheist is a person who does not believe in the existence of God. On the same lines define the following terms, using the defining relative 'who' and the information given in the box below.

a. a teetotaller	b. a hypocrite	c. a jingoist
d. a feminist	e. an intellectual	f. a lotus-eater

1. believes in the superiority of his/her country and stridently proclaims it
2. lives an idle, comfortable life and does not care very much about anything
3. abstains from alcoholic drinks
4. says one thing and does another
5. believes that women should have the same rights, power and opportunity that men have
6. reads a lot and thinks a great deal about ideas and issues

Exercise 4

Underline the relative clauses in the following sentences and say whether they are defining or non-defining. The first two are examples.

a. Opposite the park is the school <u>which I went to</u>. (defining)

b. Opposite the park is St Paul's School, <u>which is the oldest in the city</u>. (non-defining)

c. The bank is situated in Napier Road, which runs parallel to Mahatma Gandhi Road.

d. He is the person you must meet for the purpose.

e. I ran into a friend of mine whom I had not seen for twenty years.

f. My brother, who lives in Delhi, is visiting us next week.

g. My brother who lives in Delhi is visiting us next week.

Do (f) and (g) mean the same?

Exercise 5

Join the sentences below by changing the second sentence into a defining relative clause. Use contact clauses, where possible. The first two are examples.

a. He works for a company. The company makes garments for export.
Ans: He works for a company <u>which makes garments for export</u>.

b. I like the dress. You bought it for me in the sale.
Ans: I like the dress <u>you bought me in the sale</u>. (contact clause)

c. She hit upon an idea. The idea seemed absolutely brilliant.

d. We explored a cave. A twentieth century saint had lived in the cave.

e. The friends were no longer there. I had hoped to meet the friends.

f. The girl did not show up. The man was waiting for the girl.

g. The car was the envy of the neighbours. The owner had imported it from Japan.

Exercise 6

First, make defining relative clauses with these sentences with the relative pronoun left out. Then, find a suitable predicate to go with the antecedent and complete the sentence. The first one is an example.

a. I bought a two-wheeler.
   1. The two-wheeler I bought...
   2. The two-wheeler I bought cost me thirty thousand rupees.

b. We had a guest for the weekend.

c. She sent home a telegram.

d. They moved to a luxury apartment.

e. The old lady lived in a cottage.

f. We boarded a bus.

Relative pronouns cannot be omitted:

1. When they function as objects of verbs or prepositions in non-defining clauses:
   My father, *whom* you met recently, has gone abroad.
   My uncle, with *whom* you have been friends for years, is arriving today.
2. When they function as subjects of relative clauses, defining or non-defining:

I met a friend of mine *who* was at school with you.

My father, *who* is well over seventy, still lives an active life.

Study the following tables carefully. They summarise the different functions of relative pronouns.

defining relative clause		
	people	things
	who/that	that/which
subject of the clause	The man *who/that* is going to marry Rita is tall and handsome.	Here is a book *that/which* costs nearly five hundred rupees.
	whom/(that)	which/(that)
object of verb	The man *whom/(that)* Rita is going to marry is tall and handsome.	The book *which/(that)* you ordered has arrived.
	whom/(that)	which/(that)
object of preposition	The man *whom/(that)* Rita is engaged to is tall and handsome.	The book *which/(that)* you have been waiting for has arrived.

<u>*Note*</u>

The relative pronoun within brackets may be omitted.

non-defining relative clause		
	people	things
	... who ...	... which...
subject of the clause	My father, *who* is well over seventy, still lives an active life.	Mathematics, *which* is a compulsory subject of study in school, is a very useful subject.
	... whom ...	... which ...
object of verb	My father, *whom* you met recently, is over seventy years of age.	Mathematics, *which* I disliked intensely at school, is actually an exciting subject to me now.
	... preposition whom ...	... preposition which...
object of preposition	My father, for *whom* a five-mile walk is a must, is over seventy years of age.	Mathematics, for *which* I had no liking, is so useful now.

22.1.2 Prepositional Relative Clauses

Prepositional relative clauses are clauses which have a preposition preceding the relative pronoun or ending a relative clause:

1. This is the plan *about which I wanted to talk to you.*
2. This is the plan (*that*) *I wanted to talk to you about.*

When the preposition precedes the relative pronoun, it must be followed by 'whom' (for people) and 'which' (for things):

3. The boy *of whom he had high hopes* failed him badly.
4. This is the house *on which he spent quite a fortune.*

The sentences 1, 3 and 4 above (in which the preposition precedes the relative pronoun) are formal and more likely to occur in written English. In spoken English and even in informal writing, they would be rephrased as in example 2:

5. The boy (*that/whom*) *he had such high hopes of* failed him badly.
   The boy *he had such high hopes of* failed him badly. (contact cl)
6. This is the house (*that/which*) *he spent quite a fortune on.*
   This is the house *he spent quite a fortune on.* (contact cl)

However, in a non-defining relative clause, the preposition generally comes before the relative pronoun:

The book *Spycatcher, about* which I was telling you, was banned in Britain in 1988.

Here is my wife, *for* whom you expressed such admiration.

Exercise 7

Pick out the relative clauses in the following sentences and say whether they are defining or non-defining. Note that the punctuation that marks the non-defining clause has been deliberately left out.

a. This is the story of a man who loses his memory in the middle of a crowd.
b. The children waved to the soldiers who were marching by.
c. He is the sort of man whom people love to hate.
d. The drug which is being tried out on an experimental basis is expected to be on sale by next year.
e. I bought a dozen bananas three of which were found to be rotten.

Exercise 8

Here are pairs of sentences. The first of the pair is a complete sentence while the second is a skeletal one. Join each pair by making the skeletal sentence a relative clause, defining or non-defining. The first two are examples.

a. Yesterday I met an old woman. she/go/to school/with my grandmother

   Ans: Yesterday I met an old woman *who had gone to school with my grandmother.* (defining)
b. She gave me her telephone number. I/jot it down/somewhere

   Ans: She gave me her telephone number, *which I have jotted down somewhere.* (non-defining)
c. That was Lawrence's last novel. it/not published/in England/for well over thirty years
d. These are questions. no easy answers/to them
e. Corruption in high places is an issue. it/unlikely/to exercise/the minds of the common people
f. The landlady did not take kindly to the new tenant. the agent/found/for her
g. The new railway timetable is a great improvement on the old. it/is/very user-friendly
h. *Hamlet* is Shakespeare's best known tragedy. more books/written/about *Hamlet*/ than about any other play/ancient or modern

22.2 Relative Clauses Introduced by the Relative Adjective 'Whose'

Relative clauses may be introduced by the relative adjective 'whose':

An equilateral triangle is a triangle *whose sides are equal.*

Note that the relative adjective, unlike the relative pronoun, does not function as subject or object in the relative clause; that function is done by the noun modified by 'whose':

We heard of a man *whose great uncle had lived to a hundred and five years.* ('great uncle', subject of 'had lived')

I would much rather discuss this question with someone *whose intellectual calibre I respect.* ('calibre', object of 'respect')

I would much rather discuss this question with someone *for whose intellectual calibre I have respect.* ('calibre', object of the preposition 'for')

The relative adjective 'whose' refers to persons as well as things:

I met a funny old man *whose hair was a bright shade of red.*

That is a country *whose problems are largely a colonial legacy.*

We use the relative clause introduced by 'whose' to describe people:

Mr Sobjohn is a man *whose after-dinner stories seldom fail to entertain,* though oft-repeated.

Exercise 9

Think of three people you know and say something about them, using a relative clause beginning with 'whose'. Here is an example to guide you:

Mr Mulroy is a man whose public face is radically different from his private one.

Exercise 10

Express each pair of sentences as one sentence, using 'whose' as a defining or non-defining relative. Insert the appropriate punctuation to mark the non-defining relative.

a. This is the new English teacher. Her arrival has long been awaited.
b. He works for a non-governmental organisation. Their services to the tribals of Orissa recently came in for high praise.
c. The Prime Minister spoke to the back-benchers of his party. Their demeanour in Parliament brought little credit to the party.
d. We present to you, ladies and gentlemen, Ravi, the city's leading architect. His design for a new community centre has just won a prize.

22.3 Relative Clauses Introduced by Relative Adverbs

Relative adverbs are like relative pronouns in that they refer to a noun antecedent in the main clause. At the same time they function like adverbs in the relative clause:

Do you know the time *when* the Rajdhani Express from Delhi arrives?

I remember the house *where* I was born.

This is the reason *why* we lost the match to New Zealand.

'When', 'where' and 'why' in the above examples refer back to their antecedents ('time', 'house', 'reason') just like relative pronouns. They also function like adverbs in that they modify the verbs in the relative clause ('arrives', 'was born', 'lost').

The modification is typically adverbial: time, place, reason.

Compare:

I remember the house *where* I was born.

I remember the house *in which* I was born.

Both sentences have relative clauses, which mean the same. The relative clause 'where I was born' begins with a relative adverb, while the relative clause 'in which I was born' begins with the relative pronoun 'which' preceded by the preposition 'in'. The second clause, in other words, is a prepositional relative clause.

Exercise 11

Supply the missing relative adverb in the following sentences.

a. This is a country ____________ the old are respected and cared for.

b. In the nineteen twenties ____________ expeditions to Mount Everest came to be organised, many Sherpas from Darjeeling were engaged as high-altitude porters.

c. I know the reason ____________ he didn't show up at your party but I wouldn't tell you.

d. Tourist to a local: Can you suggest a hotel ____________ we can stay for a few days without being cheated?

Like the relative pronouns, relative adverbs may be defining or non-defining:

I still remember the sleepy little town in south Malabar <u>where I spent my childhood.</u> (defining)

While on a visit to the United Kingdom, the delegation of M.P.'s made it a point to go to Sandhurst, <u>where army cadets receive their pre-commission training</u>. (non-defining)

The three years I spent in the city reading English Honours were the best years of my life. I can't think of a time <u>when I was happier</u>. (defining)

He neglected his studies until a month before the examination, <u>when he started working in right earnest</u>. (non-defining)

'Why' as a relative adverb introduces only defining clauses:

Give me one good reason <u>why any country must intervene in the affairs of another</u>.

Exercise 12

Replace the underlined words by the relative adverbs 'where', 'when' and 'why'.

a. Jane Austen wrote about an age <u>in which</u> England was still largely rural and the fastest mode of transport was a horse-driven carriage.

b. That is a country <u>in which</u> all nature is beautiful and only man is vile.

c. Three days before she died, they sent for a doctor <u>and by then</u> it was too late to save her.

d. At the invitation of Prof. Hardy, Ramanujan left for Cambridge <u>and there</u> he established himself as a world-class mathematician.

Exercise 13

Think of three important times in your life and say why they are important to you. Here is an example:

That was the day when I met the woman who later became my wife.

Exercise 14

Think of three places that have been important to you and say why they have been important to you. Here's an example:

Chennai, that is the place where, at the age of ten, I saw the sea for the first time.

23 Phrases

A phrase, we defined in the chapter on noun phrases (Chapter 8), is a cohesive meaningful word-group having no subject-predicate of its own. A clause, on the other hand, is a meaningful word-group with its own subject-predicate structure. Look at these two sentences:

The people living upstairs are moving to the suburbs.

The people who are living upstairs are moving to the suburbs.

The word-group 'living upstairs' has no subject or predicate of its own. It has a participle ('living') but participles, as you know, are non-finite verbs, and non-finite verbs cannot make clauses.

The word-group 'who are living upstairs', on the other hand, is a clause consisting of a subject ('who') and a predicate ('are living upstairs'). Note that the predicate contains a finite verb ('are living').

Note

Non-finite verbs may make phrases;
only finite verbs make clauses.

A phrase is best understood by comparison with a clause. Look at these sets of sentences, rather the underlined word-groups in each set, and know a phrase from a clause:

a. We eat to live a healthy life. (phrase)
   We eat so that we may live a healthy life. (clause)
b. After listening to the news, we sat down to dinner. (phrase)
   After we listened to the news, we sat down to dinner. (clause)
c. Candidates short-listed for the interview will soon be hearing from us. (phrase)
   Candidates who are short-listed for the interview will soon be hearing from us. (clause)
d. She insisted on attending the function despite her ill health. (phrase)
   She insisted that she must attend the function despite her ill health. (clause)

23.1 Kinds of Phrases

Phrases may be classified on the basis of their function or on the basis of their form. Based on their function, phrases are divided into noun phrases, adjective phrases and adverb phrases. (We have already dealt with the first of these types in Chapter 8.) But it is more usual – and certainly more profitable to the learner of English – to divide them on the basis of their form.

In form a phrase may be:

a. an infinitive phrase (beginning with an infinitive):
   Fools build houses for wise men to live in them.
b. a participle phrase (beginning with a participle, present or past):
   The gentleman sporting a goatee is the leader of the group.
   Devastated by the cyclone, the villages along the coast presented a sorry sight.

c. a gerund phrase (beginning with a gerund):

Having the right connections is a great advantage in business. (subject of 'is')

She denied having seen him. (object of 'denied')

Note

A gerund phrase is a participle phrase with a difference: the participle phrase functions like a noun.

d. a prepositional phrase (beginning with a preposition):

The audience in the assembly hall was visibly bored and getting impatient.

e. a prepositional gerund phrase (beginning with a preposition followed by a gerund phrase):

The time for making excuses is past; we want results.

Note

A prepositional gerund phrase consists of a preposition followed by a gerund phrase, the gerund phrase serving as object of the preposition. Thus, the phrase 'for making excuses' begins with the preposition 'for', followed by the gerund phrase 'making excuses', object of the preposition 'for'.

Exercise 1

Underline the phrases in the following passage. Classify them by entering each phrase in the appropriate column, as shown below. The phrases in the opening sentence have been underlined and classified for you.

Sydney

Oct 27, 1992

A huge comet is on course to collide with the earth on August 14, 2116 and could kill most forms of life with an explosion more powerful than a million nuclear bombs, an expert on asteroids told a space conference on Sunday. The five-kilometre-wide ball of ice and rock is travelling so fast that if it collides head-on with the earth, it could plunge the world into the dark ages. The International Astronomical Union (IAU) noted the comet's discovery on October 15 and for the first time since keeping records of such finds, could not rule out a collision with the earth. Astronomers have since been watching the comet, travelling at sixty kilometres per second. 'We need to track it for five or six years,' said the expert on asteroids. 'If it is going to hit, it will be on August 14, 2116 because that is the day when the comet's path intersects the earth's.'

Asteroids are spinning pieces of space rock and there are millions of them circling the sun between the orbits of Mars and Jupiter.

Infinitive phrase	participle phrase	prepositional phrase	prepositional gerund phrase
to collide with the earth		on course; on August 14, 2116; with an explosion; on asteroids; on Sunday	

We have already dealt with the prepositional phrase in some detail in Chapter 13, so in this chapter we confine ourselves to the other four types of phrase—the infinitive phrase, the participle phrase, the gerund phrase, and the prepositional gerund phrase.

23.1.1 The Infinitive Phrase

An infinitive phrase actually represents the reduction of a clause to a phrase. The full subject-predicate form of the clause is reduced to the infinitive form, with the subject implied, understood, or appearing elsewhere in the sentence, often in a preceding prepositional phrase. In most cases the subject of an infinitive phrase is a person. Look at the underlined infinitives:

a. 'subject' implied

It may be wise sometimes to suppress the truth. (subject: anyone, everyone)

It is not good to be too smart. (subject: people)

In these examples the 'subject' of the infinitive is a generic person, that is, a whole class of people, or all people.

b. 'subject' understood from the general context

It was most painful to go through that experience. (subject: those who went through the experience)

The lady of the house left instructions to clean the house in her absence. (subject: the servant)

c. 'subject' elsewhere in the sentence

i. The 'subject' of the infinitive is the same as the subject of the main verb:

Some people live to eat. (Some people live to do something. Some people eat.)

ii. The 'subject' of the infinitive is the object of the main verb:

The yoga instructor urged the stressed-out executives to unwind.
(The yoga instructor urged the stressed-out executives to do something. The executives should unwind.)

iii. The 'subject' of the infinitive in a preceding prepositional phrase:

For you to achieve anything out of the ordinary is not very difficult. ('subject' of the infinitive 'you')

The speaker's appeal to the back-benchers to behave went unheeded. ('subject' of the infinitive: 'back-benchers'. The speaker appealed to the back-benchers. The back-benchers must behave.)

iv. In some clauses, the 'subject' of the infinitive may represent a thing or an idea:

For the gum to stick properly, it must be spread evenly. ('subject of the infinitive: 'gum')

He never allowed these disappointments to deflect him from his course of action. ('subject' of infinitive: 'disappointments')

Exercise 2

In each sentence below, underline the word that refers to the person who would go. The first one is done for you.

a. She urged me to go. (I would go)

b. We wanted to go.

c. I was forced by them to go.
d. Were you asked to go?
e. What they very much wanted was for me to go.
f. What he wanted to do was to go with her.
g. Did they permit her to go with him?

That the infinitive represents a clause in a reduced form is borne out by the fact that in many cases the infinitive phrase may be replaced by the original clause:

He has a train to catch at ten. (phrase)
He has a train which he must catch at ten. (clause)
He went to the airport to see off his father. (phrase)
He went to the airport so that he might see off his father. (clause)
She decided to accept the job on offer. (phrase)
She decided that she should accept the job on offer. (clause)

Look at these pairs of sentences:

Stanley went to Africa a second time to do something.
He would settle the question of the Nile.

We may combine the two sentences into one by:

i. reducing the finite verb in the second sentence ('would settle') to an infinitive ('to settle') and
ii. replacing the infinitive phrase in the first sentence ('to do something') by the new infinitive phrase ('to settle the question of the Nile'): Stanley went to Africa a second time to settle the question of the Nile.

This example, again, goes to prove that the infinitive phrase represents a reduction of what was originally a clause.

Exercise 3

Combine the following pairs of sentences into one by turning the second sentence into an infinitive phrase.

a. He would read all the books he could get hold of on Mahatma Gandhi to do something. He would learn all about Gandhi's method of non-violent resistance.
b. I persuaded my parents to do something. They should let me marry the girl of my choice.
c. In the spring of 1890 Helen Keller learned to do something. She spoke.
d. Well-meaning friends tried to do something. They discouraged him from going through with his plan.

Exercise 4

Turn the underlined clauses into infinitive phrases. The first one is done for you.

a. If you want to speak French like a Frenchman, you must go to Paris and spend some years there.

Ans: For you to speak French like a Frenchman, you must... there.

b. I have a dozen telephone calls which I must make during the next half-hour.

c. They stopped using electrical appliances so that they might save on electricity.

d. The police's repeated appeals to the crowd that they should disperse peacefully finally bore fruit.

e. I advised her that she should seek a second opinion before deciding on surgery.

23.1.2 Forms of the Infinitive

The infinitive has only one form for all persons and numbers:

I/We/You/They love to go to the movies.

He/She loves to go to the movies.

I am planning to go...

She is planning to go...

They are planning to go...

It has, however, two forms for indicating time. One is the general form, which we may call the present infinitive ('to go', 'to run', 'to sing'), which expresses the same time as the main verb, present, past, or future:

He is glad to see her. (present time) He was glad to see her. (past time)

He will be glad to see her. (future time)

The other form of the infinitive is a perfect form which expresses time preceding that of the main verb:

You are lucky to have found a vocation to your liking. (You are now lucky because you found earlier a vocation to your liking)

We expect them to have gone to bed by the time we arrive.

These fly-by-night operators were found to have cheated hundreds of small investors. (The cheating happened first and then the finding)

The forms of the infinitive are tabulated below:

	active voice	**passive voice**
present infinitive	to take	to be taken
continuous form	to be taking	_______
perfect form	to have taken	to have been taken
perfect continuous form	to have been taking	______

23.1.3 Functions of Infinitive Phrases

An infinitive phrase may function as an adjective, adverb or noun.

function	**example**
a. adjectival	'Thank you, ladies and gentlemen, I still have a few pearls to cast before you.' — Herbert Beerbohm Tree, one of the outstanding actors of the 19th century, to his audience when a performance of *Hamlet*, with him in the lead role, was greeted with boos and hisses

b. adverbial	To tell you bluntly, you acted most irresponsibly in the matter. (modifying an entire sentence)
	They had a big do at the Taj to celebrate their daughter's wedding. (modifying the verb 'had')
	I am sorry to see you in this state . (modifying the adjective 'sorry')
c. nominal (functioning like a noun)	
i. as subject	To forgive you is out of the question.
	To make mistakes and be able to learn from them is the mark of a wise man.
ii. as object of verb	I forbid you to come to this house again.
	She hopes to pass the sessional exam.
iii. as subject complement	To see something for yourself is to believe it implicitly.
iv. as appositive	It is out of the question for me to forgive you. (in apposition to 'it')
	He has only one desire—to set up a trust in memory of his mother.

Exercise 5

Underline the infinitive phrases in the following sentences and say what function each one of them does. The first two are done for you.

a. I was as surprised to see him in that company as you were. (modifying the participle adjective 'surprised')
b. To be frank with you, you don't have even the minimum qualifications for the job. (modifying the sentence 'You don't have...for the job')
c. He seems to be right just for once.
d. To plead ignorance of the law is no defence.
e. She declined to go into the details.
f. He is the very man to meet for the purpose.
g. He went to Mumbai to look for a better job.

23.1.4 The Split Infinitive

Note the underlined infinitive in the following sentence:

They have too many problems to even consider which one to tackle first.

That brings us to one of the hardy perennials in all grammar books—'the spilt infinitive'. There are grammarians, purists mostly, who say that an infinitive should never be split, that is, that no adverb or adverbial should be placed between 'to' and the verb of the infinitive. 'What the grammarian hath joined, let no man part'—that about sums up the purists' stance.

A blanket ban on the split infinitive is, on the face of it, absurd. For one thing, the natural position for an adverb when it comes with a finite verb is before the verb:

She did not actually mention his name.

Suppose we reduce the finite verb 'mention' to an infinitive:

She did not bring herself to actually mention his name.

Now, if 'actually' is rightly positioned with respect to the finite verb in the first example, so is it with respect to the infinitive in the second. The alternatives to splitting the infinitive are two:

She did not bring herself actually to mention his name.

She did not bring herself to mention his name actually.

Both these alternatives are unsatisfactory. In the first one, the adverb 'actually' modifies the finite verb 'did (not) bring' and distorts the meaning intended, while in the second 'actually' is placed too far away from the infinitive it modifies.

The second reason in favour of splitting the infinitive in certain places is to avoid ambiguity. Look at the following sentence:

They are planning quietly to scrap the entry requirement regarding age.

What is being done quietly? Is it the 'planning' or the 'scrapping'? Most probably the author meant 'scrapping' but not wanting to split the infinitive and cause a flutter among grammatical dovecotes, placed the adverb before the infinitive. In the process, he has unwittingly changed the meaning—it is the 'planning' that is being done 'quietly' according to the sentence, not the 'scrapping'.

The split infinitive could be an ugly thing in places like this one:

It was obviously an attempt to in some way vindicate the fascist leader.

It would be more natural to say 'an attempt to vindicate in some way...'.

Finally, there is always an appeal from grammar to usage, and usage approves of split infinitives, examples of which can be had in plenty from reputable authors of earlier centuries—examples like 'to further limit the hours', 'to further complicate our problem', and so on.

This is not to suggest that we can split infinitives by the dozen. The sensible rule to follow is to avoid splitting the infinitive where there is no need to split, and to boldly split it if splitting helps to avoid ambiguity or preserve the natural rhythm of an English sentence, as it does in this sentence:

He used to secretly admire her from afar.

Try to place 'secretly' elsewhere and see how it disrupts the natural rhythm of the sentence.

23.2 The Participle Phrase

A participle phrase is a phrase that begins with a participle—present, past, or perfect:

Anyone applying to this college must sit a stiff entrance test.

Candidates called for interview must bring with them their testimonials in original.

Having done a day's work, she decided to go shopping.

23.2.1 Forms of the Participle Phrase

Like the infinitive, the participle in a participle phrase has only one form for all persons and numbers:

Applying to this college, I/we/you/he/she/they sat a stiff entrance test.

Having done a day's work, he/she/I/we/you/they decided to go shopping.

Devastated by the news, I/we/you/he/she/they broke down.

The participle, however has two forms for indicating time. One is a general form which is neutral with respect to time. The time is determined by the main verb in the sentence and the participle, present or past, indicates the same time as the main verb:

The minister is making an aerial survey of the areas affected by the floods. (present time)

The minister was making an aerial survey of the areas affected by the floods. (past time)

The minister will be making an aerial survey of the areas affected by the floods. (future time)

The other form is a perfect form (called the perfect participle) which indicates time preceding that indicated by the main verb:

Having done a day's work, she decided to go shopping.

She first did a day's work and then decided to go shopping. The deciding to go shopping happened later. This is because the perfect participle in the phrase 'having done a day's work' corresponds to the past perfect tense:

After she had done a day's work, she decided to go shopping.

However, the perfect participle may indicate time that corresponds to the present perfect tense and in such cases the verb of the main clause may be in the present or future tense:

He takes his time to decide but having made up his mind, he does not change it.

He takes his time to decide but having made up his mind (after he has made up his mind), he will never change it.

Never having lived away from her parents (because she has never lived away from her parents), she will most probably feel homesick for the first few days.

23.2.2 Functions of the Participle Phrase

Like the infinitive phrase, the participle phrase may function as an adjective or adverb. (It may function as a noun too and when it does, it is called a gerund phrase.)

function	example
a. adjectival	The lady facing the camera (who is facing the camera) is the leader of the delegation. (modifying the noun 'lady')
	Moved by the sight of the sea in front of her, she stood speechless with wonder. (modifying the pronoun 'she')

b. adverbial	Returning from work (=as he was returning from work), he met with an accident. (modifying the verb 'met') Having completed the day's assignments (= after he had completed the day's assignments), he went for a swim. Fearing capture by the police (= because they feared capture by the police), the dacoits went into hiding and grew beards.

Most participle phrases have adjectival function, especially those beginning with a present participle:

Students arriving late will not be allowed to enter the exam hall. (= who arrive late)

Notice that the 'subject' of the participle phrase is the same as the subject of the main verb: 'students'. Here are some more examples of the same kind:

The house standing diagonally opposite this is his.

The gentleman sitting next to the President is the British Prime Minister, the special invitee to this year's Republic Day parade.

Anyone wanting to go places will have to walk the extra mile.

Exercise 6

Replace the underlined relative clause in the following sentences by a participle phrase. The first one is done for you.

a. There lay the mirror which was broken into a hundred pieces.
   Ans: There lay the mirror broken into a hundred pieces.
b. I saw a chimpanzee which was wearing a red cap.
c. Their mouths watered as the children saw the grapes which hung over the garden wall.
d. Those who die in a great cause are sure to be remembered by posterity.
e. For your sake, I will willingly sell the jewels which were given me by my parents.
f. The Prime Minister went round the villages which were hit by the earthquake.

23.2.3 Position of Participle Phrases

1. The adjectival participle phrase usually occurs after the noun or pronoun it modifies:

   Students applying to this college...

   Anyone wanting to go places...

   The adjectival participle phrase may be defining or restrictive, as in the two examples above, or non-defining or non-restrictive, as in this:

   Shridhar, wanting to go places, worked extremely hard.

   In either case, the phrase comes immediately after the noun or pronoun it modifies. In the case of the non-defining phrase, you put commas on either side of the phrase, as you do with the non-defining relative clause.

2. The participle phrase may occur at the beginning of the sentence:

   Hoping to reach our destination before nightfall, we left early.

   Not wanting to disturb the residents, the traveller chose to sleep in the open.

3. The phrase may occur at the end of the sentence:

   We left early, hoping to reach our destination before nightfall.

   The traveller chose to sleep in the open, not wanting to disturb the residents.

23.2.4 Meanings of Adverbial Participle Phrases

An adverbial participle phrase usually expresses:

a. time

   Having done a day's work, she decided to go shopping.

   Returning from work, he met with an accident.

   or

b. cause

   Feeling hot, she switched on the fan.

   Not having slept for three days in succession, he was feeling groggy.

23.2.5 The 'Dangling' or Misrelated Participle

When the participle phrase occurs at the start of the sentence, it modifies the subject of the main clause that follows:

Breaking into the shop, the burglar removed most of the jewellery.

The underlined participle phrase refers to, and modifies, the subject of the main clause— 'burglar'. And quite rightly too, for the person who broke into the shop and the person who removed the jewellery are both the same person, the burglar himself. But in the following sentence, the participle phrase is left 'dangling':

Feeling rather warm, the woollens seemed a useless burden.

The phrase in the above sentence refers to 'woollens', the subject of the sentence, which is absurd. It is not the 'woollens' which were feeling warm but the wearer of the woollens, so the sentence should be corrected to:

Feeling warm, he/she found the woollens a useless burden.

Rushing through the sky, I saw a fighter plane.

The sentence, as it stands, means: I was rushing through the sky! Correct it to:

I saw a fighter plane rushing through the sky.

Here is another example of a 'dangling' or misrelated participle:

While undoing an unclaimed parcel, care must be taken...

This must be corrected to:

While undoing an unclaimed parcel, one must take care... (or) you must take care...

Exercise 7

Each of these sentences contains a 'dangling' participle phrase. Rewrite the sentence so that the phrase relates to the right noun or pronoun.

a. Driving at 80 km.p.h., the distance was covered in less than two hours.

b. Lying in the puddle, the man saw a bright silver coin.

c. Being a naturally curious child, everything new fascinated him.
d. Before paying a bill, it must be properly scrutinized.
e. Not knowing that he was being watched by hidden television cameras, a couple of silk handkerchiefs were shop-lifted by the tourist.

23.3 The Gerund Phrase

Gerunds are participles, present or perfect, functioning as nouns:

Seeing is believing. (bp 5)
(subject) (subject complement)

He regrets having declined the offer.
(direct object of 'regrets')

The more common form, however, is the present participle. The past participle cannot function as a gerund.

Gerunds being participles functioning like nouns, they can perform any of the functions of the noun. Look at the underlined '-ing' word in the following sentences. The noun-function it does in the sentence is indicated in parentheses.

Swimming is a good exercise. (subject of verb)

I like swimming. (object of verb)

I am fond of swimming. (object of preposition)

The exercise I like best is swimming. (subject complement)

He stands in knee-deep water and splashes about, and he calls it swimming. (object complement)

He likes only one exercise—swimming. (noun in apposition)

We call 'swimming' (in the above examples) a gerund because it is a participle performing one or the other of the half-dozen functions that the noun is capable of doing in a sentence.

A gerund phrase is a phrase beginning with a gerund, that is, a participle phrase doing the work of a noun.

Reading a few hours every day is an excellent habit. (subject of the verb 'is')

He enjoys walking in the early hours of the morning. (object of 'enjoys')

Stanley knew that any clinching evidence he could provide about the origin of the Nile would hinge on his circumnavigating Lake Victoria. (object of the preposition 'on')

Exercise 8

Identify the gerunds/gerund phrases in the following sentences. Note that all the participles/participle phrases are not gerunds/gerund phrases. The first two are done for you.

a. They are used to waiting for long hours in queues.
(gerund phrase, object of the preposition 'to')

b. Not knowing the language of the region, he found it difficult to make friends with the locals. (participle phrase, adverbial)
c. How can you object to his wanting to have his say?
d. He prefers curling up with a thriller to going out for a walk.
e. *The Guinness Book of Records* has over the years attracted a number of crazy people wanting to find themselves a place in the book.
f. Slicing cucumbers, bursting hot water bottles, and dropping eggs intact from great heights are some of the events registered by these people.
g. Breaking records in such events earns for the record-breakers a little space in the local or national press.

Exercise 9

Think of three things you enjoy doing, you hate doing, you don't mind doing. Here is an example to help you:

I enjoy going to parties. I hate rising early in the morning.
I don't mind helping a colleague with her shopping.

Write three sets of sentences on the same lines as above with the verbs 'enjoy', 'hate' and 'don't mind'. You may vary the verbs if you like. Here is a list of verbs for you to choose from:

like	dislike	adore	love
be fond of	detest	loathe	

23.3.1 Forms of the Gerund Phrase

The gerund phrase is headed by a present or perfect participle but never by a past participle. The present participle form is neutral with respect to time; the time intended is determined by the tense of the main verb:

Working longer hours is not the solution to the problem. (present time)
Working longer hours did not help to solve the problem. (past time)
Working longer hours will not help to solve the problem.(future time)

The perfect participle expresses time precedent to the time expressed by the main verb. If the main verb is present or future, the perfect form corresponds to the present perfect tense:

His having worked as a party cadre is no bar to his being appointed to a government post. (=That he has worked as a party cadre...post)
Ask him, and he will never admit having worked as a party cadre. (=he will never admit that he has worked as a party cadre...)

It the main verb is past, the perfect form of the gerund corresponds to the past perfect tense:

He disclaimed having ever accepted a bribe during his entire working life.
(=He disclaimed that he had ever accepted a bribe...)
They vaguely remembered having left the house keys with their neighbour.
(=that they had left their house keys...)

Like the infinitive phrase, the gerund phrase represents a reduction of a clause. Thus, a basic sentence pattern like:

The hunter killed the tiger (bp 2)

becomes:

the hunter's killing the tiger (or) the hunter's killing of the tiger (or) the killing of the tiger by the hunter.

Notice carefully the changes that take place in the reduction of clause to phrase. The finite verb 'killed' of the clause is reduced to a non-finite participle ('killing'); the subject 'hunter' of the clause is contained in the gerund phrase as an inflected possessive ('hunter's') or as object of preposition ('by the hunter'); the object 'tiger' of the clause becomes object of gerund with or without the preposition 'of':

The hunter's killing the tiger (or)

The hunter's killing of the tiger.

Note that the gerund 'killing' serves as the headword of the gerund phrase.

These changes from the full subject-predicate form of the clause permit the gerund phrase to be embedded as a noun within another predication;

<u>The killing of the tiger by the hunter</u> (new subject derived from the clause 'the hunter killed the tiger') <u>reassured the villagers.</u> (new predicate)

Exercise 10

Reduce each of the clauses below to a gerund phrase and add a new predicate (making use of the clues given in brackets) to complete the sentence. The first one is done for you.

a. C.N. Janaki crossed the English Channel in 1992. (remarkable feat/for a physically challenged person)

   Ans: C.N. Janaki's crossing the English Channel in 1992 was a remarkable feat for a physically challenged person to bring off.

b. I met my future wife. (on board a crowded bus/not a romantic event)

c. She carried an umbrella, rain or shine. (much comment and many jokes)

d. Rohan lives in Delhi. (a matter of anxiety/old parents in far-off Kerala)

e. They play with guns. (potentially dangerous)

23.3.2 Subject of Gerund

The subject of a gerund or gerund phrase usually refers to a person or living thing.

1. In the case of a large number of gerund phrases, the 'subject' is understood as a generic person (everyone, anyone, all people):

   <u>Making mistakes</u> is so human.
   There is nothing demeaning about <u>being a manual labourer.</u>
   <u>Smoking in these premises</u> is strictly forbidden.

2. Very often the 'subject' of a gerund phrase is found in another part of the sentence:

   They commended Roger for <u>undertaking such a difficult task.</u>

(The 'subject' of the underlined gerund phrase is 'Roger', the object of the main verb 'commended')

3. The 'subject' of the gerund phrase can at times be inferred from the context:

Meeting him alone is not advisable. I suggest you go with some one.
(the 'subject' is obviously 'you')

I suggest postponing a decision till a later date.

(The subject of the underlined phrase is 'we')

4. The 'subject' of the gerund phrase is found in the possessive form of a noun or pronoun:

Anita resented her younger sister's getting more attention than she did.
('subject'of phrase 'younger sister)

The idea of his junior colleague's being promoted over his head was anathema to Ram.('subject'of gerund phrase 'junior colleague')

We use the possessive form only in formal usage. In informal usage, the non-possessive form of the noun or personal pronoun is used, the object form in the case of the personal pronoun:

Anita resented her younger sister getting more attention than she did.

The idea of him being passed over and his junior colleague being promoted was anathema to Ram.

However, if the gerund phrase functions as subject of the sentence, the possessive form is a must, both in formal and informal usage:

His being passed over and his junior colleague's being promoted was an affront to Ram.

The girl's risking her life to save a friend from drowning was widely admired and commended.

5. The 'subject' of a gerund phrase coming after main verbs like 'imagine', 'not mind', 'miss', 'remember', 'understand' etc takes the non-possessive form in informal usage:

I remember him behaving like a child (instead of 'I remember his behaving like a child...').

In those days we never minded our teachers being strict with us (instead of 'In those days we never minded our teachers' being strict with us'); we rather expected it.

Who could imagine him (instead of 'his') doing a volte-face like that ?

Such gerund phrases may come as objects of main verbs, as in the examples above, or as objects of prepositions, as in these:

I object to him serving as our spokesperson.

I thoroughly disapprove of my son moving in such company but I can't stop him.

*volte-face : change to a completely opposite opinion

All such phrases are best treated as object complements considering that they are so closely related to the object nouns or pronouns. However, conservative grammarians object to these constructions and insist on the possessive forms being used, especially with the personal pronouns. They may pass, grudgingly, a gerund phrase with a non-possessive noun like:

I object to the man serving as our spokesperson

but not a gerund phrase with a non-possessive pronoun like:

I object to him serving as our spokesperson.

According to them, it should be:

I object to his serving as our spokesperson.

6. If the 'subject' of a gerund phrase is accompanied by a modifier, it does not take the possessive form even in formal usage:

We don't like the Head of State getting embroiled in an argument with the Prime Minister. (The 'subject' of the gerund phrase is 'the Head of State', 'of State' being the modifier)

Fancy the captain of a leading cricket team being in the doghouse!

7. In gerund phrases derived from sentences beginning with 'it' or 'there', 'it' takes the possessive form, while 'there' remains unchanged:

They continued with their exploration of the jungle despite its being unsafe.

We had no notion of there being a bandh in town.

*in the doghouse: in a state of shame

23.3.3 Object of Gerund

1. Often the 'object' of the gerund phrase comes in an 'of phrase', especially if the gerund phrase is introduced by 'the':

The hunter's killing of the tiger reassured the villagers.

The burning of fossil fuels leads to global warming.

The gerund phrase may begin with some other determiner than 'the':

This wasting of gas is senseless and must be stopped.

Some substantial saving of electricity may result from these measures.

2. If there is no 'the' or possessive 'subject' preceding the gerund, the 'object' of the gerund remains unchanged:

Renovating the house will be highly expensive. (instead of 'the renovating of the house' or 'his renovating of the house')

3. Sometimes a choice of 'objects' is possible. You may either say:

   a. Shooting those dreaded man-eaters (where 'man-eaters' is the 'object' of the gerund ' shooting')

   or

   b. the shooting of those dreaded man-eaters (where 'man-eaters' is the 'object' of the preposition 'of').

Similarly, you may say: the government's promulgating an ordinance (or)the government's promulgating of an ordinance. Of the two constructions, the second is preferable.

4. A gerund phrase with an 'of phrase' may sometimes result in ambiguity. Thus, the gerund phrase 'the killing of the tiger' may be derived from the clause:

The tiger killed someone or something (where 'tiger' is subject).

(or) Someone or something killed the tiger (where 'tiger' is object).

Similarly, the phrase 'the sinking of the ship' may mean that the ship sank or it was sunk by, say, pirates. The ambiguity may be removed with a 'by phrase' :

The killing of the cattle by the tiger disturbed the villagers.

The killing of the tiger by the hunter reassured the villagers.

Note

The word 'to' coming after the following verbs is a preposition and not the sign of the infinitive and therefore requires a gerund after it—accustom oneself; allude; confess; confine oneself; dedicate oneself; resign oneself; resort; revert. In the same way, the word 'to' after certain adjectives, especially participle adjectives ending in '-ed', is a preposition and requires a gerund after it—accustomed; addicted; averse; dedicated; disposed; given; opposed; used.

On being quizzed, he confessed to copying in the maths examination.

Would you please confine yourself to commenting on the topic under discussion and not get too personal?

From a very young age she had dedicated herself to serving the poor.

He resigned himself to letting things take their course.

He was not used to working long hours.

He is averse to doing work of any kind, though not to supervising people at work.

Given, as he was, to dropping names, he was not very popular with his neighbours.

23.3.4 Functions of the Gerund Phrase

Like a gerund, a gerund phrase may perform all the functions that a noun is capable of fulfilling:

function	example
subject of verb	His smoking (of) a cigar after dinner irritated his wife.
object of verb	His wife resented his smoking (of) a cigar after dinner.
object of preposition	His wife objected to his smoking (of) a cigar after dinner.
subject complement	The thing that his wife resented most was his smoking (of) a cigar after dinner.
object complement	He considered his cigar smoking after dinner the only male prerogative left to him.
appositive	He was very particular about one thing – his smoking a cigar after dinner.

Note

The preposition 'of' in parentheses is optional.

*male prerogative: special right by virtue of his being a man

23.3.5 Gerund Phrase as Subject

You may use a gerund phrase as subject to express a general statement with 'be' as the main verb:

Fishing in troubled waters is a mean thing to do.

Eating to live is a must; living to eat is a disease.

You may use a gerund phrase as subject to express a variety of other meanings:

His springing a surprise on her disconcerted her for a while.

Taking the easy way out of trouble now may finally prove expensive.

Being taken for a ride enraged him.

You may use a gerund phrase subject after the anticipatory 'it' + an adjective:

It is very embarrassing, your losing your memory in a crowd.

It is foolish, throwing good money after bad.

It is not worthwhile, paying so much for a three-day holiday.

You may use a noun instead of an adjective after the anticipatory 'it':

It was a pleasure meeting her after all those years.

It is a terrible thing for these children, missing out on their childhood.

Exercise 11

Join the sentence opening in column 1 to an appropriate gerund phrase in column 2.

1	2
It is shameful	the child's surviving a boat capsize
It is a sad thing	offering to donate one of your kidneys
It is a frightening prospect	wasting money on conspicuous consumption
It was noble of you	losing both parents at a tender age
It was a miracle	living in a world taken over by computers

23.3.6 Gerund Phrase as Object of Verb

Certain verbs are followed by gerunds, which are regarded as their objects. Here is a list of verbs commonly used with gerund phrase objects.

acknowledge admit avoid cannot help consider contemplate defer delay deny detest enjoy escape evade fancy (=imagine) give up (=stop) grudge imagine keep mention miss postpone resent risk stop suggest tolerate urge withhold

He acknowledged receiving the money due to him.

Living in the same street, I cannot avoid running into him.

She could not help borrowing money from her neighbours.

He successfully gave up smoking cigarettes, only to put on weight.

We don't grudge your watching television after you have done your chores.

He resented their making fun of his buckteeth.

The following verbs may take a gerund or infinitive phrase as object:

attempt begin cannot bear cease commence continue
dread hate hesitate intend like love neglect
plan prefer propose remember start try

They began to practise/practising in right earnest.

He ceased to work/working from the day of his disablement.

We mustn't neglect to buy/buying the tickets rightaway.

Note

The verbs 'remember', 'try' and 'stop' have one meaning when used with the gerund, and a different meaning when used with the infinitive. Compare:

a. i. He remembered to set the alarm before going to bed, so he had no difficulty getting up at the intended hour. (He remembered first and then set the alarm.)

ii. Getting up late, he wondered why the alarm didn't wake him up at five. He clearly remembered setting the alarm for five o'clock. (He set the alarm first, and then, next morning, remembered having done so.)

b. i. I tried to give up smoking. (but didn't succeed; I continued to smoke.)

ii. I tried giving up smoking but it didn't do me much good.
(I succeeded in giving up smoking but it didn't do me much good.)

c. i. She stopped to watch the TV serial; she found it so absorbing.
(She stopped because she wanted to watch.)

ii. She stopped watching the TV serial because she found the later episodes boring.
(She was in the habit of watching the serial but later stopped watching it.)

23.3.7 Stylistics of Gerund Phrases

Compare the following:

1. Louis Pasteur's inoculating a nine-year-old boy with the rabies virus horrified the doctors of Paris.
2. Louis Pasteur's inoculating of a nine-year-old boy with the rabies virus horrified the doctors of Paris.
3 The inoculation by Louis Pasteur of a nine-year-old boy with the rabies virus horrified the doctors of Paris.

All the three sentences are formally correct and mean the same but there is a subtle difference in emphasis. In sentence 1, the emphasis is on the act of inoculating; in sentence 3, the emphasis is on the idea of inoculation; in the middle sentence the emphasis is about evenly distributed between the act and the idea. Notice that there is no gerund phrase in example 3.

23.3.8 Prepositional Gerund Phrases

A prepositional gerund phrase is a gerund phrase preceded by a preposition:

After listening to the news, we sat down to dinner.

Notice that the gerund phrase 'listening to the news' is preceded by the preposition 'after', of which the gerund phrase is the object. The preposition, together with the gerund phrase, is called the prepositional gerund phrase.

The time for making excuses is past; we want results.

23.3.9 Functions of Prepositional Gerund Phrases

Prepositional gerund phrases can function as nouns, adjectives or adverbs.

a. nominal function

I must warn you against acting impulsively. (=that you should not act impulsively)

She insisted on attending the function. (=that she should attend the function)

b. adjectival function

She spoke of the need for reforming the judicial system. (modifying the noun 'need')

That is not the right way of putting the idea across. (modifying the noun 'way')

c. adverbial function

He supplemented his regular income by working as a part-time book-keeper. (modifying the verb 'supplemented')

He went in for a hefty medical cover for himself and his family before leaving for the U.S. (modifying the verb 'went in for')

Prepositional gerund phrases functioning as adverbs may modify a predicate adjective:

She was visibly embarrassed at being named the guest of honour. (modifying 'embarrassed')

You are very quick at spotting other people's errors while overlooking your own. modifying 'quick')

We were all disgusted at his making a fool of himself in public. (modifying 'disgusted')

Exercise 12

Complete the following sentences with appropriate prepositional gerund phrases. The first one is done for you.

a. She is afraid ______________________________

Ans: She is afraid of going against her parents' wishes.

b. They were terribly annoyed ______________________________

c. You must be content ______________________________

d. The old man is rather careless ______________________________

e. Your present income is adequate ______________________________

f. He was disappointed ______________________________

Exercise 13

Identify the prepositional gerund phrase in the following sentences and say what function it does in the sentence.

a. We enjoyed your visit and look forward to having you again with us.

b. The police had made elaborate preparations for ensuring the security of the visiting dignitary.

c. You can't make an omelette without breaking eggs.

d. She finally decided on giving up a secure job at home with an assured future and starting afresh in a foreign country.

e. The measures for combating urban crime outlined by the police were generally felt to be inadequate.

23.3.10 Position of Gerund Phrases and Prepositional Gerund Phrases

A gerund phrase occurs wherever a noun does, so its position in the scheme of the sentence is fixed like that of the noun.

A prepositional gerund phrase, on the other hand, is relatively free but its position will depend on the function it does in the sentence. If it functions as an adverb, it may occur in the initial or final position:

After listening to the news, we sat down to dinner.

We sat down to dinner after listening to the news.

If you place the prepositional gerund phrase at the beginning, you must take care to see that there is no 'dangling' modifier. You must not say, for instance:

On entering the house, strange sounds were heard by us

but say instead:

On entering the house, we heard strange sounds.

An adverbial prepositional gerund phrase modifying a predicate adjective will come immediately after the adjective:

Ali was embarrassed at hearing himself praised so effusively in public.

If the prepositional gerund phrase performs an adjectival function, it will occur immediately after the noun or pronoun it modifies:

The time for making excuses is past; we want results.

If the phrase performs a nominal function, it takes its place immediately after the main verb:

She insisted on attending the function despite her illness.

Certain verbs like 'insist', 'agree', 'care', 'caution', 'decide', 'forget', 'plan', 'warn' may take a prepositional gerund phrase after them:

Did you finally agree on sharing the profits between yourselves?

The two batches of students decided on going to the same place for their picnic.

That was not a wise thing to do. I would have cautioned them against doing that if I had known.

You had better forget about recovering your dues from your customers.

Given the choice of a free holiday abroad, would you care about going to Timbuctoo?

Final note on the prepositional gerund phrase

Most pedagogic grammar books treat the prepositional gerund phrase as no different from the gerund phrase but the two are clearly distinguishable and must be distinguished. A gerund phrase, like a gerund, functions as a noun and noun only. The prepositional gerund phrase, on the other hand, is capable of functioning as a noun, adjective or adverb. As a matter of fact, its nominal function is minimal confined, as it is, to appearing after certain verbs like 'decide', 'insist', and so on. Its adjectival and adverbial functions are more numerous and significant.

23.4 The Absolute Construction

The absolute construction is in a class by itself, added here almost as a postscript to the chapter.

Look at the underlined phrases in these sentences:

The wind being favourable, the Greek fleet set sail for Troy.

The last guest having left, the hosts settled down to watch a late-night movie on television.

Her work for the day done, she went to bed.

The underlined phrases are called absolute constructions or absolute phrases. An absolute construction is so called because it is absolute or free—the phrase has no grammatical connection with the rest of the sentence. Compare:

The wind being favourable, the Greek fleet set sail for Troy.

As the wind was favourable, the Greek fleet set sail for Troy.

The underlined phrase and clause in the above sentences mean the same but the clause, unlike the phrase, is grammatically connected with the rest of the sentence—as an adverb clause of reason, it is joined to the main clause by the subordinate conjunction 'as' and modifies the predicate 'set sail for Troy' in the main clause, which is the rest of the sentence. The phrase, on the other hand, is independent of the clause that follows.

An absolute phrase, like the infinitive phrase and the gerund phrase, represents the reduction of a clause to a phrase—the finite verb of the clause is changed to a non-finite participle present, past or perfect, while the subject is retained intact.

original clause	absolute phrase
The wind was favourable	The wind being favourable (pres. part.)
The last guest had left	The last guest having left (per. part.)
Her work for the day was done	Her work for the day done (past part.)

Since the subject of the original clause remains unchanged in the absolute construction, it is sometimes called a nominative absolute. (The subject of a clause is always in the nominative case.) If the finite verb in the original clause is 'be', it is sometimes omitted in the absolute phrase:

Her work for the day over, she sat down to catch up on her correspondence.

Here are two more examples of an absolute construction without the participle:

His job now a certainty, he looked forward to his future with confidence.

His job assured, he looked forward to his future with confidence.

Notice that in the above examples, the 'subject' of the absolute construction appears with a predicate noun, predicate adjective, or adverb, as shown in the following analysis:

'subject' of absolute construction	omitted participle	complement
His job	(being)	a certainty(predicate noun)
His job	(being)	assured (predicate adjective)
Her work for the day	(being)	over(adverb)

Sometimes, the absolute construction comes in the final position:

The man who sold for cash sat there, his face wreathed in a self-gratulatory smile, a cigar stuck in his mouth.

It was what they called a 'relay fast', the participants taking turns at fasting.

The bride looked radiantly beautiful, her black-and-gold conjeevaram saree shimmering in bright neon lights.

Time expressed by the absolute construction

The participle used in the absolute construction expresses the same kind of time as it does in a participle phrase. If the participle used is present or past, it expresses the same time as the main verb:

Present participle

Half the staff being on leave, the bank manager himself is sitting at the counter cashing cheques. (present time)

Half the staff being on leave, the bank manager himself was sitting at the counter cashing cheques. (past time)

God willing, we will soon have a house of our own. (future time)

Past participle

The cadets march past the saluting base, their heads held erect and turned towards the dignitary taking the salute. (present time)

The cadets marched past the saluting base,their heads held erect and turned towards the dignitary taking the salute. (past time)

The cadets will march past the saluting base, their heads held erect and turned towards the dignitary taking the salute. (future time)

If the participle used is perfect, it expresses time that precedes that of the main verb:

All land routes having been cut off by the torrential rains, they finally chose to fly.

Law and order having been restored, the government set about the job of rehabilitating the victims of the violence.

You must have noticed by now that the 'subject'of the absolute construction does not refer to the same person or thing as the subject of the main clause. Here are additional examples to illustrate the point:

The day dawning clear and bright, the summit party began their preparations for the climb.

The absolute construction may even begin with the impersonal 'it' or 'there':

It being Friday and a holiday in Dubai, we could do no shopping.

There being no real grievance behind the workers' agitation, it petered out soon enough.

We don't normally use a personal pronoun as 'subject' of an absolute construction, except in conversational English:

Our maid was on leave. She being on leave, I helped my wife with the household chores.

I having declared myself against the scheme, they went ahead without me.

23.4.1 Meaning of Absolute Constructions

Although the absolute construction has no grammatical connection with the rest of the sentence, it has a semantic connection with it; otherwise the construction wouldn't be there!

An absolute construction usually expresses time or cause:

1. Time

   Her work for the day over, she went to bed. (in the sense of 'after'—After her work for the day was over...)

   The party being over, the hosts began to wash up.

   The cadets of the Academy marched past, the band playing *auld lang syne*. (in the sense of 'while' – while the band was playing....)

   The lake looked beautiful, the moonlight glimmering on its surface.

2. Cause

   Half the staff being on leave, the bank manager was himself sitting at the counter cashing cheques.

   The debtors having defaulted on their loans, the banks seized their assets.

In certain stereotyped phrases, the absolute construction expresses a conditional meaning:

weather permitting (if the weather permits); God willing; all things being equal; everything considered.

24 Sentence Expansion

In Chapter 2, we learned a set of seven basic sentence patterns—patterns like 'Dogs bark' (bp1), 'The hunter killed the tiger' (bp2), and so on.

The basic sentence patterns, we noted further, do not by themselves make for good communication, since as adults we are most unlikely to say 'Dogs bark' or 'Birds fly'. We might, however, say:

> The dogs in this street bark through the night, making it impossible for the residents to sleep in peace.
>
> Frigate birds fly at a speed of 100-160 km.p.h.

Sentences like the above sound more like adult communication and yet they are both basic sentence pattern 1 expanded. The subject-noun 'dogs' of bp 1 has been expanded to 'The dogs in this street' with the addition of two modifiers—the determiner 'the' and the adjectival prepositional phrase 'in this street'. The predicate 'bark' of bp 1 has been expanded to 'bark through the night, making it impossible for the residents to sleep in peace' with the addition of two adverbial modifiers—the prepositional phrase 'through the night' and the participle phrase 'making it impossible for the residents to sleep in peace'.

This is what we do as adults all the time—we expand the basic sentence patterns. The English sentence is so wonderfully plastic that it can be enlarged, condensed, combined, adjusted as finely as you want to accommodate your thought in all its complexity. All grammatical or well-formed sentences, howsoever long or complex, are little more than changes rung on the basic sentence patterns through expansion and transformation.

In this chapter, we deal with sentence expansion.

There are three methods of sentence expansion:

1. expansion through modification or the use of modifiers;
2. expansion through subordination or through the use of subordinate clauses;
3. expansion through coordination or through the use of coordinate clauses.

24.1 Sentence Expansion through Modification

The modifiers we use to expand basic sentence patterns are four:

1. adjectives	The big, black dog barked.
	The dog is a friendly, useful animal.
2. adjective phrases, which could be	
a. prepositional phrases	Dogs in the country bark.
b. participle phrases	She photographed the tiger playing with its cubs.
c. infinitive phrases	The man to engage for this purpose must be a detective.

d. prepositional gerund phrases	The money for building the new hostel has already been used up.
3. adverbs	The dog barked furiously.
4. adverb phrases, which could be:	
a. prepositional phrases	The dog barked through the night.
b. participle phrases	We spent the afternoon playing cards.
c. infinitive phrases	The party elected her leader to ensure success at the polls.
d. prepositional gerund phrases	By electing her leader, the party ensured success at the polls.

Note

Strictly speaking, adjective clauses and adverb clauses are also modifiers of nouns and verbs respectively but in this book they are dealt with under the heading—'Expansion through Subordination'.

Exercise 1

Insert suitable adjectives/adjective phrases to modify the nouns (N) in the following basic sentence patterns. The nouns are underlined. The first one is done for you as an example.

a. The girls wept. (bp 1)

   The girls of class V wept. The girls of class V, numbering about thirty, wept. Disappointed at the cancellation of the picnic, the girls of class V, numbering about thirty, wept.

b. A storm devastated the countryside. (bp 2)

c. The teacher read the children a story. (bp 3)

d. The woman was a spy. (bp 5)

Exercise 2

Insert suitable adverbs/adverb phrases to modify the verbs (V) in the following basic sentence patterns. The first one is done for you.

a. The men groaned. (bp 1)
   The men groaned in pain.
   The men groaned in pain through the night.
   The men groaned in pain through the night with no hope of relief.

b. The woman looked a stranger. (bp 5)

c. The President awarded the sergeant the Vir Chakra. (bp 3)

d. The company appointed her manager. (bp 4)

When you expand through modification, the sentence that results still remains a simple sentence. Consider this example:

The woman broke the vase. (N-V-N)

The sentence conforms to basic sentence pattern 2, consisting of subject–noun plus finite verb plus object-noun. We can modify all the three. Let us begin with the object-noun 'vase':

1. The woman broke the antique vase.
2. The woman broke the antique vase in the house.
3. The woman broke the antique vase in the house, costing a small fortune.
4. The woman ... costing a small fortune, treasured by the entire family.

We can expand the sentence further by modifying the subject-noun 'woman':

5. The sullen, old woman broke the antique vase...family.
6. The... woman, smarting under a sense of injustice, broke...family.

We can expand the sentence still further by modifying the verb 'broke':

7. The sullen, old woman deliberately broke... family.
8. In a desperate effort to get even with her employers, the...woman deliberately broke...family.

The final sentence resulting from all this modification runs as follows:

In a desperate effort to get even with her employers, the sullen, old woman, smarting under a sense of injustice, deliberately broke the antique vase in the house, costing a small fortune, treasured by the entire family.

The above example gives you a fair idea of the possibilities by way of sentence expansion through modification.

But no matter how often you modify the N and V in the basic sentence patterns, the sentence that results still remains a simple sentence. It remains a simple sentence because it has only one finite verb: 'broke'.

Exercise 3

Expand each of the following sentences, using a variety of modifiers to go with the underlined word or words.

a. The car crashed.

b. He found his wife a maid.

c. The bride thinks her husband handsome.

d. His words rang hollow.

Exercise 4

Here is a set of expanded sentences. By inserting appropriate labels, identify the basic sentence pattern of each of the sentences. The first one is done for you as an example.

a. At the end of the seventh round, the weary boxer suddenly
(adverb phrase) (adj.) N (adverb)

collapsed against the ropes. (bp 1)
V (intrans) (adverb phrase)

b. Because of the excitement of that night in Delhi, sleep was impossible for most people.

c. Tempted by the piece of cheese held in the crow's beak, the wily fox flattered the crow, calling him the wonder of the wood.

d. Not wanting to disturb his wife and children, he let himself into the house, using a latchkey.

e. The young bridegroom, alighting from a flower-decked car, looked smashing in that two-piece suit of his.

24.2 Sentence Expansion through Subordination

A second method of expanding a basic sentence pattern is through the use of one or more subordinate clauses. Look at this simple piece of information:

The car ground to a halt. (bp 1)

If that is all that you want to say, the sentence says it clearly and economically. But you may want to particularise the car:

The car <u>that we had won in a recent raffle</u> ground to a halt.

You may want to give a reason for the car grinding to a halt:

The car... ground to a halt <u>because we had run out of petrol</u>.

You may want to add more circumstantial detail: when did the car grind to a halt?

<u>When we had a good eighty odd kilometres to cover to reach our destination</u>, the car...ground to a halt...petrol.

And what happened as a result?

...<u>so that we were well and truly stuck</u>.

Where were you stuck and how badly?

...in a part of the country <u>from where the nearest petrol bunk was 25 km away.</u>

Thus, to a given piece of information, simple to start with and contained in a simple sentence, more and more detail is added until the final sentence tells us the whole story of how a particular car ground to a halt and with what result:

The car that we had won in a recent raffle ground to a halt when we had a good eighty odd kilometres to cover to reach our destination, because we had run out of petrol so that we were well and truly stuck in a part of the country from where the nearest petrol bunk was 25 km away.

The resultant sentence is a complex sentence consisting of one main clause and five subordinate clauses, as may be seen from the following analysis:

1. The car ground to a halt – main clause
2. that we had won in a recent raffle – relative clause, modifying the antecedent noun 'car' in clause 1
3. because we had run out of petrol – adverb clause of reason, modifying the predicate 'ground to a halt' in clause 1

4. when we had a good eighty odd kilometres to cover to reach our destination – adverb clause of time, modifying the predicate 'ground to a halt' in clause 1
5. so that we were well and truly stuck in a part of the country – adverb clause of result, modifying the predicate 'ground to a halt' in clause 1
6. from where the nearest petrol bunk was 25 km away – relative clause, modifying the noun phrase 'part of the country' in clause 5

What we have done in the final sentence is to synthesise (or combine into one single sentence) the following simple sentences:

The car ground to a halt. We had won the car in a recent raffle. We had run out of petrol. We had a good eighty odd kilometres to cover to reach our destination. We were well and truly stuck in a part of the country. The nearest petrol bunk (in that part of the country) was 25 km away.

Notice that the main clause states the main idea—the car ground to a halt. The other clauses fill us in on the details—the identity of the car and the circumstances (like time, reason, result) that attended on the event stated in the main clause. These details being subordinate in importance to the main idea, are rightly put in subordinate clauses.

Here is another example illustrating the second method of sentence expansion:

The Indian experiment with parliamentary democracy since 1947 shows that, although the country has had several general elections since Independence which were by and large free and fair, it still has a long way to go before it can call itself a genuine democracy.

The above is a complex sentence consisting of a main clause and four subordinate clauses:

1. The Indian experiment with parliamentary democracy since 1947 shows – main cl.
2. that it still has a long way to go – noun clause, object of the verb 'shows' in cl. 1
3. although the country has had several general elections since Independence – adverb clause of concession, modifying the predicate 'has a long way to go' in cl. 2
4. which were by and large free and fair – relative clause, modifying the antecedent noun phrase 'general elections' in cl.3
5. before it can call itself a genuine democracy – adverb clause of time, modifying the predicate 'has a long way to go' in cl. 2

Exercise 5

Combine each of the following sets of simple sentences into one complex sentence, with the underlined clause as the main clause. The first two are done for you as examples.

a. The first master of English prose was John Dryden. He wrote in the 17th century. Dryden's prose was conversational in the best sense of the term.

Answer: The first master of English prose was John Dryden, who wrote in the 17th century and whose prose was conversational in the best sense of the term.

(or)

The first master of English prose was John Dryden, a 17th century writer, whose prose was conversational in the best sense of the term.

Note that both the answers above are complex sentences; in the second, we have reduced the number of subordinate clauses from two to one, the clause 'who wrote in the 17th century' becoming an appositive phrase to 'John Dryden':

John Dryden, a 17th century writer

b. The England of Dryden's time gave birth to the coffee houses. In these houses men gathered regularly to discuss topics of the day. The topics ranged from poetry to politics.

Answer: The England of Dryden's time gave birth to the coffee houses, where men gathered regularly to discuss topics of the day which ranged from poetry to politics/ranging from poetry to politics.

c. Medical researches have established something. Cigarette smoking is the cause of lung cancer and a host of other illnesses. These illnesses are potentially fatal.

d. A person builds a house today. He spends an enormous sum of money on the comfort of his future residence. His counterpart in an earlier age was more concerned with the beauty and impressiveness of the building.

e. Think of the sun as a cricket-ball. Then the smallest stars of the Milky Way are like pinheads. The largest of them will be like barrage-balloons.

*Barrage-balloons: large balloons filled with lighter-than-air gas attached to wires around sensitive targets to prevent enemy aircraft from coming in at low level for strafing or bombing

f. Our forefathers believed in many things. Today we do not believe in them. Our faith in a bottle of medicine remains the same as theirs.

g. The man is illiterate. He has been on trial for various offences. The offences include kidnapping and murder. Such a man should not go unpunished.

24.3 Sentence Expansion through Coordination

The third and last method of sentence expansion is through coordination. Coordination, as we saw in the section on coordinate conjunctions in Chapter 15, is a process of addition. When you expand a sentence through coordination, you put together two or more main clauses by means of the coordinate conjunction:

The man disappeared from his house one morning, and his family never saw him again.

Twenty-two thousand candidates sat the common entrance test but only two thousand three hundred passed.

You may join two main clauses by means of the conjunctive adverb:

The rice was slightly undercooked; otherwise the dinner was good.

The road to the shrine is very rough; besides it is impassable during the rains.

When you expand a sentence through coordination, you get a compound sentence, double or multiple. A compound (double) sentence consists of two main clauses, while a compound (multiple) sentence consists of three or more main clauses.

He bolted his breakfast and ran towards the bus stop. (compound double)

He got up at six, had a bath, said his prayers, ate his breakfast and ran towards the bus stop. (compound multiple)

Theoretically, there is no limit to the number of main clauses that may be combined into one single sentence but most writers limit their use of coordination. Instead, they combine all three methods of sentence expansion:

Very few English sentences are limited to the elements that make up the basic patterns, and most English sentences that you come across in speech or writing are basic sentences expanded. (two main clauses plus two subordinate clauses – complex-compound)

The peace which Oxford once knew, and which a great university city should always have, has been ruined by the motor industry, and no benefactions or research endowments can make up for the change in character which the city has suffered. (two main clauses plus three subordinate clauses – complex-compound)
*benefactions: handsome donations (made to the university)

Exercise 6

Combine each of the following sets of simple sentences into a complex or complex-compound sentence. The first two are done for you as examples.

a. Early settlers in Australia introduced the European rabbit into the continent. This rabbit had no natural enemies in its new habitat. It multiplied with that abandon characteristic of rabbits. A whole continent was soon overrun by rabbits.

Answer: Early settlers in Australia introduced into the continent the European rabbit, which, because it had no natural enemies in its new habitat, multiplied with that abandon characteristic of rabbits, and as a result a whole continent was soon overrun by rabbits. (two main plus two subordinate clauses – complex-compound)

b. Both television and printing are mass media. They depend on reaching great numbers. The printed word can communicate to numbers of like minds over centuries. Television communicates to millions of unlike minds at the same moment in time.

Answer: Both television and printing are mass media which depend on reaching great numbers but whereas the printed word can communicate to numbers of like minds over centuries, television communicates to millions of unlike minds at the same moment in time. (two main plus two subordinate clauses – complex-compound)

c. Until 1957 the Earth had only one satellite—the Moon. The Moon is still the Earth's only natural satellite. In recent years the Moon has been joined by various other bodies. These bodies were made on Earth. They were launched into space by means of rocket power.

d. In the mid-fifties of the last century, the Dupont company in America made a survey of the shopping habits of American housewives. They found out something. The housewives mostly bought on impulse. Seven out of ten purchases were made in the store.

e. Cricket is, in a sense, warfare in miniature. A cricket match should be fought out by both sides with all the resources of spirit and technique at their command. At the same time it should always be a recreation, a game to be played according to an unwritten code of chivalry and good temper.
*in miniature: on a small scale

f. Parents may be good both as parents and as individuals. Children's disillusionment with parents is in some degree inevitable. Most children have a very high ideal of their parents. No parent can live up to that ideal.

g. Noise is the curse of modern civilisation. Noise is nobody's responsibility. Noise is the byproduct of almost every human activity. The deaf, the victims of noise, fail to rouse human pity. For these reasons the problem of controlling and limiting noise was neglected for a long time.

24.4 Embedding

'Embedding' may be said to be the opposite of expansion. The English sentence, we said earlier, is capable of being expanded indefinitely. On the other hand, it lends itself to condensation as well. You may, for instance, want to condense ideas expressed in one or two sentences into one single short sentence. We call this 'embedding'. Embedding is a technique of concision. Here is an example to illustrate the process of embedding:

1. Annie Joseph is a champion runner.
2. She has won a dozen competitions.
3. She is expected to make it to the Olympics.

Here are three ideas expressed in three different sentences. Suppose that the idea in sentence 3 is your main idea or message. The final sentence would then be:

4. Annie Joseph, a champion runner, who has won a dozen competitions, is expected to make it to the Olympics.

You may condense differently:

5. Having won a dozen competitions, champion runner Annie Joseph is expected to make it to the Olympics. (or)
6. Champion runner Annie Joseph, winner of a dozen competitions, is expected to make it to the Olympics.

Notice that in all the three versions 4-6, sentence 3, which carries your main idea or message, is the main clause. Sentences 1 and 2 are reduced to modifiers serving to support the main idea.

Suppose you want to highlight a different idea, say, the idea expressed in sentence 1. You would then say:

> Olympic prospect Annie Joseph, who has won a dozen competitions, is a champion runner. (or)
>
> Annie Joseph, who is expected to make it to the Olympics and who has won a dozen competitions, is a champion runner. (or)
>
> Annie Joseph, Olympic prospect and winner of a dozen competitions, is a champion runner.

The way you combine and condense two or more sentences into one single short sentence will depend on what you consider the main idea and what you consider the supporting details. The main idea will be expressed in the main clause while the supporting details or subordinate ideas will be expressed in the form of modifiers.

Exercise 7

Combine each of the following sets of sentences into one sentence through embedding.

a. My brother is an artist. His name is Samuel. He likes to paint weird animals.

b. Jonathan Swift is the author of 'Gulliver's Travels'. 'Gulliver's Travels' is a brilliant satire. The novel satirises human pride, greed and vanity.

c. Last night I dreamt I was a Labrador. This was the third time I had the dream. I had won the first prize at a dog show.

d. Eventually the sun will consume all of its energy. It will bloat out to ten times its current size. Then it will shrink into a black cinder. This will happen fifty billion years from now.

e. There are seven wonders of the ancient world. The Taj Mahal is one of them. The Taj Mahal is in India. It was erected by Shah Jahan in memory of his wife Mumtaz Mahal. It took about a dozen years to build. (more than one possibility)

25 Transformations

When you transform a sentence, clause or phrase you change the form of the sentence, clause or phrase without changing the meaning. The sentence 'He affirmed his innocence' means the same as 'He affirmed that he was innocent' but formally the two sentences are different: the first one is a simple sentence, while the second is a complex one. We call either sentence a transform of the other.

In the same way, we may change a clause into a phrase, or a phrase into a clause.

clause into phrase

He learned Chinese while he was staying in Beijing. (clause)

He learned Chinese during his stay in Beijing. (phrase)

phrase into clause

He failed his examination despite his working hard. (phrase)

Although he worked hard, he failed his examination. (clause)

A sentence, clause or phrase and its transform may mean the same thing, as in the examples cited above. Sometimes there is a small but subtle change in meaning or emphasis, as when we change active to passive voice; all the same the accent in all transformations is on the form and not on the meaning.

25.1 The Importance of Transformations

Transformations are important in a number of ways. For one thing, they are crucial to understanding the meaning of a sentence, especially when two or more sentences look superficially alike but mean different things – sentences like:

John is eager to please;

John is easy to please.

Both sentences are structured the same way; they are in fact identical in form except for the difference in the predicate adjective. However, in 'John is eager to please', 'John' is the nominal as well as the real subject – he is the one who does the pleasing:

John pleases people and John is eager to please them.

John is eager to do something. John pleases people.

In the other sentence, however, 'John', though nominally the subject, is really the object of the infinitive 'to please', while the real subject is 'people':

People please John and it is easy for people to please him.

It is easy for people to do something. People please John.

The underlying difference in subject-object relationship accounts for the difference in meaning between the two sentences – a difference, incidentally, obscured by the superficial similarity of structure – and this difference in meaning becomes apparent only when we try to transform the sentences. The sentence 'John is easy to please' may be transformed into 'It is easy to please John', while the other sentence cannot be transformed into: 'It is eager for John to please people'.

In the same way, superficially similar sentence structures like:

1. He hates growing cabbages;
2. He hates growing children;
3. He hates boring company

are in fact very different in meaning, while seemingly different sentence structures like each of the following pairs of sentences:

4. He hates growing cabbages. He hates to grow cabbages;
5. He hates growing children. He hates children that are growing;
6. He hates boring company. He hates company that bores him

mean the same. These similarities and differences in meaning are best understood through exercises in transformations on families of sentences.

Secondly and more importantly, transformations furnish the learners of the language with a variety of sentence structures to choose from, especially in writing. Spoken as well as written English, written more than spoken, is a matter of linguistic choice—choice of words and choice of sentence structures. For the potential users of the language to make the right choice of sentence structure, they should in the first instance know what choices are available to them. Here comes the relevance of transformations; exercises in transformation help to teach the learners what choices of sentence structures are available to them and what, if any, are the stylistic effects peculiar to one sentence structure vis-à-vis another, very similar to it.

25.2 Types of Transformations

There are the simpler transformations in which the subject-predicate structures are unchanged or least changed, as for example in noun, adverb and adjective clauses:

a. He said something. He was framed by his political opponents.
   He said that he was framed by his political opponents. (noun clause)
b. He was taking his customary walk in the morning. He saw a dog run over by a speeding lorry.
   As he was taking his customary walk in the morning, he saw a dog run over by a speeding lorry. (adverb clause)
c. I met a man. The man had been to school with my grandfather.
   I met a man who had been to school with my grandfather. (adjective clause)

Notice that in changing a sentence into a noun, adverb and adjective clause, you keep the subject-predicate structure of the clause practically intact. All that the transformation involves is little more than the addition of a subordinate conjunction to join the subordinate clause to the main clause.

Changing a statement into a question or a positive declarative into a negative declarative are other examples of the simpler transformations.

There are the not-so-simple transformations (such as active to passive and positive to comparative to superlative degree of comparison) in which the subject-predicate structures are changed. Among the more complex transformations are participle, gerund and infinitive phrases in which the subject or the finite verb is either reduced or altogether omitted.

We have covered the simpler and the not-so-simple transformations in the previous chapters. In this chapter we take up the more complex transformations.

25.2.1 Conversion of Complex to Simple Sentences

In this type of transformation, we convert the subordinate clause of the complex sentence to a phrase. When you convert a subordinate clause to a phrase, any kind of subordinate clause for that matter, all that you need to do is to leave out the subordinate conjunction and the subject of the subordinate clause. As for the finite verb of the subordinate clause, you usually reduce it to a non-finite verb—participle or infinitive.

1. We begin with the adverb clause.

a. Adverb clause of time

Using an adverb clause of time is only one way of expressing time. There are other ways. For instance, you may change a time-clause into a phrase—participle, prepositional, prepositional gerund or absolute.

time-clause into participle phrase

We went to bed after we finished dinner. (cl)

Finishing dinner, we went to bed. (ph)

We went to bed after we had finished dinner. (cl)

Having finished dinner, we went to bed. (ph)

time-clause into prepositional gerund phrase

We went to bed when we finished dinner. (cl)

On finishing dinner, we went to bed. (ph)

Make sure that the guest pays all his bills before he leaves the place. (cl)

Make sure that the guest pays all his bills before leaving the place. (ph)

Notice that in changing the time-clause into a participle phrase or prepositional gerund phrase, we reduced the finite verb to a participle or gerund:

time-clause	phrase
finishing ~~after~~ ~~we~~ ~~finished~~ dinner	finishing dinner
having finished ~~after~~ ~~we~~ ~~had finished~~ dinner	having finished dinner
finishing (on) ~~when~~ ~~we~~ ~~finished~~ dinner	on finishing dinner
leaving (*before) ~~before~~ ~~he~~ ~~leaves~~ the place	before leaving the place

*preposition

Note

A word by way of explanation of the signs used above and in the examples to follow:

Sign X means the word is deleted.

Sign ____ means the form of the word is changed, the new word written above the old one.
The brackets (   ) contain any new word or words added in the act of transformation.

Notice that the subordinate conjunction and the subject of the subordinate clause are deleted from the phrase.

time-clause into prepositional phrase

If the phrase you reduce the time-clause to is a prepositional phrase, the transformation procedure is slightly more complicated. You may then use a preposition – a one-word preposition or a phrasal preposition – followed by a noun phrase headed by a noun derived from the verb in the original clause:

Teaching in the school has improved since the new syllabus was introduced. (time-clause)
Teaching in the school has improved since/with the introduction of the new syllabus. (prepositional phrase)

Note that the prepositional phrase is made up of 'since' or 'with' plus the noun phrase 'the introduction of the new syllabus'. Note further that 'since' here is a preposition and not a subordinate conjunction, as in the time-clause.

As they discussed the matter, a number of interesting points came up. (time-clause)
In the course of their discussion of the matter, a number of interesting points came up. (prepositional phrase, made up of phrasal preposition 'in the course of' plus noun phrase 'their discussion of the matter')

Sometimes, particularly when the finite verb of the time-clause is the verb 'be', we think up an appropriate noun to go with the preposition:

I went to school when I was five. (time-clause)

I went to school at the age of five. (prepositional phrase)

time-clause into absolute phrase

We went ot bed after we finished dinner. (time-clause)

Dinner finished, we went to bed. (absolute phrase)

b. Adverb clause of reason and result

reason-/result-clause into participle phrase

being
~~As he was~~ ill, he did not attend the conference. (adverb clause of reason)

Being ill, he did not attend the conference. (participle phrase)

being
~~He was 'so'~~ ill ~~that~~ he did not attend the conference. (adverb clause of result)

Being ill, he did not attend the conference. (participle phrase)

reason-/result-clause into prepositional phrase (made up of phrasal preposition plus abstract noun)

(because of)
(on account of) } his ~~As he~~ illness ~~was ill~~, he did not attend the conference.
(owing to)

Owing to his illness/On account of his illness/Because of his illness, he did not attend the conference.

Notice that the predicate adjective 'ill' in the subordinate clause 'as he was ill' has been changed to its noun form 'illness', preceded by the possessive adjective 'his' derived from the subject 'he' of the subordinate clause. If the reason-clause were 'As they were ill…' the resultant phrase would be 'owing to their illness'.

reason-/result-clause into prepositional phrase made up of phrasal preposition plus gerund

his being

(on account of) ~~As~~ ~~he was~~ ill, he did not attend the conference.

On account of his being ill, he did not attend the conference.

We have the gerund phrase 'being ill' in the above example instead of the abstract noun 'illness'. The gerund comes in particularly handy when the predicate adjective in the subordinate clause does not have an abstract noun form, as in the following example:

being

(on account of) ~~As~~ his house ~~was~~ adjacent to hers, he could not help running into her often.

On account of his house being adjacent to hers, he could not help running into her often.

Note that 'his house' in the prepositional phrase 'on account of his house being adjacent' should, strictly speaking, be 'his house's'. However, the form without the apostrophe plus 's is allowed in informal English. Besides, the possessive form 'his house's' would be awkward here, its only virtue being that it conforms to a grammatical rule.

reason-/result-clause into an infinitive phrase

Every two-wheeler rider tries to get ahead of every other vehicle on the

(in order) road ~~because~~ ~~they~~ ~~want~~ to reach the office in time. (adverb clause of reason)

Every two-wheeler rider tries to get ahead of every other vehicle on the road in order to reach the office in time. (inf. ph.)

too to attend

He was so ill ~~that~~ ~~he~~ ~~did not attend~~ the conference. (adverb clause of result)

He was too ill to attend the conference (inf.ph.)

Notice that the finite verb of the result-clause 'did not attend' is reduced to the infinitive phrase 'to attend', with the negative 'not' left out of the infinitive phrase. This is because the adverb 'too' in 'He was too ill' contains a negative. Here is another example of the same kind:

He was ~~so~~ timid that he did not speak to the girl for over a year.

He was too timid to speak to the girl for over a year.

reason-/result-clause into absolute phrase

turning

~~As~~ the weather on the mountain ~~turned~~ worse, the summit party gave up the attempt to reach the top.

The weather on the mountain turning worse, the summit party gave up the attempt to reach the top. (absolute phrase)

Note that in changing the subordinate clause into an absolute phrase, we retain the subject of the clause ('the weather'), while reducing the finite verb to a non-finite participle. Remember the absolute construction is also known as the nominative absolute.

reason-/result-clause into an appositive adjective phrase

(extremely)

~~He was so~~ complacent ~~that~~ he did not see the danger ahead of him. (adverb clause of result)

Extremely complacent, he did not see the danger ahead of him. (appositive adjective phrase, in apposition to the pronoun 'he')

The appositive phrase can be an adjective phrase, as in the above example, or a noun phrase as in this:

An extremely complacent man, he did not see the danger ahead of him. (appositive noun phrase, in apposition to the pronoun 'he')

Note that in changing the subordinate clause into an appositive phrase, we delete both the subject and the finite verb.

Exercise 1

Turn the underlined adverb clauses into phrases without changing the meaning. Follow the directions given in parentheses.

a. When I first heard of the collision, I didn't imagine there would be so many survivors. (into a prepositional gerund phrase)

b. I am in a dilemma because I have had two offers, both equally interesting. (into a participle phrase)

c. Before the white man colonised Africa, the continent was just a blank space on the map of the world. (into a prepositional phrase)

d. The meeting of the standing committee had to be postponed because only a handful of members had turned up. (into an absolute phrase)

e. The room is so tiny that it cannot accommodate a bed. (into an infinitive phrase)

Exercise 2

Rewrite the following complex sentences as simple sentences by turning the subordinate clause into a phrase.

a. After the prayers were over, they ate a frugal meal.

b. She has not written to me since she emigrated to Australia.

c. The job is so tough that a teenager like you cannot do it single-handed.

d. The crowd was so large that it filled the entire stadium.

e. Surgery became painless after chemicals like nitrous oxide and ether were introduced.

c. Adverb clause of purpose

purpose-clause into infinitive phrase

to study/in order to study

People in the third world learn English ~~so that they may study,~~ science and technology. (adverb clause of purpose)

People in the third world learn English to study/in order to study science and technology. (inf. ph.)

purpose-clause into prepositional gerund phrase

(for the purpose of) studying

People in the third world learn English ~~so that they may study~~. science and technology. (adverb clause of purpose)

People in the third world learn English for the purpose of studying science and technology. (prepositional gerund phrase)

d. Adverb clause of concession

concessive clause into prepositional phrase (made up of phrasal preposition plus abstract noun)

(in spite of) (despite) (with all)(for all)

his cleverness

Although ~~he was clever,~~ he was not successful in life. (adverb clause of concession)

In spite of his cleverness/despite his cleverness/with all his cleverness/for all his cleverness, he was not successful in life. (prep. ph.)

concessive clause into prepositional phrase (made up of phrasal preposition plus gerund phrase)

(in spite of) (despite)

his being

Although ~~he was~~ clever, he was not successful in life. (adverb clause of concession)

Despite his being clever/in spite of his being clever, he was not successful in life. (prep. ph.)

Notice that the transformation procedure is the same as the one followed when converting a reason-/result clause into a prepositional phrase:

clause	phrase
As he was ill, he did not attend the conference. (adv. cl. of reason) Although he was clever, he was not successful in life.(adv. cl. of concession)	On account of his illness... On account of his being ill In spite of his cleverness... In spite of his being clever... (prep. ph.)

e. Adverb clause of condition

conditional clause into infinitive phrase

(for)

~~If~~ you ~~want~~ to pass the test, you must work hard. (adverb clause of condition)

For you to pass the test, You must work hard. (inf. ph.)

conditional clause into prepositional gerund phrase

(by) working

~~If you~~ work hard, you will pass the test. (clause)

By working hard, you will pass the test. (prep. ger. ph.)

(without) working

~~If you do not work~~ hard, you will never pass the test.

Without working hard, you will never pass the test.

conditional clause into prepositional phrase

(in the event of)

Prime Minister's dying

~~If~~ the ~~Prime Minister dies~~ in harness, he will be succeeded by his deputy. (cl)

In the event of the Prime Minister's dying in harness, he will be succeeded by his deputy. (prep. ph.)

(in case of)/(in the event of)

~~In~~ case ~~there~~ ~~is~~ a constitutional breakdown, the President will proclaim an emergency. (cl)

In case of/in the event of a constitutional breakdown, the President will proclaim an emergency. (prep. ph.)

(but for)

your intervention

~~If you had not intervened,~~ we would have fallen apart. (cl)

But for your intervention, we would have fallen apart. (prep. ph.)

Notice that the prepositional phrase 'but for' is followed by the noun form of 'intervene', preceded by the possessive adjective 'your' (from the subject of the clause 'you')—'but for your intervention'.

In the same way, the conditional clause in:

If the rains had not arrived in time, there would have been a severe drought in this part of the country

would become:

But for the timely arrival of the rains, there would have been a severe drought in this part of the country.

Note that the noun 'arrival' derived from the finite verb of the conditional clause is now modified by the adjective 'timely'—as the finite verb of the clause changes from verb to noun, the adverbial modifier 'in time' modifying the verb 'had (not) arrived' becomes the adjectival modifier 'timely' to modify the new noun 'arrival'.

If the finite verb of the conditional clause is 'be', as in these sentences:

If the rains had not been timely/If it had not been for the timely rains, there would have been a severe drought... country,

the equivalent prepositional phrase will then be:

But for the timely rains, there would have been a severe drought in this part of the country.

Exercise 3

Turn the underlined adverb clauses into phrases without changing the meaning. Follow the directions given in parentheses.

a. The family live quite simply and unostentatiously although they are rich. (into a prepositional phrase)

b. If you want to make a success of your project, you must enlist the support of the local community. (into an infinitive phrase)

c. Although he has many faults, people in the office still like him. (into a prepositional phrase beginning: 'with all...)

d. Unless we get substantial help from the government, we cannot undertake the project on our own. (into a prepositional phrase)

e. She had locked herself in so that she might ponder the situation calmly. (into an infinitive phrase)

Exercise 4

Rewrite these complex sentences as simple sentences by turning the subordinate clauses into phrases.

a. If a story should appeal to children, it should have a great deal of action.

b. In case the engine fails, lock the car and look for the nearest garage.

c. He sat in the last row so that he might not be noticed.

d. If it had not been for the trucking strike, we wouldn't have faced such an acute shortage of essential goods.

e. You must master your temper if you want to make an impact as team leader.

25.2.2 The Adjective/Relative Clause

The adjective or relative clause may be transformed into a phrase—participle, prepositional, prepositional gerund, infinitive or appositive.

a. Adjective clause into participle phrase

studying
A person ~~who studies~~ the voting behaviour of people in elections is called a psephologist. (cl)

A person studying the voting behaviour of people in elections is called a psephologist. (ph)

ever made
It was the funniest movie ~~that was ever made~~ by Charlie Chaplin. (cl)

It was the funniest movie ever made by Charlie Chaplin. (ph)

b. Adjective clause into prepositional phrase

Can you get me the book ~~that is~~ on the top shelf? (cl)

Can you get me the book on the top shelf? (ph)

(of) (of) occurrence
The exact time ~~when~~ the accident ~~occurred~~ is not known. (cl)

The exact time of occurrence of the accident is not known. (ph)

The first of the transformations in (b) is quite easy: you simply strip the adjective clause of its subject and finite verb. The second transformation is not so easy; in this the subject, along with the finite verb, of the adjective clause is converted into a prepositional phrase—the verb 'occur' is changed to its noun form 'occurrence', and the subject ('the accident') becomes part of a prepositional phrase ('of the accident'). The entire phrase 'of occurrence of the accident' becomes a larger prepositional phrase, modifying the noun 'time'.

Here is a similar example:

The teenage years are the best time when character is formed.

The teenage years are the best time for the formation of character.

c. adjective clause into a prepositional gerund phrase

(of) making
There are several ways ~~in which we can make~~ money/in which money can be made. (cl)

There are several ways of making money. (ph)

(for) making

The time ~~when one could~~ make excuses is past. (cl)

The time for making excuses is past. (ph)

d. adjective clause into infinitive phrase

to do

There is nothing ~~that you can do~~ now. (cl)

There is nothing for you to do now. (ph)

to spare

I have no money ~~that I can spare~~ for you. (cl)

I have no money to spare for you. (ph)

Prepositional relative clauses (see the relevant section in Chapter 22) can also be transformed into infinitive phrases:

to dump

She found a room ~~in which she could dump~~ all the old magazines. (cl)

She found a room to dump all the old magazines in. (ph)

to buy

He has no money ~~with which he can buy~~ a ticket . (cl)

He has no money to buy a ticket with. (ph)

adjective clause into appositive phrase

New Delhi, ~~which is~~ India's federal capital, is a highly polluted city. (cl)

New Delhi, India's federal capital, is a highly polluted city. (ph)

Our neighbour's son, ~~who is~~ barely six years old, is already a computer whiz kid. (cl)

Our neighbour's son, barely six years old, is already a computer whiz kid. (ph)

f. Sometimes it is possible to replace an entire adjective clause by an equivalent adjective:

He had always wanted to go back to the village where he was born. (cl)

He had always wanted to go back to his native village. (adj)

He is back home from hospital recovering from an illness which he had recently. (cl)

He is back home from hospital recovering from a recent illness. (adj)

Of all the pains that can afflict the body, the dental is the transcendental. (cl)

Of all the bodily pains, the dental is the transcendental. (adj)

Exercise 5

Turn the underlined adjective clauses into phrases, following the directions given in parentheses.

a. The best time when one can learn a foreign language is between the ages of four and fourteen. (into a prepositional gerund phrase)

b. Oscar Wilde wrote a hilarious comedy which he called 'The Importance of Being Earnest'. (into participle phrase)

c. He spoke on William Wordsworth, who is arguably England's greatest nature poet.

(into an appositive phrase)

d. The first problem that attracted Louis Pasteur's attention as a chemist was the problem of fermentation. (into an infinitive phrase)

e. Those who suffer from high blood pressure should not do the halasana. (into a participle phrase)

Exercise 6

Replace the relative clauses in the following sentences by equivalent adjectives.

a. We must distinguish between problems that concern the nation as a whole and those that concern a particular region.

b. He is not just an ordinary liar but a liar who is too far gone to be corrected.

c. That is the ward where ailing old people are treated and cared for.

d. A person who is capable of using both his hands with equal skill is indeed at an advantage.

e. Islam, not Christianity, is the religion that forbids alcohol altogether.

25.2.3 The Noun Clause

A noun clause may be transformed into an infinitive phrase, a gerund phrase or an abstract noun phrase. Consider the underlined noun clause in this sentence:

That she should marry him after all these years is surprising. (cl)

The clause may be turned into:

a. an infinitive phrase – For her to marry him after all these years is surprising.

b. a gerund phrase – Her marrying him after all these years is surprising.

or

c. an abstract noun phrase – Her marriage to him after all these years is surprising.

Study these additional examples of conversion:

to plead

(For them) ~~That they should plead~~ ignorance of the law is unbelievable. (noun cl)

For them to plead ignorance of the law is unbelievable. (inf. ph.)

your not knowing

~~That you did not know~~ of the existence of such a regulation is no defence. (noun clause)

Your not knowing of the existence of such a regulation is no defence. (gerund phrase)

your decision

~~That you decided~~ to stand by your friend does you honour. (noun clause)

Your decision to stand by your friend does you honour. (abstract noun phrase)

(The manner of)

dacoits' escape

~~How~~ the ~~dacoits escaped~~ from police custody is a mystery. (cl)

The manner of the dacoits' escape from police custody is a mystery. (noun phrase)

Exercise 7

Turn the underlined noun clauses into phrases, following the directions given in parentheses.

a. She suggested that I should consult a doctor at once. (into a gerund phrase)
b. He claimed that he had seen with his own eyes the Abominable Snowman. (into an infinitive phrase)
c. That he didn't report the accident to the police does not speak well of him. (into an abstract noun phrase)
d. They are hoping that the good old days will return. (into a prepositional phrase)
e. Whether the police would succeed in recapturing the escaped dacoits is doubtful. (into a noun phrase)

Exercise 8

Rewrite these complex sentences as simple sentences by turning the noun clauses into phrases.

a. The fact that he was well connected certainly helped him in his business.
b. Her belief that her husband will eventually return still remains unshaken.
c. What Stanley wrote of his meeting with Dr Livingstone turned out to be the biggest scoop of the century.
d. No one knows why he behaved so secretively.
e. How long the emergency will last is anybody's guess.

25.3 Conversion of Simple to Complex Sentences

In this kind of transformation, you do the opposite of what you did earlier: you pick a word or phrase in the simple sentence and expand it into a subordinate clause - noun, adjective or adverb clause.

Study carefully the following examples of conversion:

His manner proclaimed his guilt. (noun phrase, object of 'proclaimed')
His manner proclaimed that he was guilty. (noun clause, object of 'proclaimed')
She can hardly conceal her dislike of her employer. (noun phrase, object of 'can conceal')
She can hardly conceal the fact that she dislikes her employer. (noun clause, in apposition to the noun 'fact', object of 'can conceal')
He took over a virtually bankrupt company. (adj., modifying the noun 'company')
He took over a company that was virtually bankrupt. (adj. cl., modifying the noun 'company')
She is the person to consult on a matter like this. (adjectival infinitive phrase, modifying the noun 'person')
She is the person whom you should consult on a matter like this. (adjective clause, modifying the noun 'person')
The box is too heavy for you to lift. (adverbial infinitive phrase)

The box is so heavy that you cannot lift it. (adverb clause of result)

Despite his years of living in London, he still writes in Punjabi. (adverbial prepositional phrase)

Although he has lived for years in London, he still writes in Punjabi. (adverb clause of concession)

I would have been a soldier but for my father. (adverbial prepositional phrase)

I would have been a soldier if it had not been for my father. (adverb clause of condition)

Notice that the word/phrase in the simple sentence and the clause that replaces it in the complex sentence perform the same function, nominal, adjectival or adverbial.

Exercise 9

Transform these simple sentences into complex sentences by turning the underlined words/phrases into subordinate clauses.

a. For a man of his age to wear such loud shirts is extraordinary, to say the least.
b. The police enforced strict security measures in the area following the sudden and mysterious disappearance of a dozen school children.
c. We can't assume his guilt or innocence by simply looking at him.
d. Situated on the outskirts of the city, the house was vulnerable to attacks by dacoits.
e. Their ramshackle huts having collapsed, these people have nowhere to go.

Exercise 10

Rewrite these simple sentences as complex sentences.

a. A person opening a current account at a bank is actually lending the bank money.
b. His being rude to her was bad enough.
c. No one can hope to become an efficient reader except through systematic practice.
d. People are in fact selling off their cars on account of the steep rise in the price of petrol.
e. To be really happy, one ought to have one or two real hobbies.

25.4 Conversion of Compound to Complex Sentences

The problem in this kind of transformation is choosing aright the main clause for subordination, and that would depend on your understanding of the kind of relationship expressed by the compound sentence – whether it is cause and effect, condition and effect, concession or contrast, and so on.

Look at these two sentences:

He was so likeable, so no one could get angry with him.

Give us the tools, and we will finish the job.

The first sentence expresses a cause-and-effect relationship, while the second expresses a condition-and-effect relationship. You may convert either of the clauses in the first sentence into an adverb clause:

As he was likeable, no one could get angry with him. (adverb clause of reason)

He was so likeable that no one could get angry with him. (adverb clause of result)

Either way, the resultant sentence is a complex sentence, consisting of one main clause and one subordinate clause.

In the second sentence, the first main clause expresses a condition; the second the 'effect' that will follow if the condition is fulfilled. You may convert the first main clause into a conditional clause:

If you give us the tools, we will finish the job.

Sometimes one or the other of the main clauses making up the compound sentence may express or suggest a relationship of time, place, purpose, concession, contrast, and so on. You then convert the clause into an equivalent adverb clause, as illustrated below:

I was called to the Bar in 1980 and since then I have been in politics. (time-relationship)

I have been in politics ever since I was called to the Bar in 1980. (adverb clause of time)

They didn't want any misunderstanding later, so they put everything down on paper. (purpose)

They put everything down on paper so that they might not have any misunderstanding later. (adverb clause of purpose)

It was an inter-caste marriage with his own share of problems but it proved to be stable and enduring. (concession)

Although it was an inter-caste marriage with his own share of problems, it proved to be stable and enduring.
(adverb clause of concession)

I like him as a person but I wouldn't have him as my doctor. (contrast between 'person' and 'doctor')

While I like him as a person, I wouldn't have him as my doctor. (adverb clause of contrast)

Exercise 11

Convert the following compound sentences into complex sentences by turning the underlined main clause into a subordinate clause.

a. He is one of the country's leading educationists and his views are naturally listened to with respect.
b. Word of the minister's visit went round the office and within minutes everyone was at their desk pretending to be busy working.
c. She had no high hopes of passing the audition test; nevertheless she applied for a part in the serial.
d. The neighbours think my uncle to be a harmless old man but he is not really so harmless.
e. He had to sign on the dotted line; otherwise they would have expelled him.

Exercise 12

Rewrite these compound sentences as complex sentences by changing either of the main clauses into a subordinate clause.

a. She heard a knock on the door and at once she rushed to answer the door.

b. First, insist on a living wage, and then, agree to work for him.
c. That country was wholly dependent on imported oil until recently but by now has progressed far towards achieving self-sufficiency in oil.
d. The speaker knew his facts but his conclusions were rather confused.
e. He must have more than his share of luck this year; otherwise he will be ruined.

25.5 Conversion of Complex to Compound Sentences

In this kind of transformation, we convert the subordinate clause of the complex sentence into a main clause. This is relatively easy to do since in most cases the subordinate clause, particularly if it is an adverb clause, clearly indicates the relationship binding it to the main clause. Study these examples of conversion:

If you pay the admission fee, we will have your name registered straightaway. (complex)

Pay the admission fee, and we will have your name registered straightaway. (compound)

Even if he is very expensive, he is still the best doctor in town. (complex)

He is very expensive; nevertheless he is still the best doctor in town. (compound)

Although he hadn't met William Sharp, he had met Wilfrid Blunt. (complex)

He hadn't met William Sharp; however, he had met Wilfrid Blunt. (compound)

Can you prove the murder charge that you have made against him? (complex)

You have made a murder charge against him/You have charged him with murder but can you prove the charge? (compound)

I have no doubt that he will come out of the trial unscathed. (complex)

He will come out of the trial unscathed and I have no doubt about that. (compound)

Exercise 13

Convert these complex sentences into compound sentences.

a. The three main sources of power are coal, oil and water, all the three of which are exhaustible.
b. We sometimes refer to electricity, gas or petrol as if they were the actual sources of power.
c. We are pretty certain that of all the planets in our own solar system the Earth alone supports life.
d. Science and technology have become so pervasive in our lives that society is changing at an unprecedented speed.
e. Although in man's early days competition with other creatures was tough, even critical, it is no longer so.

Exercise 14

Rewrite these complex sentences as compound sentences.

a. If you are speaking the truth, then she must be lying.
b. After a discussion that lasted several hours, the General Body approved the action taken on their behalf by the club's office-bearers.

c. Bad as the situation is, it is by no means desperate.

d. The practice of having more than one wife, which is still in use in many parts of Africa, seemed peculiar to the early Christian missionaries.

e. If you miss this chance, you may not get another for a long time.

25.6 Conversion of Compound to Simple Sentences

In this kind of transformation, you convert one of the main clauses into a phrase. But which one? The choice would depend upon the kind of relationship between the two main clauses.

Look at the following compound sentence:

He played a game of tennis and (then) went for a swim.

The coordinate conjunction 'and' (with or without the adverb 'then') sets up a simple time-relationship: he first played a game of tennis and then went for a swim.

You now reduce the first of the main clauses to a phrase:

Having played a game of tennis, he went for a swim. (or)
After playing a game of tennis, he went for a swim.

The procedure of conversion of a main clause to a phrase is the same as the procedure you followed earlier when converting a subordinate clause to a phrase except that there is no subordinate conjunction for you to leave out.

You leave out the subject and reduce the finite verb to a non-finite verb.

This is how it is done:

having played playing
~~He played~~ a game of tennis. /(After)~~He played~~ a game of tennis.

Having played a game of tennis… /After playing a game of tennis…

Here is another example illustrating this kind of transformation, compound-to-simple:

She had everything going for her, yet she was not a happy woman.

The relationship set up in the above compound sentence is one of contrast, as may be seen from the use of the coordinate conjunction 'yet'.

You change the first of the main clauses into a prepositional phrase plus a gerund phrase:

In spite of her having everything going for her, she was not a happy woman.

He not only helped me with money but gave me some valuable tips.

The relationship set up here is one of plain addition: he did one thing and then he did another. You change the first of the main clauses to:

Besides helping me with money, he gave me some valuable tips.

Exercise 15

Convert the following compound sentences into simple sentences.

a. He is terribly absent-minded and forgetful, so he often fails to keep his appointments.

b. Children have a tendency to imitate grown-ups; it is natural to them.
c. He is an ardent admirer of George Bernard Shaw and he thinks him the greatest British dramatist ever.
d. The floods have uprooted thousands of villagers, and relief workers are trying to provide them with some makeshift shelter.
e. They tried him for a month, and after finding him incompetent, they dismissed him.

Exercise 16

Rewrite these compound sentences as simple sentences.

a. Some people cannot help gambling; the impulse to gamble is much too strong for them to resist.
b. The South Col is a bare, frozen plain of rock and ice and it lies at a height of 25,850 feet between the final peaks of Everest and Lhotse.
c. He not only urged his men to be punctual but set a personal example to them by making it a point to arrive in time for work.
d. Life in Sherpa land was very hard, and many were forced to move out in search of a living.
e. The club's secretary proposed a vote of thanks to the speaker of the evening, and with that the meeting ended.

25.7 Conversion of Simple to Compound Sentences

In converting a simple sentence into a compound sentence, you look for a word or phrase potentially expandable into a main clause. Study the following examples of conversion (the expandable bits are underlined for you):

The audience resented the reference made by the speaker to the government's reservation policy. (simple)

The speaker made a reference to the government's reservation policy and the audience resented it. (compound)

Despite his discovering the principle behind all vaccination, Louis Pasteur never bothered himself about the many applications of the principle. (simple)

Louis Pasteur discovered the principle behind all vaccination but he did not bother himself about the many applications of the principle. (compound)

That was a most gratuitous insult. (simple)

That was an insult and it was entirely uncalled for. (compound)

Stanley met Dr Livingstone at Ujiji in the year 1872. (simple)

Stanley met Dr Livingstone at Ujiji, and that was in the year 1872. (compound)

Exercise 17

Convert the following simple sentences into compound sentences by expanding the underlined phrases into main clauses.

a. On his complaining of severe pain in the stomach, he was rushed to hospital.
b. The police arriving on the scene, the demonstrators dispersed in all directions.

c. The workers called off the strike following a settlement reached by their leaders with the management.
d. With the circumnavigation of Lake Victoria, Stanley realised the first of his three aims.
e. The new measures introduced by the government to control urban crime did not work for want of the will to enforce them.

Exercise 18

Rewrite these simple sentences as compound sentences.

a. Ever since his appointment as head of the department, he has had no time for teaching.
b. In view of the extreme positions held by the two parties to the dispute, no agreement was possible.
c. In the old days people used to die like flies at the outbreak of an epidemic.
d. Astrology is a multi-million dollar business, thanks to a widely held belief in the influence of the stars over people's personal lives.
e. Nearly all the sports practised nowadays are competitive.

26 Punctuation

The purpose of punctuation is practical: it is to make the meaning of a written passage clear. Punctuation marks have their own meanings, and these supplement the meanings of words.

How important is punctuation in clarifying meaning? For an answer, compare the sentences in each of the following sets:

a. (i) The group consisted of five-year-old children. (The group consisted of a certain number of children who were five years old.)

(ii) The group consisted of five year-old children. (The group consisted of five children who were one year old.)

b (i) King Frederick says Voltaire is an ass. (Kind Frederick says that Voltaire is an ass.)

(ii) King Frederick, says Voltaire, is an ass. (Voltaire says that King Frederick is an ass.)

c. (i) He has a brother, who works in the ministry. (He has one brother, presumably only one, and he works in the ministry.)

(ii) He has a brother who works in the ministry. (He has a brother who works in the ministry; he has presumably other brothers working elsewhere.)

d. (i) These are my subordinates. (These people are my subordinates.)

(ii) These are my subordinate's. (These things belong to my subordinate.)

(iii) These are my subordinates'. (These things belong to my subordinates.)

Notice, incidentally, that the sentences in the last example can be distinguished in their written form only with the help of punctuation.

Punctuation is essential to written communication; it is not an optional frill.

26.1 Functions of Punctuation

Punctuation has four specific functions:

a. to end or round out:

Is burning good for firewood?
What a silly question!
I thought you would say that.

b. to introduce:

He has one answer to every request—a blunt no.

c. to separate:

Those who can, do; those who cannot, teach.

d. to enclose or set off:

Sidney Smith once said to his prosperous brother: "You and I are exceptions to the rules of nature. You have risen by your gravity and I have sunk by my levity."

26.1.1 Types of Punctuation

There are three types of punctuation, and these are tabulated on the next page. The table, however, is not complete. Complete it.

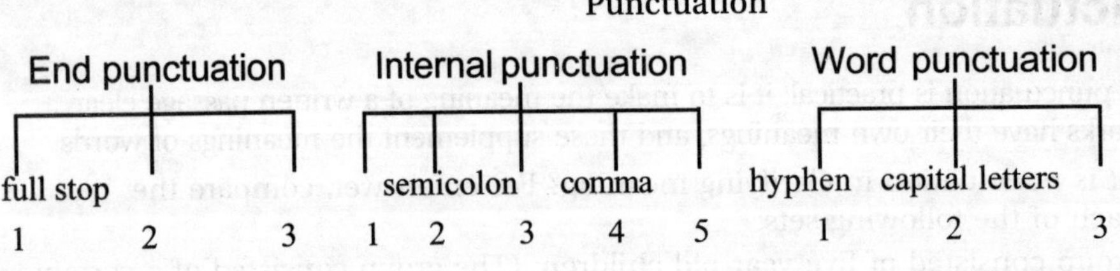

Note

Capital letters, though not strictly part of punctuation, are generally treated as part of it.

26.2 End Punctuation

26.2.1 Full Stop

a. The full stop indicates the end of a declarative sentence, an imperative sentence, or a request in interrogative form:

He snored his way into the Guinness Book of Records..

Fetch a doctor at once.

Would you please pass that piece of cake.

The declarative sentence may consist of more than one clause, even a reported question:

That a dog should play cricket was news to him.

I never could understand why he did such a silly thing.

The declarative sentence, or even a fragment of a declarative sentence, may appear within quotation marks.

She said, 'I have never heard of such a thing.'
'Never?'
'Never.'
'Sure?'
'Sure.'

b. Full stops are widely used after abbreviations:

M.A. (Master of Arts); a.m. (ante meridian); e.g. ('exempli gratia' meaning 'for example'); S. C. Bose (Subhas Chandra Bose)

Exceptions to rule (b)

(i) There is a tendency to leave out full stops in abbreviations which consist entirely of capital letters—BBC (British Broadcasting Corporation); TLS (Times Literary Supplement)

(ii) If the capital letter in the abbreviation does not stand for a complete word, it does not take a full stop—TB (tuberculosis); TV (television); MS (manuscript)

(iii) Full stops are omitted in acronyms, that is, strings of letters or syllables that are pronounced as if they spelt a complete word—NATO (North Atlantic Treaty Organisation); UNESCO (United Nations Educational, Scientific and Cultural Organisation)

26.2.2 Question Mark

The question mark is used:

a. after a direct question:

Why ever did you do that?
Will he be home early?

The questions may be in the form of words or phrases and not necessarily in the form of a completed sentence:

What? Yes? Over there? Why not here? Right now?

Sometimes, the question may not even have the typical form of a question:

She said when?

He went there?

Surely that's wrong?

b. after a question within quotation marks:

Mohan asked his mother, 'Where's my pet alligator?'

The little girl said, 'Was the man fined for biting his neighbour's dog?'

but not after an indirect or reported question:

Mohan asked his mother where his pet alligator was.

The little girl wondered whether the man was fined for biting his neighbour's dog.

c. after a 'tag' question:

You saw the car knocking down the man, didn't you?

You didn't actually see the car knocking down the man, did you?

26.2.3 Exclamation Mark

The exclamation mark is used:

a. after an emotional expression, that is, a word, phrase, or sentence expressing strong feeling such as pleasure, surprise, anger, shock, dismay and so on:

Hurrah! Bravo!

If only I had thought of that!

What a delightful party it was! How beautiful she looks!

b. after an emphatic interjection or one-word exclamation:

Ah! Alas! Help! Thieves!
Police!

When an interjection is followed by a sentence, it may be followed by an exclamation mark or a comma, depending on the degree of emphasis required:

Oh! you startled me.
Oh, you startled me.

c. after an imperative verb when it is charged with feeling:

Shut up! Get out at once!

Note

Use the exclamation mark sparingly. It is rather unfashionable nowadays and is probably used far less than in previous times.

Exercise 1

In column A are the full forms of the words. Write the abbreviated forms of these in column B, putting in full stops where necessary. The first one is done for you.

A	B
Bachelor of Arts	B.A.
Mohandas Karamchand Gandhi	
Indian Administrative Service	
Madhaya Pradesh	
World Health Organisation	
American Broadcasting Corporation	
United Nations International Children's Emergency Fund	
Kilogram	
Member of Parliament	
Postscript	

Exercise 2

Use the appropirate end punctuation mark (full stop, question mark, or exclamation mark) with the following.

a. A man is presumed innocent until he is proved guilty
b. Can you tell us how you did the trick
c. How kind of you to have thought of us
d. Stop that chatter for God's sake
e. You can't change people, can you

Exercise 3

End each of the following sentences with a full stop, question mark, or exclamation mark.

a. If only I were a millionaire
b. I thought he was stupid to believe that
   Surely you didn't say that
c. Will you please post this letter for me
d. Get the hell out of here
e. She is one of the finest women I have known
   That such a thing should happen to her

Exercise 4

The following passage is a typed report of defence witness Mrs Benson being cross-examined by the prosecuting counsel Mr Olliphant. The typist, however, has left out of the quotations all full stops and question marks. Can you insert them in the proper places?

When Andover sat down after the short examination of her, Mrs Benson got up and was about to leave the witness box.

'Just a moment, please, Mrs Benson,' said the judge. 'Mr Olliphant will want to ask you some questions'

'I apologise for asking, but how old are you, Mrs. Benson'

'I'm eighty-three next birthday'

'I'll settle for eighty-two,' said Olliphant, 'and your eyesight as good as ever, Mrs. Benson'

'Excellent'

'And your hearing excellent too' asked Olliphant.

'Perfect'

'Just dates not too good' went on Olliphant.

Mrs Benson admitted that her memory for dates was not very good.

–Adapted from Henry Cecil, *Independent Witness*

26.3 Internal Punctuation

26.3.1 Semicolon

a. The semicolon, though apparently an internal punctuation mark, is really an end punctuation mark like the full stop. It is used chiefly to separate two or more main clauses if they are closely connected in meaning.

The sun shone; we went out for a picnic.

He fell ill suddenly; he did not go to work.

Notice that the two clauses are bound together in a cause-effect relationship.

Since the semicolon is as good as a full stop, it is possible to rewrite the above examples using a full stop instead of a semicolon:

The sun shone. We went out for a picnic.

He fell ill suddenly. He did not go to work.

The full stop, however, would break the line of thought by separating ideas which are closely linked. Hence the semicolon, which is more natural in such places.

b. More usually, the semicolon is followed by a conjunctive adverb which makes the relationship between the main clauses even more plain:

The sun shone; <u>consequently</u> we went out for a picnic.

She knew she stood little chance of winning a prize; <u>all the same</u> she took part in the competition.

c. The semicolon is used to separate items in a list which are more than one in number and already have commas:

The all-India debating team consisted of Vinod Kumar, from Karnataka; John Thomas, from Kerala; Abdul Samad, from Uttar Pradesh; and Mohan Paradkar, from Maharashtra.

On the table were knives, forks and spoons; cups and saucers; plates and bowls; and glasses of all kinds.

<u>*Important Note*</u>

If the main clauses are joined together by a coordinate conjunction, the mark to use to separate the clauses is the comma, not the semicolon:

He fell ill suddenly, <u>so</u> he did not go to work.

She knew she stood little chance of winning a prize, <u>but</u> that did not stop her from taking part in the competition.

Occasionally, however, a semicolon is used between main clauses joined by a coordinate conjunction if internal commas appear in one or both of the clauses:

When I saw London for the first time, I thought I was watching the grandest show on earth; but when I went to Paris, I felt that London was not such a grand show after all.

Finally, notice the alternative ways of punctuating the same sentence:

They tried hard; they failed. (semicolon only)

They tried hard; however, they failed. (or)

They tried hard, but they failed. (comma plus coordinate conjunction)

Exercise 5

Supply semicolons where necessary.

a. There was nothing wrong with the engine of the car we had just run out of petrol.
b. The capitals of the South Indian States are: Kerala, Trivandrum Tamil Nadu, Chennai, Karnataka, Bangalore Andhra Pradesh, Hyderabad.
c. You can count on her to come on time she is much too punctual.
d. The monsoon failed for the third year in succession the country was in the grip of a famine.
e. My mother was not just annoyed she was absolutely furious.

Exercise 6

Each of the following sentences consists of two or more main clauses. The comma is correct in some of them; the semicolon in others. If the two clauses are joined by a coordinate conjunction, then the comma is enough to separate them; if there is no such conjunction and the clauses remain separate (with or without conjunctive adverbs), use the semicolon.

a. They never leave anything to chance/they plan most carefully whatever they want to do.
b. He was not very helpful/he just glanced at my letter of application and passed it on to the man sitting next to him.
c. I was present at the meeting/however, I took no part in the discussion.
d. My neighbour has pots and pots of money/yet he is not a contented man.
e. The troops were desperately short of supplies/so they decided to surrender.

26.3.2 Colon

a. The colon is used to anticipate a series of items if, and only if, the series functions in apposition to an earlier part of the sentence:

   We had the following plays of Shakespeare for detailed study: 'Romeo and Juliet', 'Julius Caesar' and 'The Merchant of Venice'.

   There are three kinds of men: the clever, the handsome, and the majority.

b. The colon is used to anticipate a specific explanation of a general statement or an explanation of some kind:

   Malaria at one time was a great killer: it killed two million people a year.

   This car is very expensive to run: it gives barely ten kilometres a litre.

Used in this way, the colon has an anticipatory function: it tells you in advance that the material that follows explains, amplifies or interprets what has gone before. What precedes the colon need not be a complete sentence any more than what follows the colon:

> 29 May 1953: It was on that day that Hillary and I set foot for the first time on Mount Everest. (Tenzing Norgay)
>
> The day dawned bright and clear: another fine day.

Note that the colon is never used with a conjunction. If a conjunction is used, a comma is enough to mark the end of the first clause:

> This car is very expensive to run, for it gives barely ten kilometres a litre.

c. A colon is sometimes used instead of the more usual comma to introduce a quotation, particularly when the quotation is a long one:

> Bertrand de Jouvenal once said of Western man: 'He tends to count nothing as an expenditure, other than human effort; he does not seem to mind how much mineral water he wastes, and far worse, how much living matter he destroys. He does not seem to realise at all that human life is a dependent part of an ecosystem of many different forms of life.'

Exercise 7

Replace the dashes in the following sentences by suitable stops (comma or colon).

a. Here's some good news for you – you have passed your finals.
b. He must be an extremely fond father – for he never seems to notice any fault in his son.
c. The audience was getting more and more restless – and he knew that his speech was not going down well.
d. My advice to you is this – consult a specialist at once.
e. He is a poor typist – he types less than twenty words a minute and makes far too many mistakes.

Exercise 8

Supply appropriate internal and end punctuation (full stop, question mark, exclamation mark; comma, semicolon, colon) for the following.

a. Doctors no longer rely on quinine for the treatment of malaria they use more efficient modern drugs
b. "Why do you want me to meet Mr. Sharma"
   "He is a most helpful man besides he is thoroughly reliable"
c. This is how he mended the puncture first he found the puncture by putting the tube in water then he cleaned the tube round the puncture next he put on a patch with the help of a sticky substance finally he put the tube and tyre back on wheel and blew up the tyre
d. We would like to order the following two dozen notebooks two reams of paper four boxes of clips a dozen dusters two dozen file covers

26.3.3 Dash

a. The dash often signals an appositive phrase, usually long:

> The new Prime Minister had a difficult problem facing him – the problem of widespread dissidence in States ruled by his party.

At last he came to a decision – a decision of great importance to his career.

It is possible to use a comma instead of a dash before the appositive phrase in the above examples. The dash, however, is the more usual mark before a long appositive phrase or before an appositive phrase, long or short, when the writer wants to give it some degree of emphasis.

b. The dash is sometimes used to set off a word or phrase intended to achieve suspense, climax or anticlimax:

There is only one person he has loved all his life – himself.

A letter usually contains a greeting, a body and – a postscript.

c. A single or double dash is used:

(i)to mark off a parenthesis from the main clause or sentence:

He believed – wrongly, as we now know – that science could provide an answer to any problem that man might face. (By 'parenthesis' we mean an additional word, phrase or sentence inserted into a passage which would be complete even without it.)

(ii) to mark a sudden shift in the thought or structure of a sentence:

This man's uncle – I remember meeting him way back in 1960 – is the only one I know, who has survived an air crash. (shift in thought)

Blue, green, red and yellow – these are the colours we have selected for decoration. (shift in structure)

Exercise 9

Supply dashes, single or double, where necessary.

a. Louis Pasteur was the first to prove that all forms of fermentation were caused by microbes or germs living creatures so small that they could be seen only through a microscope.

b. Pasteur's work on chicken-cholera led to the discovery of the principle of immunity the principle behind all protective vaccination.

c. After Pasteur found a way of preventing hydrophobia, he became a household name all over the world and people went to him in tens and hundreds people bitten by mad dogs or wolves.

d. I met her in London I was then a student at Oxford when she was on her way to New York to preside over the General Assembly session.

26.3.4 Comma

The comma is the most frequently used mark of punctuation. It is used:

a. to separate or set off words, phrases, dependent clauses occurring in a series:

The crowd consisted of men, women, and children.

She was a brilliant scientist, a charming conversationalist, and a fine writer.

He said that his father had been taken ill, that he had gone home to look him up, and that he had just returned.

Note that the comma is optional before the conjunction 'and'/'or' that joins the last item of the series.

b. to set off introductory phrases – prepositional, participial, infinitive or gerundial:

In his pre-budget report on the state of the economy, the Finance Minister sounded hopeful about the future. (prep. ph.)

Born in Khumbu, Tenzing Norgay had grown up in the very shadow of Mount Everest. (part. ph.)

c. to set off a sentence modifier, that is, a word or phrase modifying a whole sentence:

Yes, he is better now, though not yet out of danger.

To put it bluntly, he was just an adventurer out to make a fortune for himself.

d. to set off an appositive phrase, particularly when it is short:

New Delhi, India's federal capital, was designed by Edwin Lutyens. (commas on both sides of the phrase; but if the sentence ends with the phrase, only one comma)

e. to set off words in direct address:

Policeman: You know, Mr Menezes, your driving licence expired long ago.

Mr Menezes, your driving licence expired long ago, you know.

f. in letters, after the greeting and following the complimentary close:

Dear Susan, Yours sincerely,

g. to set off a short quotation:

She said, 'I was just settling down to a nap when the telephone rang.'

'I was just settling down to a nap,' she said, 'when the telephone rang.' (comma, one on either side of the introductory part 'she said')

h. to set off coordinate, consecutive adjectives preceding the noun they modify:

The lead actor was a tall, handsome man of twenty-five. (Both adjectives are of equal rank and they separately modify 'man'.)

Compare:

She is an agreeable old lady. (No comma between 'old' and 'agreeable' because the adjectives are not coordinate. 'Agreeable' modifies the entire phrase 'old lady'.)

i. after words like 'well', 'oh', 'ah', 'oh yes', 'oh no':

Well, your prediction has come true.

Oh, what a nuisance! Ah, I'm relieved.

Exercise 10

Insert commas, where necessary, in the following sentences.

a. The streets were narrow crowded and filthy.
b. The crowd shouted whistled and clapped when the film star arrived.
c. After reading Louis Pasteur's paper Surgeon Lister came to know that the air around him was full of germs. There were germs on his hands on his clothes and on his instruments.
d. A small white rabbit hopped across the path.
e. Born poor brought up in an orphanage and poorly educated he had to struggle hard for a living.

Exercise 11

Here is a transcript of a telephonic conversation between Mr Motwani and Mr Kishanchand. Punctuate the transcript supplying commas, where necessary, and end punctuation marks.

Motwani: Hongkong Fancy Goods Emporium
K. Chand: Can I speak to the Manager
Motwani: Speaking
K. Chand: I am Kishanchand speaking
Motwani: Good morning Mr Moolchand What can I do for you
K. Chand: I am Kishanchand not Moolchand
Motwani: Oh I'm sorry I thought you said Moolchand Well what can I do for you Mr Kishanchand
K. Chand: Have you any Turkish carpets with you
Motwani: Well we usually have some in stock Right now we don't have any We have some splendid Kashmiri carpets Would you be interested Mr Kishanchand
K. Chand: What size are they
Motwani: All sizes from very large to small ones

The comma is also used:

j. to separate adverb clauses:

<u>Although she was not a movie buff</u> she was familiar with the roles of many popular stars, both Indian and foreign.
<u>If I had a million rupees</u> I would go on a world tour.

The above is the general rule but it is not an absolute rule. For instance, if the adverb clauses are short, no comma is used:

<u>If it rains</u> we will cancel the picnic
I will come <u>as soon as I can.</u>

k. to separate two main clauses if they are joined together by a coordinate conjunction such as 'and', 'for', 'or', 'yet', 'so':

You have to be hard-working and lucky, <u>or</u> you will never succeed in life.
(alternative: You have to be hard-working and lucky; otherwise you will never succeed in life.)
She had never had a holiday for years, <u>so</u> she decided to go on a long holiday.
(alternative: She had never had a holiday for years; therefore she decided to go on a long holiday.)

l. to set off a parenthesis:

The last elections, <u>many people feel,</u> were not fair. (parenthetical sentence in the middle; comma on both sides)
<u>His home work done,</u> Mohan sat down to eat his breakfast. (parenthetical absolute phrase)

m. to set off non-restrictive modifiers:

(A non-restrictive modifier may be a word, phrase or clause furnishing additional but non-essential information about the thing modified. The restrictive modifier, on the other hand, is needed to identify, or limit the meaning of the modified word; therefore it is not set off by commas. Yet another difference between the two: the non-restrictive modifier can be omitted from the sentence without much loss; the restrictive modifier cannot be omitted.)

(i) non-restrictive appositive phrase:

Pandit Nehru, free India's first Prime Minister, was educated at Cambridge.

Compare: For having mis-spelt the word 'continuous', Vinod had to write it a hundred times. (restrictive)

(ii) non-restrictive adjective phrase:

Bihar, with its rich natural resources, should be able to ensure a better deal for its people.

Compare: Any territory with rich natural resources will attract investors. (restrictive)

(iii) non-restrictive adverb phrase:

The queue in front of the fair price shop stood in the sun, without complaining, for the shop to open.

Compare:

The queue in front of the fair price shop waited in the sun. (restrictive)

(iv) non-restrictive adjective or relative clause:

My grandfather, who is well over seventy, still goes for a five-mile walk every day.

Compare:

Anyone who is well over seventy needs someone to look after him or her. (restrictive)

n. to set off particular introductory and concluding expressions like 'for example', 'namely', 'that is', 'and so on':

I have recently reread the major novels of Thomas Hardy like, for example, *The Mayor of Casterbridge* and *Tess of the d 'Urbervilles.*

An efficiently run public transport system has two advantages, namely, cheapness and availability.

Exercise 12

Supply commas where necessary.

a. The platform was deserted and he knew he had missed the train.
b. The car skidded and went off the road but no one was hurt fortunately.
c. Success is yours if you listen to me carefully if you promise to act on my advice and if you act as you promise.
d. Slowly steadily relentlessly the enemy advanced upon us.
e. Your decision to accept the post offered it seems to me is a wise one.

Exercise 13

Here is a passage on Tenzing Norgay, the co-conqueror of Mount Everest with Edmund Hillary. The commas, however, are missing from the passage. Supply the missing commas.

Tenzing Norgay the co-conqueror of Mount Everest was probably born in the year 1914. He was born a Sherpa. The Sherpas are a people who belonged originally to Tibet. From Tibet they came south many years ago and settled in Solo Khumbu in north-eastern Nepal which is now their homeland.

Tenzing's first expedition to Everest was in 1935. During the next seventeen years he went with five other expeditions including a 'one-man' expedition by Earl Denman who wanted to climb Mount Everest all by himself! Before long Tenzing made his mark as a climber. In the 1938 expedition led by H.W. Tilman Tenzing's third he went up to a height of 27,200 feet and for this he was awarded the 'Tiger Medal'. (The Tiger Medal an award given to all Sherpas with a distinguished climbing record was instituted officially by Tilman in 1938.) That was his highest until in the spring of 1952 he with Lambert climbed to a height of 28,250 ft. setting up a new world record in Himalayan climbing. He was again with the Swiss the following autumn when they made their second unsuccessful attempt on the mountain this time as a full expedition member. In 1953 with such outstanding achievement behind him all that was left for Tenzing to do was to get to the top which he did with Hillary in his seventh attempt on the mountain.

26.3.5 Quotation Marks

Quotation marks or quotes are commas put in the opposite way and above the line of writing instead of along the line of writing. (For this reason, they are also called 'inverted commas'.)

Quotes, single (' ') or double (" ") are used:

a. to indicate the exact words spoken by someone, real or imagined, and to separate these words from the words of the author or writer:

> Speaking about the German writer's love of long sentences, Mark Twain once said, "Whenever a literary German dives into a sentence, it is the last you are going to see of him till he emerges on the other side of the Atlantic with his verb in his mouth."

Examine carefully the punctuation of the above passage, and you will notice that:

(i) Mark Twain's words (Whenever a literary German... in his mouth) are enclosed in quotes and separated from the author's words (Speaking about... once said);

(ii) the quotes indicate the beginning and the end of Mark Twain's words;

(iii) internal and end punctuation marks belonging to the sentence quoted (in the example there is one comma and one full stop) are inside the quotes;

(iv) a comma – it could be a comma or colon – is placed immediately after the sentence introducing the quotation and immediately before the actual quotation.

Remember that the first word of the quotation must always begin with a capital letter unless the word is in continuation of a sentence already begun and included within the quotes. Look at these two examples:

> Napoleon the pig said, "Man is the only creature that consumes without producing anything."
>
> "Man," said Napoleon the pig, "is the only creature that consumes without producing anything." (Note that we don't capitalise 'is'.)

The words that introduce the quotation may come before, after, or in the middle of the quoted words. This introductory part is usually set off from the quotation by a comma or commas:

> She said, "No, you cannot do that to me."
> "No," she said, "you cannot do that to me."
> "No, you cannot do that to me," she said.

Notice that the word 'you' in the above examples has a small rather than a capital, accurately reflecting the original quotation. If the original text consisted of two sentences (No, you cannot do that to me./It is most unfair.) this too will be reflected in the punctuation, thus:

"No, you cannot do that to me," she said, "It is most unfair."

When there is a great deal of conversation or dialogue, single quotes are often used instead of double to enclose the speakers' actual words. Also, the words of each speaker are put in a separate paragraph, as in this example:

'Are you free now?' he asked.

'Why do you ask?' she said in reply.

'Can I come over? I have something important to discuss with you.'

'Right now?'

'Yes, right now.'

b. to enclose titles of stories, plays, poems, chapters, essays, articles appearing in a larger work:

'The Leech Gatherer' is my favourite among Wordsworth's poems. I like it better than 'The Solitary Reaper'.

Did you read the article 'Advertising Gimmicks' that appeared in yesterday's paper?

c. to enclose a word or expression that is being defined:

The word 'panacea' means 'remedy for all diseases or troubles'. A 'bareback rider' is one who rides a horse without a saddle.

d. to enclose tongue-in-cheek expressions, that is, expressions meant or intended ironically:

He was the only one in the village who could read a little and count up to a hundred. He was the village 'scholar'.

Among the Everest expeditions that Tenzing Norgay had gone with was a one-man 'expedition' by Earl Denman.

Exercise 14

Arrange the following passages of conversation in paragraphs, supplying capitals and punctuation.

a. mummy can I go out and play what with all those holes in your vest oh no with the boy next door

b. arun will you keep quiet your father is trying to read gosh amma I learned to do that years ago

c. do you believe in free speech I certainly do good may I use your telephone

Exercise 15

Here is a piece of dialogue between a patient and her doctor. Rewrite the dialogue supplying capitals and punctuation.

i am an old woman said the patient and i have no fear of sickness or medicine but i do not want my family to be infected by it will the infection spread

yes if you are not cured of it replied the doctor

will i get the infection again if i do the washing

if you go into the same pond you probably will

26.4 Word Punctuation

26.4.1 Using Capitals

Capitals are used:

a. with first words:

(i) with the first word of a sentence and of any phrase that is used as a sentence:

Do you agree to the proposal? Not me. Absurd.

(ii) with the first word of a sentence within quotes:

Customs official to writer Oscar Wilde: 'Have you anything to declare?'

Oscar Wilde: 'Nothing except my genius.'

(iii) with the first word of an independent question within a sentence:

What we need to consider is this: Is the project a practical one?

(iv) with the first word of each line of poetry:

The woods are lovely, dark and deep,
But I have promises to keep,
And miles to go before I sleep,
And miles to go before I sleep. (Robert Frost)

b. with proper nouns, that is, with the names of particular persons, places or things:

Mohandas Karamchand Gandhi   Mount Everest   Delhi University

c. with proper adjectives, that is, with adjective forms derived from proper nouns:

Gandhian   Bengali   Shakespearian

Some of these proper adjectives have lost their original connection and are no longer capitalised:

platonic (from Plato)   pasteurised (from Pasteur)

d. with a common noun when it is part of a proper name but not when it is used alone or in place of the proper name:

Uncle Basu but uncle   the Punjab National Bank but the bank
The Taj Hotel but the hotel

e. with personal names, along with titles that go with personal names:

Maulana Abul Kalam Azad   Mrs Vijayalakshmi Pandit   President Bush
Field Marshal Maneckshaw

f. with high-ranking government or opposition officials, heads of state, religious heads etc:

the Prime Minister   the Foreign Secretary   the Leader of the Opposition
the Chief Justice   the Queen of England   the Dalai Lama; the Pope

g. with governmental or international organisations:

South Asian Association of Regional Countries   the U.N. Security Council
the Ministry of Defence

h. with other types of organisations—political, educational, religious or social:

the Janata Dal   All India Institute of Medical Science   Pune University
the Roman Catholic Church   Society for the Advancement of Rural Women

i. with names of places, natural or man-made:

the Marina Beach   Sahar Airport   Lucknow   the Qutab Minar

j. with the names of days and months, the names of all holidays and religious days:

Wednesday   April   Ramadan   Christmas   Gurupoornima

k. with the names of historical events and the names given to historical or cultural periods:

the Battle of Plassey the Second World War the Golden Age of the Guptas
the Russian Revolution

l. with the names of tribes, races, nationalities, languages etc:

Aryan Dravidian Negro French Sanskrit Assamese

m. with the names of religions and holy books:

Buddhism Islam the Bible the Bhagavad Gita

n. with the titles of literary works:

Malgudi Days Gitanjali The Merchant of Venice
The Man Without a Country

Notice that in writing the titles, we capitalise all the important words in the title, including the first and last words, but not articles, short conjunctions like 'and' and 'but' and short prepositions such as 'of', 'by', 'to'.

Exercise 16

Punctuate and supply capitals.

a. nero the mad emperor is supposed to have fiddled while rome burned
b. about a hundred members of parliament went in a procession to the rashtrapathi bhavan to present a petition to the president
c. a depression is building up in the bay of bengal announced doordarshan in their 9.30 p.m. news some 200 km off kakinada it is expected to move in a northwesterly direction and hit the city of calcutta by midday tomorrow

Exercise 17

Puncuate the following business letter, supplying capitals.

24 harekrishna mandir road
pune 411 016
18 october 1992

the advertiser
box 1273
maharashtra herald
pune
dear sir

this is with reference to your advertisement in today's newspaper offering for sale boy's 3-speed bicycle in good condition I am interested I should be glad if you would let me know where and when the bicycle may be seen

yours faithfully

s pathak

26.4.2 Apostrophe

The apostrophe, which is a raised comma, is used as a mark of punctuation to indicate the omission of one or more letters or figures:

can't (for 'cannot') don't (for 'do not') he's (for 'he is')
they're (for 'they are') '92 (for 1992) '03 (for 2003)

'It's' is a contraction for 'it is'; don't confuse it with 'its', the possessive form of 'it'.

Exercise 18

Put in the apostrophes in the following sentences where they are needed. Then rewrite the sentences so as to do without the apostrophes.

Example

I cant say that. I can't say that. I cannot say that.

a. Didnt I tell you not to do that again?
b. Arent you sure?
c. Dont you think we should do something about it?
d. I dont think so.
e. We neednt bother about it.

26.4.3 Hyphen

The hyphen (-) is half the length of the regular dash (—) and is used to join the parts of a compound word. The present-day tendency is to avoid using the hyphen wherever possible. However, the following classes of words would ordinarily require hyphens:

a. two or more words modifying a noun and used as a single adjective:
   a soft-spoken, mild-mannered gentleman
   the ever-rising cost of living
b. compound words with 'self', 'half', 'ex', 'quarter' as the first element of the compound:
   self-defence ex-president half-measure quarter-share
c. words made up of a prefix and a proper noun:
   pro-Indian anti-American non-Asiatic
d. words of a compound noun:
   mother-in-law commander-in-chief fellow-citizen
e. single letters joined to a noun or participle:
   U-turn H-bomb T-shaped
f. Compound numerals from 21 to 99:
   twenty-one ninety-nine
g. compounds formed from fractions:
   three-fifths four-tenths one-hundredth

The hyphen is also used to indicate the break of a word divided between syllables at the end of a line.

Punctuation Revision Exercises

Exercise 19 (semicolon, colon, dash)

Rewrite each of the following sentences as directed and change the punctuation accordingly. Keep the same punctuation if no change is called for.

The first one is done for you as an example.

a. Now listen to this carefully: send word to me if the man shows up and don't ever let him go until I come. (Put 'now listen to this carefully' after 'send word to me')
Answer: Send word to me – now listen to this carefully – if the man shows up and don't ever let him go until I come.

b. The wind at last turned favourable; the Greak fleet set sail for Troy. (Change 'turned' to 'having turned')

c. In junior college he excelled in all the games offered. These were football, hockey, basketball and tennis. (Remove 'these were')

d. I attended the meeting, but I did not participate in the discussion or the voting that followed. (change 'but' to 'however')

e. In reading the eyes move along a line of print in jerks, in a rapid series of stop-and-go movements; this fact is one of the curious revelations of high-speed photography. (remove 'this fact is')

Exercise 20 (commas)

Rewrite each of the following sentences as directed and change the punctuation accordingly.

a. There is no hope for you unless you change your ways at once. (Begin the sentence with 'change your ways at once' and use 'or' or 'otherwise')

b. She finished her chores. She then went shopping. (Combine the sentences into one and begin the new sentence with 'her chores finished')

c. The crowds waited at the airport for the Prime Minister to arrive. They were patient and uncomplaining. (Combine the sentences into one simple sentence beginning 'the crowds waited')

d. Her mother had decided to see a movie, so Priya had to stay at home in the afternoon and look after her baby brother. (Begin the sentence with 'her mother having decided…')

e. She was born into poverty; she was abandoned at the age of five; she was reared in an orphanage; she knew what it was to be a deprived child. (Combine into one sentence beginning 'born into poverty…')

f. Written English is not spoken English reduced to writing. (Insert 'as many people suppose' after 'not')

Exercise 21 (quotation marks and related marks)

Supply commas, quotation marks, and capitals for the following passages.

a. do you suppose he said that I am going to give up my ways just because you don't like them?

b. are you absolutely certain demanded the prosecuting counsel that you saw the motorist knock the old man down and drive off?

c. although they look very different the words crab and chancellor are in fact related the teacher told the class did anyone tell you that before? (all marks of punctuation)

Exercise 22

Punctuate, supplying capitals.

you have raised the veil said the visiting english surgeon which for centuries had covered infectious diseases you have changed the treatment of wounds from an uncertain and too often dangerous business into a scientific and certainly helpful art

the words were joseph listers and they were addressed to a seventy year old man too deeply moved for words lister then turned to embrace the old man and the audience burst into cheers like schoolboys it was an unusual reaction from an audience which consisted for the most part of professors members of the french academy representatives of scientific societies and distinguished visitors from abroad but the occasion itself was an unusual one the seventieth birthday of louis pasteur the year was 1892 a great number of people both french and foreign had gathered at the sorbonne in paris to honour one of the greatest scientists of all time

many were the speeches made on that day but the speech that stood out from the rest was certainly listers a distinguished english surgeon joseph lister had come as the repesentative of the royal societies of london and edinburgh and his speech more than any other confirmed the international recognition that had come the way of pasteur some ten years before

shortly after in 1895 pasteur died some years after his death a poll was taken among the french they were asked to name the man they regarded as the greatest among their countrymen the answer was not napoleon but louis pasteur pasteur like napoleon had been a soldier all his life but his battles had been fought in the laboratory with the microscope for a weapon the only weapon used who was his enemy something far more numerous and deadly than any napoleon in all his warmaking years had to contend with the invisible microbe

Appendix 1

Concord or Agreement of Verb and Subject

The rule of concord is that a verb must agree with its subject in number and person. However, there are hardly any cases in English where the form of the verb depends on both the number and person of the subject. The one exception is the auxiliary verb 'be': it has different forms for all the three persons in the present tense ('am', 'are', 'is') and two different forms for the past singular and the past plural ('was' and 'were'). The other two auxiliaries – 'have' and 'do' – have the same forms in the present tense except for the third person singular ('has', 'does'), and they have the same forms in the past tense for all the three persons, both singular and plural ('had', 'did'). What is true of 'have' and 'do' is true of the lexical verb as well. The verb 'take', for example, has the same form in the present tense except for the third person singular ('takes'), and it has the same form in the past tense for all the three persons, both singular and plural ('took').

What, in effect, we mean by concord or agreement of verb and subject is simply this: the verb must agree with the subject in number:

This tooth of mine is giving me trouble. (singular subject, singular verb)

All his teeth are false. (plural subject, plural verb)

If the verb consists of more than one word – one or two auxiliaries plus the lexical verb – agreement with the subject occurs only in the first auxiliary verb:

I am going.	He has been going.
They have gone.	The train is being delayed for some reason.

In most cases there is no problem matching the subject and the verb in number. Problems arise, however, when the number of the subject is doubtful, or where there is a conflict between form and meaning.

The following guidelines should be taken note of:

1. When the subject consists of two singular words coordinated by 'and', it normally becomes a plural subject and must take a plural verb:

    Your father and mother have arrived.

    Both lunch and dinner were bad.

    He and I are friends. Fire and water do not agree.

If the two coordinated terms refer to the same person, the verb is singular:

My friend and former colleague, Mr Pai, is in town.

My son and heir is going to be eighteen next Monday.

If the two coordinated terms refer to parts of a whole or two closely related things – like 'bread and butter', 'fish and chips', 'whisky and soda' – a singular verb often follows:

There was fish and chips for lunch.

Whisky and soda was the drink favoured by most.

Also, if the coordinated terms represent a single idea, a singular verb is used:

The tumult and the shouting was unbearable.

All coming and going was strictly forbidden.

The threat and fear of nuclear power is, curiously enough, the best safeguard for peace.

2. When the two nouns of a subject are joined by 'or', 'either...or', 'neither...nor', the verb is singular if each of the nouns is singular but plural if each of the nouns is plural:

Susan or her mother has the keys.

Either John or James is the culprit.

Neither the boys nor the girls have done well in the exam.

When one of the nouns is singular and the other plural, the verb agrees with the nearer noun:

Neither Arun nor his parents were at the party.
Neither the Mathais nor their son Arun was at the party.

Either your eyesight or your brakes are at fault.
Either your brakes or your eyesight is at fault.

A better way of expressing the idea would be to rephrase the sentences as follows:

Arun was not at the party, nor his parents.

Your eyesight is at fault, or your brakes.

3. A singular subject modified by a prepositional phrase beginning with 'as well as', 'along with', 'together with', 'in addition to', is followed by a singular verb:

John as well as James is to blame for what happened.
The heavy college curriculum, along with the periodic tests and the sessional exam, imposes an intolerable burden on the students.
The minister, together with his aides, was seen leaving the hall in a huff.

4. When the subject is a noun phrase consisting of a singular noun as headword and a modifier containing one or more plural nouns, the verb agrees with the singular headword:

The employment of young children is a punishable offence.

The cost of repairs is to be borne by the landlord.

The appearance of many things in this country reminds me of my own country.

In the above examples, the headword is boxed and the modifier underlined.

5. Though grammatically singular, 'a number of', when it means 'several' or 'many', is treated as plural and takes a plural verb:

A number of dignitaries were present on the occasion.

A large/small number of people were left behind.

But when 'number' means a numerical total, it takes a singular verb:

The number of people who attended was much greater than we had expected.

The number of car owners in the city is increasing day by day.

Conversely, though 'more than one' is notionally plural, it is treated as singular:

More than one party member was involved in cross-voting.

More than one explanation is possible.

When 'one of' is followed by a plural noun, the verb agrees with 'one', the headword:

One of the windowpanes was broken.

One of the children has been missing.

6. Many indefinite pronouns such as 'anyone', 'everyone', 'anybody', 'everybody', 'anything', 'everything', 'something', 'nobody', 'nothing', 'either', and 'neither' are singular in form, though plural in meaning, and all these take a singular verb:

   Everyone dreams of a holiday in the Bahamas.

   Neither of them was willing to make the first move.

   Anybody is welcome to join the club.

   Nothing is known of his parents or his early life.

We may use a singular or plural verb with the indefinite pronoun, depending on whether the pronoun stands for a noncountable noun or a plural countable noun:

I was looking for some milk but there was none. (The indefinite pronoun 'none' stands for the noncountable noun 'milk')

As many as thirty candidates were called for interview but none of them were found suitable. ('None' stands for the countable plural noun 'candidates').

A lot of food was laid on the table but none of it was tasty, so most of it was left over. (The indefinite pronouns 'none' and 'most' refer to the noncountable noun 'food')

In the case of the indefinite pronouns like 'all', 'more', 'most', 'half', the number of the verb is decided by the noun the pronoun refers to:

There was a lot of petrol in the can but all of it seems to have been used up.

Over 400 people had been invited but only half of them were present.

7. When the subject is a number or a fraction denoting a fixed quantity of something, it usually takes a singular verb:

   Two weeks is a long time in politics.

   Ten rupees isn't enough for a square meal these days.

   Eight kilometres is too far for you to walk.

   Three-fourths of the area is under water.

8. When the subject and the subject complement are of different numbers, the verb agrees with the subject only:

   Peas are my favourite vegetable.

   My favourite vegetable is peas.

9. Collective nouns may take a singular or plural verb.

   i. Nouns like 'clothing', 'furniture', 'luggage', 'crockery' always take a singular verb:

      Food is cheap out there but clothing is expensive.

      Has your luggage been unloaded from the train?

Note that these nouns have no plural form, nor can they be preceded by a singular indefinite article: we cannot speak of 'luggages' or 'a luggage'.

ii. Collective nouns like 'people', 'public', 'folk', 'laity' always take a plural verb:

Country folk are easy to get on with.
The public have a right to know how decisions are being made in their name.

iii. Collectives referring to professions or occupations usually take a plural form:

The police were informed of the accident.
The army were called in to bring the situation under control.
The local Bar comprise some of the best legal brains in the country.

iv. Group collectives like 'committee', 'crowd', 'congregation', 'audience', 'team', 'school', 'family' (many of which have plural forms of their own) may be treated as singular or plural:

The family was/were seated round the table.
The jury was/were convinced of the prisoner's guilt.
The government has/have decided...

The plural is more common in British English. However, no matter what we choose, singular or plural, we need to be consistent, at least throughout the same sentence. The following example ignores this guideline:

If the staff is determined to go on strike – and they say they are – they should in fairness inform the public...

'Staff' in the above example is treated as a singular noun attracting a singular verb and this is followed by three plural personal pronouns ('they'), resulting in an uncomfortable inconsistency.

V. In some cases, however, we may have to choose between the singular and the plural, depending on whether we are thinking of the group as a group or as a number of people forming the group. Thus, while we can say:

'The audience was getting bored and impatient', we cannot say:
'The audience was requested to be in its seat fifteen minutes before the start of the show'.

The audience in example 1 is rightly thought of as a group but in the second we need to think of the audience not as a group but as made up of different people arriving at different times within the fifteen-minute gap, and say:

The audience were requested to be in their seats fifteen minutes before the start of the show.

In the same way, we can say 'The crowd was getting restive' if we are thinking of the crowd as a group but we must say: 'The crowd were seen running in all directions at the approach of the police'.

10. When a sentence begins with 'there', the verb agrees with the real subject of the sentence:

There is one other question I want to ask you.
There are two other questions I want to ask you.

Usage, however, varies, as may be seen from the following exceptions to the rule.

A singular verb is used, even if a plural noun or pronoun follows, when:

i. the plural form denotes a single sum or amount:

There is only another two miles to go.

There is just ten rupees left.

ii. When a combination of two or more nouns represents a single idea:

There is rice, sambar, green peas and pappad for dinner.

For those members who do not want to sweat it out on the tennis court, there is bridge, billiards and cards.

iii. When the reference is to a whole situation:

There is my wife and family to consider.

There is just two packets of biscuits, a few packets of tea, and a litre of milk.

11. The introductory 'it' occurring as nominal subject takes a singular verb, even though the complement that follows is plural:

It was vegetables and rice again for supper.

It is ten kilometres from here to the nearest petrol station.

12. The emphatic 'it' always takes a singular verb, even though the complement that follows is plural:

It is the ordinary people, the poor and the downtrodden, that we have to consider.

It was the bad weather conditions that prevented the Swiss team from climbing Mount Everest for the first time in 1952, a year ahead of the British.

Note, however, that when the complement is modified by a relative clause with 'who', 'which', 'that' as subject, the verb of the relative clause agrees in number with the preceding complement:

It is his manner that annoys me.

It is his manners that annoy me.

It is John who is to blame.

It is John and James who are to blame.

13. The following words call for special care:

i. 'News' is always singular and it takes a singular verb:

No news is good news. The news that we received was most disturbing.

ii. Words like 'trousers', 'scissors', 'tweezers' and 'pincers' are plural in form and take a plural verb:

My trousers are torn. Can you please mend them?

Where are my scissors? I can never find them when I want them.

iii. Words ending in '-ics' usually take a singular verb when they denote a science, a study or an activity thought of as a unit:

Physics depends a great deal on mathematics.

Athletics is being given too much importance in this college.

I prefer politics to economics. Politics is interesting; economics, I'm afraid, is rather boring.

Appendix 2

Irregular Verbs with their Basic Forms (present, past and past participle)

1. All the three forms are different

arise	arose	arisen
awake	awoke	awoken (awoke)
be	was	been
bear (carry)	bore	borne
bear (produce)	bore	born
begin	began	begun
bid (wish, ask)	bade	bidden
bite	bit	bitten
blow	blew	blown
break	broke	broken
choose	chose	chosen
do	did	done
draw	drew	drawn
drink	drank	drunk
drive	drove	driven
eat	ate	eaten
fall	fell	fallen
fly	flew	flown
forbear	forbore	forborne
forbid	forbade	forbidden
forget	forgot	forgotten (forgot)
forgive	forgave	forgiven
forsake	forsook	forsaken
freeze	froze	frozen
give	gave	given
go	went	gone
grow	grew	grown
hew	hewed	hewn
hide	hid	hidden
know	knew	known
lie	lay	lain

mistake	mistook	mistaken
overdraw	overdrew	overdrawn
partake	partook	partaken
ride	rode	ridden
ring	rang	rung
rise	rose	risen
saw	sawed	sawn
see	saw	seen
sew	sewed	sewn
shake	shook	shaken
show	showed	shown
shrink	shrank	shrunk
sing	sang	sung
sink	sank	sunk
slay	slew	slain
smite	smote	smitten
sow	sowed	sown
speak	spoke	spoken
spring	sprang	sprung
steal	stole	stolen
stink	stank	stunk
strew	strewed	strewn
stride	strode	stridden
strive	strove	striven
swear	swore	sworn
swell	swelled	swollen
swim	swam	swum
take	took	taken
tear	tore	torn
throw	threw	thrown
tread	trod	trodden
wake	woke	woken (woke)
wear	wore	worn
weave	wove	woven
withdraw	withdrew	withdrawn
write	wrote	written

2. The second and third forms are alike

bend	bent	bent
beseech	besought	besought
bind	bound	bound
bleed	bled	bled
breed	bred	bred
bring	brought	brought
build	built	built
buy	bought	bought
catch	caught	caught
cling	clung	clung
creep	crept	crept
deal	dealt	dealt
dig	dug	dug
dream	dreamt (dreamed)	dreamt (dreamed)
feed	fed	fed
feel	felt	felt
fight	fought	fought
find	found	found
flee	fled	fled
fling	flung	flung
get	got	got
grind	ground	ground
hang (hang a shirt)	hung	hung
hear	heard	heard
hold	held	held
keep	kept	kept
kneel	knelt	knelt
lead	led	led
leap	leapt	leapt
leave	left	left
lend	lent	lent
lose	lost	lost

make	made	made
mean	meant	meant
meet	met	met
read	read	read
rend	rent	rent
say	said	said
seek	sought	sought
sell	sold	sold
send	sent	sent
shine	shone	shone
shoot	shot	shot
sit	sat	sat
sleep	slept	slept
slide	slid	slid
sling	slung	slung
slink	slunk	slunk
speed	sped	sped
spin	spun	spun
stand	stood	stood
stick	stuck	stuck
sting	stung	stung
strike	struck	struck
string	strung	strung
sweep	swept	swept
swing	swung	swung
teach	taught	taught
tell	told	told
think	thought	thought
understand	understood	understood
weep	wept	wept
win	won	won
wind	wound	wound
withstand	withstood	withstood
wring	wrung	wrung

3. All the three forms are alike

bet	bet	bet
bid (offer money at an auction)	bid	bid
broadcast	broadcast	broadcast
burst	burst	burst
cast	cast	cast
cost	cost	cost
cut	cut	cut
hit	hit	hit
hurt	hurt	hurt
knit	knit (knitted)	knit (knitted)
let	let	let
put	put	put
quit	quit	quit
set	set	set
shed	shed	shed
shut	shut	shut
slit	slit	slit
split	split	split
spread	spread	spread
thrust	thrust	thrust

4. The first and third forms are alike

come	came	come
become	became	become
overcome	overcame	overcome
run	ran	run
overrun	overran	overrun

5. The first and second forms are alike

beat	beat	beaten (beat)

Appendix 3

Glossary of Grammatical Terms

Note

This glossary includes nearly all the grammatical terms used in the text but it is by no means a complete list of grammatical terms. The definitions given here are simpler and cruder and the illustrative examples have been kept to a minimum. For a fuller treatment, we refer the reader to the relevant sections in the main text.

absolute construction: A phrase consisting, usually, of a participle plus the subject of the participle:

The wind being favourable, the ship set sail.

The phrase is not as absolute as the term suggests; it generally functions, as in the example above, as an adverbial modifier. It is called absolute all the same in that it is not so closely related to the rest of the sentence as, say, a subordinate clause is to a main clause. Compare:

The wind being favourable, the ship set sail.

As the wind was favourable, the ship set sail.

Notice how loosely bound the absolute phrase is to the main clause, unlike the equivalent adverb clause of reason 'As the wind was favourable'. Since the phrase retains the subject ('the wind'), it is also called a nominative absolute. If the subject were a pronoun instead of a noun, it would be in the nominative case:

He being my nextdoor neighbour, I couldn't possibly say no to him.

abstract noun: A noun standing for, or referring to, an abstraction, that is, a concept or idea like 'honesty', 'simplicity', 'faith'.

active voice: Voice is one of the attributes of a verb. A verb may be in active or passive voice. It is said to be in active voice when the subject is thought of as the doer, rather than as the receiver, of the action:

John loves Mary.

John is the one who does the 'loving' and 'John' is also subject, so the verb 'loves' is said to be in active voice. We may change the verb into the passive form:

Mary is loved by John.

In this sentence, 'Mary' is subject but she is not the doer of the action. The doer is John still, Mary is the 'loved' one, the receiver of the action, the one who is affected by the action; so the verb 'is loved' is said to be in passive voice. The two forms, however, are not freely interchangeable.

adjective: A class of words which describe, or give information about, people and things:

The old lady lived in a small cottage on the edge of a dense forest.

The underlined word are adjectives, which, in the language of grammar, are said to modify the nouns that follow them. Adjectives are usually marked by adverbs of degree like 'very', 'extremely', 'rather':

a very clever boy; an extremely poor performance; a rather slow learner

Descriptive adjectives in particular are marked by inflection for comparison ('-er','-est'): small–smaller–smallest.

Adjectives have several endings characteristic of their class—'-ful', '-less', '-able', '-ous', '-ive' etc.

adjective clause: A clause, that is, a group of words with a subject and predicate of its own, modifying a noun:

Do you recall the face of the man who gave you these keys?

The train which was due to arrive at 7 a.m. arrived two hours late.

The girl with whom you went to school is my cousin.

This is the house that I was born in.

The adjective clause is one of three types of subordinate clause, the other two being the noun clause and the adverb clause. The adjective clause is more commonly known as the relative clause. See relative clause.

adjective phrase: A phrase, that is, a group of words without a subject-predicate structure of its own, modifying a noun:

a. The man standing behind the Prime Minister is his principal aide. (participle phrase)

b. How did you get past the sentry at the gate? (prepositional phrase)

c. He is the authority to consult on matters of personal tax. (infinitive phrase)

d. The media, both visual and print, are the principal means of building up an image of oneself. (prepositional gerund phrase)

The underlined adjective phrases modify the nouns preceding them. (The nouns are boxed.) In form an adjective phrase may be a participle phrase, a prepositional phrase, an infinitive phrase, or a prepositional gerund phrase, as in the above examples.

adverb: A class of words which usually modify verbs:

She sang beautifully.

Less usually adverbs modify adjectives and other adverbs:

She has a very beautiful voice.

She sang very beautifully.

Adverbs, especially those derived from descriptive adjectives, are marked by the '-ly' ending: beautiful-beautifully; abundant-abundantly. Adverbs generally answer questions like 'when?', 'where?', 'how?', 'how much?' 'why?'.

Less commonly, adverbs modify phrases, clauses, or sentences:

They live close to the church.

The police knew exactly where the dacoits were hiding.

Luckily, he wasn't at home to face the wrath of the crowd.

adverb clause: A clause, that is, a word-group with a subject and predicate of its own, functioning like an adverb. The adverb usually modifies a verb and sometimes a whole predicate.

Come and see us whenever you are in town.

Although he had some money on his person, he refused to part with it.

You had better take a look at the cottage from here so that you have a better view of it.

I'm telling you this because I thought it my duty to tell you.

The adverb clause expresses time, place, reason, result, concession, condition, purpose or manner so that we have as many as eight types of adverb clauses. The adverb clause is one of three types of subordinate clauses, the other two being the adjective (relative) clause and the noun clause.

adverb phrase: A group of words without a subject-predicate structure of its own, functioning as an adverb. It usually modifies a verb, an adjective, or an entire sentence. In form, the adverb phrase can be:

a. a participle phrase — Returning home from school, the children raided a mango grove.

Having completed a year's probation, he was hoping to be confirmed in his post.

b. an infinitive phrase — To put it bluntly, the whole thing was an act of folly on your part.

He is all set and ready to leave at a moment's notice.

c. a prepositional phrase — They met at a party for the first time.

d. a prepositional gerund phrase — On learning of the stock market crash, the man collapsed.

agreement: Agreement between the parts that make up a sentence, namely, subject and verb. The rule is that the subject and the finite verb of the predicate must agree in number and person. However, there are very few cases in English where the form of the verb depends on both the number and person of the subject. What in effect, we mean by agreement is simply this: the subject and the verb must agree in number, that is to say, they should be of the same number:

My tooth is aching.

All his teeth are false.

This rule applies also to a pronoun and its antecedent:

Everyone must do his duty.

Sheila and Victor haven't yet decided where they are going for their honeymoon.

The man who lives next door is a foreigner.

The people who live in this street are an argumentative lot.

antecedent: A noun or noun-equivalent to which a pronoun, in particular a relative pronoun, refers:

The income that they earn is barely sufficient for their needs.

People who work in mines are to be admired.

The relative pronouns in the above examples are underlined and their antecedents boxed.

anticipatory 'it': Refers to the 'it' that begins sentences like these:

It is fun (learning a foreign language) when one is young.

It might be interesting (to speculate about her motives.)

It is widely believed (that some of the cricketers were into betting and match-fixing.)

The word 'it' in the above sentences fills the subject position, yet it is only a nominal subject, anticipating the real subject, which comes after the predicate. (The real subject is enclosed in parentheses in the examples.) Hence it is called the anticipatory 'it'. It is also called expletive 'it'.

apostrophe: The mark (') used in English to indicate the omission of part of a word ('can't for 'cannot', 'I'll' for 'I will', 'that's' for 'that is', 'didn't' for 'did not'). It is also used to form the possessive of nouns: boy–boy's; boys–boys'; John–John's.

article: A group term for 'a', 'an' and 'the'. 'A' and 'an' are called indefinite articles, and 'the' is called the definite article. The articles belong to the class of determiners.

attributive adjective: The normal position of an adjective is before the noun it modifies:

a rich merchant; a brown envelope; his latest novel

When the adjective occurs in that position, it is called an attributive adjective, as opposed to the predicative adjective and the appositive adjective. See predicate adjective, appositive adjective.

auxiliary verb: A finite verb may be a single-word verb, as in the simple present tense and the simple past tense:

The children attend a night school.

The monkey played on the harmonica.

Elsewhere the finite verb comprises two or more words:

The children were attending a night school until recently.
(aux.) + (lexical verb)

The monkey has been playing on the harmonica for an hour.
(aux.) + (aux.) + (lexical verb)

The underlined are called verb phrases, made up of one or more auxiliary verbs plus a lexical verb. The lexical verbs are the meaning-bearing verbs: 'attend', 'play'. They are also called the main verbs. The auxiliary verbs, on the other hand, combine with the main verbs to express tense, as in the two examples above, or voice, interrogation and negation, as in these examples:

The suspect was questioned by the police. (aux; voice)

Do these men make a living out of rag-picking? (aux; interrogation)

I swear that I did not inform on you. (aux; negation)

Auxiliaries besides may combine with lexical verbs to modify their meaning:

You may go. (You have my permission to go.)

She can sing. (She has the ability to sing.)

Notice that in the verb phrase, it is always the auxiliary verb that is inflected for person, number and tense and never the lexical verb.

Auxiliaries are of three types: tense auxiliaries, 'do' auxiliaries, and modal auxiliaries.

basic parts of verb: Chiefly three: the simple form of the verb or the stem, the past tense, and the past participle:

'do' (stem); 'did' (past tense); 'done' (past participle).

To these may be added a fourth: the present participle of the verb 'doing'. We call these the basic parts of the verb because without them we cannot make up the various tense forms of the verb like the continuous, the perfect, the perfect continuous, as may be seen from the following tables:

	continuous	perfect
present	am/is/are + doing	has/have + done
past	was/were + doing	had + done
future	shall be/will be + doing	shall/will have + done

	perfect continuous
present	has/have + been + doing
past	had + been + doing

clause: A group with a subject and predicate of its own, the predicate containing a finite verb. Some grammarians extend the term to include infinitive phrases, participle phrases, and gerund phrases, calling them non-finite clauses. In this book we stick to the traditional distinction between clauses and phrases: clauses are made by finite verbs and phrases may be made by non-finite verbs like infinitives, gerunds and participles.

Clauses are of two kinds: main and subordinate. See main clause, subordinate clause.

collective noun: A type of noun. A collective noun is a name given to a group of beings or things like–'crowd', 'mob', 'flock', 'herd', 'team', 'family'. The choice of a collective noun depends to some extent on the person or the thing that is being named. Thus, we say 'a herd of cattle' but 'a flock of sheep' rather than 'a flock of cattle' and 'a herd of sheep'. A collective noun, when used as a subject, may take a singular or plural verb:

The government has decided/have decided...

common noun: A type of noun that names a class of persons or things or an individual as a representative member of a class, as opposed to a proper noun, which names a particular person or thing. Thus 'man', 'woman', 'city', 'country', 'river', are common nouns, whereas 'Robert', 'Yasmin', 'Paris', 'Russia', 'the Nile' are proper nouns.

countable noun: A noun that refers to a person or thing that can be counted: 'man', 'woman', 'house', 'tree', 'apple'. Nouns in English may be countable or noncountable nouns. Examples of noncountable nouns: 'water', 'petrol', 'cheese', 'milk', 'sugar', 'sand'. Only countable nouns have plural forms. A singular countable noun is usually preceded by an article – 'a', 'an', or 'the':

A dog is man's best friend.

They went on an excursion, sailing down the river.

comparative degree: See comparison.

comparison: Most descriptive adjectives and adverbs of manner may be compared. They may be compared to express a quality (positive degree), more of a quality (comparative degree), or most of a quality (superlative degree). You add the inflectional endings '-er' and '-est' (or the adverbs 'more'/'less' and 'most'/'least') to adjectives and adverbs in the positive degree to get the comparative and the superlative forms: hard–harder–hardest; strenuous–more/less strenuous–most/least strenuous. A few adjectives and adverbs are compared irregularly: good–better–best; badly–worse–worst.

Examples of comparision

Fishing is as relaxing as walking. (positive degree)

Fishing is more relaxing than walking. (comparative degree)

Walking is less relaxing than fishing. (comparative degree)

Reading is the most relaxing of all hobbies. (superlative degree)

complement: A term used to indicate a word or word-group that completes a sentence:

Abdul is a doctor.

The class was noisy.

The people elected him leader.

A complement is not a part of speech. Complements are of two kinds–subject and object complements. In the above examples, 'a doctor', 'noisy' are subject complements (referring, as they do, to the subject), while 'leader' in the third example is an object complement (referring, as it does, to the object 'him'). Some grammarians extend the term to include direct object, indirect object, indeed any part of the predicate that completes the meaning but in this book the term 'complement' is restricted to subject and object complements only–subject complements occurring in basic sentence patterns 5, 6 and 7 and object complements occurring in basic sentence pattern 4.

subject complements

The king was a tyrant. (bp 5)

The crowd seems restless. (bp 6)

The man is here. (bp 7)

object complements

The parents named the baby-girl Sudha. (bp 4)

The teacher thought the book silly.

They painted the town red.

We consider her trustworthy.

A complement, particularly a subject complement, can be a noun, a pronoun, a gerund, an adjective, a phrase, or a clause:

The boy over there is Latif.

I am he.

Seeing is believing.

Sheila is beautiful.

They were in a great hurry.

The fact is that we cannot count on a normal rainfall this year.

The underlined are all subject complements.

complex sentence: A sentence that consists of one main clause and one or more subordinate clauses:

If I were born a prince, I would be by now a king. (one main + one subordinate clause)

Although she knew that she was the least prepared of the lot, she would never admit it. (1 main + two subordinate clauses)

The complex sentence is one of four types of sentence, the other three being the simple sentence, the compound sentence, and the complex-compound sentence.

complex-compound sentence: A sentence that consists of two or more main clauses plus one or more subordinate clauses:

He knew all along who she was but he pretended not to know. (2 main clauses plus one subordinate clause)

When we heard of the accident in which our friends were involved, we rushed at once to the spot but the police had cordoned off the area and would not let us get anywhere near our friends. (3 main clauses plus 2 subordinate clauses)

The complex-compound sentence is one of four types of sentence, the other three being the simple sentence, the complex sentence and the compound sentence.

compound sentence: A sentence that consists of two or more main clauses. Some grammarians distinguish between compound (double) and compound (multiple). A compound (double) sentence consists of two main clauses; a compound (multiple) sentence three or more main clauses.

He returned home late but left again within minutes for an undisclosed destination. (compound double sentence)

You helped me with my maths homework and I helped you with your English homework, so we are quits. (compound multiple sentence)

The compound sentence is one of four types of sentence in English, the other three being the simple sentence, the complex sentence, and the complex-compound sentence.

concord: See agreement.

concrete noun: A noun which stands for an object that exists in the real world, something that we can see, touch, smell ('pot', 'flower', 'cottage'), as opposed to an abstract noun, which names a concept or idea which exists in our minds only ('truth', 'beauty', 'justice').

conditional clause: An adverb clause (also known as an adverb clause of condition) that states or stipulates a condition that must be realized for the idea in the main clause to happen. Conditional clauses are usually introduced by 'if' or 'unless':

If you complete your probation satisfactorily, we will confirm you in your job.

Unless funds are forthcoming, we won't be able to take up the second phase of the project.

The condition stated may at times be unreal:

If I were you. I wouldn't touch that offer with a pair of tongs.

If I had known of your problems, I would have done my bit to help you.

conjunction: A word whose primary function is to join words or word-groups. Conjunctions are of two types – coordinate conjunctions and subordinate conjunctions. There is a third type called the correlative conjunction, which is but a variation of the coordinate conjunction. See coordinate conjunction, subordinate conjunction.

conjunctive adverb: A word which is both a conjunction and an adverb at the same time:

It rained heavily in the catchment area; therefore the dam gave way.

The car is expensive to buy; besides, it hardly gives eight kilometres a litre.

The underlined words connect the two main clauses like conjunctions and at the same time modify the clauses that come after them, or the verbs in those clauses, like adverbs.

contact clause: If a defining relative clause is introduced by a relative pronoun functioning as object of a verb or a preposition in the relative clause, the relative pronoun is usually omitted from the defining relative clause, and such a clause is called a contact clause:

The man (whom) I wanted to see was on vacation.

The book (that) you were looking for has arrived in the library.

contracted form: The form of a word or phrase shortened by the omission of one or more of the sounds in the middle of the word or phrase. In writing, the contraction is indicated by an apostrophe, as in:

can't (for 'cannot'); won't (for 'will not'); don't (for 'do not'), that's (for 'that is')

coordinate conjunction: A conjunction that connects words or word-groups of the same class: nouns with nouns, adjectives with adjectives, adverbs with adverbs, phrases with phrases, clauses with clauses:

single words – bread and butter; clever but lazy; slowly and steadily;

phrases – boys in uniform/and/girls in skirts;

clauses – The band played /and/ the crowd cheered.

The coordinate conjunction is one of two types of conjunction, the other being the subordinate conjunction.

correlative conjunction: A name given to a small group of conjunctions which always go together like 'not only...but also', 'either...or', 'neither...nor', 'both....and':

She is not only beautiful but also intelligent and articulate.

You must either fend for yourself or find a woman willing to look after you.

Notice that in the examples above, the correlatives are placed immediately before the elements that are coordinated: 'not only' before 'beautiful' and 'but also' before 'intelligent and articulate'; 'either' before 'fend for yourself' and 'or' before 'find a woman willing to look after you'.

dangling participle: A participle so used that it does not seem to modify anything in the sentence or seems to modify the wrong word. When, for instance, a sentence begins with a participle, we expect it to modify the subject of the clause that follows:

Breaking into the shop, the burglar removed most of the jewellery.

The underlined participle modifies the subject of the clause 'the burglar' and quite rightly, for the person who broke into the shop and the person who removed most of the jewellery are both the same person, the burglar himself. But in the following sentence, the participle is left 'dangling' because it modifies the wrong subject:

Breaking into the shop, most of the jewellery was removed.

Here are some more examples of the 'dangling' modifier:

Being a hardened thief with several convictions, the judge sentenced the prisoner to three years' R.I.

Born poor, orphaned at five, brought up in an orphanage, life was no bed of roses for him.

declarative sentence: A sentence that makes a statement; it is also called a statement:

None of us in the family went into business.

They come from Kerala.

He visited London way back in the seventies.

A declarative sentence is one of four types of sentence, the other three being an interrogative sentence, an imperative sentence, and an exclamatory sentence.

defining relative clause: One of two types of relative clause, the other being the non-defining relative clause. The defining relative clause defines the antecedent noun:

The man who lives next door is a poet.

Out of thousands of men the clause selects a particular man. The clause answers the question: What man? The man who lives next door (and not any other man). The defining relative clause is an essential part of the sentence, since without it the sentence does not make much sense. The defining relative clause is also known as the restrictive relative clause. See non-defining relative clause.

definite article: The word 'the' as in 'the house opposite', 'the Holy Roman Empire', 'the Subcontinent'. The definite article, along with the indefinite articles ('a', 'an'), belongs to the class of determiners. See determiners.

demonstrative adjective: An adjective that 'demonstrates' or points out which of the things named by the noun is meant:

Take this book home. That girl is going to fall off the stool.

These factors have to be considered. Those men are from Delhi.

Apart from 'this', 'these', 'that' and 'those', the word 'such' is also thought of as a demonstrative adjective if it is followed by a noun:

Look at that lean and hungry Cassius. Such men are dangerous.

demonstrative pronoun: A pronoun used to point to a following noun as the one intended. The forms are the same as for the demonstrative adjective: 'This', 'these', 'that', 'those' and 'such'. But while the demonstrative adjectives are followed by nouns, the demonstrative pronouns stand alone and function as nouns in the sentence:

This is the gentleman I was telling you about.

These are the pictures which will come under the hammer at next week's sale.

Such was the pattern of his life: an unhappy childhood, a long and bitter struggle through youth and early manhood, and eventual recognition when he was in his early fifties.

The nouns pointed to by the demonstrative pronouns are boxed in the above examples.

dependent clause: See subordinate clause.

descriptive grammar: Grammar that confines itself to a statement and explanation of the facts and refuses to pronounce on the relative correctness of different usages, as opposed to prescriptive grammar, which seeks to lay down the law in regard to what is correct and what is not correct. Henry Sweet's *New English Grammar,* 1892 is a pioneering example of descriptive grammar. For examples of prescriptive grammar, see Robert Lowth's

A Short Introduction To English Grammar, 1762 and Lindley Murray's *English Grammar Adapted To Different Classes Of Learners,* 1795.

determiners: A group name for a whole class of words which always come before nouns, helping to identify the persons or things named by the nouns. Determiners are of two kinds: general determiners and specific determiners. The former identify the persons or things named by the nouns in a general way, while the latter identify them in a specific way.

general determiners

A man called at our place the other day. (could be any man)

A few people turned up for the meeting. (doesn't say how few)

specific determiners

The woman chased the thief down the street. (A particular woman chased a particular thief down a particular street)

What do you call that joke on wheels? A moped?

Determiners comprise seven grammatical categories: articles, demonstrative adjectives, possessive adjectives, indefinite adjectives, numeral adjectives, interrogative adjectives and relative adjectives.

direct object: A noun or noun-equivalent on which the action of a verb is directed. Usually the direct object comes immediately after the verb, as in basic sentence pattern 2:

The hunter killed the tiger.

When the sentence contains an indirect object, the direct object usually follows the indirect object, as in basic sentence pattern 3:

The children gave the elephant peanuts.
(I.O.) (D.O.)

I bought my sister a present. Mother baked me a pie.
(I.O.) (D.O.) (I.O.) (D.O.)

Will you please pass me the salt?
(I.O.) (D.O.)

The direct object, unlike the indirect object, is an indispensable part of the sentence. Thus, we can say: 'I bought a present' but not 'I bought my sister'.

direct question: A question that appears within quotes, as in direct speech:

"What were you doing at that hour in your office?"

"How long have you known the defendant?"

As opposed to this, is the indirect question, the question as it appears in indirect or reported speech:

The policeman asked John what he was doing at that hour in his office.

The lawyer asked the defence witness how long he had known the defendant.

direct speech: Speech which is reported in the words actually used by the original speaker, as against indirect speech, in which the speaker's original speech is rephrased by someone else, usually a third person. Direct speech is enclosed in quotes.

direct speech

He said, "I'm going home tomorrow."

indirect speech

He said that he was going home the next day.

ditransitive verb: A transitive verb which takes two objects, a direct object and an indirect object, as in basic sentence pattern 3:

The children gave the elephant peanuts.
(I.O.) (D.O.)

I sold him the antiques,
(I.O.) (D.O.)

'do' auxiliary: An auxiliary verb which is used only with verbs in the simple present and the simple past tense to form questions and negatives:

statement	question	negative
He goes to school.	Does he go to school?	He doesn't go to school.
They go to school.	Do they go to school?	They don't go to school.
They went to school.	Did they go to school?	They didn't go to school.

The 'do' auxiliary is one of three types of auxiliary verb, the other two being the tense auxiliary and the modal auxiliary. See tense auxiliary, modal auxiliary.

elliptical clause: An adverb clause from which the subject and the verb, or part of the verb, has been omitted:

When in Rome, do as the Romans do.(= when you are in Rome)

The police will impose a curfew, if necessary. (= if it is necessary)

When completed, the dam will be dedicated to the nation. (= when the dam is completed)

emphatic pronoun: A pronoun which is made up of a personal pronoun plus the suffix '-self' or '-selves' and which is used to emphasize a noun or pronoun in a sentence:

Did John write this essay himself?

She herself made it/She made it herself.

The question 'Did John write this essay himself?' may be asked with or without the emphatic pronoun 'himself'. Either way the question remains the same, only the emphasis will be missing if 'himself' is dropped. The emphatic pronoun has the same form as the reflexive pronoun but unlike the reflexive pronoun, the emphatic pronoun is dispensable. See reflexive pronoun.

emphatic 'it': Is used to emphasize a particular piece of information:

It was in 1965 that he met his future wife. (Compare: He met his wife in 1965.)

Any one piece of information in a sentence can be highlighted, as shown below:

Sheila played the piano at last night's concert.

It was Sheila who played the piano at last night's concert.

It was the piano that Sheila played at last night's concert.

It was at last night's concert that Sheila played the piano.

The underlined word or phrase carries the emphasis in each of the above sentences beginning with 'it'.

exclamatory sentence: A sentence which begins with an exclamatory phrase consisting of 'what' or 'how' followed by a part of the predicate. The exclamatory phrase is followed by the subject and the rest of the predicate:

What a memorable day that was!

How calm the evening is!

Sometimes the exclamatory phrase stands along without the rest of the predicate following it:

What a memorable day!

How beautiful!

An exclamatory sentence is an emphatic way of expressing emotion. The exclamatory sentence is one of four types of sentence, the other three being the declarative sentence, the interrogative sentence, and the imperative sentence.

expletive 'it': See anticipatory 'it'.

expletive 'there': A term for the word 'there', as used in these sentences:

There were thirty-three men in all.

The expletive 'there' has no meaning. It is used only to begin the sentence, since we cannot have a sentence like:

*Were thirty-three men in all.

The subject of the sentence is 'men', as the plural verb clearly indicates.

Here are two more examples of the expletive 'there':

There is just one question I want to ask you.

There will be time enough for us to decide.

feminine gender: See gender.

finite verb: A verb that can make a statement about a person or thing referred to by the subject:

Dogs bark. The little girl hates onions.

Secondly, a finite verb can express person and number:

I am going to the cinema/You are going to the cinema/He is going to the cinema. See non-finite verb.

foreign plurals: A term used to denote nouns borrowed from Latin and Greek which retain their plurals–in English: stimulus-stimuli; crisis-crises; criterion-criteria.

formal definition: A definition based on form, that is, sound and spelling. Thus, a noun may be formally defined as a word that forms its plural by adding '-s' and its possessive by adding 's. A formal definition may be distinguished from a syntactic definition, which is based on the relationship of a given word with other words, and a notional definition which is based on meaning.

functional definition: Same as syntactic definition.

future continuous tense: A tense made up of the auxiliary verb 'shall' or 'will' plus the auxiliary 'be' plus the present participle of the lexical verb:

I wonder what I will be doing ten years from now.

future perfect tense: A tense made up of the auxiliary verb 'shall' or 'will' plus the auxiliary verb 'have' plus the past participle of the lexical verb:

By this time next year, I will have completed my house.

future tense: A tense composed of the auxiliary verb 'shall' or 'will' and the infinitive form of the lexical verb 'shall come', 'will play', 'shall be', 'will have'. The lexical verbs: 'come', 'play', 'be' and 'have' are infinitive but without the sign of the infinitive 'to'.

gender: The grammatical expression of sex distinctions in nouns and third person pronouns. Gender in English is generally based on sex. In life we think of people and things as male, female, either male or female, neither male nor female. Corresponding to these divisions in real life, we have In grammar masculine gender ('boy', 'man', 'bull'), feminine gender ('girl', 'woman', 'cow'), common gender ('parent', 'doctor', 'teacher') and neuter gender ('chair', 'basket', 'cloud'). A noun in English belongs to one of these four genders. As for the third person pronouns, we have 'he' for masculine, 'she' for feminine, and 'it' for neuter. Sometimes neuter gender is given to babies and small animals although they are not sexless:

The tiny tot put out its foot, sucking its thumb.

The boys chased the dog, throwing stones at it.

genitive case: A case of nouns marked either by 's or by the form 'of'. The first is called apostrophe genitive; the second phrasal genitive or 'of genitive':

The policeman's function (or) the function of the policeman. Most grammar books use the term 'possessive' for 'genitive'. The term is misleading since the so-called possessive does not always indicate possession. A better, more inclusive term is 'genitive', of which the possessive genitive is one aspect. Apart from the possessive genitive, we have the appositive genitive, the descriptive genitive, and so on.

gerund: A participle, present participle or perfect participle (but not past participle), functioning like a noun in a sentence:

Seeing is believing.
(subject) (subject complement)

He regrets having wasted his time in college. (object of verb)

By wasting his time in college, he put himself at a great disadvantage. (object of the preposition 'by')

He stands in knee-deep water and splashes about, and he calls it swimming. (object complement)

He likes only one exercise–swimming. (appositive to the noun 'exercise')

The more common form of the gerund, however, is the present participle.

gerund phrase: A phrase or word-group headed by a gerund:

Having the right connections is a great advantage in business.

The man was fined for smoking in the auditorium.

She denied having ever seen the man.

grammatical gender: A gender system that does not have a close correspondence to the male-female distinction observed in real life. For example, in Sanskrit every noun has gender stamped on it as masculine, feminine, or neuter, and the classification is not based on sex. This is known as grammatical gender, as opposed to 'natural gender', a gender system, like the one in English, based by and large on sex.

grammatical meaning: The meaning a word-group may have, considered purely as a grammatical unit. Thus, a nonsense sentence like:

They slantered folicly until a vagan weened to famble them

sounds acceptable for the following reasons:

i. The structure words 'they', 'until', 'a', 'to' and 'them' provide an acceptable framework to the nonsense words;

ii. Some of the nonsense words are marked by endings which are typically English–'slantered' and 'weened' by the past tense ending '-ed' and 'folicly' by the adverbial ending '-ly'.

iii. The words are so arranged that they conform to a familiar sentence pattern in English, consisting of a main clause ('They slantered folicly') and an adverb clause ('until a vagan weened to famble them').

headword: The word that is being modified by a modifier, the modifier being an adjective, adverb, adjective phrase or adverb phrase. Thus, in the sentence:

Most of the candidates called for interview were found wanting,

'most' is a headword modified by the prepositional adjectival phrase 'of the candidates'. The word 'candidates', part of the modifier, is itself a headword, modified by the participle phrase 'called for interview'. Here is another example:

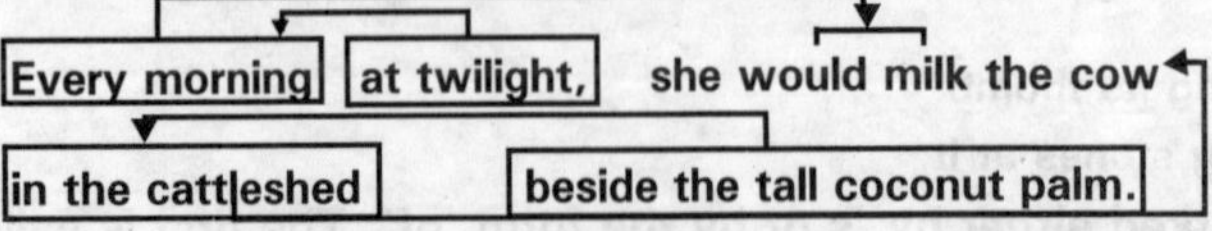

In the above example, 'every morning', an adverb phrase, modifies the headword 'would milk'; 'at twilight', a prepositional adjective phrase, modifies the headword 'morning' in 'every morning', itself a modifier; 'in the cattleshed', a prepositional adjectival phrase, modifies the headword 'cow'; beside the tall coconut palm', another prepositional adjectival phrase, modifies the headword 'cattleshed', itself part of the modifier 'in the cattleshed'. In the above example, the modifiers are boxed and the headwords indicated by means of arrows.

historic present: The use of the present tense to report an action that occurred in the past. The present tense is used with a view to making the narration more lively and vivid:

Well, there I am, standing in a queue at the bus stand, waiting for Bus 301. I see a bearded old man in dark glasses, his head covered, coming down the queue, begging for alms. He comes up to me, stops, looks at me, and the next thing I see is the man dashing down the queue and disappearing but not before I recognize in him our servant Chotu on his afternoon off!

imperative sentence: A sentence beginning with a verb, with 'you' as the implicit subject:

Wait for a little while. Be quiet.

The imperative sentence is used to give orders or instructions ('Keep reading silently'), or to make a request or to appeal to someone for help ('Please hurry up and ring for the ambulance').

impersonal 'it': A term used to refer to 'it' in sentences like these:

It was a fine day. It is going to rain. It was a cold November morning.

The word 'it' in the above examples has no meaning since it does not stand for, or refer to, an inanimate noun. It is used for the simple reason that a declarative sentence must have a subject. It merely introduces the sentence, and for this reason it is called the introductory 'it'. The impersonal 'it' has three uses: the introductory 'it', the emphatic 'it', and the anticipatory 'it'. See emphatic 'it', anticipatory 'it'.

indefinite adjective: A word like 'any', 'each', 'either', 'neither', 'some', 'little', 'less', 'much', 'more', 'most', 'few', 'enough', 'one', 'several', 'all' etc, used to modify a noun:

Have you any money on you? Either boy may go.

There is little milk and even less sugar.

See indefinite pronoun.

indefinite article: A term for 'a' and 'an', which are weakened forms of the indefinite adjective 'one'. 'A' and 'an' are used to refer to a person or thing in a general way without identifying the person or thing:

A man called at our place the other day.

At the end of the day there was an unclaimed parcel.

'A' is used before words beginning with a consonant sound ('a book', 'a round table', 'a university'; 'an' is used before words beginning with a vowel sound ('an egg', 'an uneasy calm', 'an hour').

indefinite pronoun: A pronoun which refers to an indefinite person ('someone', 'somebody', 'nobody', 'everybody', 'anybody', 'anyone', 'everyone') or an indefinite thing ('something', 'nothing', 'everything', 'anything') or an indefinite quantity ('any', 'some', 'much', 'many', 'more', 'most', 'little', 'a little', 'few', 'a few', 'several', 'none', 'each', 'either', 'neither'). They are called indefinite because they do not refer to any definite person, thing or quantity. The term, however, is not a happy one: 'all', 'each', 'none', 'either', 'neither' are by no means indefinite but traditionally they have been treated as such.

Examples

Someone called. Either of the boys will do. Neither of them sent his regrets. None of us knew anything about it. Some of the mangoes were rotten. Many are called but only a few are chosen.

indirect object: See direct object.

indirect question: See direct question.

indirect speech: See direct speech.

infinitive: One of the four non-finite verbs in English, the other three being the present participle, the past participle and the perfect participle. The infinitive consists of the simple form of the verb, usually but not always, preceded by the sign of the infinitive 'to':

To know her is to love her. He was keen to visit his ancestral home. Please try to recall what happened that day. The boy scouts were helping the blind to cross the road.

infinitive phrase: A phrase (that is, a word-group with no subject-predicate of its own) headed by an infinitive:

The minister refused to go into the details.

To forget one's own name when one is among strangers can be very embarrassing.

For once he decided to speak extempore.

We must eat sensibly to live a healthy life.

An infinitive phrase may function as a noun, as an adjective, or as an adverb.

inflected language: A language in which the words change their forms or endings with a change in their grammatical function like, for example, Sanskrit, as opposed to an analytic language like English. Modern English has a few inflectional endings like, for example, the '-ed' ending added to most English verbs to form the past tense, the 's added to nouns to indicate the genitive case, and so on but it is still largely an analytic language.

inflection: A form or ending added to a word to indicate a change in number, person, case, gender, tense, voice etc. Pronouns in English inflect more than nouns. For example, the first person pronoun is 'I' in the singular, 'we' in the plural. It is 'I' when it comes as subject (nominative case) but 'me' as object of verb (objective case). The third person pronoun is 'he' for masculine, 'she' for feminine, and 'it' for neuter. The possessive forms of pronouns also inflect: 'me' and 'mine', 'our' and 'ours', 'your' and 'yours', and so on. The plural ending '-s' added to nouns, the 's added to nouns to form the genitive, and the past tense ending '-ed' added to verbs in the present tense are the other examples of inflection in English.

interrogative adjective: A 'wh-' word that introduces a question and at the same time modifies a noun. The 'wh-' words used are: 'what', 'which' and 'whose'.

What day is it? Which book would you like to borrow?

Whose umbrella is this?

The same words can be used as interrogative pronouns as well. See interrogative pronoun.

interrogative adverb: A 'wh-' word that introduces a question and at the same time functions as an adverb, modifying a verb, an adjective, or an adverb. The 'wh-' words used are– 'when' 'where', 'why' and 'how':

When did you report for work?

Where were you hiding all these days?

How tall is the Empire State Building in New York?

Why don't you speak up?

How badly was he beaten up?

interrogative pronoun: A 'wh-' word that introduces a question and at the same time functions as a pronoun, that is, as subject of verb, object of verb, subject complement etc. The 'wh-' words used are: 'who' ('whom', 'whose'), 'what' and 'which':

Who was that man you were talking to last evening at the club?

Someone seems to have left his wallet. Whose could this be?

Tell me: What is your problem?

Which came first, the chicken or the egg?

interrogative sentence: One of four types of sentence in English, the other three being the declarative sentence, the imperative sentence, and the exclamatory sentence. The interrogative sentence asks a question:

Is your father by any chance a psychiatrist?

Do you think you can take on a whole community?

Shall we eat out tonight?

What do you think you are doing? Who was that captive listener of yours that you were haranguing last night? When do you expect to finish your course?

The question may be a 'yes-no' question (like the first three above), or a 'wh-' question (like the last three).

irregular plurals: A term used to indicate nouns that do not form their plurals the regular way, that is, by having '-s' added to the singular. An irregular plural may take the form of an internal change (man–men; tooth–teeth; louse–lice) or an '-en' ending (ox–oxen; child–children).

irregular verb: See regular verb.

lexical verb: A meaning-bearing verb. The lexical verb carries the meaning of the action or the description, depending on whether the verb is a verb of doing or verb of being:

The children screamed in delight.

The other boy looked unhealthy.

Skiing seems a dangerous sport.

They hanged him for murder.

A lexical verb is also called a main verb. Every sentence must have a lexical verb. Lexical verbs may be distinguished from auxiliary verbs, which do not carry much meaning but which combine with the lexical verbs to express tense, interrogation, negation, etc. 'Lexical' is the adjective of 'lexis', meaning the body of words in a language.

linking verb: A verb that links or joins what goes before it (the subject) to what comes after it (the subject complement). The commonest linking verb is the verb 'be' but many other verbs like 'seem', 'become', 'feel', 'look', 'remain', 'appear', 'continue' etc are also used as linking verbs.

Dr Jones is the leading cardiologist in town.

He lost heavily and became bankrupt.

The situation remains tense.

The weather on the mountain continued calm and sunny.

Linking verbs are one of two types of lexical verb, the other being action verbs or verbs of doing, as shown in the chart below:

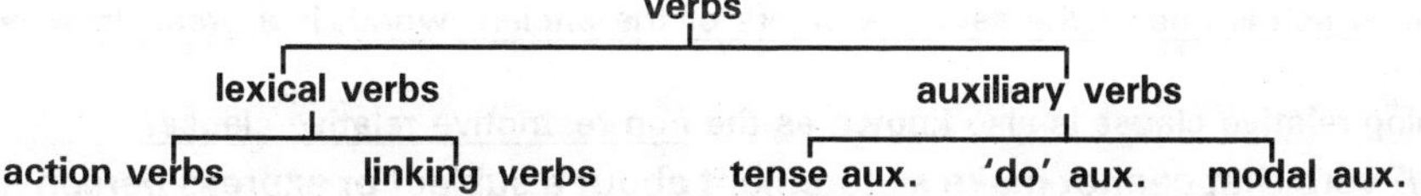

main clause: A clause that stands by itself, as opposed to a subordinate clause that depends on some other part of the sentence. Both the main clause and the subordinate clause have a subject-predicate structure of their own; the chief difference between the two is that the main clause is complete and independent while the subordinate clause is incomplete and dependent. Examples of main clauses:

The one-eyed monster was always hungry.

He left in a huff, vowing never to return.

We were well and truly ripped off at that tourist hotel.

We had informed them of our coming but no one come to meet us at the station. (2 main clauses)

He fell off the ladder; however, he came out of the fall without a scratch. (2 main clauses)

main verb: See lexical verb.

masculine gender: See gender.

mass nouns: Words for concrete objects which are referred to as a mass, as a quantity:

Cheese is good food but high cholesterol.

The French are very fond of wine.

I prefer tea to coffee.

Mass nouns are a type of noncountable nouns in English.

modal auxiliary: One of three types of auxiliary verb in English, the other two being the tense auxiliary and the 'do' auxiliary. Modal auxiliaries are different from the other two types of auxiliaries in that they (and they alone) combine with the lexical verbs to modify their meaning. This they do by adding to the lexical verb an idea such as ability, permission, possibility, obligation, necessity, and so on. Compare:

He is swimming.

He can swim. (meaning 'he has the ability to swim now or in the future').

There are twelve modal auxiliaries in all consisting of four paired items (can-could; may-might; shall-should; will-would) and four single forms (must, ought, need, dare).

neuter gender: See gender.

nominative absolute: See absolute construction.

non-defining relative clause: One of two types of relative clause, the other being the defining relative clause. The non-defining clause gives non-essential and therefore dispensable information about the antecedent noun:

My father, who is past seventy, still goes for a three-mile walk every morning.

The term 'my father' is fully defined; the clause 'who is past seventy' is therefore non-defining, as opposed to the underlined relative clause in the following sentence, which is defining:

The man who is sitting next to the chief guest is my father.

Here are some more examples of the non-defining relative clause:

The Visiting Professor spoke on William Shakespeare, who is England's greatest dramatist.

Alec Guinness, who won an Oscar for his role as the English colonel in *The Bridge On The River Kwai*, was an outstanding actor equally at home on the stage, on the screen and on television.

The Taj Mahal, which is one of the seven wonders of the ancient world, is a great draw with foreign tourists.

The non-defining relative clause is also known as the non-restrictive relative clause.

non-finite verb: A verb that cannot make a statement about a subject or express person and number – unlike a finite verb, which can do both. The non-finite verbs are four: the infinitive ('to go'), the present participle ('going'), the past participle ('gone'), and the perfect participle ('having gone'). The non-finite verb cannot express person or number because it has only one form. The underlined verbs in the following passage are all non-finite verbs:

For want of work to do or anything else to engage their bodies and minds, these young men are roaming the streets from morning till late at night, trying to find ways of spending time and generally making themselves a nuisance to their parents and the public at large.

See finite verb.

non-restrictive relative clause: See non-defining relative clause.

notional definition: One of three kinds of definition, the other two being formal definition and functional (or syntactic) definition. The notional definition is based on the meaning of whatever is defined. Thus, a noun may be defined as the name of a person, place, animal or thing; a verb as a word that expresses action, being or state of being; an adjective as a word that describes, or gives information about, the person or thing represented by the noun, and so on.

noun: A word that is the name of a person ('John'), place ('Moscow'), animal ('camel'), or thing ('chair'). A noun forms its plural by adding '-s' to the singular (dog-dogs) and its possessive by adding 's (man-man's). It can perform one of six syntactic functions–it can serve as subject of verb, object of verb, object of preposition, subject complement, object complement, and appositive. The underlined words in the following passage are all nouns:

The home of Martin Luther King was a deeply religious one, and as a boy Martin had been brought up to look upon the Bible as a guide-book to living. The question, however, was how to apply the teachings of Jesus to the problems of everyday life. The answer came to him while he was in Boston.

noun clause: A subordinate clause functioning as a noun in a sentence, that is, as subject, object, subject complement etc. The noun clause is one of three types of subordinate clause, the other two being the adjective (relative) clause and the adverb clause. The underlined clauses in the following sentences are noun clauses:

That he did not know is no defence; it was his business to know. (subject)

I can see that you don't like your employer. (object of verb)

Your continuance in the job will depend on how well you do during the period of probation. (object of preposition)

The most remarkable thing about the charge of the Light Brigade was that it happened. (subject complement)

It is well known in the locality that X is a scoundrel. (in apposition to the anticipatory 'it')

noun phrase: A phrase or word-group without a subject-predicate structure of its own, functioning as a noun, that is, as subject, object, subject complement, object complement etc. The noun phrase is usually headed by a noun, called its headword. The underlined phrases in the following sentences are noun phrases. (The headword in each phrase is boxed.)

The big, black dog barked. (subject)

Jim Corbett killed several man-eating tigers of Kumaon. (object of verb) The ruler was an infamous tyrant loathed by his subjects. (subject complement)

A noun phrase may in addition take the form of an infinite or gerund phrase:

To own up one's mistakes calls for courage of a rare kind.

Owning up one's mistakes calls for courage of a rare kind.

numeral adjective: An adjective that tells us how many persons or things we are talking about or the order in which a particular person or thing stands:

A year has twelve months and January is the first month of the year.

A numeral adjective may be cardinal (like 'one', 'two', 'twenty-five') or ordinal (like 'first', 'second', 'twenty-fifth').

object: A noun or noun-equivalent that receives, or is affected by, the action expressed by a verb. The objects of verbs are underlined in the following sentences:

He crushed the fly with a swatter. (noun)

She met him at a seaside town. (pronoun)

He admitted that he made a big mistake. (noun clause)

He denied stealing the watch. (gerund)

She declined to sign on the dotted line. (infinitive phrase)

Apart from the verb, the preposition also takes an object; the noun or noun equivalent coming after the preposition is the object of the preposition:

We went to Mulund by the suburban train.

The father objected to her meeting him. (gerund phrase)

She stood by him in his hour of need.

object complement: See complement.

'of' genitive: See apostrophe genitive.

participle: A word made from a verb. Participles are of three kinds: present participle ('going'), past participle ('gone') and perfect participle ('having gone'). Participles – present and perfect – may function as gerunds:

Swimming is a good exercise.

I like swimming.

He denied having met her.

She regretted having declined an earlier offer.

More usually, participles, present, past and perfect, act as modifiers:

Haven't you repaired the leaking tap yet?

That is a broken chair.

Shattered by the news, the old man broke down.

Having spent sleepless nights, the man looked haggard.

Raising his voice, the chairman asked the heckler to shut up.

participle phrase: A phrase (or word-group without a subject-predicate of its own) headed by a participle, present, past, or perfect:

1. Stung by the insult, the man rushed forward to hit him.
2. The man walked into the hall, clad in a safari jacket.
3. Not wishing to make herself conspicuous, she sat in the last row.
4. Anyone listening to you must be off his head.
5. Having been a smoker for over fifty years, he found it impossible to give up the habit.

A participle phrase may function as an adjectival or adverbial modifier. The phrases in examples 2 and 4 above are adjectival, those in 1, 3 and 5 are adverbial.

participle prepositions: Words like 'concerning', 'considering', 'during', 'excepting', 'including', 'excluding', 'notwithstanding', 'regarding', 'pending':

Considering his young age, the judge let him off with a light sentence.

I would like everyone of you to be present, including the girls.

Notwithstanding his exceptional ability, he never rose above mediocrity.

parts of speech: The major categories into which the vocabulary of a language is divided. English has eight parts of speech–the noun, the pronoun, the adjective, the verb, the adverb, the preposition, the conjunction, and the interjection. This book deals with all but the last.

passive voice: See active voice.

past participle: One of three participles in English, the other two being the present participle and the perfect participle. The past participle of most verbs has the same form as the past tense: walk–walked–walked; cling–clung–clung; feel–felt–felt. A few dozen verbs have a past participle different from the past tense: take–took–taken; begin–began–begun; come–came–come; know–knew–known; give–gave–given.

Normally the past participle functions as an adjective:
frozen food; stolen jewellery; a deserted village; a torn shirt; a split infinitive.
Mistaken for a burglar, the metre reader was badly beaten up.
Hurt and humiliated, the boy ran away from home.

past perfect tense: A tense made up of the auxiliary 'had' plus the past participle of the lexical verb: had gone; had eaten; had finished. The past perfect passive consists of 'had' plus 'been' plus the past participle of the main verb: had been eaten; had been finished. The past perfect continuous consists of 'had' plus 'been' plus the present participle of the main verb: had been going; had been taking; had been eating.
The past perfect refers to some other past time:
By the time we reached the station, the train had left.
They disconnected my electricity; I had forgotten to pay the bill.
The servant had already been given a week's notice.
I had been thinking of you when you phoned me.

past tense: One of the three or four basic parts of a verb, the others being the simple form of the verb, the past participle, and the present participle. Most verbs form their past tense with the addition of the sounds 'it', 'd' or '-ed': stop–stopped; prove–proved; end–ended. Some verbs form the past tense by changing the vowel sound: take–took; freeze–froze; see–saw. A few verbs have a past tense identical with the present: cut–cut; set–set; put–put. The past passive is formed with 'was' or 'were' plus the past participle form: was taken; were taken. The past continuous tense is formed with 'was' or 'were' plus the present participle of the lexical verb: was going, were going. The past tense is chiefly used to indicate past time:
That was the biggest air accident in recent years. All those on board were killed.
Those were days when might was right.
I saw him as he was boarding a bus.

perfect tense: A tense made up of the auxiliary 'have' plus the past participle of the lexical verb: 'has gone', 'have gone', 'had gone', We have besides the following perfect continuous forms: 'has been going', 'have been going', 'had been going'. See present perfect tense, past perfect tense, future perfect tense.

person: There are three persons which distinguish the three possible subjects of discourse: the person speaking (the first person), the person spoken to (the second person), and the third person or thing spoken about (the third person). These distinctions are chiefly made by the personal pronouns:

	singular	plural
1st person	I	we
2nd person	you	you
3rd person	he/she/it	they

personal pronoun: A pronoun standing for, or referring to:
a. the speaker (1st person);
b. the person spoken to (2nd person);
c. the person or thing being spoken of (3rd person).
Modern English has the following forms as personal pronouns:

	1st person singular	2nd person singular	3rd person singular
Nominative case	I	you	he, she, it
Possessive case	my, mine	your, yours	his, her, hers, its
Objective case	me	you	him, her, it

phrasal verb: A monosyllabic word like 'come', 'go', 'set', 'carry', 'bring', 'look', 'take', 'stand', 'put' plus a particle, meaning a preposition or adverb. The particle too is monosyllabic like 'at', 'by', 'for', 'in', 'on', 'to', 'up', 'down' except for three of them–'across', 'over' and 'upon'. The verb and the particle are so closely related in meaning that they together form a single unit. Examples of phrasal verbs: go up, bring in, turn out, bring up, pick up, put off etc. Most phrasal verbs are made up of a verb plus one particle. A few are made up of a verb plus two particles - like 'come in for', 'burst in upon', 'come up against', 'look forward to', 'look down upon'.

phrase: A word-group having no subject-predicate of its own, as opposed to a clause, which is a word-group with its own subject and predicate. Based on their function, phrases may be classified as noun phrases, adjective phrases, and adverb phrases. Formally, a phrase may be an infinitive phrase, a participle phrase, a prepositional phrase, or a prepositional gerund phrase. For the various kinds of phrases, see under the relevant section.

phrasal preposition: A preposition made up of two or more words. Phrasal prepositions may be two-word prepositions like 'ahead of', 'because of', 'instead of', 'aside from', 'inclusive of' or prepositions consisting of three or more words like 'by dint of', 'at the cost of', 'in spite of', 'in the event of', 'in the name of'.

possessive case: Another term for genitive case. See genitive case.

possessive pronoun: The personal pronoun in its possessive form. See personal pronoun. The possessive pronoun, like the possessive adjective, says that someone owns something:

This house is ours. Theirs is in the next street.

That car is mine. This box is hers. These books are ours.

The only difference between the pronoun and the adjective is that the possessive pronoun functions as a noun (that is, as subject, subject complement etc), while the possessive adjective is followed by a noun which it modifies:

possessive adjective	possessive pronoun
This is our house.	This house is ours.
Did you find your car key?	Yes, mine is here, in my trouser-pocket.

positive degree: The form of an adjective or adverb that either does not compare the word modified to other things, or compares it to another thing to an equal or unequal degree:

Adjectives

X is clever. (no comparison)

X is as clever as Y. (compared to an equal degree)

Y is not as clever as X. (compared to an unequal degree).

Adverb

She sang well. She sang as well as her sister. She did not sing as well as her sister.

See comparison.

possessive adjective: One of several types of adjectives. The possessive adjective says that someone owns something:

This is our house. Their house is in the next street.

That is my car. His box is green. See possessive pronoun.

predicate: One of the two essential parts of a sentence, the other being the subject. The predicate is something that we say about the subject. It normally comes after the subject and consists of a finite verb. The predicate may contain, apart from the finite verb, an object or two, a complement, and modifiers of the verb:

Dog bark. (finite verb only)

The dog chased the boy. (verb plus object)

She gave him a letter. (verb plus two objects)

They made him leader. (verb plus object plus object complement)

The dog chased the boy down the road. (verb plus object plus modifier)

The king was a tyrant. (verb plus subject complement)

predicate adjective: An adjective used as subject complement:

The streets are noisy and crowded.

Doesn't she look beautiful? The medicine tastes bitter.

He is able and hard-working.

predicate noun: A noun used as subject complement:

The king seems an autocrat.

Cyclops was a one-eyed monster.

He is a doctor by profession.

predicate pronoun: A pronoun used as subject complement:

It is he. What is this? This house is ours.

The responsibility is yours.

preposition: A word that relates a noun or noun-equivalent to some other word in the sentence:

The sentry is at the gate. He has been ill for some weeks.

They went from house to house. He was dismissed for incompetence.

Prepositions may be single-word prepositions like 'at', 'by', 'for', 'from', 'to', 'in', 'on' etc, or phrasal prepositions consisting of two or more words like 'abreast of', 'irrespective of', 'subject to', 'for fear of', 'in the light of'. See phrasal prepositions. Prepositions commonly indicate adverbial relationships like time, position, direction, reason, purpose, concession, comparison, manner etc.

prepositional idiom: A prepositional phrase made up of a single preposition plus a noun or noun phrase with which it is closely linked:

The men were at work. They were on duty. They met by accident.

She came in time for the rehearsal.

The ring leaders are under arrest.

prepositional phrase: A phrase made up of the preposition plus the object of the proposition:

The sentry is at the gate. He has been ill since last Monday.

He walked into the departmental store. I woke up with a start.

prepositional gerund phrase: One of the four types of phrase, the other three being the infinitive phrase, the participle phrase, and the prepositional phrase. The prepositional gerund phrase consists of a preposition followed by a gerund phrase, the gerund phrase serving as object of the preposition:

On hearing the good news, she danced in joy.

The principal insisted on punishing the late-comers by fining them.

Prepositional gerund phrases can function as nouns, adjectives, or adverbs:

I must warn you against acting impulsively. (=that you should not act impulsively; nominal function)

The minister spoke of the need for opening more branches in the countryside. (modifying the noun 'need'; adjectival function)

After listening to the news, we played a game of Scrabble. (modifying the verb 'played'; adverbial function)

prescriptive grammar: See descriptive grammar.

present participle: One of three participles in English, the other two being the past participle and the perfect participle. We add the ending '-ing' to the simple form of the verb to form the present participle: go–going; run–running; take–taking. The present participle is used to form the continuous tense forms: 'is going', 'was going', 'will be going', 'has been going', 'had been going'. The passive cortinuous forms use the present participle of 'be': 'is being taken', 'was being taken'.

present perfect tense: A tense made up of the auxiliary 'have' plus the past participle of the lexical verb: has taken, have taken. In its passive form, the simple perfect tense consists of the auxiliary 'have' plus 'been' plus the past participle of the main verb: has been taken; have been taken. The perfect continuous tense is made up of the auxiliary 'have' plus 'been' plus the present participle of the lexical verb: has been taking; have been taking.

present tense: A tense that is identical in form with the stem of the verb, except in the third person singular, where '-s' is added:

love--loves; run–runs; do–does; have–has; hurry–hurries.

In its passive form, it consists of the auxiliary 'be' plus the past participle of the lexical verb:

is loved; am loved; are loved.

The present continuous tense is made up of the auxiliary 'be' plus the present participle of the lexical verb: am going; is going; are going.

pronoun: A word that belongs to a subclass of nouns occupying the same position, and performing the same function, as a noun. Often it takes the place of a noun. Pronouns are never preceded by articles or other limiting adjectives. The underlined words in the following sentences are pronouns:

I don't know when he will be back home.

We are a pluralistic society. Who told you that?

I knew nothing about the matter. They are themselves to blame.

A practical scientist is one who applies science to the solving of everyday problems.

proper noun: See common noun.

proper adjective: An adjective derived from a proper noun: a Chinese restaurant, an African pop singer; a Burmese monk; the Victorian Age.

reciprocal pronoun: A term for 'each other' and 'one another':

The brothers resemble each other.

The party leaders congratulated one another when their party won the election.

The reciprocal pronouns may be used in their possessive form:

They hated each other's guts.

The alcoholics draw comfort from one another's experience.

reflexive pronoun: A pronoun made up of a personal pronoun plus the suffix 'self' or '-selves': 'myself', 'ourselves', 'yourself', 'yourselves', 'himself', 'themselves'. The reflexive pronoun generally refers to a living thing, usually a person:

He stretched himself on the divan. (direct object)

Jane mixed herself a cup of coffee. (indirect object)

You must learn to manage your home by yourself. (object of preposition)

The reflexive pronoun has the same form as the emphatic pronoun but unlike the emphatic pronoun, the reflexive pronoun is an essential part of the sentence. Also, a reflexive pronoun always functions as object of verb or preposition. See emphatic pronoun.

regular verb: A type of verb that forms its past tense by the addition of a 'd', 't' or '-ed' sound (represented in written language by the letters '-ed') without any other change, as opposed to an irregular verb, which forms its past tense usually (thought not always) through a vowel change. Examples of regular verbs: walk–walked; love–loved; thin–thinned; end–ended. Examples of irregular verbs: read–read; take–took; put–put; go–went.

relative adjective: A word that introduces a relative clause, and within the relative clause, it functions as an adjective modifying the noun that follows it. The form commonly used as relative adjective is 'whose', which refers to persons as well as things:

He is a man whose word can be relied on.

That is a country whose development has been outpaced by the growth in population.

relative adverb: A word that introduces a relative clause, and within the relative clause, it functions as an adverb. The forms commonly used as relative adverbs are: 'when', 'where', and 'why'.

Examples

Does anyone here know the time when he left home?

I have vague memories of the village where I was born.

He was found cheating. That was the reason why they gave him the sack.

'When', 'where' and 'why' in the examples above have their antecedent nouns ('time', 'village', 'reason') like a relative pronoun but at the same time they modify the verbs in the relative clauses. The modification is typically adverbial: time, place, reason.

relative clause: One of three types of subordinate clause, the other two being the noun clause and the adverb clause. The relative clause is most commonly introduced by a relative pronoun, less commonly by a relative adjective or adverb. The relative clause modifies a noun or noun-equivalent preceding it, called its antecedent:

Countries which are not weighed down by too much tradition are at an advantage.

Those who live in glass houses must not throw stones.

The relative clause does the work of an adjective; hence it is also known as an adjective clause. See adjective clause.

restrictive relative clause: See defining relative clause.

sentence: Normally an independent unit of thought or feeling expressed through a logically related subject and predicate. An English sentence, in other words, consists of a predication: something is predicated, or said, about a subject. Thus, in 'Dogs bark', we are saying something about 'dogs' (subject) and the thing that we are saying about 'dogs' is that they 'bark' (predicate). The sentence is the basic unit of communication. A sentence may consist of one or more clauses, at least one of which must be a main clause. Theoretically, there is no limit to the number of clauses that a sentence may have but in practice a sentence seldom consists of more than four or five clauses.

sentence adverb: An adverb which modifies a whole sentence and is often the equivalent of a whole clause:

Luckily, there were no casualties. (It was lucky that there were no casualties.)

Surprisingly, he didn't react to the allegations made against him. (It was surprising that he didn't react to the allegations...him.)

sequence of tenses: A special requirement, mostly with noun clauses. If the verb in the main clause is in the past tense, the verb in the subordinate clause must also be in the past tense even if the verb in the subordinate clause points to present or future time:

He said that his father was ill. (From: He said, "My father is ill.")

He said he was going home tomorrow. (From: He said, "I am going home tomorrow.")

If, one the other hand, the verb in the main clause is in the present tense, the verb in the noun clause may be present, past or future. In that case, there is no sequence of tenses:

He says that his father is ill. He says that his father was ill for a few weeks. He says his father will be ill if he doesn't go on a long vacation.

simple sentence: A group of words containing only one main clause and no subordinate clause:

He loves to talk about his children.

They tried to negotiate a settlement.

They argued for an hour. The roses are in bloom right now.

The simple sentence is one of four types of sentence, the other three being the complex sentence, the compound sentence, and the complex-compound sentence.

split infinitive: A construction in which an adverb or adverbial phrase is placed between the sign of the infinitive ('to') and the infinitive verb:

to quietly forget; to openly admire; to more or less finish. Prescriptive grammarians of old forbade the splitting of the infinitive in any circumstances; modern grammarians are more permissive—they favour splitting if splitting helps to convey the intended meaning or remove ambiguity.

strong verb: A verb that forms the past tense and past participle by a change in the vowel sound (take-took-taken; sing-sang-sung; freeze-froze-frozen), as distinct from a weak verb, which adds a 'd', 't' or '-ed' sound to the present tense (walk-walked-walked; bury-buried-buried; shun-shunned-shunned). The terms 'strong' and 'weak' verbs, roughly but only roughly, correspond to 'regular' and 'irregular' verbs: all regular verbs are weak but not all weak verbs are regular, some having undergone various sound changes–verbs like 'teach-taught', 'tell-told'.

subject: The word or word-group about which the predicate makes a statement:

The children waved to the soldiers marching by.

Our car broke down mid-way. Skipping classes is an offence.

Most of the recruits were upto scratch. To know her is to love her.

The underlined are the subjects, while the boxed words are the headwords or the subjects proper.

subject complement: See complement.

subordinate clause: A clause (that is, a word-group with a subject-predicate of its own) functioning as a noun, an adjective, or an adverb and therefore dependent on, or subordinate to, some other word-group in the sentence, as opposed to a main clause, which can stand by itself. The underlined are subordinate clauses, the rest of the sentence being the main clause:

When I heard of his coming home, I wasn't very excited, to tell you the truth.

If promises have been made, they must be kept.

He was the only minister who was accessible to the public.

I assure you that the mistake will not be repeated.

None of us knows whether or not she will attend the party.

He finally found the keys that he had been looking for the whole day.

See main clause.

subordinate conjunction: A conjunction that introduces a subordinate clause and joins it to the main clause. A relative pronoun is also in a sense a subordinate conjunction introducing, as it does, a relative or adjective clause but it does more than introduce the clause: it functions at the same time as the subject or object in the relative clause. The subordinate conjunction introducing a noun clause or adverb clause merely introduces the clause and joins it to the main clause; it has no additional function. The underlined are subordinate conjunctions:

Check the man's credentials before you hire him.

Although I had my doubts about the viability of the scheme, I kept my own counsel.

Come whenever you happen to be in town.

That the prisoner was guilty was the unanimous opinion of the jury.

I was wondering if I could borrow your lawn mower for a day.

superlative degree: See comparison.

syntactic definition: The same as functional definition.

syntax: That part of grammar which deals with the arrangement of words in sentences as subjects, verbs, objects, complements, modifiers etc.

tense: The mode of expressing concepts of time through verb forms. 'Tense' comes from a Latin word meaning 'time' but there is no close correspondence between tense and time in English. For instance, the present tense indicates not only present time but past and future time as well:

Vinoba is a tailor. (was yesterday, is today, will be tomorrow)

Water freezes into ice at 0 degree centigrade. (did yesterday, does now, will do in the future)

The past tense often refers to the future, as in conditional 2. English has six tenses: present, past, future, present perfect, past perfect, and future perfect.

tense auxiliary: One of three types of auxiliary verbs, the other two being 'do' auxiliary and modal auxiliary. The tense auxiliary verb combines with the lexical verb to form the various tenses. Thus, in the sentence 'He has been working in the garden since morning', the verb phrase 'has been working' is made up of the auxiliary 'has' plus the auxiliary 'been' plus the main verb. Only the simple present tense and the simple past tense do not have tense auxiliaries; all other tenses make use of the auxiliary 'be' or the auxiliary 'have' or both.

transitive verb: A verb that takes an object. The word 'transitive' means 'moving across'. The action referred to by the verb moves the verb from the subject to the object:

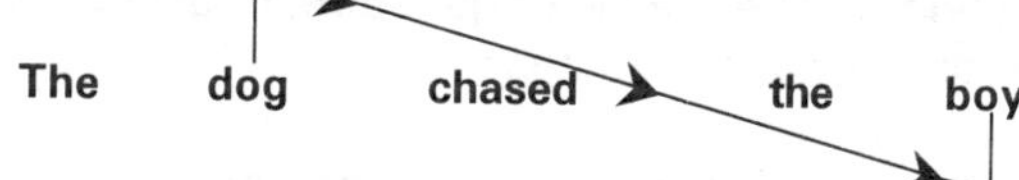

The tennis ace dominated the game right from the start.

They admired her for her integrity.

The committee discussed the proposal thoroughly.

Can you handle the situation?

transformation: a process by which you change the form of a sentence, clause or phrase without changing the meaning. Given below are pairs of sentences each of which is a transform of the other:

India beat Sri Lanka in the finals.	Sri Lanka was beaten by India in the finals.
He learned French while he was staying in France.	He learned French during his stay in France.
As this was his first interview, he was feeling nervous.	This being his first interview, he was feeling nervous.
Although he was exceptionally gifted, he never rose above mediocrity.	His exceptional gifts notwithstanding, he never rose above mediocrity.

usage: The customary way of speaking or writing a language. There are levels of usage and these are determined largely (though not solely) by the education of the language users. Also, usage varies depending on whether one is dealing with spoken English or written English. Thus, 'Who were you talking to?' is standard usage in conversation but in formal writing, it would be: 'Whom were you talking to?' or 'To whom were you talking?' Similarly, the use of 'like' as a conjunction (as in 'Speak like I do if you want to improve your pronunciation') will pass muster in spoken English but will not be condoned in formal writing.

verb: A word that expresses action or being. It may be identified by its position in the sentence as well as by certain characteristic endings. The verb is the most important element in the sentence; all other elements like subject, object, complement etc are defined in relation to the verb.

verb phrase: A verb consisting of two or more words, made up of one or more auxiliaries plus a lexical verb. Examples of verb phrases:

aux. +	lexical verb	aux. +	aux. +	lexical verb
has	gone	has	been	going
is	going	will	be	going
are	sending	are	being	sent
would	go	would	have	gone

vocative: A noun is direct address:

Sam, can you get me a glass of water? Well done, John.

weak verb: See strong verb.

'wh-' question: One or two types of questions commonly used in English, the other being the 'yes–no' question. The 'wh-' question begins with a word whose initial letters are 'wh-': who, whom, whose, what, which, why, where, when and how.

Who are you? Where do you come from? How did you come to know? Whose watch is this?

The 'wh-' question is an open-ended one, the answer to which cannot be predicted with any certainty. See 'yes–no' question.

'yes-no' question: The 'yes-no' question, unlike the 'wh-' question, begins with an auxiliary verb and admits of a simple 'yes' or 'no' for an answer:

Are you a doctor by any chance?

Has she already left?

Do you need a break?

May I go an hour early, sir?

Is leprosy contagious?

Can he do it?

The auxiliary verb introducing a 'yes–no' question may be a tense auxiliary ('be' or 'have'), a 'do' auxiliary, or a modal auxiliary.